WORLD OUTSIDE THE WINDOW

THE SELECTED ESSAYS OF
KENNETH REXROTH

BOOKS BY KENNETH REXROTH

POEMS

The Collected Shorter Poems
The Collected Longer Poems
Sky Sea Birds Trees Earth House Beasts Flowers
New Poems
The Phoenix and the Tortoise
The Morning Star
Selected Poems

PLAYS

Beyond the Mountains

CRITICISM & ESSAYS

The Alternative Society
American Poetry in the Twentieth Century
Assays
Bird in the Bush
Classics Revisited
Communalism, from the Neolithic to 1900
The Elastic Retort
With Eye and Ear
World Outside the Window: Selected Essays

TRANSLATIONS

100 Poems from the Chinese
100 More Poems from the Chinese: Love and the Turning Year
Fourteen Poems of O. V. Lubicz-Milosz
Seasons of Sacred Lust: The Selected Poems of Kazuko Shiraishi
    (*with Ikuko Atsumi, John Solt, Carol Tinker, and*
    Yasuyo Morita)
Women Poets of Japan (*with Ikuko Atsumi*)
Women Poets of China (*with Ling Chung*)
100 French Poems
Poems from the Greek Anthology
100 Poems from the Japanese
100 More Poems from the Japanese
30 Spanish Poems of Love and Exile
Selected Poems of Pierre Reverdy
Li Ch'ing-chao: Complete Poems (*with Ling Chung*)

AUTOBIOGRAPHY

An Autobiographical Novel

EDITOR

The Continuum Poetry Series

WORLD OUTSIDE THE WINDOW

THE SELECTED ESSAYS OF

KENNETH REXROTH

EDITED BY BRADFORD MORROW

A NEW DIRECTIONS BOOK

Grateful acknowledgment is made to the editors and publishers of the journals, magazines, and individual volumes in which many of these essays first appeared. Details of first publication are given on the opening page of each essay.

Manufactured in the United States of America
First published clothbound and as New Directions Paperbook 639 in 1987
Published simultaneously in Canada by Penguin Books Canada Limited

Library of Congress Cataloging-in-Publication Data

Rexroth, Kenneth, 1905–1982
    World outside the window.
    (A New Directions Book)
    Includes index.
    1. Morrow, Bradford II. Title.
PS3535.E923W6   1987   814'.52   86-28610
ISBN 0-8112-1024-3
ISBN 0-8112-1025-1 (pbk.)

New Directions Books are published for James Laughlin
by New Directions Publishing Corporation,
80 Eighth Avenue, New York 10011

Table of Contents

Preface by Bradford Morrow   vii

The Function of the Poet in Society (1936)   1

Poetry, Regeneration, and D. H. Lawrence (1947)   8

The Visionary Painting of Morris Graves (1955)   26

Simon Weil (1957)   35

Disengagement: The Art of the Beat Generation (1957)   41

San Francisco Letter (1957)   57

Rimbaud as Capitalist Adventurer (1957)   65

Jazz Poetry (1958)   68

Revolt: True and False (1958)   73

The Hasidism of Martin Buber (1959)   77

Sung Culture (1960)   102

The Students Take Over (1960)   113

Turner and Whistler (1960)   127

Gnosticism (1960)   132

The Influence of French Poetry on American (1961)   143

The Poet as Translator (1961)   171

What's Wrong with the Clubs (1961)   191

The Institutionalization of Revolt, the Domestication of Dissent
(1963)   197

Why is American Poetry Culturally Deprived? (1963)   209

Community Planning (1964)   218

The Heat (1966)   222

The Spiritual Alchemy of Thomas Vaughan (1967)   243

The Cubist Poetry of Pierre Reverdy (1969)   252

Who Is Alienated from What? (1970)   259

The Influence of Classical Japanese Poetry on Modern American
    Poetry (1973)   267

The Art of Literature (1974)   275

Lafcadio Hearn and Buddhism (1977)   303

Index   321

Preface

. . . independently, widely, and seriously educated, at home in those provinces of art and thought, distant in time or space, which interest him. He has assimilated only what he wanted, but he has wanted much, and he has been thorough about it . . .

Reviewing a retrospective exhibition of Mark Tobey's paintings in 1951, Kenneth Rexroth sketched as evocative a portrait of his own homegrown auto-didacticism as exists in any of his poems, essays, or autobiographical works. He had a singularly tenacious memory; if memory is, as Beckett suggests in his early study on Proust, a function of the intensity of the original perception of an idea or a thing, then it is a function finally of desire. Like Tobey, Rexroth "wanted much": he perhaps assimilated more than any other American poet of his generation. Alchemy, gnosticism, pre-literate poetry, post-apocalyptic communalism, jazz, "Country gentlemen and Cornbelt Metaphysicals," the thousands of years from sand-shuffling shamans to dispensers of the Social Lie, the convergences of cultures in their religions, their literatures and painting, their philosophies and politics—here is a range of interests rarely encountered in an individual in any age, let alone in an age of specialization. Rexroth's particular genius for making not just the fine distinctions, but unexpected associations and distillations, gives torque to his numerous judgments, stances, opinions. "Purposive construction of any kind is a species of communication, just as any kind of communication must be structured. I cannot get paid for this lecture," he once said, "by babbling to you incoherently."

These essays represent not quite half a century's work. The earliest (only the half-finished "Examen de Conscience"—a letter to Louis Zukofsky protesting emendations made against his wishes in the cubist "Prolegomena to a Theodicy"—precedes it) was a speech delivered in November 1936 to the Congress of Western Writers in San Francisco. Published here for the first time, "The Function of the Poet in Society" shows just how early on Rexroth had developed the richness of knowledge, profound socio-political altruism, and courageous, even combatative individuality that were to be the signature of all his later works. The last, an Introduction to a collection of Lafcadio Hearn's writings on Buddhism, was dictated—as were many of his essays, without reference to notes or sources—in the late seventies.

In assembling this selection, I have attempted to give some sense of not merely the breadth of Rexroth's work, which is clearly immense—twenty-seven more essays might have displayed twenty-seven more facets of imagination—but its depth. A dynamic associative quality of thought is present in nearly every paragraph. Here was a mind which was both ideative and thoroughly morally engaged. His style may vary from that of the brash, cool, streetwise raconteur-commentator of "The Heat" to the polymathic educator of "The Art of Literature," but each voice he adopts has a fundamental humanism at its center. That he read through the encyclopedia each year as a "lentative" (his term) exercise, lying in the bath with a board laid across the lips of the tub, is an amusing bit of San Francisco literary lore. But nothing garnered from all this vast reading was embraced as knowledge for knowledge's sake, nor does he, even in his most opinionated moments, betray the dogmatism of a closed mind. Everything was applicable to the world outside the window.

Prefacing the 1959 collection *Bird in the Bush*, Rexroth claimed that his essays were journalism, not criticism, and asserted that—with the exception of his paper on Buber—had they not been "assigned in advance, written to a requested wordage and for an agreed fee," he would never have written any of them. "Poets are very ill advised to write prose for anything but money," he continued. "The only possible exceptions are anger and logrolling for one's friends." One pragmatic eye, then, was cast toward keeping bread on the table. At the same time, he hoped his essays would "find a modest place" in the tradition of James Huneker, H. L. Mencken, and Edmund Wilson—a tradition which Eric Mottram has aptly defined as non-academic, non-*Partisan Review*, and personal. Just as he paraphrased Eliot paraphrasing Dryden, inspiration isn't always at its peak; essay-writing can, in a manner similar to translation, "be a way to keep your tools sharp until the great job, the great moment, comes along." To essay—the verb "essay" being, after all, a refashioned form of *assay*: put to the proof, practice by way of trial—might have been the second best way for him to hone words and thoughts.

Rexroth was a prolific essayist, to say the least. Counting uncollected book reviews and newspaper columns, he wrote well over four hundred pieces. In making any selection from such a mass of materials there are going to be individual essays which but for lack of space one would have included. While this book is no exception, I would like to express my appreciation to my editor Peggy Fox, and Griselda Ohannessian, vice-president of New Directions, who, reading through a final manuscript which was almost twice the length originally planned, accommodated the idea that more pages were needed to demonstrate properly the scope of Rexroth's studies. But, still, choices had to be made. In 1944, when he wrote "Les Lauriers Son Coupé—Mina Loy" Rexroth's was the single voice calling for a closer reading of this great, erotic poet; similarly, his essay on D. H. Lawrence's poetry, which served as an Introduction to a *Selected Poems*, came at a time when Lawrence's reputation as a poet was low, and urged a reappraisal of his work. I have chosen to include the latter. "The Holy Kabbalah" is a key essay from what must be the most significant period of his critical writings, the middle fifties through the early sixties, the period from which most of these essays come; but both "Gnosticism" and "The Hasidism of Martin Buber," two essays I've included, will serve to give the reader a notion of Rexroth's acumen as a commentator on religion, mysticism, be it Catholic, Jewish, Buddhist. Inclusion of his reviews of Lawrence Durrell or Henry Miller might have demonstrated that he was, over the years, willing to change his mind about things—his criticism of the progressive collapse of *The Alexandria Quartet*, whose first volume he'd written about with such enthusiasm, is a revelatory document, for which there was, unfortunately, no room. A comparative essay on Mark Twain and Henry James in which the former is canonized, the latter disparaged, is present in strategy and spirit in

"Turner and Whistler." The editor can only recommend that if readers enjoy what they find here, they would be well advised to read *Bird in the Bush* and *Assays* in their entirety.

Several further editorial matters. I have left out of the selection altogether the chapters of *American Poetry in the Twentieth Century* as they were written not as individual essays but to be read in sequence. I have chosen not to collect any of the numerous book reviews Rexroth himself did not determine to preserve in his books of essays. Many of the finest of Rexroth's shorter essays are to be found in his *Classics Revisited* series. I have omitted the sixty brief essays originally published under that title in 1968 since they were reissued only last year by New Directions. I have also excluded the twenty-nine "More Classics Revisited" from *The Elastic Retort*, as well as a number of other pieces—"Mark Twain," "Franz Kafka's *The Trial*," "Moll Flanders," the Introductions to Herbert Read's masterpiece *The Green Child* and Leo Tolstoy's *The Kingdom of God Is Within You*, as well as several uncollected essays on Ssu-ma Ch'ien's *Records of the Grand Historian* and Gibbon's *Decline and Fall*—all soon to be gathered into a volume of *More Classics Revisited*.

Bradford Morrow
New York City
December 1986

The Function of Poetry
and the Place of the Poet
in Society

I believe that to a certain extent always, but in modern times especially, the poet, by the very nature of his art, has been an enemy of society, that is, of the privileged and the powerful. He has sometimes been an ally and spokesman of the unprivileged and the weak, where such groups were articulate and organized, otherwise he has waged an individual and unaided war.

In the past he has usually been in the latter position, but I believe that the period of increasing isolation of the poet in common with all artists is drawing to a close. I wish to indicate briefly the nature and significance of poetic activity and its relation to past societies and to open up a discussion of its future possibilities.

Some years ago in New York I met two young men. One of them was an active revolutionist, a critic who had specialized in the cinema, and poet of extraordinary promise. Some may remember him. His name was Harry Allen Potamkin. The other, who will have to be unnamed, was probably the most precocious boy I have ever met. At that time he had just completed a translation of the entire work of Arthur Rimbaud. He sat up all night reading it to me, and telling me his ideas of poetry, philosophy, economics, morals. There were few things we did not discuss. I do not believe I have ever encountered a mind of greater intensity and brilliance. In the morning, before we went out to breakfast, he took off his shirt to wash. He was horribly, unbelievably, emaciated. I discovered later

Delivered in November 1936 to the Conference of Western Writers in San Francisco, not previously published.

that he had lived for two years by panhandling and petty thievery. Today he has apparently ceased to write.

Harry Allen Potamkin was at that time, without doubt, one of the most acute critics of the arts in America. In a period when the general run of Marxist criticism was shallow and immature, he was developing in his discussion of the moving picture a critical apparatus which was to be of inestimable value to the critics who were to come after him. Unfortunately, the character of the Left press at that time prevented him from being widely published as a poet. Had this not been the case he might have devoted himself more entirely to poetry. The promise that is apparent in his few published poems might have been fulfilled.

However, he died in 1932 of an illness which was the direct result of semi-starvation. His funeral was a mass demonstration. Hundreds of the common people of New York attended to honor a spokesman whom they had loved and respected. Small minded intellectuals who had accused him of obscurity, who had called him a metaphysician, who had said he was incomprehensible to the workers, were dumbfounded at his popularity.

These two cases made a tremendous impression on me. Although I had always been a very decided radical, both politically and in the forms of my writing, I had not realized that in the concrete social status of the poet lay an explanation of the nature of his function. I had accepted my position as a social outcast and had identified myself with the forces striving for a better social system, a system in which the humanity and leisure for vital appreciation of the arts would be the common property of all men, but I had never had to pay any very terrible penalties for my decision. I had always managed to get by.

Since then I have thought a great deal about the status of the poet in an exploitative society. About Greene, Nashe, Peele, and Marlowe and their friends—starving and roistering, writing plays and lyrics in which a new philosophy of man was emerging—dying obscurely and violently, while the new British ruling class grew fabulously rich. About Ben Jonson and Dryden, hungry in their old age. About Blake and Burns and Keats. About Baudelaire and Rimbaud, who rejected absolutely the society in which they found themselves, and who were accordingly penalized with the maximum severity that society could muster.

I believe that a class which owes its power to the exploitation of others has always had very little use for the poet. When such a class is struggling for power and later, for a short time, when it is consolidating the structure of the world outlook characteristic of it, the poet may be suffered to exist as a sort of refined court jester. Once the zenith of power is passed and the struggles of the ruling group become increasingly defensive and regressive, both in the fields of economics and ideas, as its position becomes increasingly desperate, that dominant class rejects the poet in fear. It has use only for the most venal, propagandistic rhymesters.

Due to the fact that the movement represented by the French Revolution both established an exploiting class in power and gave the hope and promise of liberty, equality and fraternity to the exploited, the present system of social relationships has been challenged continuously from its inception. Concomitantly, the poet in modern times has usually been an outcast.

What is it in poetry which makes it so disruptive a force, so dangerous to ideas and systems which have outlived their usefulness? Even Plato found it necessary to banish poets from his Republic if an admirable, but admittedly artificial, status quo was to be preserved. I think there are several factors concerned here.

First, poetry is pre-eminently the art of language. The poet is continuously reorganizing the vast complex web of communication which makes our social life possible. Every great poem and every great poet has left the language different than they found it. Some writers today, notably Joyce in his recent work, and Gertrude Stein, have concentrated almost exclusively on aspects of this function of literature. At least their most important and durable contributions have been linguistic, whatever their intentions.

The poet is constantly trying to make the language a more efficient instrument for the control and appreciation of experience. As soon as the forms of society come to rest on artificially preserved methods of controlling experience any such deeply critical approach to the mechanism of communication becomes dangerous to the group. What we call reaction is an insistence upon regressive techniques of living. In his most abstract activities the poet is a menace to reaction.

Secondly, almost all schools of thought have agreed that the final criteria of the arts are in some sense moral. Certainly the arts are concerned with the weighing of values. Thus the poet is occupied not only with the intensification and enlargement of the techniques of experience, but with the evaluation of its contents. In fact, when the individual writer places intensity before judgment he soon lapses into a triviality in which intensity itself evaporates. This can be seen by comparing, for example, Verlaine and Rimbaud, or Ezra Pound and T. S. Eliot. If all the poets in the world wrote like Ernest Dowson a decaying social order would have little to fear from them. At least not until decadence and chaos made even romantic sexual satisfaction impossible.

Any activity which presumes to control the most fundamental elements of individual and concurrently of group experience, and to pass very trenchant judgment upon them, to constantly revise and reorder processes of evaluation, to not only change and reconstruct the mechanisms of communication, but to give these mechanisms new purposes, will obviously find itself in conflict with those sections of the population which owe their privileges to communication kept on the most debased, uncritical and uncreative levels.

Thirdly, the poet is not only concerned with the immediate relations of the individual to experience, or with judgment, however cognizant of the purpose and significance of the details of nature. Most, perhaps all the greatest poets of the past have been well aware of the more extensive implications of their world. Some have written with definite and clearly expressed programs. Dante, Milton, Shelley, Lucretius, Abelard, Aquinas, Rimbaud are a very few examples of conscious philosophic content. Others, probably the majority, have preferred to make such content implicit in the structure of lyric and dramatic interests. Keats and his correspondents claim that he was the most valid exponent of the ideals of the French Revolution in the England of his time. Dante, in his commentary on his own lyric work, shows that he was aware of the function of psychological and even subconscious symbolism. Perhaps some of his interpretations sound a little far-fetched and *post hoc* today, but his method is perfectly sound.

Walter Savage Landor's neo-Classicism was a typical expression of the revolutionary ideas of his time. His notions of the nature of Greek democracy and Roman republicanism, his philosophy of history, were ultimately Jacobean in their origins. It was this, a vastly different neo-Classicism to that of Pope, which determined his choice of subject and his style. He may be compared with the painter David.

Elements of this tradition go back a long way in English literature. They begin as a quality of mind and a type of taste rather than as an explicit philosophy. Thus Ben Jonson and Dryden, both loyal to the Stuart dynasty which grudgingly supported them, inaugurated a movement of reasonableness and order in verse which was part of the general growth of a rational, realistic empiricism. This empiricism, before the death of Dryden, was to destroy the power of the Stuarts and the anachronistic feudalism they represented.

These two examples (and many more could be quoted) show that it is possible for the poet, writing as a practical man, with material loyalties in his environment, but with a sensitivity acutely attuned to the shifting forces of an evolving world outlook, to write other than he is aware.

The world today is a far more self-conscious place than it was in the days of Dryden. There are proportionately fewer writers who are able to enjoy the privileges of such a divided personality. Where such men now exist, they have adopted not points of view subservient to the dominant class, but systems which, considered in abstraction, are deeply critical, but which as systems, are socially ineffective and anachronistic. William Butler Yeats, with his involved theosophical mythology, T. S. Eliot, with his Anglo-Catholicism and royalism, have both written some of the most profound poetry of our time, and poetry which I believe to be, as they believed it to be, truly revolutionary in its final implications. This is due to the fact that this theosophy and this Anglo-Catholicism have little to do with the actual cults, but are personal systems, built up by men of wide and erratic reading, in defiance of the reigning ideology.

Most of us, however, have been more subject to the principles of a self-conscious producing class on the one hand and to the narcotics and coercions of an exploiting class on the other, than we have been to the speculations of Arabian Mystics, Renaissance Rosicrucians or to devotional literature of the early Anglican church. I don't believe that any of us are as great writers as Mr. Yeats or Mr. Eliot, but I am afraid we are too aware of the grosser issues of our contemporary world to take refuge in their admirable personal philosophies.

There are several poets in California who have not chosen to commit themselves to the program of this Congress. In this connection I quote a very wise passage from John Stuart Mill's essay on poetry:

> For, depth and durability of wrong as well as of right opinions is proportionate to the fitness of the material; and they who have the greatest capacity for natural feeling are generally those whose artificial feelings are the strongest. Hence, doubtless, among other reasons, it is that in an age of revolutions in opinion, the contemporary poets, those at least who deserve the name, if they are not before their age, are almost sure to be behind it. An observation curiously verified all over Europe in the present century. Nor let it be thought disparaging. However urgent may be the necessity for a breaking up of old modes of belief, the most strongminded and discerning, next to those who head the movement, are generally those who bring up the rear.

Vanguard or rear guard, it makes very little difference today. Our most significant poets, whatever limited prestige and reputations they may enjoy, are nonetheless outcasts from this society. We may not all of us be extraordinarily distinguished or considered tremendously significant in the world of letters, but insofar as we are poets, we are enemies of this present society. None of us is in the position of my friend in New York. We either have some non-literary source of income, or we are employed by the WPA, but it is only an accident that we are all not so many Villons. The forces which control much of the world, forces which in America and in California are striving to suppress the democracy and creative freedom we have, have little use for us. They are committed to the belief that the sword is mightier than the pen. We are outcasts in their eyes already. None of us makes a living by poetry, although we think it one of the most important activities man has ever had or could ever hope to have as long as society remains as it is.

We have met to preserve the minimum conditions under which creative work is possible. We have not met to form a literary school or to persuade each other of the advisability of our individual techniques. We have not met to discuss Proletarian art, Surrealism, or heroic couplets. As writers we can make a significant gesture of defiance in the faces of those who are trying to remove America from the civilized world. But alone we cannot do very much else. There is a potential audience of all the producing classes of the West, which obviously we have not reached. We are conscious of the dangers which threaten what civilization we have. It is our job to awaken this audience to these dangers and to ally ourselves with the common people who have already awakened. It is they, not we, who will be the deciding factors in the coming struggle. Any moderately efficient fascist police could in a month silence or exterminate every honest writer in America. But they could not so easily dispose of farmers and workers, the common people upon whom the life of the country depends. It is still possible to rally the American people to the defense of their democracy.

This is our responsibility. If we enter upon it without losing our sense of proportion, without trying to save ourselves by embracing a cult, without abandoning the special, individual values we bring, we can accomplish much. The objective conditions for a regional renaissance are strong in the West today. Presumably we know what we are about or we would not be here. If we can leave here with a consciousness of the solidarity of our purposes, with a cohesion which we have not hitherto enjoyed, and, most important, if we can lay the foundations for a regional periodical which will be financed and edited with stability, which will be truly representative of the writers of the West, and which will address itself to the broadest possible audience of mature people, the effort which has gone to make this Congress will not have been wasted.

In conclusion, I hope that we do not fall into futile discussion of the relative merits of various contemporary literary groupings. Our ranks are not so crowded that there isn't still lots of room and, after all, it is quite conceivable that a sonnet about the moon, written by someone thoroughly aware of what he was talking about, might be much more effective than an agitational lyric by someone not so blessed. From each according to his ability, unto each according to his needs.

Poetry, Regeneration, and D. H. Lawrence

At the very beginning Lawrence belonged to a different order of being from the literary writers of his day. In 1912 he said: "I worship Christ, I worship Jehovah, I worship Pan, I worship Aphrodite. But I do not worship hands nailed and running with blood upon a cross, or licentiousness, nor lust. I want them all, all the gods. They are all God. But I must serve in real love. If I take my whole passionate, spiritual and physical love to the woman who in turn loves me, that is how I serve God. And my hymn and my game of joy is my work. All of which I read in . . ."

Do you know what he read all that in? It makes you wince. He thought he found that in *Georgian Poetry, 1911–1912!* In Lascelles Abercrombie, Wilfred Gibson, John Drinkwater, Rupert Brooke, John Masefield, Walter de la Mare, Gordon Bottomley! What a good man Lawrence must have been. It is easy to understand how painful it was for him to learn what evil really was. It is easy to understand why the learning killed him, slowly and terribly. But he never gave up. He was always hunting for comradeship—in the most unlikely places—Michael Arlen, Peter Warlock, Murry, Mabel Dodge. He never stopped trusting people and hoping. And he went on writing exactly the gospel he announced in 1912, right to the end.

Lawrence thought he was a Georgian, at first. There are people

Originally published as the Introduction to D. H. Lawrence, Selected Poems (*New York: New Directions, 1947), and, under the title "The Poems of D. H. Lawrence," in* Now *magazine the same year. Collected in* Bird in the Bush, *1959.*

who will tell you that his early poetry was typical Georgian country-side poetry—*Musings in the Hedgerows,* by the Well Dressed Dormouse. It is true that early poems like "The Wild Common," "Cherry Robbers," and the others, bear a certain resemblance to the best Georgian verse. They are rhymed verse in the English language on "subjects taken from nature." Some of the Georgians had a favorite literary convention. They were anti-literary. Lawrence was the real thing. His "hard" rhymes, for instance, "quick-kick," "rushes-pushes," "sheepdip-soft lip," "gudgeon-run on." I don't imagine that when Lawrence came to "soft lip" he remembered that bees had always sipped at soft lips and that, as a representative of a new tendency, it was up to him to do something about it. I think his mind just moved in regions not covered by the standard associations of standard British rhyme patterns. At the end of his life he was still talking about the old sheep dip, with its steep soft lip of turf, in the village where he was born. Why, once he even rhymed "wind" and "thinned," in the most unaware manner imaginable. That is something that, to the best of my knowledge, has never been done before or since in the British Isles.

The hard metric, contorted and distorted and generally banged around, doesn't sound made up, either. Compulsion neurotics like Hopkins and querulous old gentlemen like Bridges made quite an art of metrical eccentricity. You turned an iamb into a trochee here, and an anapest into a hard spondee there, and pretty soon you got something that sounded difficult and tortured and intense. I think Lawrence was simply very sensitive to quantity and to the cadenced pulses of verse. In the back of his head was a stock of sundry standard English verse patterns. He started humming a poem, hu hu hum, hum hum, hu hu hum hu, adjusted it as best might be to the remembered accentual patterns, and let it go at that. I don't think he was unconscious of the new qualities which emerged, but I don't think he went about it deliberately, either.

This verse is supposed to be like Hardy's. It is. But there is always something a little synthetic about Hardy's rugged verse. The smooth ones seem more natural, somehow. The full dress, Matthew Arnold sort of sonnet to Leslie Stephen is probably Hardy's best poem. It is a very great poem, but Arnold learned the trick of talking like a highly idealized Anglican archbishop and passed it on to Hardy.

That is something nobody could imagine Lawrence ever learning; he just wasn't that kind of an animal.

Hardy could say to himself: "Today I am going to be a Wiltshire yeoman, sitting on a fallen rock at Stonehenge, writing a poem to my girl on a piece of wrapping paper with the gnawed stub of a pencil," and he could make it very convincing. But Lawrence really was the educated son of a coal miner, sitting under a tree that had once been part of Sherwood Forest, in a village that was rapidly becoming part of a world-wide, disemboweled hell, writing hard, painful poems, to girls who carefully had been taught the art of unlove. It was all real. Love really was a mystery at the navel of the earth, like Stonehenge. The miner really was in contact with a monstrous, seething mystery, the black sun in the earth. There is a vatic quality in Lawrence that is only in Hardy rarely, in a few poems, and in great myths like *Two on a Tower.*

Something breaks out of the Pre-Raphaelite landscape of "Cherry Robbers." That poem isn't like a Victorian imitation of medieval illumination at all. It is more like one of those crude Coptic illuminations, with the Christian content just a faint glaze over the black, bloody "Babylonian turbulence" of the Gnostic mystery. I don't know the date of the "Hymn to Priapus"—it seems to lie somewhere between his mother's death and his flight with Frieda—but it is one of the Hardy kind of poems, and it is one of Lawrence's best. It resembles Hardy's "Night of the Dance." But there is a difference. Hardy is so anxious to be common that he just avoids being commonplace. Lawrence *is* common, he doesn't have to try. He is coming home from a party, through the winter fields, thinking of his dead mother, of the girl he has just had in the barn, of his troubled love life, and suddenly Orion leans down out of the black heaven and touches him on the thigh, and the hair of his head stands up.

Hardy was a major poet. Lawrence was a minor prophet. Like Blake and Yeats, his is the greater tradition. If Hardy ever had a girl in the hay, tipsy on cider, on the night of Boxing Day, he kept quiet about it. He may have thought that it had something to do with "the stream of his life in the darkness deathward set," but he never let on, except indirectly.

Good as they are, there is an incompleteness about the early poems. They are the best poetry written in England at that time, but they are poems of hunger and frustration. Lawrence was looking for completion. He found it later, of course, in Frieda, but he hadn't found it then. The girl he called Miriam wrote a decent, conscientious contribution to his biography. She makes it only too obvious that what he was looking for was not to be found in her. And so the Miriam poems are tortured, and defeated, and lost, as though Lawrence didn't know where he was, which was literally true.

Between Miriam and Frieda lies a body of even more intense and troubled poems. Those to his mother, the dialect poems, and the poems to Helen are in this group. The "mother" poems are among his best. They are invaluable as direct perspectives on an extraordinary experience.

From one point of view Lawrence is the last of a special tradition that begins with St. Augustine and passes through Pascal and Baudelaire amongst others, to end finally in himself. There is no convincing evidence for Freud's theory that the Oedipus Complex dates back to some extremely ancient crime in the history of primitive man. Least of all is there any Oedipus Complex in the Oedipus myth or plays. There is ample evidence that Western European civilization is specifically the culture of the Oedipus Complex. Before Augustine there was nothing really like it. There were forerunners and prototypes and intimations, but there wasn't the real thing. The *Confessions* introduce a new sickness of the human mind, the most horrible pandemic, and the most lethal, ever to afflict man. Augustine did what silly literary boys in our day boast of doing. He invented a new derangement. If you make an intense effort to clear your mind and then read Baudelaire and Catullus together, the contrast, the new thing in Baudelaire, makes you shudder. Baudelaire is struggling in a losing battle with a ghost more powerful than armies, more relentless than death. I think it is this demon which has provided the new thing in Western Man, the insane dynamic which has driven him across the earth to burn and slaughter, loot and rape.

I believe Lawrence laid that ghost, exorcised that demon, once for all, by an act of absolute spiritual transvaluation. "Piano," "Silence," "The Bride," and the other poems of that period, should be read with the tenth chapter of the ninth book of the *Confessions*. It is the beginning and the end. Augustine was a saint. There are acts of salvation by which man can raise himself to heaven, but, say the Japanese, a devil is substituted in his place. Lawrence drove out the devil, and the man stepped back. Or, as the Hindus say, with an act of absolute devotion from the worshiper, the goddess changes her aspect from maleficent to benign.

It is not only that Lawrence opened the gates of personal salvation for himself in the "mother" poems. He did it in a special way, in the only way possible, by an intense realization of total reality, and by the assumption of total responsibility for the reality and for the realization. Other people have tried parts of this process, but only the whole thing works. This shows itself in these poems, in their very technique. There, for the first time, he is in full possession of his faculties. He proceeds only on the basis of the completely real, the completely motivated, step by step along the ladder of Blake's "minute particulars." Ivor Richards' *Practical Criticism* contains a symposium of his students on Lawrence's "Piano." It makes one of the best introductions to Lawrence's poetry ever written. And one of the qualities of his verse that is revealed there most clearly is the uncanny, "surreal" accuracy of perception and evaluation. Objectivism is a hollow word beside this complete precision and purposiveness.

From this time on Lawrence never lost contact with the important thing, the totality in the particular, the responsibility of vision. Harassed by sickness and betrayal, he may have faltered in fulfilling that most difficult of all the injunctions of Christ, to suffer fools gladly. He may have got out of contact with certain kinds of men at certain times. He may have become cross and irritable and sick. But he never lost sight of what really mattered: the blue vein arching over the naked foot, the voices of the fathers singing at the charivari, blending in the winter night, Lady Chatterley putting flowers in Mellors' pubic hair.

The "Helen" poems are strange. (See "A Winter's Tale," "Return," "Kisses in the Train," "Under the Oak," "Passing Visit to Helen," "Release," and "Seven Seals.") They all have a weird, dark atmosphere shot through with spurts of flame, a setting which remained a basic symbolic situation with Lawrence. It is the atmosphere of the pre-War I novel, young troubled love in gas-lit London—draughty, dark, and flaring, and full of mysterious movement.

Probably the girl's name was not Helen. Lawrence thought of her as dim, larger than life, a demi-goddess, moving through the smoke of a burning city. For certain Gnostics Helen was the name of the incarnate "female principle," the power of the will, the sheath of the sword, the sacred whore who taught men love. Helen seems to have been the midwife of Lawrence's manhood. At the end, something like her returns in the Persephone of "Bavarian Gentians." Re-birth. No one leaves adolescence cleanly without a foretaste of death.

Ezra Pound said that the dialect poems were the best thing Lawrence ever wrote. This is just frivolous eccentricity. But they are fine poems, and in them another figure of the myth is carefully drawn. They are poems about Lawrence's father, the coal miner who emerges nightly from the earth with the foliage of the carboniferous jungles on his white body. Lawrence's little dark men, his Gypsies, and Indians, and Hungarians, and Mexicans, and all the rest, are not dark by race, but dark with coal dust. The shadow of forests immeasurably older than man has stained their skins. Augustine was never at peace until he found his father again in the pure mental absolute of Plotinus. Lawrence found his father again in the real man, whose feet went down into the earth. In certain poems where he speaks as a fictional woman, the erotic intensity is embarrassing to those of us who still live in the twilight of the Oedipus Complex. What had been evil in the father image becomes a virtue, the source of the will; deeply behind the mother image lies the germ of action, the motile flagellate traveling up the dark hot tube, seeking immortality.

The boy watching the miners rise and descend in the yawning maw of the earth in Nottinghamshire grows into the man of forty watching the Indians pass in and out of a lodge where an old man is interminably chanting—there is a sense of strangeness, but no estrangement. There is no effort to violate the mystery of paternity because it is known in the blood. Lawrence knew by a sort of sensual perception that every cell of his body bore the marks of the striped Joseph's coat of the paternal sperm.

All this world of the early poems, and of the novels, *The White Peacock, The Trespasser,* the first draft of *Sons and Lovers,* is an unborn world, a cave, a womb, obscure and confused. The figures have a mythic vagueness about them. The sensual reality seems to be always struggling beneath an inhibiting surface of flesh, struggling to escape into another realm of meaning. So many of the images are drawn from birth, escape, confinement, struggle. Critics have found much of their Freudianism in the work of this period. Had they been better read they would have found Jung above all else, and certainly Rank. Lawrence had yet to read Freud or Jung and may never have heard of Rank.

Some shockingly ill-informed things have been written about Lawrence's relation to psychoanalysis. In the first place, he was not a Freudian. He seems to have read little Freud, not to have understood him any too well, and to have disliked him heartily. In the winter of 1918-19 he read Jung, apparently for the first time, in English. Presumably this was *The Psychology of the Unconscious.* Jung was very much in the air in those days, as he is again. There was probably a great deal of amateur talk about his ideas among Lawrence's friends. But Lawrence does not seem to have had much more to go on, and *The Psychology of the Unconscious* is only the beginning of the system later elaborated by Jung. Nor did he ever become intimate with any of Jung's students. Later Mabel Dodge tried to bring the two together by correspondence. The story goes that Jung ignored her letters because they were written in pencil. So much for that.

Lawrence wrote quite a bit on psychoanalysis. There are the two books, *Psychoanalysis and the Unconscious,* a somewhat sketchy popularization of some of Jung's basic concepts, and *Fantasia of the Unconscious,* of which more in a moment. And then there are the reviews of Trigant Burrow's book, and miscellaneous remarks scattered through correspondence and reviews. This is all of the greatest importance to the understanding of Lawrence.

Fantasia of the Unconscious is an extraordinary book. It is foully written, unquestionably Lawrence's worst writing, but it is certainly a landmark in the history of psychoanalysis. It is an attempt to combine the empirical neurology of Kundalini Yoga with his own interpretation of Jung's psychology and with a theory of sexuality which may be either his own or derived from popular, occultist expositions of certain Gnostic sects and rumors of the practices of Shakti-Yoga. When it appeared, it must have seemed like pure fantasy of the Lost Atlantis variety. Jung's *Secret of the Golden*

Flower, and his studies of "spiritual alchemy" lay in the future. The "psychology of the autonomic system" was unheard of. It is all there, in Lawrence's inspired guesses. The white race is going mad, but it is the autonomic nervous system which is out of kilter; what goes on in the head is secondary—and the autonomic nervous system is, as a whole, the organ of communion.

To return to the poems. There is an hallucinatory quality in the images of the poems which precede Frieda which it is interesting to compare with the induced hallucination of H.D. The conflict in H.D. is hidden in herself. It is still there to this day, although her latest prose work has been the journal of a Freudian analysis. Her images are purified of conflict; then the intensity which has been distilled from the sublimation of conflict is applied from the outside. ("Your poetry is not pure, eternal, sublimated," she told Lawrence.) What results is a puzzling hallucination of fact, a contentless mood which seems to reflect something tremendously important but whose mystery always retreats before analysis.

Lawrence's early poems are poems of conflict. The images are always polarized. Antagonisms struggle through the texture. But the struggle is real. The antagonisms are struggling toward the light. The conflict yields to insight, if not to analysis. It is like the propaedeutic symbolism of the dream, as contrasted to the trackless labyrinths of falsification which form the patterns of most waking lives. The hallucination is real, the vision of the interior, personal oracle. Its utterance has meaning, more meaning than ordinary waking reality because the subjective is seen in the objective, emerging from it, the dream from the reality—not dislocated or applied from outside the context.

The poems of *Look! We Have Come Through* fall into three groups. First there are the structurally more conventional pieces like "Moonrise," which sounds a little like Masefield's sonnets though it is incomparably finer, and the "Hymn to Priapus," and the others— they are all probably earlier and have already been discussed. Second, there are the poems of the Rhine Journey, "December Night," "New Year's Eve," "Coming Awake," "History"; erotic epigrams, intense as Meleager, more wise than Paul the Silentiary. Lawrence was still a young man, and had many great poems to write—but put these beside the few poets who have survived from that day, Sturge Moore, Monro, De La Mare . . . they look like pygmies. Only Yeats stands up against Lawrence. And last, there are the Whitmanic free verse manifestoes, "explaining" marriage to a people who had forgotten what it was.

With Frieda the sleeper wakes, the man walks free, the "child" of the alchemists is born. Reality is totally valued, and passes beyond the possibility of hallucination. The clarity of purposively realized objectivity is the most supernatural of all visions. Bad poetry always suffers from the same defects: synthetic hallucination and artifice. Invention is not poetry. Invention is defense, the projection of pseudopods out of the ego to ward off the "other." Poetry is vision, the pure act of sensual communion and contemplation.

That is why the poems of Lawrence and Frieda on their Rhine Journey are such great poetry. That is why they are also the greatest imagist poems ever written. Reality streams through the body of Frieda, through everything she touches, every place she steps, valued absolutely, totally, beyond time and place, in the minute particular. The swinging of her breasts as she stoops in the bath, the roses, the deer, the harvesters, the hissing of the glacier water in the steep river—everything stands out lit by a light not of this earth and at the same time completely of this earth, the light of the Holy Sacrament of Marriage, whose source is the wedded body of the bride.

The accuracy of Lawrence's observation haunts the mind permanently. I have never stood beside a glacier river, at just that relative elevation, and just that pitch, with just that depth of swift water moving over a cobbled bed, without hearing again the specific hiss of Lawrence's Isar. These poems may not be sublimated (whatever Y.M.C.A. evasion that may refer to), but they are certainly pure and eternal.

Again, it is fruitful to compare the Rhine Journey poems with the only other poems of our time which resemble them much, Ford Madox Ford's *Buckshee.* Ford was writing about something very akin to what Lawrence was, about an aspect of marriage. But he was writing about its impossibility, about how life had bled away its possibility from both him and his girl, and how they had taken, in middle age and in the long Mediterranean drought, the next best thing—intense erotic friendship. And about how, every once in a while, marriage comes and looks in at the window. The contrast with Lawrence and Frieda, sinking into the twilight in the fuming marsh by the Isar, "where the snake disposes," is pathetic past words.

Ford's "L'Oubli—Temps de Secheresse" and Lawrence's "River Roses" and "Quite Forsaken" are things of a kind and the best of their kind, but like the north and south poles, there is all the difference in the world between them. There is more communion in Frieda's temporary absence than in the closest possible kiss "under the catalpa tree, where the strange birds, driven north by the drought, cry with their human voices." "Singular birds, with their portentous, singular flight and human voices," says Ford. This is the Persephone of "Bavarian Gentians" and the Orphic birds which flutter around the dying who are withdrawing themselves, corpuscle by corpuscle, from communion. Lawrence would come there one day, with the dark blue flowers on the medicine table and Frieda sleeping in a chair beside him, but he was on the other side of the universe then—the early summer of 1912, in the Isartal, the snow leaving the mountains.

After the Rhine Journey come the poems of struggle for a living adjustment. The ceremonial glory of the sacrament passes from the forefront of consciousness, and the period of adjustment to the background of life begins. Every detail of life must be transformed by marriage. This means creative conflict on the most important level.

Sacramental communion is bound by time. Mass does not last forever. Eventually the communicant must leave the altar and digest the wafer, the Body, and Blood must enter his own flesh as it moves through the world and struggles with the devil. The problem lies in the sympathetic nervous system, says Lawrence. And it is not easy for two members of a deranged race, in the twentieth century, to learn again how to make those webs mesh as they should.

Some of these poems are, in a sense, Frieda's—records of her own interior conquest. It is amazing how much they accomplished, these two. Today, revisiting this battlefield between love and hate that is so carefully mapped in certain of the poems, it is like Gettysburg, a sleepy, pastoral landscape dotted with monuments and graves. Only maimed women and frightened men are Suffragettes anymore. Hedda Gabler is dead, or lurking in the suburbs. We should be grateful to Frieda. It was she who gave the dragon its death blow, and the Animus no longer prowls the polls and bedrooms, seeking whom it may devour.

The Whitmanic poems seem to owe a good deal to "Children of Adam" and "Calamus". They look like Whitman on the page. But if read aloud with any sort of ear, they don't sound much like him. Whitman flourished in the oratorical context of nineteenth-century America. He isn't rhetorical in the invidious sense; that is, there is nothing covert or coercive about him. He says what he means, but he says it in the language of that lost art of elocution so popular in his day. There is little of this in Lawrence. At this period his long-lined free verse is derived almost entirely from the poetry of the Bible, the Psalms, the song of Deborah, the song of Hezekiah, of Moses, the Benedicite, the Magnificat, the Nunc Dimitus. All the devices of Hebrew poetry are there, and in addition the peculiar, very civilized, self-conscious, "sympathetic" poetry of St. Luke— those poems which have made his the "women's Gospel," and which all good Englishmen must learn in childhood as part of the Morning and Evening Prayer of the Church.

In the volume *Look! We Have Come Through* Lawrence was just beginning to learn to write free verse. I don't think some of the poems are completely successful. They are diffuse and long-winded. He tries to say too much, and all at the same pitch of intensity; there are no crises, no points of reference. On the whole the most successful is "New Heaven and Earth." It may not be a perfect object of art but it is a profound exhortation.

Beyond Holy Matrimony lies the newly valued world of birds, beasts, and flowers—a sacramentalized, objective world. "Look, we have come through"—to a transformed world, with a glory around it everywhere like ground lightning. The poems of *Birds, Beasts, and Flowers* have the same supernatural luster that shines through the figures of men and animals and things, busy being part of a new redeemed world, as they are found carved around the mandala of the Blessed Virgin above some cathedral door or on some rose window.

Birds, Beasts, and Flowers is the mature Lawrence, in complete control of his medium, or completely controlled by his demon. He never has any trouble. He can say exactly what he wants to say.

Except for the death poems, he would never write better. (And too, after this, he would never be well again.) He seems to have lived in a state of total realization—the will and its power, positive and negative, at maximum charge, and all the universe streaming between them glowing and transformed. The work of art grows in that electric field, is a "function" of it. It is the act of devotion in the worshiper that forces the god to occupy the statue. It is the act of devotion in the sculptor that forces the god to occupy the stone which the artist then pares to his invisible limbs, tailors like cloth. It is never theology in the first; it is never aesthetics or any teachable craft in the second. The craft is the vision and the vision is the craft.

Good cadenced verse is the most difficult of all to write. Any falsity, any pose, any corruption, any ineptitude, any vulgarity, shows up immediately. In this it is like abstract painting. A painting by Mondrian may look impersonal enough to be reduced to code and sent by telegraph. Maybe. But it offers no refuge, no garment, no mask, no ambush, for the person. The painter must stand there, naked, as Adam under the eye of God. Only very great or very trivial personalities dare expose themselves so.

Think of a few typical writers of cadenced verse: Whitman, Sandburg, Wallace Gould, F. M. Ford, F. S. Flint, Aldington, Lola Ridge, and James Oppenheim. (H.D.'s verse is primarily a counterpointing of accentual and quantitative rhythms in patterns of Greek derivation. Pound's verse is Latin in reference, and usually quantitative.) How the faults stand out! Every little weakness is revealed with glaring cruelty. Whitman's tiresome posturing, Sandburg's mawkishness, Aldington's erotic sentimentality, the overreaching ambition of Lola Ridge and Oppenheim—what a lot of sore thumbs standing out! Yet in many ways these are good poets, and Whitman is a very great one.

Gould, Flint, and Ford were never dishonest, never overreached themselves, did their best to say what they meant and no more, never bargained with art. "The sentimentalist," said Daedalus, "is he who would enjoy, without incurring the immense debtorship for a thing done." They are not prophets, but they are good poets because they rendered a strict accounting with their own souls.

Sentimentality is spiritual realization on the installment plan. Socially viable patterns, like conventional verse, are a sort of underwriting or amortization of the weaknesses of the individual. This is the kernel of sense in the hollow snobbery of Valéry. The sonnet and quatrain are like the national debt, devices for postponing the day of reckoning indefinitely. All artistic conventions are a method of spiritual deficit-financing. If they were abandoned, the entire credit structure of Poets, Ltd., would be thrown into hopeless confusion. It is just as well that the professors have led the young, in my lifetime, away from free verse to something that can be taught. No one could be taught to be Lawrence, but in a world where the led lead the leaders, those who might pretend to do so are sure to be confidence men.

Lawrence's free verse in *Birds, Beasts, and Flowers* is among the small best ever written. It can be analyzed, but the paradigms produced by the analysis are worthless. It cannot be explained away, demonstrated in a mathematical sense. Neither, certainly, can any other great poetry; but at least a convincing illusion can be created, and the young can be provided with something to practice. A poem like "Bat" or the "Lion of St. Mark" moves with a stately, gripping sonority through the most complex symphonic evolutions. The music is a pattern of vibration caught from the resonant tone of Lawrence himself. The concerto is not on the page, little spots with flags and tails on a stave, but the living thing, evolving from the flesh of the virtuoso. It is like Gregorian chant or Hindu music, one thing when sung at Solesmes, or in the ruins of Konarak, another when "rendered" by the Progressive Choral Group or at a concert of the Vedanta Society of Los Angeles.

Again, the faults of *Birds, Beasts, and Flowers* are the excess of virtue. Like anyone who knows he has something intensely important to say, Lawrence found it hard to keep from being long-winded. I think a good deal of his over-expansiveness and repetition is due to his methods of composition.

Some poets meditate in stillness and inactivity, as far away as possible from the creative act. We know that Baudelaire and T. S. Eliot, by their own testimony, spent long periods of time quiescent, inert as artists, turning over and over the substance of vision within themselves. Sometimes, as in Baudelaire, this process is extremely painful, a true desert of the soul. Months went by in which the paper and pen were red hot, it was impossible for him to read, his whole personality seemed engulfed in a burning neurasthenia. And then there would come a period of peace, and slowly growing exaltation, and finally the creative act, almost somnambulistic in its completion. Actual composition by this sort of personality tends to be rare, and usually as perfect as talent permits.

Lawrence meditated pen in hand. His contemplation was always active, flowing out in a continuous stream of creativity which he seemed to have been able to open practically every day. He seldom reversed himself, seldom went back to rework the same manuscript. Instead, he would lay aside a work that dissatisfied him and rewrite it all from the beginning. In his poetry he would move about a theme, enveloping it in constantly growing spheres of significance. It is the old antithesis: centrifugal versus centripetal, Parmenides versus Heraclitus. He kept several manuscript books of his verse, and whenever he wanted to publish a collection he would go through them and pick out a poem here and there, the ones he considered had best handled their themes. Behind each poem was usually a group of others devoted to the same material. His selection was always personal, and sometimes it was not very "artistic." *Nettles*, for instance, is a selection of what are, by any standard, the poorer poems of the collections of epigrams printed in *Last Poems*.

There are those who think these epigrams, the ones in *Pansies*, and those in *Last Poems*, aren't art. This opinion is the product of a singular provincialism. It is true that, due to the reasons just mentioned, they aren't all successful, but they belong to a tradition, are members of a species, which has produced some of the greatest poetry. Epigram or maxim, Martial or La Rochefoucauld, the foundations of this tradition are far more stable than those of the neo-metaphysical poetry produced, with seven ambiguities carefully inserted in every line, by unhappy dons between the wars.

Any bright young man can be taught to be artful. It is impossible to teach taste, but you can teach most anybody caution. It is always the lesser artists who are artful, they must learn their trade by rote. They must be careful never to make a false step, never to speak out of a carefully synthesized character. The greater poetry is nobly disheveled. At least it never shows the scars of taking care. "Would he had blotted a thousand lines," said Ben Jonson of Shakespeare. Which thousand? Lawrence was always mislaying those manuscript books of poetry and writing around the world for them, just as Cézanne left his paintings in the fields. Not for any stupid reason—that they were not Perfect Works of Art—but simply because he forgot.

Eliot (who does not write that way), writing of Pound's epigrams, points out that the major poet, unlike the minor, is always writing about everything imaginable, and so is in good form for the great poem when it comes. Practice makes perfect, and those who wait for the perfect poem before putting pen to paper may wait mute forever. I suppose it is the absolutism which swept over popular taste in the wake of Cubism that has encouraged the ignorant to expect a canzone of Dante's in each issue of their favorite little magazine, a School of Athens in every WPA mural. This is just greediness, like children who want it to be Christmas every day. And it produces an empty, pretentious, greedy art. Meanwhile, Pound's "Les Millwin," and Lawrence's "Willy Wet-Legs," quietly pre-empt immortality, a state of being only rarely grandiose.

As far as I know the poems in the novel *The Plumed Serpent* have never been printed separately. This book is one of the most important (he thought it the most important) Lawrence ever wrote. It has brought forth all sorts of pointless debate. People are always saying: "Well, I have lived in Mexico for years and it *simply* isn't like that." Lawrence was not an idiot. He knew it wasn't. And in the first chapter he gave a very accurate and pitiful picture of the "real" Mexico—sterile, subcolonial, brutal, with the old gods gone, and the church gone, and the revolution a swindle, and nothing left but a squalid imitation of Ashtabula, Ohio. And he knew the other side too, the pasty frigid nymphomaniacs, the deranged women of Europe and America, who consider themselves disciples of Lawrence and prowl the earth seeking Dark Gods to take to bed. He wrote a story which should have destroyed them forever—"None of That." It should be read with *The Plumed Serpent.*

Every year there is less, but in Lawrence's day there was still something, of the primeval Mexico—at the great feast in Oaxaca, in the life of the peasants in the remote villages, in the Indian communities in the back country. Lawrence did not make any very definite contact with the ancient Mexico but he could see and sense it, and he was fresh from a much less-touched primitive world—that of the

Navaho and Pueblo Indians of the Southwest. His materials were not as abundant as they might have been but they were enough to build a book of ritual, of the possible that would never be, of potentialities that would never emerge. It is a book of ceremonial prophecy, but prophecy uttered in the foreknowledge that it would never be fulfilled.

The reawakening of mystery, the revival of the old Aztec religion, the political "Indianism"—even if it all came true, one knows it would be a fraud, a politician's device, as Indianism is in Latin America today. Lawrence knew that, of course, and so the book is dogged with tragedy. One constantly expects the characters to go out in a blazing *Götterdämmerung* in some dispute with the police, like a gangster movie. They don't, but maybe it would have been better if they had, for eventually they tire; they seem to become secretly aware that all this gorgeous parading around in primitive millinery, this Mystery, and Fire, and Blood, and Darkness, has been thought up. There is something Western European, British Museum, about it. The protagonist, Kate, submits to her lover's insistent Mystery, but rather out of ennui and loathing of Europe than out of any conviction, and one feels that the book could have no sequel, or only a sequel of disintegration, like *Women in Love.*

Still, in the middle of the book, before the fervor dies out, Lawrence wrote as nearly as he could what he believed should be. If the religion of Cipriano and Ramón is taken as an other-worldly system of values, it is profound and true, and, due to the freshness of its symbols, tremendously exciting. Also, it differs very little from any other religion that has maintained its contacts with its sources. Ramón and Cipriano short-circuit themselves where Christianity was short-circuited by Constantine, in the desire to have both worlds, to found a political religion—a Church. That, if any, is the "message" of the book.

The mystery survives in the poems, just as the sacraments survived Constantine. They are not the greatest poems Lawrence ever wrote, but they are among the most explicit. This is Lawrence's religion. Wherever he found it he is now in complete possession of a kind of orthodoxy, the orthodoxy of the heterodox—the symbolic world of the Gnostics, the Occultists, Tantrism, Jung. In a sense they are failures, these poems, in the way that the Indian songs published by the United States Bureau of Ethnology are not failures. But, again, that is the message of the book. Finally you discover that you cannot make up paganism. What you make up is a cult. There is nothing primitive about Gnosticism, anymore than there is anything primitive about Theosophy. It is the creation of over-civilized Hellenistic intellectuals. Tantrism too grew up in India, in Buddhism and Hinduism, when civilization was exhausting itself. Jung comes, with Lawrence, at the end of the career of Western European Man. Lawrence, after all, was a contemporary of Niels Bohr and Picasso. And so his poems are mystical poems—and the Aztecs were not mystics, they were just Aztecs. This doesn't invalidate the poems. They have very little to do with ancient or modern Mexico, but they do express, very well, the personal religion of D. H. Lawrence. They may be full of "occult lore," but behind the machinery is an intense, direct, personal, mystical apprehension of reality.

In the last hours Lawrence seems to have lived in a state of suspended animation, removed from the earth, floating, transfigured by the onset of death. Poems like "Andraitix," "Pomegranate Flowers," have an abstracted, disinterested intensity, as though they were written by a being from another planet. Others are short mystical apothegms. There is no millinery anymore, no occultism; they differ only in their modern idiom from any and all of the great mystics. And finally there are the two death poems, "Bavarian Gentians" and "The Ship of Death." Each was written over several times. There exists a variant which can be taken as a final, or pre-final, version of "Bavarian Gentians," but both are clusters of poems rather than finished products.

"The Ship of Death" material alone would make a small book of meditations, a contemporary *Holy Dying*. It is curious to think that once such a book would have been a favorite gift for the hopelessly ill. Today people die in hospitals, badgered by nurses, stupefied with barbiturates. This is not an age in which a "good death" is a desired end of life.

All men have to die, and one would think a sane man would want to take that fact into account, at least a little. But our whole civilization is a conspiracy to pretend that it isn't going to happen— and this, in an age when death has become more horrible, more senseless, less at the will of the individual than ever before. Modern man is terribly afraid of sex, of pain, of evil, of death. Today childbirth, the ultimate orgiastic experience, has been reduced to a meaningless dream; dentists insist on injecting Novocain before they clean your teeth; the agonies of life have retreated to the source of life. Men and women torture each other to death in the bedroom, just as the dying dinosaurs gnawed each other as they copulated in the chilling marshes. Anything but the facts of life. Today you can take a doctor's degree in medicine or engineering and never learn how to have intercourse with a woman or repair a car. Human self-alienation, Marx called it. He said that was all that was really wrong with capitalism. "Let us live and lie reclined" in a jet-propelled, streamlined, air-cooled, lucite incubator. When we show signs of waking, another cocktail instead of the Wine of God. When we try to break out, flagellation instead of Holy Matrimony, psychoanalysis instead of Penance. When the machinery runs down, morphine for Extreme Unction.

In a world where death had become a nasty, pervasive secret like defecation or masturbation, Lawrence re-instated it in all its grandeur—the oldest and most powerful of the gods. "The Ship of Death" poems have an exaltation, a nobility, a steadiness, an insouciance, which is not only not of this time but is rare in any time. It doesn't matter who: Jeremy Taylor, the Orphic Hymns, the ancient Egyptians—nobody said it better. And there is one aspect of the "Ship of Death" which is unique. Lawrence did not try to mislead himself with false promises, imaginary guarantees. Death is the absolute, unbreakable mystery. Communion and oblivion, sex and death, the mystery can be revealed—but it can be revealed only as totally inexplicable. Lawrence never succumbed to the temptation to try to do more. He succeeded in what he did do.

The Visionary Painting
of Morris Graves

It is not well-known around the world that there existed in the nineteenth-century United States a very considerable visionary art. William Blake and his disciples, Samuel Palmer and Edward Calvert, Francis Danby and John Martin, the later Turner, the Pre-Raphaelites, Odilon Redon, Gustave Moreau, the Nabis, were popular in America and had considerable influence. Most of the painters of this tendency are now forgotten, but one, Albert Pinkham Ryder (1847–1917), has survived in popular esteem as one of America's greatest artists. In our own time visionary painting has been at a discount all over the world, in spite of some interest stirred up a generation ago by the Surrealists, but it is quite possible that the re-evaluation which has brought back Palmer, Calvert, and Redon, may in time to come restore many more forgotten reputations, even Moreau, who, say what you will, is the master of Rouault at least.

It is to this tendency of American painting that Morris Graves belongs. However, he is beyond question a richer and more skillful artist than any of his predecessors, and, to put it simply, a better, "greater" painter than any of them, except possibly Ryder. In recent years a whole new school of American painting, abstract-expressionism, has come to maturity and begun to influence painting around the world. Painters such as Rothko, Still, Pollock, Motherwell, de Kooning, and Ferren now seem to be the forerunners of what may be the international style of the coming decade. Morris Graves,

---

First published in Perspectives USA #10 *in Winter 1955. Collected in* Bird in the Bush, *1959.*

however, stands apart from the expressionist group, as, at the other extreme of contemporary style, does a figure of comparable stature, Ben Shahn.

Morris Graves is less provincial, far more a "citizen of the world" than any of his predecessors of the visionary school. It is curious to reflect on this fact, a symptom of the terrific acceleration of the civilizing process of this continent, for Graves was born, raised, and came to maturity as an artist in the Pacific Northwest, a region that was a wilderness until the last years of the nineteenth century. Greatly as I admire Graves's work, it must be admitted that certain of its characteristics are those found, not at the beginning, but at the end of a cultural process—hypersensitivity, specialization of subject, extreme refinement of technique. Nothing could show better the essentially world-wide, homogeneous nature of modern culture than that this successor to the great Sung painters sprang up in a region that was created out of a jungle-like rain forest by the backwash of the Alaska gold rush.

People in the rest of the United States and in Europe have difficulty in adjusting to the fact that the Pacific Coast of America faces the Far East, culturally as well as geographically. There is nothing cultish about this, as there might be elsewhere. The residents of California, Oregon, and Washington are as likely to travel across the Pacific as across the continent and the Atlantic. Knowledge of the Oriental languages is fairly widespread. The museums of the region all have extensive collections of Chinese, Japanese, and Indian art. Vedantist and Buddhist temples are to be seen in the coast cities. And of course there are large Chinese and Japanese colonies in every city, and proportionately even more Orientals in the countryside. It is interesting to note that besides the direct influence of the Orient on them, the Seattle painters, Graves, Tobey, and Callahan, the Portland painter, Price, the San Francisco abstract-expressionists, have all avoided the architectural limited-space painting characteristic of Western Europe from the Renaissance to Cubism, and show more affinity to the space concepts of the Venetians. Venice, of course, was for centuries Europe's chief window on the East, an enclave of Byzantine civilization, and the first contact with China. There are drawings by Tintoretto that might have been done in his contemporary China. I do not believe that this has been a conscious influence in most cases, but rather an example of what anthropologists call convergence.

Graves was born in 1910 in the Fox Valley of Oregon and has lived in the state of Washington, in or near Seattle, all his life, except for short visits to Japan in 1930, to the Virgin Islands in 1939, to Honolulu in 1947, and a year in Europe in 1948, after his personal style was fully developed and "set." He studied at the Seattle Museum, with the old master of Northwest painting, Mark Tobey, and had his first one-man show there in 1936. His first New York shows were in 1942 at the Willard Gallery and the Museum of Modern Art. His paintings are now to be found in the permanent collections of most of the major American museums, including the Metropolitan in New York.

Except for the emphasis on deep complex space and calligraphic skill which he learned from Tobey, but which he could just as well have learned from the Far Eastern paintings in the Seattle Museum, Graves's style, or styles, his special mode of seeing reality and his techniques of handling it, have come, like the spider's web, out of himself, or, at the most, out of the general cultural ambience of a world civilization, syncretic of all time and space. Therefore, influences and resemblances which seem certain to a historian of art may never in actual fact have existed. Since today Graves's painting is an extremely specialized view of reality and his concept of space differs from that usually thought of as the contribution of modern painting, it is fruitful to compare him in his development with other painters of other times around the world, always realizing that, with the exception of Chinese, specifically Sung, and Japanese, specifically Ashikaga, and particularly the painter Sesshu, Graves himself may never have known of any resemblance let alone influence.

The first of Graves's paintings after his apprentice days are in a rather thick medium, often laid in like cloisonné between broad, abrupt, dark, single brush strokes. The colors are all "local." There is no attempt to achieve deep space or movement in space by juxtaposition of color. In fact the color is limited to a small gamut of earths, dull reds, browns, and yellows, with occasionally a slate blue. The line, however, has a great deal of snap, while the movement is very shallow, almost Egyptian. If there are receding planes in these pictures, they are kept to a minimum and the lines stick to the silhouette, never crossing from plane to plane to fill the space. The thing that identifies these paintings immediately is a peculiar, individual sense of silhouette, a silhouette defined by an eccentric calligraphic stroke.

As is well known, a highly personal line of this type comes late, if at all, to most artists. Yet it seems to have been the first thing Graves developed. I can think of nothing quite like it. The brush drawings of the early Jean de Bosschere—not the commercial book illustrations but rather those for his own *Portes Fermées*—have somewhat the same feeling. I rather doubt that Graves has ever seen these.

This is also somewhat the style of very early Klee. It is generally identified with the magazine *Simplicissimus*, a German satirical publication of the years before the First War. Graves, very likely, has never heard of it.

Already in this period, which incidentally was roughly that of the WPA Art Project (1935–42), Graves was beginning to concentrate on birds and sometimes small animals as masks of man and as symbols of the personae, the forces, operating in man—a kind of transcendental Aesop.

Certainly the best picture of this period is a large *Game Cock* (1933), many times life size, caught in a thick perimeter that whips across the picture plane like jagged lightning. There is no sign of the easy line so attractive to young artists who are beginning to pay attention to their drawing—the decorative sweeps of Beardsley, Botticelli, or the Book of Kells, those perennial favorites of the innocent. Neither is there any of the impressionist line of the Rodin water colors, the other and great influence on the young—and on Matisse and his descendants. This line is tooled to the last millimeter and, with the exception of the Bosscheres I spoke of, there is nothing like it except certain painted ceramics, Greek and Oriental, some Romanesque illumination, and the akimbo linearity of the Moissac Portal. It is simply not a line usually found in painting. Later this cock was to be repainted, smaller, more compact and secretive, in the two *Game Cocks* of 1939.

In his early twenties Graves had begun to concentrate on calligraphy, under the influence of Mark Tobey's "white writing," which Tobey himself was just then beginning. Graves shared practically on equal terms with the older man in its development.

At this time too Graves took a short trip to Japan and later traveled in the eastern United States and the Caribbean. The paintings of this period parallel—they cannot really be said to be influenced by—the major paintings of Tintoretto in the treatment of the picture space as a saturated manifold quivering with three-dimensional lines, really tracks of force. The best analogy is to the whorls of iron filings in a magnetic field. But in this case the field is both three dimensional and possessed of more than two poles, and all of varying intensity. This space concept reaches its highest development only in the Venetian baroque in the West, but of course it is basic in the greatest periods of Sung and Ashikaga ink painting.

In writing of Sesshu, I have said, "The brush, which never departs from the calligraphy of the square Chinese characters, is as quick, precise, powerful, and yet effortless as Japanese sword play. 'The sword,' say the Zen fencing masters, 'finds channels opened for it in space, and follows them without exertion to the wound.' This is the central plastic conception of Sesshu. The picture space is thought of as a field of tangled forces, a complex dynamic web. The brush strokes flow naturally in this medium, defining it by their own tensions, like fish in a whirlpool of perfectly clear water."

Both Tobey and Graves can be considered as direct descendants of Sesshu. In Graves there is an additional factor, a deliberate formal mysteriousness, a conscious seeking for uncanny form, analogous to that found in primitive cult objects—sacred stones and similar things. There are several series of studies of just such objects—stones and driftwood—notably the nine water colors of 1937 called *Purification*.

From 1939 to 1942 were the years of the *Little Known Bird of the Inner Eye, Bird in Moonlight,* and *Blind Bird,* now in the New York Museum of Modern Art collection, paintings which achieved an instantaneous fame when they were first exhibited. Every critic seems to have been aware that here was a really different yet thoroughly competent artist.

Incidentally, the haunted, uncanny character of these pictures, which reaches its height, representationally at least, in *Young Rabbit and Foxfire* and *Bird with Possessions* of 1942, owes little or nothing to Surrealism. There is much more conscious knowledge of mystery, and much less unconscious Freudian or Jungian symbolism.

On into the war years the mastery of calligraphy developed, until finally the line, sometimes "white writing," sometimes black, reaches a climax in the *Joyous Young Pine* series of 1944, *Black Waves* (1944), *In the Air* (1943), and the two great ideographs called *Waning Moon* (1943), in the Seattle Art Museum. These paintings are fully the equal of anything, East or West, of the kind. *Waning Moon* passes out of the realm of ordinary painting altogether and can be compared only with the ominous, cryptic characters which Shingon monks write on six-foot sheets of paper while in trance.

To 1945 belongs the series called *Consciousness Assuming the Form of a Crane.* I own what I consider the best of these, and for nine years I have found its ephemeral simplicity inexhaustible. In these paintings the old dynamic hyperactive space of Sesshu has been surpassed. The background is a vague cloudy diagonal drift of red and green, overcast with a frost of white. From this, in a few faint strokes of white with touches of somber red, emerges a slowly pacing, more than life-size crane-being rising from flux into consciousness, but still withdrawn, irresponsible, and stately. There is nothing exactly like this in the world's art, for it is not simply a literary or a mystical notion but a plastic one as well. Form, an ominous, indifferent form, emerges from formlessness, literally seems to bleed quietly into being.

The great dragon painters of the Orient whose dragons are confused with and only half emerge from vortexes of clouds and rain were seeking the same kind of effect, but of course their paintings are far more active. Graves's *Cranes* are not active at all. They are as quiet as some half-caught telepathic message.

In 1948, Graves traveled in Europe. Much of this time was spent at Chartres. Just before leaving America he had done a series of what can only be described as intensely personal portraits of Chinese Shang and Chou bronzes. Objects of great mystery in their own right, in Graves's paintings they become visions, supernatural judgments of the natural world. *Individual State of the World*, with its use of Graves's recurrent minnow, symbol of the spark of spiritual illumination, is representative of this series. Contemporary with these bronzes is a series of vajras (Buddhist ritual bronze thunderbolts), lotuses, and diamonds of light which can be considered as illustrations for that great refusal to affirm either being or nonbeing, the *Prajnaparamita Sutra.*

No one has seen what Graves did at Chartres. In conversation he has told me how he spent the better part of a cold foggy winter there, painting every day, details of the cathedral, fragments of statues, bits of lichened masonry, and several pictures of the interior of the cathedral in early morning—the great vault, half filled with thick fog, dawn beginning to sparkle in the windows. When he came back to America and reviewed the year's work he destroyed it all. I have a feeling that the painting in the Fredericks collection, *Ever Cycling*, may have survived from this time.

Shortly after this, Graves abandoned ink, gouache, and water color on paper, and returned to oil. From 1950 to the present [1955], most of the paintings are in the vein of *Guardian*—or the *Spirit Bird Transporting Minnow from Stream to Stream* of the Metropolitan collection—geese, hawks, and eagles, most of them over life size, many with mystifying accessories such as black suns or golden antlers. It would seem, looking at a sizable collection of these recent paintings, that Graves has, at least temporarily, abandoned the surcharged, dynamic, baroque space of the calligraphic paintings and returned to the intact object. Again, there is considerable resemblance to the bird painters of the Far East—the famous pair of ducks of the Sung Dynasty in the British Museum, or the early falcon painters of the Kano school. These new paintings share with them a concentration on maximum surface tension, a sense of absolutely full occupation of their separate volume, like formed globules of quicksilver, or drops of viscid oil. This particular formal quality does have a parallel in contemporary art, notably in Brancusi's sculpture of a *Fish* and those dreaming ovoids he calls *Birth*, and more especially in the most successful of Hans Arp's swollen, amoeboid figures. Piero della Francesca, of course, is the outstanding example of what might be called overloaded volume in the

Renaissance. This, by the way, is a quality that must be distinguished from Picasso's excessive specific gravity—in his case a directly representational device masquerading as "significant form." Picasso and most of his disciples simply paint things to look many times as heavy as they actually are. In Graves's recent work there is always a sense of ominous, impending meaning, as if these human-eyed birds were judging the spectator, rather than he them, and in terms of a set of values incomprehensible to our sensual world.

It is none too easy to sum up such an accomplishment as that of Graves. Certainly he is one of the greatest calligraphers of all time—not just a "master of line" but a creator of significant ideographs and, beyond that, a creator of a new and strange significance of the ideograph as well. Graves has also been one of the many around the world who in this generation have freed painting from the exhausted plasticism, the concentration on architecture alone, which formed the residue of subsiding Cubism. This he has accomplished not merely, or even primarily, by illustrative, but by plastic means, by discovering a new world of form antipodal to the Poussin rigor of Cubism. Graves has opened the plastic arts to a whole range of experience hardly found in the external world at all, let alone in art. He has created a series of objects, masks, personae, which act both as objects of contemplation, and, in contemplation, as sources of values which judge the world the spectator brings to them. On the whole this judgment has little room or time for those values known to the popular mind as "American," but which are really those of our acquisitive mass Western civilization.

Jacques Maritain asks somewhere, "What kept Europe alive for so long after it had obviously been stricken with a fatal disease?" and answers his question, "The prayers of the contemplatives in the monasteries." I am not prepared to enter into a metaphysical defense of petitionary prayer, or a sociological one of monasticism, but the empirical evidence for the social, perhaps even biological necessity for contemplation, is, in these apocalyptic hours, all too obvious. Civilizations endure as long as, somewhere, they can hold life in total vision. The function of the contemplative is contemplation. The function of the artist is the revelation of reality in process, permanence in change, the place of value in a world of facts. His duty is to keep open the channels of contemplation and to discover new ones. His role is purely revelatory. He can bring men to the springs of the good, the true, and the beautiful, but he cannot make them drink. The activities of men endure and have meaning as long as they emanate from a core of transcendental calm. The contemplative, the mystic, assuming moral responsibility for the distracted, tries to keep his gaze fixed on that core. The artist uses the materials of the world to direct men's attention back to it. When it is lost sight of, society perishes.

Although the mystique behind such evaluation is overtly Oriental, even Buddhist or Vedantist, and hence anti-humanistic, I do not feel that this type of explication is really relevant. The perfected mystic, of course, would not seek to express himself at all. In the last analysis it is the artist, the contemplator and fabricator, who speaks and judges through these embodied visions. And the united act of contemplation and shaping of reality is in its essence the truest and fullest human deed. Morris Graves has said of his own work: "If the paintings are confounding to anyone—then I feel that words (my words, almost anyone's words) would add confusion. For the one to whom the message is clear or even partially clear or challengingly obscure—then, for them, words are obviously excessive. To the one whose searching is not similar to ours—or those who do not feel the awful frustrations of being caught in our individual and collective projection of our civilization's extremity—to those who believe that our extroverted civilization is constructively progressing—those who seeing and tasting the fruits and new buds of self-destructive progress are still calling it good, to them the ideas in the paintings are still preposterous, hence not worth consideration."

Simone Weil

Simone Weil was one of the most remarkable women of the twentieth, or indeed of any other century. I have great sympathy for her,
but sympathy is not necessarily congeniality. It would be easier to
write of her if I liked what she had to say, which I strongly do not.

For an alert non-Bolshevik radical of the years of the Second
World War, the two most decisive insights, at least for those who
read only English, were Paul Mattick's "The War Is Permanent,"
published in *Living Marxism* in 1939, and Simone Weil's "The
Coming World War," published in the *International Review* in
1938, but written in 1934. Nobody who read them then is ever likely
to forget them. Mattick's theme is obvious from the title and is a
commonplace today. Simone Weil pointed out that modern technology had made social violence a supranational thing, so that,
whoever "won," modern warfare resolved itself in actual practice
into the lethal conflict of the man at the desk with the man at the
bench. The workers get killed in shop or foxhole, the college gradu-
ates get commissions or join the OWI. Unhappily, she was herself to
undergo a transvaluation of values and join the Gaullist OWI.

One of Simone Weil's books, *The Need for Roots*, was a collection
of egregious nonsense surpassed only by the deranged fantasies of
the chauvinist Péguy; it was written for De Gaulle—a program for
the moral rehabilitation of France when our side had won. It
attempted to enlist on our side the same dark irrational spirits who
seemed then to be fighting so successfully for the other side. Today

---

Review of The Notebooks of Simone Weil *originally published with the*
title "The Dialectic of Agony" in The Nation, *January 1957. Collected in*
Assays, *1961.*

it is a weird, embarrassing relic of a too immediate past. Luckily, as it turned out, they lost and we won without much effective intervention from the spirits on either side. Realities of the kind called harsh rule France today rather than any vestige of Simone Weil's odd ideals.

Simone Weil was born in Paris in 1909 to well-do-do parents of Jewish ancestry but no religion. After a brilliant academic career in philosophy she became a secondary-school teacher. In 1934 she left teaching for a year to work in the Renault plant, "to experience the life of the workers." In 1936 she went to Spain, and fought, or rather did not fight, in the Republican Army. Between her return from Spain late in the same year and the outbreak of the Second World War she broke down in health, abandoned her revolutionary ideas—which were never Marxist in any orthodox sense, but rather Communist-Anarchist of the type we associate with Alexander Berkman and Emma Goldman—and began a sort of tortured prowling outside the doors of the Catholic Church—like a starving wild animal. In 1940 she settled in Marseilles with her family, who were arranging to escape to America. In 1941 she met Fr. Perrin, a Dominican, who introduced her to Gustave Thibon, a wealthy farmer and a leading Catholic intellectual. On his farm she tried, not very successfully, to work as a "land girl." In the summer of 1942 she came to New York, and left for England in the fall with a commission to serve in the Gaullist organization in England. In the spring of 1943 she entered a hospital, and in August she died in Ashford Sanatorium in Kent. Superficially this career sounds much like that of many idealistic and rather giddy upperclass college girls of those days. Probably many such girls who are successful lady executives today did live with the same burning intensity as Simone Weil; probably a good many others came to an equally sad end. But she, like Marie Bashkirtsev, who was her nineteenth-century double, and the perfect exemplar of the type in those days, left a record quite as classic and fully as poignant.

In recent years Putnam has published several collections of her journals and correspondence: *Waiting for God, Letter to a Priest, Gravity and Grace* and *The Need for Roots.* As they have come out I have read them all again, and with them her new, unabridged notebooks.

I have the greatest respect, indeed veneration, for any tortured soul seeking peace and illumination. But in 1934 she wrote this: "War in our day is distinguished by the subordination of the combatants to the instruments of combat, and the armaments, the true heroes of modern warfare, as well as the men dedicated to their service, are directed by those who do not fight. Since this directing apparatus has no other way of fighting than sending its own soldiers, under compulsion, to their deaths—the war of one State against another resolves itself into a war of the State and the military apparatus against its own army. War in the last analysis appears as a struggle led by all the State apparatuses and general staffs against all men old enough and able to bear arms." And later in the same article: "Revolutionary war is the grave of revolution."

When war actually came she was writing things like this: "In civil society, penal death, if death is used as a punishment, ought to be something beautiful. Religious ceremonies would be necessary for it to be made so. And there ought to be something to make it be felt that the man who is being punished, on receiving death, accomplishes something great; contributes, as far as he is able in the situation in which he has placed himself, to the orderly state of the community. Let him remain in his cell until such time as he himself accepts to die?"

What would Thomas Aquinas have made of this? Or any Sicilian peasant or Irish teamster? Very much, I fear, the same as you or I. This girl killed herself seeking salvation, a salvation she identified with Catholicism. The passage above, and there are hundreds of remarks like it in the notebooks, is far from Catholicism, in fact from any religion. It has a horrible similarity to one theory of the Moscow trials, but it is a sick kind of agonized frivolity. And there are other things: a captious, misinformed playing with Hinduism and comparative mythology, worse than the confabulations of Robert Graves; a toying with modern mathematics of infinitudes and incommensurabilities—a kind of post Cantor-Dedekind Neo-Pythagoreanism.

In her last years Simone Weil seems to have sought enlightenment by a systematic cultivation of maximum hypertension. Her thought proceeded by no other way than paradox. This is not new. There is a good deal of it in Pascal, that least Catholic of Catholic thinkers, and of course in Kierkegaard. In Chesterton it sinks to the level of a vulgar journalistic trick. Paul Tillich has created, beyond the "theology of crisis" of Barth, Niebuhr and the Neo-Lutherans, a "theology of tension"—perhaps the most viable expression of that ancient science for a modern man. But there is the tension of life and the tension of death. Simone Weil was a dying girl. Hers was a spastic, moribund, intellectual and spiritual agony. We can sympathize with it, be moved to tears by it, much as we are by the last awful lunacies of Antonin Artaud, but we imitate it, allow it to infect us, at our peril. This is a Kierkegaard who refuses to leap. *Angst* for *angst's* sake. Anguish is not enough. When it is made an end in itself it takes on a holy, or unholy, folly.

It is one thing, like John Woolman, to refuse sugar because it was made by slave labor; it is another thing to refuse to eat more than the starvation rations of occupied Paris when one is dying in an English sanatorium. (What sort of doctor permitted this?) It is touching, even tragic, but it is the farcical tragedy of Lear, equally distant from the tragedy of Prometheus on his rock or Christ on his cross.

What was wrong with Simone Weil? Our grandparents used to say of learned girls who broke down, "She studied too hard. She read too many books." And today we laugh at them. I think Simone Weil had both over- and under-equipped herself for the crisis which overwhelmed her—along, we forget, immersed in her tragedy, with all the rest of us. She was almost the perfectly typical passionate, revolutionary, intellectual woman—a frailer, even more highly strung Rosa Luxemburg.

Rosa was saved from personal, inner disaster during the great betrayals of the First World War by several, all rather tough-minded, characteristics. She had a tenacious orthodoxy: she was perfectly confident of the sufficiency of Marxism as an answer, though she was more humane about it than Lenin. She had a warm, purely human love of people—physically, their smell and touch and comradeship. And a kind of Jewish indomitable guts, that ultimate unkillability which comes only from grandparents in *yamulke* and horsehair wig. Simone Weil had none of this. She made up her own revolution out of her vitals, like a spider or silkworm. She could introject all the ill of the world into her own heart, but she could not project herself in sympathy to others. Her letters read like the more distraught signals of John of the Cross in the dark night. It is inconceivable that she could ever have written as Rosa Luxemburg did from prison to Sophia Kautsky. People to Simone Weil were mere actors in her own spiritual melodrama. I doubt if she was ever aware of the smell of her own armpits. She may have called her fantasy "the need for roots," but *yamulkes*, rosaries or plain chewing-tobacco atheism, none had ever existed in her past. She was born a *déracinée* and she insisted on remaining one. She was constitutionally disengaged—the Renault plant, the Spanish Republican and the Free French armies to the contrary notwithstanding. Faced with the ordinary but definite engagement of becoming a baptized Catholic, she panicked.

Religion has been called the gap between the technology and the environment. When her intellectual and psychological environment blew up in her face, Simone Weil discovered that she had no technology whatever, and the gap was absolute. She never permitted herself access to anyone who could help her. If I were planning to enter the Catholic Church the last person I would ever approach would be the kind of priest who could make head or tail of her *Letter to a Priest.*

Fr. Perrin and M. Thibon may have been wise men in their generation, but they both fell into the trap of her dialectic of agony. They took her seriously—in the wrong way. They lacked the vulgar but holy frivolity of common sense of the unsophisticated parish priest who would have told her, "Come, come, my child, what you need is to get baptized, obey the Ten Commandments, go to Mass on Sundays, make your Easter duties, forget about religion, put some meat on your bones, and get a husband." Simone Weil knew the type, and she avoided them as a criminal avoids the police, and probably secretly disdained them as much.

Only such advice could have saved her. Only the realization of the truth—so hard to come by for the religious adventurer—that no one is "called" to be any holier than he absolutely has to be, could have given her real illumination. To anything like this she was defiantly impervious. She went to John of the Cross when she should have gone to plain Fr. Dupont, or Fr. Monahan, or Fr. Aliotto. Even Huysmans, with all his posturing, had sense enough to make St. Severin, that humble slum church, his home parish. Simone Weil assaulted the Garden of Gethsemane, and as is so often the case, was broken on the gate.

At least she speaks, again and again, of her absolutely sure sense of the suddenly descending, all-suffusing presence of God. So we know that somewhere, somehow, in all her agony, she did find some center of peace, a peace which, unless we happen to believe in God, we may find hard to explain.

Disengagement:
The Art of the Beat Generation

Literature generally, but literary criticism in particular, has always been an area in which social forces assume symbolic guise, and work out—or at least exemplify—conflicts taking place in the contemporary, or rather, usually the just past, wider arena of society. Recognition of this does not imply the acceptance of any general theory of social or economic determinism. It is a simple, empirical fact. Because of the pervasiveness of consent in American society generally, that democratic leveling up or down so often bewailed since de Tocqueville, American literature, especially literary criticism, has usually been ruled by a "line." The fact that it was spontaneously evolved and enforced only by widespread consent has never detracted from its rigor—but rather the opposite. It is only human to kick against the prodding of a Leopold Auerbach or an Andrey Zhdanov. An invisible, all-enveloping compulsion is not likely to be recognized, let alone protested against.

After World War I there was an official line for general consumption: "Back to Normalcy." Day by day in every way, we are getting better and better. This produced a literature which tirelessly pointed out that there was nothing whatsoever normal about us. The measure of decay in thirty years is the degree of acceptance of the official myth today—from the most obscure hack on a provincial newspaper to the loftiest metaphysicians of the literary quarterlies. The line goes: "The generation of experimentation and revolt is over." This is an etherealized corollary of the general line: "The bull market will never end."

First published in New World Writing #11, *1957. Collected in* The Alternative Society, *1970.*

I do not wish to argue about the bull market, but in the arts nothing could be less true. The youngest generation is in a state of revolt so absolute that its elders cannot even recognize it. The disaffiliation, alienation, and rejection of the young has, as far as their elders are concerned, moved out of the visible spectrum altogether. Critically invisible, modern revolt, like X-rays and radioactivity, is perceived only by its effects at more materialistic social levels, where it is called delinquency.

"Disaffiliation," by the way, is the term used by the critic and poet, Lawrence Lipton, who has written several articles on this subject, the first of which, in the *Nation*, quoted as epigraph, "We disaffiliate . . ."—John L. Lewis.

Like the pillars of Hercules, like two ruined Titans guarding the entrance to one of Dante's circles, stand two great dead juvenile delinquents—the heroes of the post-war generation: the saxophonist, Charlie Parker, and Dylan Thomas. If the word "deliberate" means anything, both of them certainly deliberately destroyed themselves.

Both of them were overcome by the horror of the world in which they found themselves, because at last they could no longer overcome that world with the weapon of a purely lyrical art. Both of them were my friends. Living in San Francisco I saw them seldom enough to see them with a perspective which was not distorted by exasperation or fatigue. So as the years passed, I saw them each time in the light of an accelerated personal conflagration.

The last time I saw Bird, at Jimbo's Bob City, he was so gone—so blind to the world—that he literally sat down on me before he realized I was there. "What happened, man?" I said, referring to the pretentious "Jazz Concert." "Evil, man, evil," he said, and that's all he said for the rest of the night. About dawn he got up to blow. The rowdy crowd chilled into stillness and the fluent melody spiraled through it.

The last time I saw Dylan, his self-destruction had not just passed the limits of rationality. It had assumed the terrifying inertia of inanimate matter. Being with him was like being swept away by a torrent of falling stones.

Now Dylan Thomas and Charlie Parker have a great deal more in common than the same disastrous end. As artists, they were very similar. They were both very fluent. But this fluent, enchanting utterance had, compared with important artists of the past, relatively little content. Neither of them got very far beyond a sort of entranced rapture at his own creativity. The principal theme of Thomas's poetry was the ambivalence of birth and death—the pain of blood-stained creation. Music, of course, is not so explicit an art, but anybody who knew Charlie Parker knows that he felt much the same way about his own gift. Both of them did communicate one central theme: Against the ruin of the world, there is only one defense—the creative act. This, of course, is the theme of much art—perhaps most poetry. It is the theme of Horace, who certainly otherwise bears little resemblance to Parker or Thomas. The difference is that Horace accepted his theme with a kind of silken assurance. To Dylan and Bird it was an agony and terror. I do not believe that this is due to anything especially frightful about their relationship to their own creativity. I believe rather that it is due to the catastrophic world in which that creativity seemed to be the sole value. Horace's column of imperishable verse shines quietly enough in the lucid air of Augustan Rome. Art may have been for him the most enduring, orderly, and noble activity of man. But the other activities of his life partook of these values. They did not actively negate them. Dylan Thomas's verse had to find endurance in a world of burning cities and burning Jews. He was able to find meaning in his art as long as it was the answer to air raids and gas ovens. As the world began to take on the guise of an immense air raid or gas oven, I believe his art became meaningless to him. I think all this could apply to Parker just as well, although, because of the nature of music, it is not demonstrable—at least not conclusively.

Thomas and Parker have more in common than theme, attitude, life pattern. In the practice of their art, there is an obvious technical resemblance. Contrary to popular belief, they were not great technical innovators. Their effects are only superficially startling. Thomas is a regression from the technical originality and ingenuity of writers like Pierre Reverdy or Apollinaire. Similarly, the innovations of bop, and of Parker particularly, have been vastly overrated by people unfamiliar with music, especially by that ignoramus, the intellectual jitterbug, the jazz aficionado. The tonal novelties consist in the introduction of a few chords used in classical music for centuries.

And there is less rhythmic difference between progressive jazz, no matter how progressive, and Dixieland, than there is between two movements of many conventional symphonies.

What Parker and his contemporaries—Gillespie, Davis, Monk, Roach (Tristano is an anomaly), etc.—did was to absorb the musical ornamentation of older jazz into the basic structure, of which it then became an integral part, and with which it then developed. This is true of the melodic line which could be put together from selected passages of almost anybody—Benny Carter, Johnny Hodges. It is true of the rhythmic pattern in which the beat shifts continuously, or at least is continuously sprung, so that it becomes ambiguous enough to allow the pattern to be dominated by the long pulsations of the phrase or strophe. This is exactly what happened in the transition from baroque to rococo music. It is the difference between Bach and Mozart.

It is not a farfetched analogy to say that this is what Thomas did to poetry. The special syntactical effects of a Rimbaud or an Edith Sitwell—actually ornaments—become the main concern. The metaphysical conceits, which fascinate the Reactionary Generation still dominant in backwater American colleges, were embroideries. Thomas's ellipses and ambiguities are ends in themselves. The immediate theme, if it exists, is incidental, and his main theme—the terror of birth—is simply reiterated.

This is one difference between Bird and Dylan which should be pointed out. Again, contrary to popular belief, there is nothing crazy or frantic about Parker either musically or emotionally. His sinuous melody is a sort of naive transcendence of all experience. Emotionally, it does not resemble Berlioz or Wagner; it resembles Mozart. This is true also of a painter like Jackson Pollock. He may have been eccentric in his behavior, but his paintings are as impassive as Persian tiles. Partly this difference is due to the nature of verbal communication. The insistent talk-aboutiveness of the general environment obtrudes into even the most idyllic poetry. It is much more a personal difference. Thomas certainly wanted to tell people about the ruin and disorder of the world. Parker and Pollock wanted to substitute a work of art for the world.

Technique pure and simple, rendition, is not of major importance, but it is interesting that Parker, following Lester Young, was one of the leaders of the so-called saxophone revolution. In modern jazz, the saxophone is treated as a woodwind and played with conventional embouchure. Metrically, Thomas's verse was extremely conventional, as was, incidentally, the verse of that other tragic *enragé*, Hart Crane.

I want to make clear what I consider the one technical development in the first wave of significant post-war arts. Ornament is confabulation in the interstices of structure. A poem by Dylan Thomas, a saxophone solo by Charles Parker, a painting by Jackson Pollock—these are pure confabulations as ends in themselves. Confabulation has come to determine structure. Uninhibited lyricism should be distinguished from its exact opposite—the sterile, extraneous invention of the corn-belt metaphysicals, our present blight of poetic professors.

Just as Hart Crane had little influence on anyone except very reactionary writers—like Allen Tate, for instance, to whom Valéry was the last word in modern poetry and the felicities of an Apollinaire, let alone a Paul Éluard, were nonsense—so Dylan Thomas's influence has been slight indeed. In fact, his only disciple—the only person to imitate his style—was W. S. Graham, who seems to have imitated him without much understanding, and who has since moved on to other methods. Thomas's principle influence lay in the communication of an attitude—that of the now extinct British romantic school of the New Apocalypse—Henry Treece, J. F. Hendry, and others—all of whom were quite conventional poets.

Parker certainly had much more of an influence. At one time it was the ambition of every saxophone player in every high school band in America to blow like Bird. Even before his death this influence had begun to ebb. In fact, the whole generation of the founding fathers of bop—Gillespie, Monk, Davis, Blakey, and the rest—are just now at a considerable discount. The main line of development today goes back to Lester Young and bypasses them.

The point is that many of the most impressive developments in the arts nowadays are aberrant, idiosyncratic. There is no longer any sense of continuing development of the sort that can be traced from Baudelaire to Éluard, or for that matter from Hawthorne through Henry James to Gertrude Stein. The cubist generation before World War I, and, on a lower level, the Surrealists of the period between the wars, both assumed an accepted universe of discourse, in which, to quote André Breton, it was possible to make definite advances, exactly as in the sciences. I doubt if anyone holds such ideas today. Continuity exists, but like the neo-swing music developed from Lester Young, it is a continuity sustained by popular demand.

In the plastic arts, a very similar situation exists. Surrealists like Hans Arp and Max Ernst might talk of creation by hazard—of composing pictures by walking on them with painted soles, or by tossing bits of paper up in the air. But it is obvious that they were self-deluded. Nothing looks anything like an Ernst or an Arp but another Ernst or Arp. Nothing looks less like their work than the happenings of random occasion. Many of the post-World War II abstract expressionists, apostles of the discipline of spontaneity and hazard, look alike, and do look like accidents. The aesthetic appeal of pure paint laid on at random may exist, but it is a very impoverished appeal. Once again what has happened is an all-consuming confabulation of the incidentals, the accidents of painting. It is curious that at its best, the work of this school of painting—Mark Rothko, Jackson Pollock, Clyfford Still, Robert Motherwell, Willem de Kooning, and the rest—resembles nothing so much as the passage painting of quite unimpressive painters: the mother-of-pearl shimmer in the background of a Henry McFee, itself a formula derived from Renoir; the splashes of light and black which fake drapery in the fashionable imitators of Hals and Sargent. Often work of this sort is presented as calligraphy—the pure utterance of the brush stroke seeking only absolute painteresque values. You have only to compare such painting with the work of, say, Sesshu, to realize that someone is using words and brushes carelessly.

At its best abstract expressionism achieves a simple rococo decorative surface. Its poverty shows up immediately when compared with Tiepolo, where the rococo rises to painting of extraordinary profundity and power. A Tiepolo painting, however confabulated, is a universe of tensions in vast depths. A Pollock is an object of art—bijouterie—disguised only by its great size. In fact, once the size is big enough to cover a whole wall, it turns into nothing more than extremely expensive wallpaper. Now there is nothing wrong with complicated wallpaper. There is just more to Tiepolo. The great Ashikaga brush painters painted wallpapers, too—at least portable ones, screens.

A process of elimination which leaves the artist with nothing but the play of his materials themselves cannot sustain interest in either artist or public for very long. So in recent years abstract expressionism has tended towards romantic suggestion—indications of landscape or living figures. This approaches the work of the Northwest school—Clayton Price, Mark Tobey, Kenneth Callahan, Morris Graves—who have of all recent painters come nearest to conquering a territory which painting could occupy with some degree of security. The Northwest school, of course, admittedly is influenced by the ink painters of the Far East, and by Tintoretto and Tiepolo. The dominant school of post-World War II American painting has really been a long detour into plastic nihilism. I should add that painters like Ernie Briggs seem to be opening up new areas of considerable scope within the main traditional abstract expressionism—but with remarkable convergence to Tobey or Tintoretto, as you prefer.

Today American painting is just beginning to emerge with a transvaluation of values. From the mid-nineteenth century on, all ruling standards in the plastic arts were subject to continual attack. They were attacked because each on-coming generation had new standards of its own to put in their place. Unfortunately, after one hundred years of this, there grew up a generation ignorant of the reasons for the revolt of their elders, and without any standards whatever. It has been necessary to create standards anew out of chaos. This is what modern education purports to do with finger painting in nursery schools. This is why the Northwest school has enjoyed such an advantage over the abstract expressionists. Learning by doing, by trial and error, is learning by the hardest way. If you want to overthrow the cubist tradition of architectural painting, it is much easier to seek out its opposites in the history of culture and study them carefully. At least it saves a great deal of time.

One thing can be said of painting in recent years—its revolt, its rejection of the classic modernism of the first half of the century, has been more absolute than in any other art. The only ancestor of abstract expressionism is the early Kandinsky—a style rejected even by Kandinsky himself. The only painter in a hundred years who bears the slightest resemblance to Tobey or Graves is Odilon Redon (perhaps Gustave Moreau a little), whose stock was certainly not very high with painters raised in the cubist tradition.

The ready market for prose fiction has had a decisive influence on its development. Sidemen with Kenton or Herman may make a good if somewhat hectic living, but any novelist who can write home to mother, or even spell his own name, has a chance to become another Brubeck. The deliberately and painfully intellectual fiction which appears in the literary quarterlies is a by-product of certain classrooms. The only significant fiction in America is popular fiction. Nobody realizes this better than the French. To them our late-born imitators of Henry James and E. M. Forster are just *chiens qui fument*, and arithmetical horses and bicycling seals. And there is a no more perishable commodity than the middle-brow novel. No one today reads Ethel L. Voynich or Joseph Hergesheimer, just as no one in the future will read the writers' workshop pupils and teachers who fill the literary quarterlies. Very few people, except themselves, read them now.

On the other hand, the connection between the genuine highbrow writer and the genuinely popular is very close. Hemingway had hardly started to write before his style had been reduced to a formula in *Black Mask*, the first hard-boiled detective magazine. In no time at all he had produced two first-class popular writers, Raymond Chandler and Dashiell Hammett. Van Vechten, their middle-brow contemporary, is forgotten. It is from Chandler and Hammett and Hemingway that the best modern fiction derives; although most of it comes out in hard covers, it is always thought of as written for a typical pocketbook audience. Once it gets into pocketbooks it is sometimes difficult to draw the line between it and its most ephemeral imitators. Even the most *précieux* French critics, a few years ago, considered Horace McCoy America's greatest contemporary novelist. There is not only something to be said for their point of view; the only thing to be said against it is that they don't read English.

Much of the best popular fiction deals with the world of the utterly disaffiliated. Burlesque and carnival people, hipsters, handicappers and hop heads, wanted men on the lam, an expendable squad of soldiers being expended, anyone who by definition is divorced from society and cannot afford to believe even an iota of the Social Lie—these are the favorite characters of modern postwar fiction, from Norman Mailer to the latest ephemerid called *Caught*, or *Hung Up*, or *The Needle*, its bright cover winking invitingly in the drugstore. The first, and still the greatest, novelist of total disengagement is not a young man at all, but an elderly former I.W.W. of German ancestry, B. Traven, the author of *The Death Ship* and *The Treasure of the Sierra Madre*.

It is impossible for an artist to remain true to himself as a man, let alone an artist, and work within the context of this society. Contemporary mimics of Jane Austen or Anthony Trollope are not only beneath contempt. They are literally unreadable. It is impossible to keep your eyes focused on the page. Writers as far apart as J. F. Powers and Nelson Algren agree in one thing—their diagnosis of an absolute corruption.

This refusal to accept the mythology of press and pulpit as a medium for artistic creation, or even enjoyable reading matter, is one explanation for the popularity of escapist literature. Westerns, detective stories, and science fiction are all situated beyond the pale of normal living. The slick magazines are only too well aware of this, and in these three fields especially exert steady pressure on their authors to accentuate the up-beat. The most shocking example of this forced perversion is the homey science-fiction story, usually written by a woman, in which a one-to-one correlation has been made for the commodity-ridden tale of domestic whimsy, the stand-by of magazines given away in the chain groceries. In writers like Judith Merrill the space pilot and his bride bat the badinage back and forth while the robot maid makes breakfast in the jet-propelled lucite orange squeezer and the electronic bacon roto-broiler, dropping pearls of dry assembly plant wisdom (like plantation wisdom but drier), the whilst. Still, few yield to these pressures, for the obvious reason that fiction indistinguishable from the advertising columns on either side of the page defeats its own purpose, which is to get the reader to turn over the pages when he is told "continued on p. 47."

Simenon is still an incomparably better artist and psychologist than the psychological Jean Stafford. Ward Moore is a better artist than Eudora Welty, and Ernest Haycox than William Faulkner, just as, long ago, H. G. Wells was a better artist, as artist, than E. M. Forster, as well as being a lot more interesting. At its best, popular literature of this sort, coming up, meets high-brow literature coming down. It has been apparent novel by novel that Nelson Algren is rising qualitatively in this way. In *A Walk on the Wild Side*, thoroughly popular in its materials, he meets and absorbs influences coming down from the top, from the small handful of bona fide high-brow writers working today—Céline, Jean Genêt, Samuel Beckett, Henry Miller. In Algren's case this has been a slow growth, and he has carried his audience with him. Whatever the merits of his subject matter or his thesis—"It is better to be out than in. It is better to be on the lam than on the cover of *Time* Magazine"—his style started out as a distressing mixture of James Farrell and Kenneth Fearing. Only later did he achieve an idiom of his own.

There is only one thing wrong with this picture, and that is that the high-brow stimulus still has to be imported. Algren, who is coming to write more and more like Céline, has no difficulty selling his fiction. On the other hand, an author like Jack Kerouac, who is in his small way the peer of Céline or Beckett, is the most famous "unpublished" author in America. Every publisher's reader and adviser of any moment has read him and was enthusiastic about him. In other words, anybody emerging from the popular field has every advantage. It is still extremely difficult to enter American fiction from the top down.

The important point about modern fiction is that it is salable, and therefore negotiable in our society, and therefore successful in the best sense of the word. When a novelist has something to say, he knows people will listen. Only the jazz musician, but to a much lesser degree, shares this confidence in his audience. It is of the greatest social significance that the novelists who say, "I am proud to be delinquent" are sold in editions of hundreds of thousands.

Nobody much buys poetry. I know. I am one of the country's most successful poets. My books actually sell out—in editions of two thousand. Many a poet, the prestige ornament of a publisher's list, has more charges against his royalty account than credits for books sold. The problem of poetry is the problem of communication itself. All art is a symbolic criticism of values, but poetry is specifically and almost exclusively that. A painting decorates the wall. A novel is a story. Music . . . soothes a savage breast. But poetry you have to take straight. In addition, the entire educational system is in a conspiracy to make poetry as unpalatable as possible. From the seventh-grade teacher who rolls her eyes and chants H. D. to the seven types of ambiguity factories, grinding out little Donnes and Hopkinses with hayseeds in their hair, everybody is out to de-poetize forever the youth of the land. Again, bad and spurious painting, music, and fiction are not really well-organized, except on obvious commercial levels, where they can be avoided. But in poetry Gresham's Law is supported by the full weight of the powers that be. From about 1930 on, a conspiracy of bad poetry has been as carefully organized as the Communist Party, and today controls most channels of publication except the littlest of the little magazines. In all other departments of American culture, English influence has been at a steadily declining minimum since the middle of the nineteenth century. In 1929, this was still true of American poetry. Amy Lowell, Sandburg, H. D., Pound, Marianne Moore, William Carlos Williams, Wallace Stevens—all of the major poets of the first quarter of the century owed far more to Apollinaire or Francis Jammes than they did to the whole body of the English tradition. In fact, the new poetry was essentially an anti-English, pro-French movement—a provincial but clear echo of the French revolt against the symbolists. On the other hand, Jules Laforgue and his English disciples, Ernest Dowson and Arthur Symons, were the major influence on T. S. Eliot. Unfortunately Mr. Eliot's poetic practice and his thoroughly snobbish critical essays which owed their great cogency to their assumption, usually correct, that his readers had never heard of the authors he discussed—Webster, Crashaw, or Lancelot Andrewes—lent themselves all too easily to the construction of an academy and the production of an infinite number of provincial academicians—policemen entrusted with the enforcement of Gresham's Law.

Behind the façade of this literary Potemkin village, the mainstream of American poetry, with its sources in Baudelaire, Lautréamont, Rimbaud, Apollinaire, Jammes, Reverdy, Salmon, and later Breton and Éluard, has flowed on unperturbed, though visible only at rare intervals between the interstices of the academic hoax. Today the class magazines and the quarterlies are filled with poets as alike as two bad pennies. It is my opinion that these people do not really exist. Most of them are androids designed by Ransom, Tate, and Co., and animated by Randall Jarrell. They are not just counterfeit; they are not even real counterfeits, but counterfeits of counterfeits. On these blurred and clumsy coins the lineaments of Mr. Eliot and I. A. Richards dimly can be discerned, like the barbarized Greek letters which nobody could read on Scythian money.

This is the world in which over every door is written the slogan: "The generation of experiment and revolt is over. Bohemia died in the Twenties. There are no more little magazines." Actually there have never been so many little magazines. In spite of the fantastic costs of printing, more people than ever are bringing out little sheets of free verse and making up the losses out of their own pockets. This world has its own major writers, its own discoveries, its own old masters, its own tradition and continuity. Its sources are practically exclusively French, and they are all post-symbolist, even anti-symbolist. It is the Reactionary Generation that is influenced by Laforgue, the symbolists, and Valéry. Nothing is more impressive than the strength, or at least the cohesion, of this underground movement. Poets whom the quarterlies pretend never existed, like Louis Zukofsky and Jack Wheelwright, are still searched out in large libraries or obscure bookshops and copied into notebooks by young writers. I myself have a complete typewritten collection of the pre-reactionary verse of Yvor Winters. And I know several similar collections of "forgotten modernists" in the libraries of my younger friends. People are always turning up who say something like, "I just discovered a second-hand copy of Parker Tyler's *The Granite Butterfly* in a Village bookshop. It's great, man." On the other hand, I seriously doubt whether *The Hudson Review* would ever consider for a moment publishing a line of Parker Tyler's verse. And he is certainly not held up as an example in the Iowa Writers' Workshop. There are others who have disappeared entirely—Charles Snider, Sherry Mangan, R. E. F. Larsson, the early Winters, the last poems of Ford Madox Ford. They get back into circulation, as far as I know, only when I read them to somebody at home or on the air, and then I am always asked for a copy. Some of the old avant-garde seem to have written themselves out, for instance, Mina Loy. There are a few established old masters, outstanding of whom are, of course, Ezra Pound and William Carlos Williams. I am not a passionate devotee of Pound myself. In fact, I think his influence is largely pernicious. But no one could deny its extent and power amongst young people today. As for Williams, more and more people, even some of the Reactionary Generation, have come to think of him as our greatest living poet. Even Randall Jarrell and R. P. Blackmur have good words to say for him.

Then there is a middle generation which includes Kenneth Patchen, Jean Garrigue, myself, and a few others—notably Richard Eberhart, who looks superficially as if he belonged with the Tates and Blackmurs but who is redeemed by his directness, simplicity, and honesty; and Robert Fitzgerald and Dudley Fitts. Curiously enough, in the taste of the young, Kenneth Fearing is not included in this group, possibly because his verse is too easy. It does include the major work, for example, *Ajanta*, of Muriel Rukeyser.

I should say that the most influential poets of the youngest established generation of the avant-garde are Denise Levertov, Robert Creeley, Charles Olson, Robert Duncan, and Philip Lamantia. The most influential avant-garde editor is perhaps Cid Corman, with his magazine *Origin*. Richard Emerson's *Golden Goose* and Robert Creeley's *Black Mountain Review* seem to have suspended publication temporarily. Jonathan Williams, himself a fine poet, publishes the Jargon Press.

All of this youngest group have a good deal in common. They are all more or less influenced by French poetry, and by Céline, Beckett, Artaud, Genêt, to varying degrees. They are also influenced by William Carlos Williams, D. H. Lawrence, Whitman, Pound. They are all interested in Far Eastern art and religion; some even call themselves Buddhists. Politically they are all strong disbelievers in the State, war, and the values of commercial civilization. Most of them would no longer call themselves anarchists, but just because adopting such a label would imply adherence to a "movement." Anything in the way of an explicit ideology is suspect. Contrary to gossip of a few years back, I have never met anybody in this circle who was a devotée of the dubious notions of the psychologist Wilhelm Reich; in fact, few of them have ever read him, and those who have consider him a charlatan.

Although there is wide diversity—Olson is very like Pound; Creeley resembles Mallarmé; Denise Levertov in England was a leading New Romantic, in America she came under the influence of William Carlos Williams; Robert Duncan has assimilated ancestors as unlike as Gertrude Stein and Éluard, and so on—although this diversity is very marked, there is a strong bond of esthetic unity too. No avant-garde American poet accepts the I. A. Richards-Valéry thesis that a poem is an end in itself, an anonymous machine for providing esthetic experiences. All believe in poetry as communication, statement from one person to another. So they all avoid the studied ambiguities and metaphysical word play of the Reactionary Generation and seek clarity of image and simplicity of language.

In the years since the war, it would seem as though more and more of what is left of the avant-garde has migrated to Northern California. John Berryman once referred to the Lawrence cult of "mindless California," and Henry Miller and I have received other unfavorable publicity which has served only to attract people to this area. Mr. Karl Shapiro, for instance, once referred to San Francisco as "the last refuge of the bohemian remnant"—a description he thought of as invidious. Nevertheless it is true that San Francisco is today the seat of an intense literary activity not unlike Chicago of the first quarter of the century. A whole school of poets has grown up—almost all of them migrated here from somewhere else. Some of them have national reputations, at least in limited circles. For example, Philip Lamantia among the Surrealists; William Everson (Brother Antoninus, O.P.)—perhaps the best Catholic poet. Others have come up, like Lawrence Ferlinghetti, Allen Ginsberg, Gary Snyder, Philip Whalen, David Meltzer, Michael McClure, still have largely local reputations. But the strength of these reputations should not be underestimated. The Poetry Center of San Francisco State College, directed by Ruth Witt-Diamant, gives a reading to a large audience at least twice a month. And there are other readings equally well attended every week in various galleries and private homes.

This means that poetry has become an actual social force— something which has always sounded hitherto like a Utopian dream of the William Morris sort. It is a very thrilling experience to hear an audience of more than three hundred people stand and cheer and clap, as they invariably do at a reading by Allen Ginsberg, certainly a poet of revolt if there ever was one.

There is no question but that the San Francisco Renaissance is radically different from what is going on elsewhere. There are hand presses, poetry readings, young writers elsewhere—but nowhere else is there a whole younger generation culture pattern characterized by total rejection of the official high-brow culture—where critics like John Crowe Ransom or Lionel Trilling, magazines like the *Kenyon, Hudson* and *Partisan* reviews, are looked on as "The Enemy"—the other side of the barricades.

There is only one trouble about the renaissance in San Francisco. It is too far away from the literary market place. That, of course, is the reason why the bohemian remnant, the avant-garde have migrated here. It is possible to hear the story about what so-and-so said to someone else at a cocktail party twenty years ago just one too many times. You grab a plane or get on your thumb and hitchhike to the other side of the continent for good and all. Each generation, the great Latin poets came from farther and farther from Rome. Eventually, they ceased even to go there except to see the sights.

Distance from New York City does, however, make it harder to get things, if not published, at least nationally circulated. I recently formed a collection for one of the foundations of avant-garde poetry printed in San Francisco. There were a great many items. The poetry was all at least readable, and the hand printing and binding were in most cases very fine indeed. None of these books was available in bookstores elsewhere in the country, and only a few of them had been reviewed in newspapers or magazines with national circulation.

Anyway, as an old war horse of the revolution of the word, things have never looked better from where I sit. The avant-garde has not only not ceased to exist. It's jumping all over the place. Something's happening, man.

The disengagement of the creator, who, as creator, is necessarily judge, is one thing, but the utter nihilism of the emptied-out hipster is another. What is going to come of an attitude like this? It is impossible to go on indefinitely saying: "I am proud to be a delinquent," without destroying all civilized values. Between such persons no true enduring interpersonal relationships can be built, and of course, nothing resembling a true "culture"—an at-homeness of men with each other, their work, their loves, their environment. The end result must be the desperation of shipwreck—the despair, the orgies, ultimately the cannibalism of a lost lifeboat. I believe that most of an entire generation will go to ruin—the ruin of Céline, Artaud, Rimbaud, voluntarily, even enthusiastically. What will happen afterwards I don't know, but for the next couple of decades we are going to have to cope with the youth that we, my generation, put through the atom smasher. Social disengagement, artistic integrity, voluntary poverty—these are powerful virtues and may pull them through, but they are not the virtues we tried to inculcate—rather they are the exact opposite.

San Francisco Letter

There has been so much publicity recently about the San Francisco Renaissance and the New Generation of Revolt and Our Underground Literature and Cultural Disaffiliation that I for one am getting a little sick of writing about it, and the writers who are the objects of all the uproar run the serious danger of falling over, "dizzy with success," in the immortal words of Comrade Koba. Certainly there is nothing underground about it anymore. For ten years after the Second War there was a convergence of interest—the Business Community, military imperialism, political reaction, the hysterical, tear and mud drenched guilt of the ex-Stalinist, ex-Trotskyite American intellectuals, the highly organized academic and literary employment agency of the Neoantireconstructionists— what might be called the meliorists of the White Citizens' League, who were out to augment the notorious budgetary deficiency of the barbarously miseducated Southron male schoolmarm by opening up jobs "up N'oth." This ministry of all the talents formed a dense crust of custom over American cultural life—more of an ice pack. Ultimately the living water underneath just got so damn hot the ice pack has begun to melt, rot, break up and drift away into Arctic oblivion. This is all there is to it. For ten years or more, seen from above, all that could be discerned was a kind of scum. By very definition, scum, ice packs, crusts, are surface phenomena. It is what is underneath that counts. The living substance has always been there—it has just been hard to see—from above.

It is easy to understand why all this has centered in San Francisco. It is a long way from Astor Place or Kenyon College. It is one

Published in The Evergreen Review, *1957, not previously collected.*

of the easiest cities in the world to live in. It is the easiest in America. Its culture is genuinely (not fake like New Orleans—white New Orleans, an ugly Southron city with a bit of the Latin past subsidized by the rubberneck buses) Mediterranean—*laissez faire* and *dolce far niente.* I for one can say flatly that if I couldn't live here I would leave the United States for someplace like Aix en Provence— so fast! I always feel like I ought to get a passport every time I cross the Bay to Oakland or Berkeley. I get nervous walking down the streets of Seattle with all those ghosts of dead Wobblies weeping in the shadows and all those awful squares peering down my neck. In New York, after one week of living on cocktails in taxicabs, I have to go to a doctor. The doctor always says—get out of New York before it kills you. Hence the Renaissance.

Most of the stuff written about San Francisco literary life has been pretty general, individuals have figured only as items in long and hasty lists. I want to talk at a little more length about a few specific writers and try to show how this disaffiliation applies to them, functions in their work.

In the first place. No literature of the past two hundred years is of the slightest importance unless it *is* "disaffiliated." Only our modern industrial and commercial civilization has produced an elite which has consistently rejected all the reigning values of the society. There were no Baudelaires in Babylon. It is not that we have lost sight of them in time. The nearest thing in Rome was Catullus, and it is apparent, reading him, that there stood behind him no anonymous and forgotten body of bohemians. He was a consort of the rich, of generals and senators, Caesar and Mamurra, and the girl he writes about as though she was, in our terms, an art-struck tart from the Black Cat, was, in fact, a notorious multimillionairess, "the most depraved daugher of the Clodian line." Tu Fu censured the Emperor, but he wanted to be recognized for it—he wanted to be a Censor. So the Taoism and Buddhism of Far Eastern culture function as a keel and ballast to the ship of state. The special ideology of the only artists and writers since the French Revolution who deserve to be taken seriously is a destructive, revolutionary force. They would blow up "their" ship of state—destroy it utterly. This has nothing to do with political revolutionarism, which in our era has been the mortal enemy of all art whatever. When the Bolsheviks, for a brief period, managed to persuade the culture bearers, demoralized by the world economic crisis and rising tide of political terrorism, that the political revolutionary and the artist, the poet, the moral *vates* were allies, Western European culture came within an ace of being destroyed altogether and finally. Capitalism cannot produce from within itself, from any of its "classes," bourgeois, petit-bourgeois, or proletariat, any system of values which is not in essence of itself. The converse is a Marxist delusion. This is why "Marxist aestheticians" have gone to such lengths to "prove" that the artist, the writer, the technical and professional intelligentsia, are *not* declassés in modern society, but members of the petit bourgeoisie, and must "come over," in the words of Engels' old chestnut, "to the proletariat," that is, become the prostitutes of their brand of State Capitalism. Nothing could be more false. Artist, poet, physicist, astronomer, dancer, musician, mathematician are captives stolen from an older time, a different kind of society, in which, ultimately, *they* were the creators of all primary values. They are exactly like the astronomers and philosophers the Mongols took off from Samarkand to Karakorum. They belong to the *ancien régime*—all *anciens régimes* as against the nineteenth and twentieth centuries. And so they could only vomit in the faces of the despots who offered them places in the ministries of all the talents, or at least they were nauseated in proportion to their integrity. The same principles apply today as did in the days of Lamartine. Caught in the gears of their own evil machinery, the bosses may scream for an Einstein, a Bohr, even an Oppenheimer; when Normalcy comes back, they kick them out and put tellers in their place. The more fools the Einsteins for having allowed themselves to be used—as they always discover, alas, too late.

You may not think all this has anything to do with the subject, but it is the whole point. Poets come to San Francisco for the same reason so many Hungarians have been going to Austria recently. They write the sort of thing they do for the same reason that Hölderlin or Blake or Baudelaire or Rimbaud or Mallarmé wrote it. The world of poet-professors, Southern Colonels and ex-Left Social Fascists from which they have escaped has no more to do with literature than do the leading authors of the court of Napoleon III whose names can be found in the endless pages of the *Causeries du lundi.* The *Vaticide Review* is simply the *Saturday Evening Post* of the excessively miseducated, and its kept poets are the Zane Greys, Clarence Budington Kellands and J. P. Marquands of Brooks Brothers Boys who got an overdose of T. S. Eliot at some Ivy League fog factory. It is just that simple.

There are few organized systems of social attitudes and values which stand outside, really outside, the all corrupting influences of our predatory civilization. In America, at least, there is only one which functions on any large scale and with any effectiveness. This of course is Roman Catholicism. Not the stultifying monkey see monkey do Americanism of the slothful urban backwoods middle-class parish so beautifully satirized by the Catholic writer James Powers, but the Church of saints and philosophers—of the worker priest movement and the French Personalists. So it is only to be expected that, of those who reject the Social Lie, many today would turn towards Catholicism. If you have to "belong to something bigger than yourself" it is one of the few possibilities and, with a little mental gymnastics, can be made quite bearable. Even I sometimes feel that the only constant, consistent, and uncompromising critics of the secular world were the French Dominicans.

So, William Everson, who is probably the most profoundly moving and durable of the poets of the San Francisco Renaissance, is a Dominican Tertiary and oblate—which means a lay brother in a friary under renewable vows . . . he doesn't have to stay if he doesn't want to. It has been a long journey to this point. Prior to the Second War he was a farmer in the San Joaquin Valley. Here he wrote his first book of poems, *San Joaquin.* Like so many young poets he was naively accessible to influences his maturity would find dubious. In his case this was Jeffers, but he was, even then, able to transform Jeffers' noisy rhetoric into genuinely impassioned utterance, his absurd self-dramatization into real struggle in the depths of the self. Everson is still wrestling with his angel, still given to the long oratorical line with vague echoes of classical quantitative meters, but there is no apparent resemblance left to Jeffers. During the War he was in a Conscientious Objectors' camp in Oregon, where he was instrumental in setting up an off time Arts Program out of which have come many still active people, projects, and forces which help give San Francisco culture its intensely libertarian character. Here he printed several short books of verse, all later gathered in the New Directions volume, *The Residual Years*. Since then he has printed two books, *Triptych for the Living* and *A Privacy of Speech*. In the tradition of Eric Gill and Victor Hammer, they are amongst the most beautiful printing I have ever seen. Since then—since entering the Order, he has published mostly in the *Catholic Worker*. In my opinion he has become the finest Catholic poet writing today, the best since R. E. F. Larsson. His work has a gnarled, even tortured, honesty, a rugged unliterary diction, a relentless probing and searching, which are not just engaging, but almost overwhelming. Partly of course this is due to the scarcity of these characteristics today, anything less like the verse of the fashionable quarterlies would be hard to imagine.

Philip Lamantia is generally considered by his colleagues in San Francisco to be another of the three or four leading poets of the community. He too is a Catholic. Unlike Everson, who is concerned primarily with the problems of moral responsibility, the World, the Flesh, and the Devil, Lamantia's poetry is illuminated, ecstatic, with the mystic's intense autonomy. Unfortunately, since his surrealist days, although he has written a great deal, he has published practically nothing. Poems he has read locally have been deeply moving, but each in turn he has put by and gone on, dissatisfied, to something else. As it is so often the case with the mystic temperament, art seems to have become a means rather than even a temporary end. I hope that soon he will find what he is seeking, at least in a measure, and then, of course, his previous work will fall into place and be seen as satisfactory enough to publish—I hope.

Of all the San Francisco group Robert Duncan is the most easily recognizable as a member of the international avant garde. Mallarmé or Gertrude Stein, Joyce or Reverdy, there is a certain underlying homogeneity of idiom, and this idiom is, by and large, Duncan's. But there is a difference, "modernist" verse tends to treat the work of art as purely self-sufficient, a construction rather than a communication. Duncan's poetry is about as personal as can be imagined. So it resembles the work of poets like David Gascoyne and Pierre Emmanuel, who, raised in the tradition, have seceded from it to begin the exploration of a new, dedicated personalism. What is the self? What is the other? These are the questions of those who have

transcended "the existentialist dilemma"—Buber or Mounier.
What is love? Who loves? Who is loved? Curiously, although
Duncan is very far from being a Catholic, these are the leading
problems of contemporary Catholic thought, as Gascoyne and Emmanuel are Catholics. Perhaps what this means is that, as I said at
the beginning, the Church is one of the few places one can get away
to and start asking meaningful questions. There is, however, no
reason whatever why, if one is strong enough to stand alone, the
same questions should not be asked independently. Duncan has
written a large number of books; he started out very young (Gascoyne and Emmanuel were prodigies, too) as an editor of the
Experimental Review with Sanders Russell, and later of *Phoenix*
with the neo-Lawrentian Cooney. *Heavenly City, Earthly City*;
Fragments of a Disordered Devotion; *Caesar's Gate*; *Medieval
Scenes*; *Poems 1948-49*—the use of language may have changed
and developed, but the theme is consistently the mind and body of
love.

Allen Ginsberg's *Howl* is much more than the most sensational
book of poetry of 1957. Nothing goes to show how square the
squares are so much as the *favorable* reviews they've given it.
"Sustained shrieks of frantic defiance," "single-minded frenzy of a
raving madwoman," "paranoid memories," "childish obscenity"—
they think it's all *so* negative. Also—which is much more important—they think there is something unusual about it. Listen you—
do you *really* think your kids act like the bobby soxers in those
wholesome Coca-Cola ads? Don't you know that across the table
from you at dinner sits somebody who looks on you as an enemy
who is planning to kill him in the immediate future in an extremely
disagreeable way? Don't you know that if you were to say to your
English class, "It is raining," they would take it for granted you were
a liar? Don't you know that they never tell you nothing? That they
can't? That faced with the system of values which coats you like the
insulating rompers of an aircraft carrier's "hot papa"—they simply
can't get through, can't, and won't even try any more to communicate? Don't you know this, really? If you don't, you're headed for a
terrible awakening. *Howl* is the confession of faith of the generation
that is going to be running the world in 1965 and 1975—if it's still
there to run. "The Poetry of the New Violence"? It isn't at all

violent. It is *your* violence it is talking about. It is Hollywood or the censors who are obscene. It is Dulles and Khrushchev who are childishly defiant. It is the "media" that talk with the single-minded frenzy of a raving madwoman. Once Allen is through telling you what you have done to him and his friends, he concerns himself with the unfulfilled promises of *Song of Myself* and *Huckleberry Finn*, and writes a *Sutra* about the sunflower that rises from the junk heap of civilization . . . your civilization. Negative? "We must love one another or die." It's the "message" of practically every utterance of importance since the Neolithic Revolution. What's so negative about it? The fact that we now live in the time when we must either mind it or take the final consequences? Curiously, the reviewers never noticed—all they saw was "total assault." All this aside, purely technically, Ginsberg is one of the most remarkable versifiers in America. He is almost alone in his generation in his ability to make powerful poetry of the inherent rhythms of our speech, to push forward the conquests of a few of the earliest poems of Sandburg and of William Carlos Williams. This is more skillful verse than all the cornbelt Donnes laid end to end. It is my modest prophecy, that, if he keeps going, Ginsberg will be the first genuinely popular, genuine poet in over a generation—and he is already considerably the superior of predecessors like Lindsay and Sandburg.

Lawrence Ferlinghetti runs the City Lights Pocket Bookshop, publishes the Pocket Poets Series, paints very well (a little like Redon), writes poetry (*Pictures of the Gone World*), and, with myself, has worked to bring about a marriage of poetry and jazz. He is a lazy-looking, good-natured man with the canny cocky eye of an old-time vaudeville tenor. Everybody thinks he's Irish. One of those Irish wops—like Catullus. He is actually French. I think he thinks he don't get enough done. Oh, yes, he teaches French, too. For several years after War Two he lived in Paris and his poetry, while quite, even very, American, is also quite French. He has translated most of the verse of Jacques Prévert and speaks of himself as influenced by him. Possibly, but I think he has moved up from his master into another qualitative realm altogether. Prévert is not, as some Americans seem to think, some sort of avant garde poet. He is their equivalent of our "*New Yorker* verse." This may be a sad comment on the comparative merits of two cultures, but this doesn't make Prévert any less journalistic—only a short distance above *Le Canard enchaîné* or Georges Fourrest. There is a lot more real bite to Ferlinghetti and a deeper humor. The French poet he resembles most is Queneau. It is possible to "disaffiliate," disengage oneself from the Social Lie and still be good tempered about it, and it is possible to bite the butt of the eternal Colonel Blimp with the quiet, penetrating tenacity of an unperturbed bull dog. This is Ferlinghetti's special talent and it is no mean one. e. e. cummings and James Laughlin have written this way, but few other Americans nowadays. His verse, so easy and relaxed, is constructed of most complex rhythms, all organized to produce just the right tone. Now tone is the hardest and last of the literary virtues to control and it requires assiduous and inconspicuous craftsmanship. Ferlinghetti is definitely a member of the San Francisco School—he says exactly what Everson, Duncan, Ginsberg say. I suppose, in a religious age, it would be called religious poetry, all of it. Today we have to call it anarchism. A fellow over in Africa calls it "reverence for life."

Rimbaud as
Capitalist Adventurer

Most people think of Rimbaud as the very archetype of youth in revolt, as well as the founder of modernist poetry and one of the greatest secular, that is non-religious, or in his case anti-religious, mystics. A kind of Rimbaudian orthodoxy has grown up which meets with very little protest. A few European critics have spoken in demurrer, but most interested Americans have never heard of them. I think myself that the whole Rimbaudian gospel is open to question.

The very title of his prose poems raises this question. Does it mean "illuminations," as in medieval manuscripts? The French verb is *enluminurer.* "Illuminations" is usually considered an English import into French. Does it mean mystical insights? Does it mean bits of illumination in the French sense—enlightenment? (This again in the ironic French sense; an *illuminé* is very close to being a sophisticate or, feminine, a bluestocking.) Nobody ever suggests that the first meaning to occur to an unruly adolescent boy might be "fireworks." I vote for fireworks.

The neuroses the treatment of which now consumes so much of the budget of the more fashionable members of the American upper middle class are actually, by and large, palpitations of behavior due to unsatisfied bourgeois appetites and lack of life aim. In the young, especially in the young poor, the syndrome is called delinquency. Its

---

Review of Illuminations, *by Arthur Rimbaud, translated by Louise Varese, originally published with the title "Fireworks of Adolescence" in* The Nation, *October 12, 1957. Collected under this revised title in* Bird in the Bush, *1959.*

ravages are often attributed to television. Television has a lot to do with it all right, but not the horror serials, the Westerns, and crime shockers. The real source of corruption is the commercial. It is possible to mistake a demoralized craving for Cadillacs for "revolt." Revolutionaries hitherto have not expressed themselves by snitching the gaudier appurtenances of conspicuous expenditure. Genuine revolt goes with an all-too-definite life aim—hardly with the lack of it. Whether or not there is anything genuine about the vision, whether the visionary really sees anything, is open to dispute, but there is a wide consensus as to what the genuine experience is like, and how the genuine visionary behaves. As Baron von Hugel pointed out in one of his most penetrating observations, true illumination always results in a special sweetness of temper, a deep, lyric equanimity and magnanimity. The outstanding characteristic of the mystic's vision is that it is satisfying. He is never frustrated, at least not in our worldly sense. It would be hard to find too less suitable words in any language to apply to Rimbaud than equanimity and magnanimity. This leaves us with Rimbaud as a sort of magician of the sensibility—of that specifically modern sensibility invented by Blake and Hölderlin and Baudelaire—and an innovator in syntax, the first thoroughly radical revealer of the poetic metalogic which is the universal characteristic of twentieth-century verse.

I think this is enough. I don't think anybody has ever demonstrated convincingly that behind the syntactic surface lay the profound content of a sort of combination Bakunin and St. John of the Cross. The content is the season in hell, the dark night of the soul, the struggle with God and the State, of all adolescence. This, of course, has its own common profundity. I do not doubt but what the first flares to burn in the gonads of puberty do light up the ultimate questions of the fate and meaning of man, but that is not what the Rimbaudians mean. The excitement and fury is not metaphysical, it is youthful. The cocksureness is youthful too, but it is also something else. It is bourgeois. Rimbaud did not lose himself in Africa; he found himself. The average poet turns to writing because he can't compete with his schoolmates in track and football. High school dances frighten him. He never learns the proper passes that score with a chick in the back seat of a convertible. In fact, he never gets near one. But there are always a few girls, not very appetizing, most of them, who will be nice to a fellow who has made "The Lit." So, he invests in a set of Dowson, Housman, and T. S. Eliot and starts in. This was not Rimbaud's approach. He applied to literature, and to litterateurs, the minute he laid eyes on them, the devastating methods of total exploitation described so graphically in the *Communist Manifesto.* Some of them were not very applicable. He "ran" the vowels like he later ran guns to the Abyssinians, with dubious results. Usually, however, he was very successful—in the same way his contemporaries Jim Fiske and P. T. Barnum were successful. He did things to literature that had never been done to it before, and they were things which literature badly needed done to it . . . just like the world needed the railroads the Robber Barons did manage to provide.

Not for nothing is *Bateau Ivre* a schoolboy's dream of Cowboys and Indians—that's where Rimbaud belonged, on the frontier—with Cecil Rhodes. And that is where, back in his home town, he was immortalized. The old monument to Rimbaud in Charleville ignores his poetry and memorializes him as the local boy who made good as a merchant and hero of French imperialism in the Africa where the aesthetes who were never good at business think he went to die unknown, holding the Ultimate Mystery at bay.

Jazz Poetry

A little short of two years ago, jazz poetry was a possibility, a hope and the memory of a few experiments. Today it runs the danger of becoming a fad. The life of fads is most often intense, empty and short. I feel, on the contrary, jazz poetry has permanent value or I would not have undertaken it.

When it is successful there is nothing freakish or faddish about it nor, as a matter of fact, is there anything specially new. At the roots of jazz and Negro folk song, especially in the Southwest, is the "talking blues." It is not much heard today, but if you flatten out the melodic line, already very simple, in Big Bill Broonzy or Leadbelly, you have an approximation of it, and some of their records are really more talked than sung. This is poetry recited to a simple blue guitar accompaniment. Long before this, in the mid-nineteenth century, the French poet Charles Cros was reciting, not singing, his poems to the music of a *bal musette* band. Some of his things are still in the repertory of living *café chantant* performers, especially the extremely funny *Le Hareng Saur*. Even today some Rock 'n Roll "novelties" are recited, not sung, and they are some of the most engaging, with music that often verges into the more complex world of true jazz. It has become a common custom in store front churches and Negro revival meetings for a member of the congregation to recite a poem to an instrumental or wordless vocal accompaniment. I believe Langston Hughes recited poems to jazz many years ago. I tried it myself in the twenties in Chicago. In the late forties Kenneth Patchen recited poems to records. Jack Spicer, a San Francisco poet, tried it with a trio led by Ron Crotty on bass. The result, more like

Published in The Nation, *March 29, 1958, not previously collected.*

the Russian tone color music of the first years of the century, was impressive, if not precisely jazz. Lawrence Lipton has been working with some of the best musicians in Los Angeles for almost two years. William Walton's "Façade," Stravinsky's "Persephone," compositions of Auric, Honneger, Milhaud, are well-known examples of speaking, rather than singing, to orchestra in contemporary classical music. Charles Mingus and Fred Katz, two of the most serious musicians in jazz—to narrow that invidious distinction between jazz and serious music—have been experimenting with the medium for some time. The music has been impressive, but in my opinion, speaking as a professional poet, the texts could be improved.

What is jazz poetry? It isn't anything very complicated to understand. It is the reciting of suitable poetry with the music of a jazz band, usually small and comparatively quiet. Most emphatically, it is not recitation with "background" music. The voice is integrally wedded to the music and, although it does not sing notes, is treated as another instrument, with its own solos and ensemble passages, and with solo and ensemble work by the band alone. It comes and goes, following the logic of the presentation, just like a saxophone or piano. Poetry with background music is very far from jazz. It is not uncommon, and it is, in my opinion, usually pretty corny.

Why is jazz poetry? Jazz vocalists, especially white vocalists and especially in the idiom of the most advanced jazz, are not very common. Most Negro singers stay pretty close to the blues, and there is more to modern jazz than blues. Frank Sinatra, Ella Fitzgerald, there are not many singers whom all schools of jazz find congenial. Curiously enough, the poet reciting, if he knows what he is doing, seems to "swing" to the satisfaction of many musicians in a way that too few singers do. I think it is wrong to put down all popular ballad lyrics as trivial; some of them are considerable poetry in their own right, but certainly most are intellectually far beneath the musical world of modern jazz, and far less honest. The best jazz is above all characterized by its absolute emotional honesty. This leaves us with the words of the best blues and Negro folk song, often very great poetry indeed, but still a limited aspect of experience, and by no means everything, translated into words, that modern jazz has to say. In other words, poetry gives jazz a richer verbal content, reinforces and expands its musical meaning and, at the same time, provides material of the greatest flexibility.

How is it done, in actual practice? Kenneth Patchen has been working with Allyn Ferguson and the Chamber Jazz Sextet. The music is composed; it is actually written out, with, of course, room for solo improvisation, but with the voice carefully scored in. There is nothing wrong with this. Far more of the greatest jazz is written music than the lay public realizes. Some of even the famous King Oliver and Louis Armstrong records of long ago were scored by Lil Hardin, a very sophisticated musician. Duke Ellington and his arranger, Billy Strayhorn, are among America's greatest composers. For the past year I have been working with my own band, led by Dick Mills, trumpet, and including Brew Moore, tenor, Frank Esposito, trombone, Ron Crotty, bass, Clair Willey, piano, and Gus Gustafson, drums. Recently in Los Angeles, I played a two-week engagement with a fine band led by Shorty Rogers. In each case we worked from carefully rehearsed "head arrangements." The musicians had each in front of them the text of the poetry, and the sheets were used as cue sheets, scribbled with "inners and outers," chord progressions, melodic lines and various cues.

I feel that this method insures the maximum amount of flexibility and spontaneity and yet provides a steadily deepening and thickening (in the musical sense) basis, differing emotionally more than actually from a written score. The whole thing is elaborately rehearsed—more than usual for even the most complicated "band number." I would like to mention that jazz, contrary to lay opinion, is not just spontaneously "blown" out of the musicians' heads. Behind even the freest improvisation lies a fund of accepted patterns, chord changes, riffs, melodic figures, variations of tempo and dynamics, all understood by the musicians. In fact, they are there, given, as a fund of material almost instinctively come by. Even in a jam session, when a soloist gets as far out as possible, everybody has a pretty clear idea of how he is going to get back and of how everybody is going to go off together again. Then the major forms of common jazz are almost as strict as the sonata—the thirty-two bar ballad, the twelve bar blues—bridges, choruses, fillers, all usually in multiples of the basic four bar unit, in four-four time. Needless to say, the poetry is not "improvised" either. This has been tried, but with disastrously ridiculous results, and not by me. On the other hand, several poets have read over their things once with sensitive musicians and then put on a thoroughly satisfactory show. I have done this with Marty Paitch on piano or Ralph Pena on bass—both musicians with an extraordinary feeling for the rhythms and meanings of poetry. It all depends on the musician.

I hope the faddist elements of this new medium will die away. The ignorant and the pretentious, the sockless hipsters out for a fast buck or a few drinks from a Village bistro, will soon exhaust their welcome with the public, and the field will be left clear for serious musicians and poets who mean business. I think that it is a development of considerable potential significance for both jazz and poetry. It reaches an audience many times as large as that commonly reached by poetry, and an audience free of some of the serious vices of the typical poetry lover. It returns poetry to music and to public entertainment as it was in the days of Homer or the troubadours. It forces poetry to deal with aspects of life which it has tended to avoid in the recent past. It demands of poetry something of a public surface—meanings which can be grasped by ordinary people—just as the plays of Shakespeare had something for both the pit and the intellectuals in Elizabethan times, and still have today. And, as I have said, it gives jazz a flexible verbal content, an adjunct which matches the seriousness and artistic integrity of the music.

Certainly audiences seem to agree. Wherever it has been performed properly, the college auditoriums, the night clubs, the concert halls have been packed, and everybody—musicians, poets and audiences—has been enthusiastic.

In the past two years it has spread from The Cellar, a small bar in San Francisco, to college campuses, to nightclubs in Los Angeles, St. Louis, New York, Dallas and, I believe, Chicago; to the Jazz Concert Hall in Los Angeles, where Lawrence Lipton put on a program with Shorty Rogers, Fred Katz, two bands, myself, Stuart Perkoff and Lipton himself, heard by about six thousand people in two weeks. Kenneth Patchen and Allyn Ferguson followed us, and played there for the better part of two months. Dick Mills and his band have performed with me at several colleges and at the San

Francisco Art Festival, and we are now planning to take the whole show on the road.

If we can keep the standards up, and keep it away from those who don't know what they are doing, who have no conception of the rather severe demands the form makes on the integrity and competence of both musicians and poets, I feel that we shall have given, for a long time to come, new meanings to both jazz and poetry.

Revolt: True and False

You don't have to read Toynbee or Hegel to know that there is a systole and diastole to history. What goes up comes down, what swings left swings right; a literate chimpanzee could learn this from ten years or less of reading the newspapers. Alas, the merchants of words seem not, in the second postwar period, to have understood. Nobody covered his bets, nobody protected his flank. Now the spokesmen of the age of conformity are in a very exposed position. Apple-sellers are just around the corner, a shadow is haunting the leading thinktank circles—the shadow of a second Writers' Project. The younger critics are trying to pawn their pillowcase headdresses, the last Eliot anybody will admit remembering is George, every known type of ambiguity is going for ten cents on the dollar, the quality slicks and the pulpier pulps have discovered dissent, Madison Avenue is busy hunting samples of a new hot commodity—nonconformity. What goes up comes down, with as little insight. Blindly I go my way, said Adolf, like a sleep-walker—not to make an invidious comparison, but because that historic phrase is the perfect rhetoric of the enthusiastic pawn of history.

Why are the ideogogues so at the mercy of their own verbiage? Why do they always have to believe it? I think it is one of the secrets of our civilization—sell the salesman. If you sell him hard enough, he'll take care of the customers, and he's got lots of cousins. The purveyors of the Social Lie today *must* believe it. After all we're not living in the age of Burke: this merchandise has had a long time to spoil. If they didn't believe it smelled like violets, they'd die of disgust. Now a long but significant digression (like Toynbee):

I'll never forget one day, humming around Texas in the early

Published in The Nation, *April 26, 1958, not previously collected.*

twenties with a very sharp boy named Harold Mann. Just a couple of years before, he had been St. Louis district manager of Real Silk Hosiery, the famous house-to-house pitch of those days. We were busted, so he went to the local Real Silk office, perhaps it was in Pecos, and took out a kit to pick up some change. He came back early, with plenty of change, but with ashen cheeks and haunted eyes. Said he, "I have just witnessed one of the great climacterics of history, far more important than the World War. It used to be the manager told you, 'The sucker comes to the door. You say this, she says that, you put your foot in the door, she says this, you say that, you bust out the kit. The sucker says this, you say that—and so on.' Now you go down at eight in the morning and spend an hour singing *Real Silk, Real Silk,* to the tune of *Marching Through Georgia,* and listen to the boss tell you what good stockings they are—all on your own time. Mark my words, this will make a greater change in the human race than the invention of fire!"

Wise words. When Arthur Schlesinger, Jr., a member of Stevenson's writing crew, came to review Adlai's speeches for *The Reporter,* he reviewed them with the delicious surprise of a sweet new ingénue in the hands of the late Lionel Barrymore. The technical term for this is the hallucination of documents and the delusion of participation.

So now. Before all the Henry Adamses from the Bronx and the cornfield Lord Chesterfields start miscegenating, blowing jazz poetry and taking heroin, it would be a good idea to understand what that long-forgotten word "revolt" is all about. Who objects to what and why, and what is it that is wrong with what we used to call The System, anyway? How do you nonconform?

One thing for sure, you don't do it by caricaturing the values of the very civilization that debauched you in the first place. You don't dash here and yon through the night, wrecking stolen cars and going "Whee!" You don't have six deserted wives, all of them pregnant. You don't take dope. You don't "dig" jazz. (Which means you don't think it is savage jungle drums and horns blowing up a storm around the flickering fires while the missionary soup comes to a boil.) You don't Whitmanize and Rimbaudize and Artaudize that evil perversion we call, in jazz, "Crow-Jimism." Probably you shave. Probably you wear shoes. At least you plan to take up both if things get much worse. If you dress and behave eccentrically, you dress and behave the way nobody else does—not the way every high school boy who can remember Jimmy Dean does. The essence of revolt is understanding, the essence of disconformity is comprehension, and their second essence is purposeful action.

This is why the word merchants can't dig it. They haven't, don't, and can't *act*. Marx called this "human self-alienation"—the divorce of man from his work, and hence, his divorce from his fellows, and hence from himself. This is what that thing we used to call the Revolution is all about. There is good reason for disaffiliation; it's not just for kicks. But the man who has got by all his life just quivering his glottis can't, constitutionally, understand this. I am, amongst other things, a poet. My poetry is work. I write it to lay hands on an obdurate world, to make love to women and to overthrow the State, the Church and the Capitalist System. I do not write it to get it analyzed in a seminar and neither did John Donne or Arthur Rimbaud. And anybody can throw away his socks and let his feet go dirty. The billionaires all have six deserted wives, or at least they used to in the best days of the old *Masses* and *Mother Earth*. Disaffiliation from the inhuman means affiliation with the truly human.

Literature is work. Art is work. And work, said St. Benedict, is prayer. There are at least three Zen Buddhists to be found in every public toilet in every city over 250,000 in the U.S.A. after ten at night. "You just dig it man. You just let it happen. It just busts in your head like sh—t in your blood stream, you dig? It's the old whirl, man, you dig?" Have these poor disheveled children any idea of the work, years and years of it, that goes to the perfecting of a Japanese swordsman, a judo expert, one of the admirals that pulled off Pearl Harbor, a monk in a Zendo, or any other recognized exponent of the philosophy of Boddhidarma? No. "Like that's all for squares, man. Like pops, don't come around talking that old moldy fig political jive, you bug me, man. W.O.R.K., wasn't that the name of a bunch of real gone cats used to ride freight trains in Montana and Washington way back? Like why don't you make like them, pops, and dig this new Zen kick, like?" *Illumination.* The reasoned derangement of the senses. Rimbaud, Céline, Artaud, Genêt, Beckett, Ionesco—is that what they did: just let it happen?

Yes and no. Rimbaud no more than got those famous words out of his mouth than he went off and never came back and never wrote another word. Reasoned derangement of the senses is for gun runners in Africa when they relax *en famille* in a grass hut; it's a bourgeois-type kick. It is true, especially in a period of cowardice and silence, that those who are being stamped into the mud see most clearly the iron soles of Juggernaut and the clay feet within— but Céline has been ill for a very long time, and Artaud was not at all well. Genêt we can lay on the side—he has always seemed to me a one-man rubberneck bus of the sins of Paris, an up-to-date and conscienceless Eugène Sue. But anybody who thinks Beckett and Ionesco just let it happen needs to go back and take English One. The real danger, of course, is that artists like these will be hooked by the mystique they have, innocently, helped create.

An orthodoxy is forming, and like all orthodoxies it is a system of lies and evasions, a ritual of the lazy and greedy. How do you escape it? By reading Marx and Kropotkin? By joining up? Indeed not. *Playboy*, a leading socio-economic authority, says, "Rexroth says the Anarchists must organize." Excuse me; I mean, *ça ira*. It is a deliberately fostered delusion of Western Civilization, of the Old and New Testaments and the Koran, that life is hard to understand and harder still to live. It is only too obvious, every step of the way as the newspapers roll past, what should be—should have been—done.

You are right in choosing art as the one perfect instrument; you are even right in choosing jazz. The best artists of the past fifteen years of darkness have found voice in jazz for the same reason that, in the years of terror after the 1905 revolution, the Russians wrote metaphysics: the cops couldn't understand it. But do you think jazz is something you just get up and blow out of a cloud of pod? Do you think being beat comes easy? You don't get that way growing an embouchure moustache and painting nail holes on your hands and feet. Do you know about Lester Young, clinging to his saxophone in the Army stockades in the piney woods of the savage South? Do you know that story?

Be very careful you don't become what Madison Avenue wants every artist to be—a wild man.

The Hasidism of Martin Buber

The last two years in the religious book field, it's been like Old MacDonald's farm, with here a Buber, there a Buber, everywhere a Buber, Buber. There is a good reason for this. Martin Buber is practically the only religious writer a non-religious person could take seriously today. Paul Tillich probably runs him a close second, but Tillich is too much a technical theologian for secular, let alone atheist, taste. Yet Buber is one of the most important living theologians. I should say that the determinative theological works of this century have been Schweitzer's *Quest of the Historical Jesus*, Otto's *The Idea of the Holy*, Barth's *Commentary on the Epistle to the Romans*, and, to go back to the very beginning of the century, a selection, difficult to make, from the works of Baron von Hugel and Father Tyrrell, and, conversely, from the work of their opponents, the Neo-Thomists, before Neo-Thomism became a fad with French journalists and spoiled Surrealists. Towards the top of this list belongs Buber's *I and Thou*, one of the most moving books ever written.

I and Thou is a little book, a true pocket book, a *vade mecum*, to go with you on your way, like *The Little Flowers of St. Francis*, or Angelus Silesius, or *The Imitation of Christ*, or the *Bhagavad-Gita*, or Carus' *Gospel of Buddha*—"*vade mecum* . . ." and I imagine it has gone with many a person on many a strange and tortured way. After all, it is a book by a German Jew. I read it, long ago, in French on the recommendation of—of all people—Hugh MacDiarmid, and it was one of the determinative books of my life. For twenty years I have given away copies of the paperbound Scottish edition to

Published in Bird in the Bush, 1959.

whomever I could get interested. Scribner's announces a new edition of *I and Thou* for this fall [1958]. That will mean that somewhere close to twenty-five books by Martin Buber will be in print in English, many of them in paperback editions. A large number of these latter have been published in the last two years.

What kind of religious writer is Martin Buber? He is a Romantic Traditionalist. His approach to doctrine and ritual is pragmatic, symbolist, experiential. This is a tradition, actually a kind of revolution, known to most educated people as exemplified by Cardinal Newman, Father Tyrrell, Monsignor Duchesne, Baron von Hugel, William James, Carl Jung. Hard as it might be for the uninitiated to believe, this was once the prevailing philosophy of the Romanist clergy in America, until it was suppressed early in the century by the famous Papal Bull against "Modernism." The great popularity of Carl Jung has led to its proliferation in every sect. In so far as they have any, it is the philosophy of most occultists, Vedantists, self-styled Zen Buddhists, a considerable percentage of Anglo-Catholics, and a small but significant percentage of Roman Catholics who, perforce, are not very communicative about it. Since the terrible events of the war years it has become a common attitude amongst previously non-religious Jews. It is not so common amongst Protestants, for the reason that Protestantism does not provide this kind of an apologetic with sufficient materials to work on. These materials are myth, miracle, mystery, ritual, dogma. As far as the religious American Protestant layman is concerned, his religion has just spent three difficult centuries getting rid of precisely these characteristics and he does not care to return to them. Kierkegaard and Barth he never heard of; Reinhold Neibuhr he thinks of as a rather moralistic politician—like John Foster Dulles—and hence unreliable and unrealistic.

It is a clever apologetic, with a wonderful ability to sneak up on the most sophisticated and catch them unawares. Mystery, miracle, myth, ritual are considered anthropologically, in terms of their significance for a community—its living contact with its past, its internal coherence and tone, its ability to act in the present and envisage the future—exactly, of course, the way one would consider the role of religion in the study of an exotic primitive tribe. It is assumed that since some primitive tribes have been reported to be

in a better state of social health than our admittedly sick civilization, the pervasive role of mystery, miracle, myth, ritual, is responsible for this difference. They give life dignity and significance, and
with their rites of passage at birth, death, sexual maturity, marriage,
eating, drinking, bathing—the matter of all sacraments everywhere—give it a kind of grandeur which lifts it out of the frustrations and tedium and ultimate meaninglessness of "materialistic
existence." It is then assumed that since this constitutes social
health, the individual in modern society who belongs to an artificial
community which preserves these characteristics will have greater
mental health than his non-religious fellows.

If miracle, mystery, myth, ritual, are group symbols of psychological realities which can be taken over by the individual to the great
improvement of his mental health, why not dogma too? It is easier
to believe an obvious impossibility—such as the Catholic doctrine
that Christ came out of the Virgin's womb like light through glass
and left her a *virgina intacta*, "Blessed Mary *Ever* Virgin,"—than it
is to believe a simple misstatement of fact, for the simple reason that
an impossibility, to be believed, must be immediately etherealized,
made part of a system which is transmundane altogether. This is
why so estimable a religion as Mormonism has so hard a time
holding its young intellectuals. It is almost impossible to etherealize
the simply wrong geography and history of the *Book of Mormon*.
Anybody, even mathematical physicists, can believe the Athanasian
Creed by an act of transfiguration of its statements.

So today we have large sections of our most literate population
voluntarily adopting the religious behavior and beliefs of more
primitive communities for purely pragmatic, psychologistic, personal reasons. The assumption is that this is a kind of symbolic
behavior by which greater spiritual insight into reality, better interpersonal relations, and finally true realization of the self, will follow.
The fact that there is not the slightest statistical evidence for this
assumption does not matter. The fact that the entire Judeo-Chris-
tian-Muslim period in human history has been an episode of unparalleled personal and social psychosis and international barbarity is
beside the point. People have Hanukkah lights in the window or
Christmas trees at the winter solstice and take Communion at
Easter or make a Seder on Pesach because the society in which they

live provides them with no valid life aim and robs them of all conviction of personal integrity. All "neo" religions are cults of desperation in a time of human self-alienation and social disintegration. Rigid orthodoxies like Neo-Thomism are just archaizing pragmatisms of the same kind which as a final act of faith reject the personal and social instrumentalism which is their initial assumption.

It is in this context—that of the only effective apologetic of our time—that Buber functions. But this is not to belittle him. It is obvious that what I have been describing is not really the role of religion in society at all. It is the role of art. Just as the Surrealists and others have tried to substitute art for religion, so the Romantic Traditionalist, be he Jew, Catholic, Vedantist, or Buddhist, turns religion into a kind of compulsive poetry—poetry with an imperative attached. (I might point out that sometimes it isn't very well attached.)

The real reason for the popularity of the Occult Ancient East was pointed out long ago by Kipling: "Ship me somewhere East of Suez . . . where there ain't no ten commandments . . ." If your religion is just exotic enough, you don't need to bother about responsibility. You can get away with anything. There is nothing of this in Buber. For him the faith is the faith of his fathers, and the highest expression of that faith is its prayer, and prayer is the highest form of responsibility, the ultimately committed dialogue. This is an aesthetic statement, not a religious one, and in the final analysis all of Buber's major works are works of art. *I and Thou* is one of the greatest prose poems, an *Isaiah*, and a *Song of Myself.*

From *I and Thou* to his latest collection of essays, all of Martin Buber's work has been a celebration of the joys of communion. Will Herberg has recently included him in his collection, *Five Existentialist Theologians.* Now when Will Herberg was young and giddy and a Marxist, he had the reputation of being the only American of that persuasion whom the Kremlin ever took seriously as a thinker. He once wrote a pamphlet which I still treasure, called *The Stalinist Position on the American Negro,* which pretty well disposed of *that* folly forever. As he has grown older and got religion, he seems to have lost his sense of discrimination. "Existentialism" may be a fashionable term that helps sell books, but Martin Buber's connection with Existentialism is of the simplest and most fundamental kind—he is against it, and he has written more cogent polemic against it than anybody else who has ever bothered with it. He is the leading anti-Existentialist amongst modern religious writers. Maritain, one of the five, is neither a theologian nor an Existentialist. He is a religious journalist with a keen nose for catchwords that sell books.

Religious Existentialism descends directly from Augustine to Luther to Kierkegaard to Barth. It is obsessed with the absolute transcendence of the creator and the utter contingency of the creature, and it recognizes no mediation except a sort of historically instantaneous thunderbolt, the Incarnation of Jesus Christ, which must be accepted as an act of blind faith. It has no use for the responsibilities of community: Augustine put aside his wife, married after the rites of a slightly different sect, as a whore, and Kierkegaard's love life was a pitiable farce. It pictures man as ridden by the anxieties and terrors of his only spiritual ability—his realization of his own insignificance. This is why atheist Existentialism is a philosophy of despair, "the philosophy of the world-in-concentration-camp," a kind of utterly thoroughgoing masochism. Take away God and there is absolutely nothing left. Nothing but black bile. Nobody there. However Martin Buber might disagree doctrinally, take away his God and nothing important in his philosophy has changed. It remains a philosophy of joy, lived in a world full of others.

Actually, Buber's philosophy, technically speaking, is much like that of the English Hegelians, especially McTaggart, and the great forgotten American, Josiah Royce, just as his epistemology and his position in the Existentialist controversy is close to that of the contemporary English thinker, John Wisdom. The Beloved Community may not be for him, as a quasi-orthodox Jew, the Absolute, but it is the garment of the Absolute. And his epistemology is founded on the answer to the question "What is out there?"— "Other minds." And that answer is the title of John Wisdom's most seminal book. I am well aware that Buber's philosophical writings are an integral part of the modern Existentialist dispute. *Between Man and Man* is concerned almost entirely with the question of personality, the person as human being, the person as a member of society, the absolute personality. As such, written in Germany in the second

quarter of this century, it is perforce a running commentary on
Kierkegaard, Husserl, Heidegger, Scheler. But this does not make
Buber an Existentialist any more than Aquinas is a Nominalist or
an Averroist. Again, the American lectures gathered as *The Eclipse
of God*, deal with God as absolute person and man as contingent.
This is the favorite stamping ground of the Existentialists, and also,
of course, American lectures must be about things up-to-date audiences want to hear.

Existentialism is a frame of mind. For people who do not know
the maximum state of insecurity bred in most men caught in our
disintegrating social fabric as in a thicket of fire, its dilemmas, like
the epistemological dilemma that bothered the British for three
centuries, simply do not exist. The dilemma does not exist for Buber.
He cannot project himself with any success into the psychosis of
total insecurity. He is too much at home in the world. Nothing
shows this better than his treatment of Simone Weil in the essay,
"The Silent Question" (from *At the Turning*), or of Sartre in *Eclipse
of God*. Neither Weil nor Sartre is very great shakes as philosopher,
but both are certainly pure Existentialist personalities, high-level
Beatniks. Buber is very funny. Forced by popular demand to discuss
an outrageous and pathetic girl, whose writings are a farrago of
terror and misinformation, and a plain vulgar journalist, it is all he
can do to control himself. His distaste for life lived on this level, for
the most important issues exploited purely for sensationalism, for a
kind of metaphysics of delinquency, is more than his sympathy can
bear. He takes refuge from Simone Weil in his own orthodoxy.
Sartre he dismisses with a compliment as a great literary artist.
Coming from the author of the *Tales of the Hasidim* and *I and
Thou*, this is the most ironic innocence.

He is so polite, this man with the most beautiful beard since von
Hugel. He is so nice to Carl Jung. He picks his way so nicely, so
kindly through and over the *disjecta membra* of that beached whale,
the chubby corpse of Mme. Blavatsky, which is the gnostic theosophy of Jung, and even after Jung "answers" him in a half-cocked
polemic full of pleas about the "science of psychology" from one of
the most unscientific minds of all time, Buber so gently points out
that the controversy is beneath the level of a second-year student in

a good theological seminary—any time in the past fifteen hundred years. He does this, of course, purely by implication. Jung, I am sure, was completely unaware that he was thoroughly told off. Buber likes people. Had he met Simone Weil in person, he would have liked her, and it is a pity he didn't, because, had she listened, he would have done her a lot of good. Many girls and young men exactly like her must have come to him down the years. He is the kind of man whom any person in trouble would recognize on sight, or on the sight of a single book of his work, as the ideal confessor. Simone Weil did not like such people and avoided them. To her, they were what her more vulgar sisters call "the fuzz," representatives of her "Great Beast," the Social Lie.

Is Buber in any sense a representative of the Social Lie? Max Weber long ago pointed out that the use of a transcendental ideology to justify the betrayals and compromises of politics and economics is the essential social falsehood. The oncoming war is not going to be fought on either side for any sort of values whatsoever, and anybody who says it is is a liar or a dupe. We have finally reached a point where the very conditions under which they operate expose the fiction of politics and economics for what they are. If Buber were a spokesman for Judaism, or any other religion as an institution, or for Israel or any other State, then of course Simone Weil would be right.

This brings us at last to the meat and crux and essence of Buber's thought, his idea of community, his interpretation of the vocation of prophet, and hence, by implication, of his own social role vis-à-vis Hasidism. Buber's Existentialism is terminological—an accident of current talk; his Hasidism is at his heart. Now Buber's Hasidism is a very special thing, and for those who know nothing about the subject, his presentation can be not just very, but almost totally misleading. That is, for anybody seeking ordinary information. He has, practically singlehandedly, brought Hasidism to life for educated people. (The actual sect is still very much alive, especially among poorer Jews in, for instance, Williamsburg, Brooklyn.) But he has revivified only certain elements of this Jewish sect; much, in fact what most actual Hasids would have considered the most important parts, he has left dead and forgotten or has subtly reinterpreted. What is Hasidism—not Buber's Hasidism, but the historical movement as it appears in the record?

Hasidism is an ecstatic religious movement which resulted from the impact of popular Kabbalism on the folk culture of the eighteenth-century Polish ghetto. Many elements went to produce it. In part it was a pressure phenomenon like the pentecostal religions of the American Negro. Polish Jewish life in the eighteenth century was especially hard. The Messianic movement of Sabatei Zevi collapsed in spiritual demoralization when he became a Muslim. The partition of Poland subjected the Jewish communities to new problems. Life was insecure and unstable and full of disabilities and petty annoyances. Pogroms and persecutions increased. The community was driven in upon itself more than ever before, but it was driven in upon a specially rich folk culture, some of which was ancient, some of which was Russian or Polish in origin, some of which had developed *in situ*. All those folkways which one's Polish Jewish friends reminisce about with such gusto gave life in the ghetto and in the Jewish villages an intensity unlike anything in the peasant cultures of Western Europe. At the same time similar pentecostal and charismatic movements were sweeping through the Christian peasant communities of that part of the world. This was a time of great proliferation of the sects of Russian Dissenters, and of the Eastward movement of German Mennonites, Anabaptists, and Pietists.

Jews have been in Poland longer than anyone knows. The Persians settled Jewish communities on their northern borders beyond the Black Sea. The Khazar kingdom, Jewish in religion, competed with the Vikings, A.D. 600-800, for control of the waterways and the fur and amber trade of what is now Russia. In the Dark Ages the Jews were *voyageurs* much like the fur traders of French Canada centuries later, over all the Baltic-Black Sea river connections. These Jews were not Talmudists, and remnants of them still survive as Karaites—non-Talmudic Jews—in the Crimea and elsewhere.

Into the same borderlands, the Byzantine Empire had for centuries expelled incorrigible heretics. First the Paulicians and Gnostics, later the Bogomils. At one time much of the South Slav world was ruled by Bogomil dynasties. From the Bogomils by direct propaganda came the Cathari—the Albigenses of Provence. Russian dissent is strongly influenced by Bogomilism. Any unprejudiced study of Hasidism immediately reveals all sorts of ideas shared with Catharism.

Kabbalism dates back into the most obscure past of Judaism. It claims to be at least as old as Jewish orthodoxy, and it may well be right, but its basic document, *The Zohar*, was written in Spain in the Middle Ages. It is simply Jewish Gnosticism. This is disputed but it is none the less true. It shares every important feature with all the leading Gnostic sects. From the inscrutable Godhead, Ayn Soph, emanate ten *sephiroth*, with names like Rigor and Mercy, the aeons of Valentinian. The final one, Malkuth, the Queen, is the physical manifestation of Deity in the universe. This is the Wisdom that danced before Him before the beginning of days, of the Book of Proverbs, the Shekinah, the Glory that hovered over the Ark and blessed with her presence all the great rites of passage and the festivals of the year. She is thought of as a hypostasis, a Divine Woman, the Bride of God, exactly like the Shakti of Shiva. She is also the abomination of desolation against whom the prophets continuously cry out. Ishtar, Astarte, Ashtoreth, the Baalat of Baal, the most ancient Canaanite goddess reasserts herself in eighteenth-century Poland.

A great deal of Kabbalism is taken up with alphabetical magic, and the manipulation of Biblical texts, numerologically and otherwise, to make them mean something quite different from what they say. Finally, the "innermost secrets" of the Kabbalah are what are occult in all occultism, various autonomic nervous system gymnastics of the sort we identify with Yoga, and erotic mysticism. For the Kabbalist the ultimate sacrament is the sexual act, carefully organized and sustained as the most perfect mystical trance. Over the marriage bed hovers the Shekinah. The Glory of God is revealed in the most holy of duties, and new souls are reborn into the sacred community of Israel. There are other notions—reincarnation, light metaphysics, worship of the planets and the moon, the latter identified with the Shekinah. (When Hasids dance in the public parks of New York under the new moon with their hands over their heads, they are showing her her stigmata, found in the lunes of their fingernails, and celebrating her as their Great Mother.)

Kabbalism is thus one with the most ancient heterodoxy, and it well may be more ancient than any orthodoxy. Emanationism and some other doctrines are set forth in the so-called Memphite Theology, an Egyptian tractate older than the days of Moses and the Exodus. Kabbalism differs little from any other form of Gnosticism, whether of Kobo Daishi or Bardesanes, and as a full-fledged system it is certainly a few centuries older than the Christian Era. People who know of all this only through modern cultists or occult Freemasonry are under the impression that it was all thought up a couple of generations ago by Eliphas Levi and Mme. Blavatsky. On the contrary, its claims to antiquity are quite valid. There is one important particular in which Kabbalism differs from many Gnosticisms, and especially from Manicheanism-Paulicianism-Bogomilism-Catharism. It is not dualistic. The final source of all reality is One, a hidden and unknowable God. Evil is explained in the various orthodox fashions—as a term of creation, as a manifestation of the recalcitrance of matter, as the result of a Fall, the Fall of the Angels and the Exile of the Shekinah, of Adam, and a falling apart of the manifest and the transcendent worlds, and finally—a notion shared with Indian Tantrism—as the "shells" left over, like burst vessels, from previous creations. The Biblical epic, from Abraham to the closing of the canon and on to the Fall of the Temple is considered to be the essential process of the return of the *sephiroth*. Hovering above the Torah, the Rite and the Law, the Shekinah is wed, the Creative Act is a closed circuit. Outside the Covenant or in the Diaspora, she is still in Exile. The Community of Israel *is* the Bride of Jehovah.

It must be pointed out that the various sects descended from Manicheanism have all disclaimed dualism. The accusation comes from the orthodox. All this is repeated in the mystical doctrine of the Blessed Virgin—the names in the Litany of the BVM, the etherealization of the Song of Songs and the Books of Esther and Ruth, are common to Kabbalah and Mariolatry. For this reason and similar ones, conventional Jews have always been suspicious of Kabbalah as a transmission belt to Christianity. It has been so in the past and the leading twentieth-century Kabbalist, Paul Levertoff, became an Anglo-Catholic priest.

This is very heady stuff. History has proved, time and again, that when it gets out amongst the masses it can be extremely intoxicating and subversive of all decent social order. Except, reputedly, for the ancient Babylonian city of Harran, the last outpost of paganism to survive, and possibly for the Assassin inner community of Alamut, there has never been a stable polity reared on Gnosticism. The Kabbalists kept their speculations carefully confined to a very small elite. Much of the present *Prayerbook* is the work of one of the greatest Kabbalists that ever lived, but not one Jew in ten thousand is aware of it. Rabbi Israel ben Eliezer Baal-Shem, the founder of Hasidism, turned it into a popular cult, with an extremely active propaganda. He gave it a kind of organization. He imbedded it in the Yiddish folk culture. He did much more than this. He gave it an ethical content of a sort we do not know to have existed in any other Gnostic movement. Again, we know the ethical aspects of heresy only from the polemics of the orthodox. If Albigensian Provence, with all its wealth and culture, was anything like the poor villages of Poland gripped in the enthusiasm of the Hasidic movement, Europe was dealt a deadly blow by the Albigensian Crusade. Simon de Montfort and the Pope, Hitler and Himmler—perhaps there is something about the rage of the Great Beast at the sight of the pure joy of living which can be appeased only with the savor of burning human flesh.

Hasidism came to have a whole group ritual, special ways of celebrating the old Jewish holidays and rites of passage. Most conspicuous was ecstatic dancing of a peculiar character. It is like nothing else in the world, although I suppose its antecedents go back to the dancing dervishes of the Levant and through them to the Corybantic brotherhoods of the Baals and Baalats of Canaan. Great emphasis was placed on the bath of purification. For the antiquity of this we have physical evidence amongst the Essenes of the Dead Sea settlement. The Baal Shem frowned on asceticism and taught that the holy man "redeems" food and drink by consuming it. Alcohol was consumed, especially before dancing, to produce a kind of holy intoxication. Erotic mysticism and direct adoration of the Shekinah as the Bride of God were central to most rites. The ritual dance was customarily performed to singing in which all took part, dancing in a circle around a young boy with a pure unchanged voice who stood in the center of the ring dance on a table, and who was understood as a surrogate for a woman. Dances like this are referred to in both the Jewish and the Christian Apocrypha and they are common in other Gnostic sects from Japan to Bengal. This, however, did not result in any sort of orgiastic sexual promiscuity. There is no question but that sacred prostitutes, male and female, were part of the temple ritual until the revolution which "discovered the ancient documents" of the present Torah. In Hasidism their place is taken by each married couple—a temple unto themselves. All Hasidim, and especially their leaders, the Zaddiks, were expected to marry, and the final expression of erotic mysticism was centered in the marriage bed and the family. In this way Hasidism, after all its colorful and emotional detour, returns to be at one with the most orthodox mystery of Judaism—the seed of Israel.

Hasidism was organized exactly like the Albigenses. There was an elite, called Zaddiks, which means the Righteous, corresponding to the elite of the Albigenses, the Cathari or Purified Ones. They were usually rabbis, but not always, and like the imams of the Shi'ite Muslims, there were supposed to be always thirty-six Hidden Zaddiks, or sometimes only one who was a sort of bodhisattva or latent Messiah, and from whom flowed the holiness of the others. Around each of these especially devoted and illuminated leaders (they were thought of, like the Cathari, as literally filled with light) were grouped little fellowships of the rank and file Hasidim, an ecstatic, dancing, singing, gesticulating band who greatly resemble the first Franciscans and may well have resembled in actual behavior the first disciples of Christ (who, we may be sure, did *not* comport themselves like the Bench of Bishops).

The Zaddiks were direct sources of *mana*, holy power, which could be tapped by less saintly laymen, and they were equally direct advocates with God. To each Zaddik the laity brought little slips of paper inscribed with all the troubled petitions of life and with the petitioner's name and, not his father's, as is the Jewish custom, but with his mother's name. The Zaddiks spent long hours in meditative prayer, in the course of which all the day's petitions were presented before the Throne of Mercy. If this constitutes the essence of

priesthood the Zaddikkim were priests, and as such the only priesthood surviving in Jewry outside of the Falasha of Abyssinia. In the
course of time this custom and another like it, which greatly resembled the sale of indulgences that disgraced Renaissance Roman
Catholicism, came to corrupt Hasidism, and many Zaddiks ended
up rich, vain, drunken exploiters of ignorant slum and village
superstition. The Hasidic community was a genuine fellowship. The
laity spent a great deal of time with their masters, in the synagogues
and schools, and at table, eating with them if possible on all the
holidays and on every Sabbath, especially the third Sabbath meal—
the Feast of the Queen. Alcohol, dance, song, sex all played a part,
but above all else, Hasidism was a *religion of conversation*. In this,
once again, it must have been very like the earliest days of Christianity. The Marriage Feast of Cana, the Miracle of the Loaves and
Fishes, the Last Supper—these are all intensely Hasidic episodes.

This special temper seems to have been always latent in Jewry
and in eighteenth-century Poland the Hasidic propaganda fell on
fertile soil. Almost everything which the non-religious American
treasures as part of the Jewish contribution to modern culture comes
from the intense and intensely gregarious life of the Polish ghetto.
Above all else it is a frame of mind, an insouciance in the face of the
cruel absurdities of life, a very special kind of whimsical irony,
which has passed over, emasculated, to become our typical modern
American (*New Yorker*) humor, an inexhaustible, mocking fantasy, a
special kind of intimacy which is compounded of a general ebul-
lient love of man and of life and a very active interest in the
immediate partner of any dialogue. This is the Hasidic temper. It
gives the characteristic color to those typical Jewish jokes and
anecdotes which are so much funnier than other jokes. From it
come all the great Yiddish writers, from Sholem Aleichem to
Moishe Nadir, the visionary poets like Yehoash. It gives the Yiddish
theater its effervescence and poignancy. Zak, Zakkine, Soutine,
many Americans—my friends Doner and Zakheim amongst
them—these are all Hasidic artists, and the greatest of all, of course,
the pure illustrator of the Hasidic spirit, is Marc Chagall, whose
paintings find their parallel in the *Tales of the Hasidim* of Buber.
The intended canard of chauvinists that jazz is Negro and Jewish

music is perfectly correct. It is the ecstatic Hasidic heritage that
made it possible for American musicians from Avenue A and Maxwell Street and Williamsburg to meet the Negro half way.

The Hasidic movement at its height included close to half the
population of Jewish Poland. What effect did such an explosion
have on the orthodox? Surprisingly little, considering. In the first
place, Kabbalism as long as it was veiled in the decent obscurity of
learning was a perfectly respectable part of Judaism. In the second
place, all their opponents, the *mitnagdim*, shared the same folk
culture, unless they were assimilated—renegades—a good deal
worse than being Hasids. Many of the doctrines and ideas and
practices of the Hasidim were paralleled in the regular Jewish
community. The Hasidic movement just gave them a new emotional content and so shaped them to a more ecstatic form. Eventually many of the Zaddikkim became very learned, with a rather
crazy kind of learning, and were able to dispute the rabbis on their
own ground, and the power of learning, Jewish learning, is respected
by even the most bigoted.

And then, finally, there is no Jewish orthodoxy in the sense a
Christian would understand. It is possible to believe in heaven, hell,
and purgatory, or in reincarnation, or in no after life at all, and still
be a good Jew. The emanationism and hypostases of Kabbalah have
never been challenged as either polytheism or pantheism. It is
inconceivable that the world of Jewry could ever tear itself asunder
over speculations as to the exact nature of subtle psychological
processes in the structure of the Deity, or as to the exact nature and
occasion of God's saving grace. If you preserve the unity of the
Godhead and keep the Torah, you are a Jew and no rabbi, however
learned, can say you nay. The Jews are the only people who have
ever met the supposed threat of a widespread movement of the
Gnostic type without persecution to the point of extermination.
True, *mitnagdim* means "persecutors"—but the defensive measures of the conventional communities of Poland were affectionate
compared with the Albigensian Crusade, the Persian crusade
against Mani—and in our own day against the Bahai movement, or
the Lutheran suppression of the Anabaptists of the Munster Com-
monwealth. In fact, all Judaism, from Frankfort to Jerusalem, from
Lithuania to Rumania, felt the influence of the Hasidic movement

and shows it to this day. (There exists another province of Hasidism, the popular Kabbalism of Levantine and Sephardic Jews. It had demonstrable connections with the movement of Baal Shem Tov but it is not important in a consideration of Martin Buber's neo-Hasidism.) Hasidism itself is still very much alive and typical Hasidism can be seen any day—but the Sabbath—by anyone who cares to visit the fur district of New York at lunch hour. It is not only powerful in Israel, but its rites and ceremonies with their dancing and songs and joy of life are the direct source of the folk customs of the neo-Judaism of the *kibbutzim*, the Jewish cooperative communes in Israel. The "Israeli" songs and dances that have become so popular a part of the Zionist propaganda in America and that can be heard at parties of the most sophisticated Jewish young people are Hasidic, not Palestinian, in origin.

Hasidism owes its power and durability to its ethical content, and to the specific kind of ethical content. Partly this is simply Jewish, but much of it is the teaching of the Baal Shem and his first disciples. There have been lots of Baal Shems; the term means the "master of the name," a Kabbalist who has discovered or inherited one of the secret names of God and can work magic with it and summon up powers and demons. Baal Shem Tov, as Rabbi Eliezer was called, is the master of the Good Name, the Kabbalist who can work miracles in the souls of men. Actually, Baal Shem Tov seems to have been an almost illiterate man as far as Kabbalistic learning went, and many of the early Zaddikkim were simple workmen, woodcutters, coachmen, potters, butchers, tanners—many of them from occupations of dubious purity from the strict Jewish point of view. Hasidism is ethical mysticism. Its dominant characteristic is joy in the good—in the good in every sense of the word, in life, in the good things of life, in the beauty of creation, in the good in all men, and in doing good. The joke, "Good food, good drink, good God, let's eat," could well be a brief Hasidic "grace."

The great trouble with Talmudic Judaism is that it was used up emotionally—it had become a religion of rules and prescriptions, very difficult to get excited about. Hasidism changed all this. The Torah, the Law, became a source of endless intoxicating joy. To use the vulgar phrase of a bad American revivalist, they discovered that it was fun to do good and to be good. It is curious that with the

exception of the Quakers, Christianity and the religions influenced
by it teach or at least imply that it is very, very hard to be a good
human being. This is simply not true, not at least for a person
uncorrupted by manufactured guilts. It is not only easy to avoid
lying, stealing, fornication, covetousness, idolatry, lust, pride, anger,
jealousy, and the rest, it is a positive pleasure. Essential to such a life
are magnanimity, courage, and the love and trust of other men.
These are above all others the Hasidic virtues, along with humility,
simplicity, and joy. These are all virtues of direct dealing with other
men—the virtues of dialogue. To the Hasid the mystical trance is a
dialogue. The self does not unself itself, but "forgets itself" in
conversation with the Other; and from the Other, i.e., God as the
ultimate and perfect partner of dialogue, flows out the conversation
with all others—the life of dialogue, the philosophy of Martin
Buber.

What Buber has done is divest Hasidism of its Gnosticism, and of
the extremities and eccentricities of conduct which are the marks of
isolated sectarianism. Unless he himself has some personal esoter-
ism he has not divulged to us, he has discarded all of its occult lore
and practice. What he has kept is the folk spirit, the ethical gospel,
and above all the specific temper. Baron von Hugel says somewhere
that one of the essential signs of sanctity in the process of canoniza-
tion is a certain pervasive sweetness of temper—a kind of holy good
humor—or possibly just plain good humor. It is this *courtoisie*
which Hasidism shares with the early Franciscans and which is so
rare a virtue amongst the professedly religious. Least of all is it
common amongst the Romantic Traditionalists, the inventors and
followers of our modern archaizing neo-religions. Let a contemporary intellectual start reading Thomas Aquinas or Dr. Suzuki and
he immediately adopts all those lovely virtues preached by Christ or
Buddha—pride, arrogance, intolerance, bigotry, ill temper, anger. It
is not for nothing that the Pope condemned *L'Action Française*. It
was a parade of all the deadly sins in literary guise—in the guise of
Catholic polemic and apologetic. Von Hugel of course was not a
convert, he was a born Catholic of great power and influence; he
rather was trying to convert the Church. Possibly Buber is in the
same position. He has taken a movement of ghetto, slum, and

peasant enthusiasts of which most educated Jews were secretly ashamed, and has used it to reform, restate, and give new emotional meaning to what he considers to be the essence of Judaism. It is quaint to notice that his American exponent, Will Herberg, is still embarrassed by the ruffianly antecedents of Buber's philosophy and tries as best he can to ignore his Hasidism altogether and to make him out a fashionable existentialist. You can get a far more reliable picture of Buber as man and thinker from Maurice Friedman, to whom Buber's Hasidism is central and paramount.

I and Thou—the life of dialogue. We have heard something like this from that most bankrupt of all sectarian sects, American Liberal Protestantism (or Reformed Judaism). Does this mean "sharing," folksiness, "group dynamics"? I know of no more obnoxious experience than to be approached after a lecture or reading by some ass in well-shined face and well-shined shoes who says, "I'd like to share your thinking about Red China—or Birth Control—or Juvenile Delinquency." Who is he to ask a piece of my mind for a piece of his? At this moment America is bedeviled by the popinjays of Togetherness. Recently my little daughter came home from school and asked for twenty-five cents for her Good Citizen Milk. Anybody who, at this stage of the game, starts talking about this subject is treading on dangerous ground and should rightly be viewed with the greatest suspicion. What sort of dialogue is this? Certainly our current Togetherness is simply the massing of frightened ciphers and only adds up to a compulsory vacuum.

This of course is not Buber's notion. For him the reciprocal response I and Thou is the only mode of realization of the fullest potential of each party. The one realizes itself by realizing the other. *The ego is by definition the capacity to respond.* It does not lie in some inner recess of the person, but is "out there," it is built in the fullness of our intercourse with others. We respond to a person, we react to things. True, a great deal of our relations with other men is systems of reaction, but *morality is the art of substituting response for reaction.* In so far as another human being is treated as a thing he is dehumanized. This is not a new concept. We have heard the term "reification" before, here in America. Conversely, Buber says somewhere that all things come to us as more or less manifest or remote perspectives on persons, and this, certainly, is pure British Hegelian Idealism of fifty years ago. In fact, it is pure McTeggart. "All real living is meeting," says Buber.

"Pure," "Absolute," "Ideal"—such a philosophy deals in the most transcendent material and therefore, as it presents itself in the world, must show its *bona fides*. We have been far more than twice burned and the baby goes reluctantly back to the candle. McTeggart's philosophy of love led him to demand the expulsion of Bertrand Russell from his university because he was a conscientious objector, on humane grounds, to the least justifiable war in history. How much is Buber open to the accusation of Max Weber?

It is possible to put together an irreproachable catena of quotations on all the crucial questions of our violently sick social order. The community emerges out of the I-Thou relation, not conversely. "Only men capable of truly saying Thou to one another can truly say We with each other." "Individualism understands only a part of man, collectivism understands man only as a part; neither advances to the wholeness of man. Individualism sees man only in relation to himself, but collectivism does not see man at all; it sees 'society.' Individuation is a reciprocal process and hence cannot exist in autonomy. There is nothing to confirm." "Confirmation of the self through the collective is pure fiction."

Against individualism and collectivism, Buber advocates communism—that communism with a small "c" which is almost forgotten today. His ideas can be paralleled in dozens of "communitarian" writers, from the socialists Engels dismissed as "Utopian" to Bakunin, Kropotkin, the Russian Socialist-Revolutionaries, Berkman, Gorter, as well as some Roman Catholic radical social thinkers. All of these people envisaged their communities as coming about after either an overthrow of the existing society or in isolation after a total turning away, geographically as well as physically and morally, from our own moribund competitive society. Buber identifies his communitarian ideal with the actually existing *kibbutzim* in modern Israel. Now these are, most of them, committed to a peculiarly unreal Bolshevism-without-the-Bolsheviks of their own, a kind of etherealized Stalinism. Others are religious communities of various states of orthodoxy. They are quasi-military in their internal life. All basic relationships and duties are compulsory. They are directly military in their external relations. Most of them are armed out-posts, constantly on the defense against Arab invasion or infiltration. *They are almost completely devoid of privacy.* The I-Thou relation requires that the parties have an always open opportunity to be alone together. This simply is not permitted in the typical *kibbutz.* They are, of course, part of the state policy of the aggressive State of Israel. They are the perfected fulfillment of the "movement"—a depersonalizing thing of delegated responsibility, of ideological com-mand and obedience, of Zionism. Finally, without a continuing stream of American money, from Jews still deeply committed to competitive individualism and patriotic collectivism, they would not exist at all.

Buber tries hard to etherealize both the Zionist movement and the State of Israel. He considers this the redemptive role of proph-ecy, the continual confrontation of the secular state with the tran-scendental demands of an intention, a destination, beyond the world. This may give him comfort, but it does not alter the facts. Zionism remains an imperialist maneuver, invented by Napoleon and taken over by the British and used with considerable effective-ness in the First World War. Israel remains the final outcome of this maneuver, an aggressive nationalist State founded on invasion and war, and perpetuated by conscription of both girls and boys and by the militarization of wide sections of life. In New York the Hasidim of Williamsburg rioted against the conscription of women.

We have dozens of articles and speeches of Buber's, first to Zionist meetings and conferences, later to groups in the State of Israel. Again and again he stresses the responsibility of the Jews as the chosen people to redeem the world, and he states specifically that to do this, to even begin to do it—to be a chosen people in the full sense of the word—the Jews must have a "homeland," a nation with a political structure of power and discipline and a geographic location—Palestine. Of course the notion of a chosen people is a foolish and dangerous superstition which has caused untold harm in the world. If a chosen people, say the Mormons or the Jehovah's Witnesses, are utterly without real temporal power, it is possible to etherealize this calling into a spiritual vocation. But it is not possible to etherealize actual temporal power. You cannot etherealize the State of Israel any more than you can etherealize the Vatican or the

Kremlin. All three are actually there, they are not rash ideas but concrete physical masses of political power. And if you go back to the foundations of Buber's philosophy and religion, and go logically from there to the question of political power, to the nation and the State, it is all too apparent that they are evil as such, the manifest contradiction of the basic principles of his morality.

Israel he tries to etherealize by equating it with the Israel of the Old Testament. This is the people with whom the Lord swore a covenant. This is the people Moses led out of Egypt as the deputy of God. Buber's political and social writings are full of appeals to Biblical religion and to the personality of Moses. This is strange talk for a neo-Hasid. The great stumbling block for all Gnosticism has always been the Old Testament. Many Christian Gnostic sects held that it was written by the Devil. Certainly Kabbalah is nothing more nor less than an elaborate device to juggle the plain words of the Biblical narrative and make them mean the opposite of what they all too obviously do mean.

It is rather late in the day to have to recall that the Old Testament is one of the most disagreeable books in all the unpleasant history of religion. The Children of Israel are no better and no worse than the Children of Egypt or the Children of Athens. They are simply vain, foolish, and irresponsible, a prey to rumor and appetite, and always ready to let go a greater ultimate good for any immediate satisfaction. But their God is another matter. He is vindictive, jealous, angry, bloodthirsty, given to the tantrums of a child, and so thoroughly dishonest that he did not dare include "Thou shalt not lie" amongst his own ten commandments. The story of the invasion of Canaan is no more bloody and unscrupulous than any other tale of conquest, but the narrator is insufferably self-righteous about it. The early Gnostics were perfectly right. What the Old Testament teaches is not virtue but "sin," murder, adultery, deception, anger, jealousy, above all, *disloyalty*, Buber's primary sin. No other sacred book is so utterly immoral.

Buber stresses over and over again that Jehovah reveals himself to the Jews in history, that Judaism is a religion of historical revelation. It is precisely for this reason that its god is such a wretched creature. "God" does not work in history, man works in history. If God is the sum total of being viewed as a "Thou," this sum total is always frivolous. This is why the *Iliad* is so superior to the Old Testament. The universe and its separate great natural forces are neither good nor bad, but over against the works of men they are always senseless. The virtues, all the enduring values of life are products of the transient associations of mortal men—they are the heroes, and the proper attitude of a virtuous man towards the universe viewed as a whole is that it is dangerous. Viewed as a person, it is a fool. Buber goes back always to the Song of Deborah, presumably because it is the oldest of the documents of the Old Testament. It is an exciting poem, but a people who persist in believing that the stars in their courses fight for them is nothing but a nuisance and a menace. The stars in their courses do not fight, they burn, and eventually they burn out. The Heroic Age produces moving poetry, but a people who believes in its own heroic epics does so not just at its peril, but at the peril of everybody else.

Buber's *Moses* is a curious document. It is his attempt to ethereal-ize the most obnoxious part of the Old Testament narrative. He throws overboard at the beginning all the results of two centuries of Biblical criticism as beside the point and strives to return to what the experience of Exodus meant immediately to the participants. He then proceeds to pick and choose from the very textual, anthro-pological, and historical research he has discarded and to construct a narrative and a personality of Moses to suit himself. What emerges is simply a self-portrait, a kind of symbolic autobiography. In a footnote he regrets the rash and ill-informed Moses book of Freud's, but his is no different. It is better, yes, but because Buber is a far better man than Freud, not for any reasons connected with the text, Moses, or the wanderings of the Children of Israel.

It is pitiful to watch a man of Buber's intelligence and goodness struggling in the toils of an outworn and abandoned social paranoia. For thousands of years men of good will have been trying to make Judaism and Christianity morally palatable to sane and civilized men. No other religions have ever required such efforts at ethereali-zation. Today we think of Islam as a rather elementary and provin-cial religion—or at least of the *Koran* as such a book. But we forget, confused by centuries of misleading apologetics, what an enormous advance over both Christianity and Judaism Islam was. Why do people bother? If they must have a religion, the basic texts of

Taoism, Buddhism, Confucianism need no such reworking. It may be necessary, particularly of the Buddhist documents, to trim off the exotic rhetoric, but it is not necessary to make them mean exactly the opposite of what they say.

Buber does not succeed as well as the Kabbalists and Hasidim before him. Neither Moses nor Jehovah was an enlightened, humane unitarian and socialist of the Weimar Republic. There is only one kind of writer that we can afford to forgive for such willful perversions of history and present fact, especially in spiritual matters, and that is an artist. If we lay aside all Buber's pretensions as theologian and religious leader, we are left with him as poet. *I and Thou, Tales of the Hasidim, For the Sake of Heaven*—we can judge these as works of art, as symbolic criticism of value, as works of spiritual insight with their kind of veracity. Even here there are limits. We can forgive Dante for a narrow vindictive mind of shocking cruelty, very like his Old Testament god, by the way. We can, if we confine ourselves to the two great novels, forgive Céline for being an anti-Semite, but when, as the Communists used to say, "Art is a weapon," then we cannot forgive. We cannot forgive the direct, depraved political tendentiousness of T. S. Eliot, Ezra Pound, or Guillevic.

The religion of the Old Testament is morally obnoxious in the extreme. Does Buber as artist preach it? Of course he does not. There is no empiric justification for the logical drive toward simplification and concentration that leads to monotheism. Entities are multiplied without sufficient reason. The universe is not orderly in the same way as the mind of man. Only as a concept is nature a unity. Is this monotheistic deity, dredged up from the shores of the Red Sea out of the midst of a petty battle—is he essential to the understanding of these works as works of art? Certainly not. Behind all the ontological confabulation into which Buber's enthusiasm and the weight of his tradition drive him is a simple response to the most ordinary fact of life—the presence of other persons and the possibility of love.

I and Thou is a sort of Rochester in reverse. As Rochester's poems are typical seventeenth-century hymns in which the name of the Deity has been replaced by the name of his mistress, Buber's wonder and excitement at the discovery of love in a loveless world, his astonishment that there is another "out there," mount steadily to such a pitch that by the second half of the book no human object can contain the burden of awe and ecstasy. Love is essentially a relationship—it and its parties are relative, contingent, it is this which gives it its pathos. At the end of a long life, the husband of one woman, the Japanese poet says, "We thought our love would last a thousand years, and we were together only a little while." Love can be made the final value, or the most important one in the shifting and flowing of contingency, but if too great a burden is placed on it, any vehicle must break down. The contingent collapses into the absolute. The wine overflows the vessel and shatters it and spills into the sea. But the sea is not a person. "Being as a whole viewed as a Thou" self-evidently is a product of insatiable desire, not of any evidence at all. We are familiar with these love poems— Richard Rolle, Julian of Norwich, The Cloud of Unknowing, John Ruysbroeck, Walter Hilton—the beautiful but insatiable lust no earthly lover can satisfy. But saying so does not make it true, any more than saying so makes Moses a liberal traditionalist or an ethical mystic of the twentieth century, or an armed *kibbutz* a Brotherhood of Love. The pious who believe that if you just want something hard enough and pray for it hard enough you get it are alas, but fortunately, wrong. Voltaire to the contrary, no need is great enough to create an absolute satisfaction. Death perhaps, certainly nonexistence, is the only absolute man can imagine.

As a poem, *I and Thou* is very beautiful. But it is this metaphysical greed which removes it from the category of the highest art. There is amongst men no absolute need. The realization of this is what makes Homer and the Greek tragedians so much sounder a Bible than the Old or New Testaments. Love does not last forever, friends betray each other, beauty fades, the mighty stumble in blood and their cities burn. The ultimate values are love and friendship and courage and magnanimity and grace, but it is a narrow ultimate, and lasts only a little while, contingent on the instability of men and the whims of "Nature viewed as a Thou." Like life, it is Helen's tragedy that gives her her beauty or gives Achilles and Agamemnon their nobility. Any art which has a happy ending in reserve in Infinity is, just to that degree, cheating. It is, I think, this pursuit of the absolute, the Faustianism of Spengler, which vitiates

most Western art. We feel embarrassed at Goethe's paeans to the
Eternal Feminine as the conclusion of his pitiful drama.

Early in life Buber turned away from what he considered the self-
obliterative mysticism of the East. But he was wrong. Taoism is not
self-obliterative. In a sense it is not even mysticism. It is rather just a
quiet and fairly accurate assessment of the facts. Perhaps the self
which demands an Absolute Partner for its life of dialogue is
obliterating itself, or at least crippling itself. It seems to me that the
fullest realization of the self comes in the acceptance of the limits of
contingency. It is harder, but more ennobling, to love a wife as
another human being, fugitive as oneself, than it is to carry on
imaginary conversations with an imaginary Absolute. The demand
to be loved totally, irrevocably, destroys first the love and then the
lover. It is a kind of depersonalization—the opposite pole, but
exactly like prostitution. It is this over-ambition which haunts all of
Buber, Israel, Zion, "God"—these are all power concepts; they
represent "success." But the real essence of Buber's philosophy has
no place for success and no place for power. "Live unknown." "Own
nothing you can't leave out in the rain." "Never think of men except
in terms of those specific individuals whose names you know."
These old saws are exemplified once more in his Hasidism. Why
bother? They are so *easy* to act on, and the passion for power and
success is so tiring, so depersonalizing.

I think this is the reason that the most fruitful social result of *I
and Thou* is to be found not in religion, but in psychiatry. Buber's
concepts and those of his followers have given new life to the
American schools of so-called "interpersonal psychology." He is a
far greater man than any of the leaders of the Baltimore-Washing-
ton movement—Adolph Meyer, William Alanson White, Harry
Stack Sullivan, Trigant Burrow. None of these men was a very clear
thinker and they were all very bad writers. They were on the right
track, but they expressed themselves abominably. Now they are all
dead and a group of younger men, strongly influenced by Buber, are
giving their concepts new clarity and depth. Once again, as so often
in dealing with Buber's ideas, we return to the tradition of William
James.

Tales of the Hasidim, the books about Rabbi Nachman and Baal
Shem Tov, the novel, *For the Sake of Heaven,* are hardly fiction at

all, but collections of anecdotes of the Hasidim. They are filled with joy, wonder, modesty, and love. It is their own peculiar moral character which lifts them above the general run of Oriental pious tales, whether of Sufi or Shi'ite saints or of Chuang Tzu and Lieh Tzu and the Taoist adepts. Now the remarkable thing about the Hasidic response to the wonder of the world is that it implies an unconscious but none the less enthusiastic acceptance of its contingency. God is there, as he is in *I and Thou,* as a center and referrent, as the ultimate reduction, as the repository of all excess demand—but what comes through most is joy and wonder, love and quiet, in the face of the continuously vanishing world. It is called God's Will, but the movement of the universe—not from Infinity to Eternity, but just endless—is accepted on very similar terms to those of the *Tao Te Ching.* Song and dance, the mutual love of the community—these are the values; they are beautiful precisely because they are not absolute. And on this foundation of modesty and love and joy is raised a moral structure which heals and illuminates as hardly any other Western European religious expression does. "Heals and illuminates"—again we come back to the health which can be found only in a true community of true persons.

There are faults, not least of which is the careful expurgation of the erotic and intoxicated elements of Hasidism. The Shekinah herself is always referred to as "It," never as "She," whole realms of Hasidic practice and experience are quietly ignored. These are Buber's Hasidim, not the real seventeenth-century ones, and in this sense the books are fictions. But nowhere else does his philosophy come through with such poignant simplicity—or, for that matter, with such complexity. Not only does he face the actual complexities of real human relationships amongst individual men and women—rather than abstractions like "Israel" or "Zionism"—but many of the cryptic Kabbalistic sayings of the Zaddiks are given a kind of surrealist, symbolic burden, so that they function as little poems, illuminating experience in their own dark way. And finally, the morality, the ethics, the religion are all so much clearer in this living context. Nowhere is there a better criticism of the folly of using the transcendent to affect the mundane world of power politics than in *For the Sake of Heaven.* Buber has written his own best answer to his Zionism and nationalism.

Sung Culture

Spring Night*

The gold incense burner has gone out.
The water clock has stopped.
A chill breeze sends a shiver through me.
Spring troubles me and threatens my sleep.
Against my balcony, the moon casts the shadows of flowers.

So wrote the great statesman and reformer Wang An-shih (1021–86). His political opponent, the leading Sung poet and calligrapher, Su Tung-p'o (1036–1101), wrote:

Flower Shadows

It piles up, thick and formidable, on the marble terrace.
The pages, called again and again, try to sweep it away.
Just then the sun comes out and carries it off.
But never mind, the next moon,
The shadow will come back.

My, weren't they cultivated for politicians!, you think. Yes, but not precisely in the way you think. These are both political poems and refer to the influence of eunuchs, foreigners and nongentlemen of the court and to the respective authors' antagonistic parties of

*The translations of poetry are from Rexroth's *One Hundred Poems from the Chinese* (All rights reserved, 1959); used by permission of New Directions Publishing Corp.

Originally published in ARTnews Annual #3 *under the title "Speculations on the Times of Sung" in 1960 (Copyright ARTnews Associates, 1960) used by permission. Collected in* Assays, *1961.*

reform. It is as though, in the days of Dienbienphu, Mr. Eden had written:

> On the balcony overlooking the mountains,
> Muguette, the most accomplished and learned concubine,
> In red, white and blue gauze trousers powdered with gold lilies,
> Serves, with delicate, weak gestures, the Lord of the West
> The precious viands of the land of golden elephants.
> Alas, she has placed them so near the edge of the inlaid table
> That they may spoil the embroidered waves on his robe of state.

The Sung Dynasty (960–1279) was like that. It was over-civilized, but it adopted its own overcivilization as a mask. A great deal went on behind the filmy scrim of gauze and mist and incense smoke. In some ways the Sung was more tough-minded and realistic and even middle-class than any other period in Chinese history until the last, the Manchu (Ch'ing) Dynasty (1644–1912). It is in the Sung Dynasty that what we consider the specifically Chinese sensibility first came to flower. All those patterns of response to life that had developed through the earlier centuries of Chinese civilization stiffened slightly into an over-all design.

However much we try to escape them, we always tend to view Chinese history through the eyes of the Confucian scholar-gentlemen who first wrote it. They are passionately legitimist. They speak of dynasties in periods of chaos when there were no dynasties. They persist in looking at the very courts before their eyes as embodiments of the Confucian Utopia ruled by the priest-king of the harvest and surrogate for the people, although often the actual court was as polyglot as Charlemagne's and as little "sprung from the local soil." They dismiss whole cultures, for instance the northern proto-Mongol contemporaries of the Sung, as barbarians. And always they hold up as the ideal man the civilized, non-violent scholar-gentleman, with his human-heartedness and his head full of memorized texts for all contingencies. Other classes may have ruled the State and made vital contributions to the culture. They have hardly a literary or historical existence.

Han (206 B.C. to A.D. 220) and T'ang (A.D. 618–906) culture was imperial and syncretistic. Sung culture was national and synthesizing. Only in Sung times did the cultural base become narrow enough, only then was there sufficient lack of distraction from outside, for what we mean by "Confucianism" or, even more loosely, what we mean by "Chinese civilization" to set in the molds that have persisted to this century. Outlanders, what would later be Tibetans, Mongols and Manchus, had been the statesmen who had built the inner Asian empire of China for the T'ang. The T'ang fell in a welter of brigandage and ephemeral "dynasties," and as the Sung emerged and unified China, they drew in upon themselves and eventually left the inner Asian empire to the outlanders. They retreated from the old Chinese borderlands and finally from the homeland, to "South of the River"—once a land of long-haired savages, recently filling up with emigrants from "China." Here the gentlemen-scholars, undisturbed among their own people, could refine and intensify their peculiar culture, much as the Cockney prisoners could build an England more English than England in nineteenth-century Australia.

It is not altogether true that the Sung were beaten out of North China. Their shift to the South was partly economic. Islam had closed the oasis trade routes and had opened the monsoon trade through the Southern seas. It was partly hedonistic, as though older Caucasian New Yorkers should leave the city to Puerto Ricans and Negroes come North seeking opportunity, and themselves all migrate to Southern California, "for the climate" and for a new and different kind of opportunity.

This vast cultural shift had several results you might not expect and might never gather from the legitimist, orthodox histories. The standard of living rose sharply. Peasants on new land, townsmen in new trades and industries, all were better off than in the glorious days of T'ang. A huge middle class of merchants and other literates who were not scholar-gentlemen literati came into being. Soon luxuries were widespread. Prices began a steady rise. Inflation set in and increased sharply till the fall of the dynasty. Against all this the scholar-gentlemen set their faces and built their Confucian Utopia into Chinese society as a durable myth. But they did not do this without first incorporating philosophical Taoism as transmuted by popular folkways from the woods and springs and high places, and both popular and philosophical Buddhism from India, into the very foundations of what purported to be a purely aristocratic and ethnocentric system. So the society that developed in Sung times was at once adventurous and fluid, conservative and anachronistic.

This is a long introduction, but without it, to understand the period is impossible. In Sung times things are never what they seem, and this is not just due to Buddhist skepticism. Sung society and culture are permeated with contraries and contradictions which are never resolved, but, at the worst, are suspended and at the best, beautifully transcended. This is just as meaningful in pottery as in politics. The Sung synthesis, which looks so idle and dreamy on the surface, so precious and frail, is actually extremely dynamic—full of strength and tension.

A very fetching surface it must have been though. Hangchow, the Southern pleasure city turned capital, set amid waters and hills, wreathed with parks and canals and whimsical bridges, the great lake dreaming off into infinity, and the streets, in Baudelaire's phrase, "lit with prostitutes." It was like Baudelaire's Paris, the Paris of the Second Empire when all important business and politics were transacted in salons and brothels, but most of all it was like Tiepolo's Venice—the Venice of Browning's "Toccata of Galuppi's."

Read the poem again; it's sentimental, but so was Gaspara Stampa and so too was Su Tung-p'o in not a very different way:

As for Venice and her people, merely born to bloom and drop,
Here on earth they bore their fruitage, mirth and folly were the crop:
What of soul was left, I wonder, when the kissing had to stop?

"Dust and ashes!" So you creak it, and I want the heart to scold.
Dear dead women, with such hair, too—what's become of all the gold
Used to hang and brush their bosoms? I feel chilly and grown old.

Sentimentality is a middle-class quality. It is especially one of the aristocratized middle class where it occurs.

Su Tung-p'o was the greatest of the poets of Sung and the greatest poet of sentiment China ever produced. He was one of the greatest calligraphers of all time, and on his style is reared a whole tradition of Japanese fluent calligraphy. He was master of the abstract brush stroke—a painter of bamboo leaves in misty moonlight, so famous that half the bamboo scrawls in Hong Kong art shops are attributed to him to this day. While he was governor of Hangchow he was the lover of Su Hsiao-hsiao, one of the most beautiful prostitutes of Chinese legend, whose tomb was still venerated beside the West Lake of the city until our own time.

A soft breeze from the East scarcely ripples the pale water.
North of the Lake, south of the Lake, the Blue mountains
    vanish in warm mist.
Pairs of ducks play on the mud flats.
Orioles sing, mating in the new leaves.

By Sung standards this is an intensely erotic poem. It is love-making in a universe which neither is nor is not, in which the only reality is the unconditioned Void, of which it cannot be said that it is either real or unreal, and behind which lies pure undetermined consciousness, thought which does not think:

I drift alone in the middle of the Lake.
There is no rush to moor to, nor bottom to hold an anchor.
Nothing is visible beyond the prow of my little boat.
I take the wine from the picnic basket and slowly get drunk,
    while my rod hangs untended over the dim water.

The demon king Ravana asked for teaching and Buddha showed him all the mountains and palaces and jewels and harem maidens of all the universes. Suddenly Ravana's sensibility was overturned and he was utterly alone, and Buddha laughed. Why did he laugh? Because he knew that duality and nonduality are both delusions. Peace is the single point of suchness which is beyond all conditions. And then all the Buddhas and Bodhisattvas and gods and demons and people and beasts and things laughed in all the universes. So opens the Lankavatara Sutra. Again, Buddha, once while he was preaching, picked a flower and smiled, and only the disciple Kasyapa understood why he had smiled. According to tradition, Kasyapa by similar meaningless acts taught Bodhidharma, who brought Ch'an Buddhism (or Zen as it is known in Japan) to China riding on a reed.

Does this mean that the great artists and poets of Sung were all Ch'an Buddhists? They were not. Most of them were not Buddhists at all. They were mostly Confucianists, scholar-gentry who specially prided themselves on the orthodoxy of their caste philosophy. But Confucianism had changed. The welter and flow of ideas of the last two or three hundred years had created a new "universe of discourse," a new consciousness of the popular mind. Indian ideas and notions from the animistic folk background of China had mingled with and profoundly altered the old Confucian orthodoxy.

Sung times produced the two great founders of Neo-Confucianism, Chu Hsi, China's greatest "philosopher" in our sense, and Lu Hsiang-shan, Chu's leading opponent. They not only made Confucianism a more systematic philosophy, they turned it into a personal discipline of the sensibility. To use Western philosophical jargon, which is misleading but will do, Chu and Lu both developed reality from Not-Being, the unconditioned, through the interaction of form (*li*) and potentiality (*ch'i*). For Chu, these two metaphysical principles always interacted, although the world of form was, eventually, one—pure, empty—the Void of the Buddhists. For Lu, form was always primary, its substantiation an illusion. The only trouble with this glib summary is that both thought of *li* (form, principle) as itself a realm of potentiality in our sense and *ch'i* as really a sort of bare matter, serving as a principle of individuation. For Chu, man's mind was a combination of *li* and *ch'i*. For Lu, man's mind had strayed from the world of *li*, pure form, to which it had originally belonged, and the aim of the wise and good man was to find his lost mind or true nature again by quiet meditation and begin to understand its relation to the whole. At the end would come, without words or ideas, the sudden illumination, the knowledge that the individual was in fact the totality. In the words of the Upanishads—"That art thou."

Far more important to them than the metaphysics they had developed, the Ch'an Buddhists, the Neo-Confucianists, all cultivated a specific kind of sensibility, a special life attitude. This sensibility is the ideal of the Bodhisattva, the being who turns away, on the brink of vanishing into Nirvana, out of quiet, "indifferent" love, and vows that he will not enter into salvation until he can bring all other beings with him. This he does with a smile of "indifference," realizing that all beings, animals, flowers, things, atoms, have the Buddha nature, and yet realizing that there is neither being nor not-being, neither Buddha nor not-Buddha, neither Nirvana nor not-Nirvana, neither illusion nor not-illusion. This ideal reaches its most developed form in Buddhism, true, and finds its most perfect expression in the weary, oversophisticated, smiling faces of the Sung paintings of the Bodhisattvas. But, toned down and made more "practical," it is very close to the ideal of the scholar-gentry. Both Neo-Confucianism and the Bodhisattva ideal involve a real sense of responsibility behind their language of indifference. The difference with orthodox Hinduism is marked. For Arjuna in his chariot in the Bhagavad-Gita, action and inaction become one and the same, but for the Chinese this becomes a scarcely concealed imperative to the moral, socially responsible action that has ever since been identified with Confucianism.

So Su Tung-p'o was not just a dreamer of mists and mountains and foggy bamboo leaves; he was a great administrator with a love and devotion for the people of Hangchow, to whom he became a kind of demigod. And, like a modern, altruistic, overcivilized English civil servant, he was acutely conscious of the pathos of his responsibility and the gulf that it created between him and those given into his charge.

> . . . The rich prepare banquets.
> Silk and brocade decorate their halls.
> The poor have hardly anything to offer.
> Instead, they try to hide
> The family mortar from the tax assessor.
> I am a stranger in this neighborhood,
> Where gay processions fill the streets and alleys.
> I, too, sing the old folksongs.
> But I sing to myself. No one sings with me.

And again, Su's opponent, the great reformer Wang An-shih, who for a while put into effect the Utopian, semisocialistic measures of this idealized Confucianism:

> In midsummer, leaning on my thorn stick,
> I climb up the rocky trail
> Where the leaf shadows make a darkness at noon.
> I stop and listen to the quiet voice of the water.

The Sung sensibility was polarized between quiet meditation, a gentle sinking into the indeterminate profundity of an Absolute which was never absolute, and intense, active curiosity about all the manifold of life and things, which led to investigations into the riddles of nature.

This was the time when Chinese science came into its own, the full midsummer of an efflorescence of observation, speculation and technology. Printing, invented shortly before, came of age, and Sung books and style are still considered the best. T'ang stories had been as simple as the Brothers Grimm; true fiction in the vernacular begins with Sung. A whole new kind of poetry, at once freer and more complexly musical, developed—of this Su Tung-p'o is the acknowledged first master. Back to Sung is traced the beginning of modern drama, and the quieter, more subtle plays of the present repertory are still known as "Sung," although most of them are much later. Music, to which Confucius had attributed at least as much importance as ever did Plato or the Pythagoreans, was analyzed and systematized, and again, the quietest, subtlest, most civilized—to our ears—music is still known as Sung. It is likely that some of the solemn choral dances of the Japanese court date back to Sung China, little altered today. Taoism was also revived and provided with a systematic mythology and a philosophy, and it is from Taoist researches and speculations of this time that alchemy and related protoscientific practices grew and, in the case of alchemy, spread over the world. Great illustrated herbals, pharmacopoeias and manuals of medicine, acupuncture, massage, physiotherapy were compiled, as well as encyclopedias, not unlike our own, which developed six hundred years later. Chinese merchants sailed all the southern seas, at least as far as India and the Persian Gulf, and may have reached the African coast.

Painting shows the same polarity. In fact, Sung painting can be described most succinctly by saying that it sought two goals. The portrait painter, the painter of flowers, birds, animals, detailed or, so to speak, close-up studies of landscape, the genre painter of human activities, all strove to concentrate with such intensity on the realization of the subject, the Other, off there opposite their eyes, that the integument was burst asunder and the Buddha nature shown forth. This accounts for the extraordinary surface tension of Sung paintings like the famous *Two Geese* in the British Museum, so reminiscent of our own Arp or Brancusi, and, of course, it accounts for the overpowering sense of individuality in Sung portraiture, surpassed, I suppose, in our own world only by the Romans.

Especially after the conquest of the north by the Chi-Tan from the desert, on the other hand, when Southern Sung landscape almost dissolved in dream, the landscape painters sought to portray the essence of the Ch'an, Neo-Confucian or Taoist metaphysics of ultimate reality. It is significant that this type of painting, committed in principle to an aesthetic of the formless, rises to its highest achievements in a number of extremely individualistic painters. Tung Yüan's *River Landscape* in the Boston Museum establishes a kind of classic norm as early as A.D. 1000. Note that along with his fantasy, mists and illimitable waters, Tung Yüan is an acute observer of geological forms. A perfect example of a U-shaped glacial trough of the Yosemite type is the *Fishing in a Mountain Stream* by Hsu Tao-ning, also from about A.D. 1000, in the Nelson Gallery, Kansas City, Missouri. The strange, almost false-naive calligraphic paintings of Mi Fei—sugar-loaf mountains, wet windy pines, marshy meadows, all swathed in mist—are painted with discreet, horizontal spots of the brush, in a technique so obvious and so personal as to be utterly inimitable.

Ma Yüan, whose lovely fan painting *Bare Willows and Distant Mountains* is perhaps the most famous Chinese painting in America, also painted a *Fisherman Alone in His Boat*, now in Japan, an archetypal illustration of an archetypal Ch'an poem . . . just a little boat, low in the water, a single figure, a drifting line, and the slight surge of the water stretching away. In a Chinese collection there is a long scroll attributed to Hsia Kuei, *A Myriad Miles of the Yang-Tse*, whole passages of which consist of nothing but the expanse of illimitable water. Other passages, however, are of rocks, whirlpools and rapids, and busy with traffic and folk life.

Many of the paintings of the school of Hsia Kuei are specifically portrayals of the act of "quiet meditation," a sage reclining by a waterfall or a still pool, or looking out from cliffs across endless, formless distance, and sheltered by a gnarled, stunted, highly individualistic pine. This type of painting, at least for my taste, culminates in Fa-ch'ang's *Eight Views of the Tung-T'ing Lake* and in the ink-blot painting of Ying Yu-chien, in his *Eight Views of Hsiao Hsiang*. The most famous section of this latter scroll, *Haze Dispersing from around a Mountain Village*, anticipates the ink blots of the great Japanese, Sesshu, and his followers, and is certainly one of the most remarkable paintings in all history.

There is a small group of paintings, mostly by one or the other of the great artists I have already mentioned, which, it seems to me, combine all the qualities of both main types of Sung painting, the capturing of the absolutely generalized and of the intensely particular—the Buddha Nature and the Unformed Void. Chief among these is the simple and stupendous painting of Fa-ch'ang (Mu Ch'i), five Japanese persimmons in varying stages of ripeness in an irregular row, and slightly to the fore, another, the smallest, persimmon. This is certainly the most nearly perfect expression of the aesthetic principles of the Sung period, whether derived from Ch'an Buddhism or Neo-Confucianism. All similar Western paintings, those Italian bottles of Morandi, for instance, come up to it, topple over into it and vanish. Here is one of the greatest achievements of the mind and skill of man, and inconceivably simple. There is a *Woman in White* with a wicker basket and fly whisk in the Freer Gallery, Washington, D.C., which is more than one of the world's most haunting portraits. The folds of her robe conceal her feet so that she seems to float in bottomless space. The quiet surface tension of the forms is almost unbearable. As you stand before it and watch it (and I use this verb advisedly), its still rapture catches you up and marks your mind indelibly forever after. And last, by another unknown Sung painter, a dog, in the Boston Museum, a painting of a being so lonely, so poignant and yet so sure, that it might have been painted by a Bodhisattva himself, as he smiled "indifferently," turned away from promised bliss and lifted his first soul out of Hell.

This special poignancy is itself the Sung sensibility par excellence, and it finds expression in poetry too, notably in Su Tung-p'o's "Gold Hill Monastery," "Terrace in the Snow," and Lu Yu's "I Walk Out in the Country at Night" and the poems by the poetesses Li Ch'ing-chao and Chu Shu Chen (which can be found translated in my own *One Hundred Poems from the Chinese*). In the poetesses the sense of vertiginous ecstasy reaches a point verging on hysteria. Here is a poem by Li Ch'ing-chao:

> The lascivious air of Spring
> Overflows the narrow garden
> Beyond my open windows.
> Across the pulsating curtains
> Confused flower shadows flicker.

All alone in the summer house,
Wordless, I stroke a rose jade lute.
Far off in the lingering early
Twilight a cliff falls from a mountain.
The faint wind breathes with a light rain,
Delicate as a falling shadow.
O, pepper plant, you do not need
To bow and beg pardon of me.
I know you cannot hold back the day.

No art requires more refined perception than pottery. Here all forms are at least as subtle as the subtlest Brancusis and the slightest error of taste jars like a noisy racket. It is not surprising then that the Sung Dynasty produced the greatest pottery ever made. Pure, ethereal celadons, Tingware plates that look as though they had been made on the moon, stoneware bowls and jugs with brown hare's fur or oil-spot glaze, Chün ware with a purplish mottled glaze like the breast of a bird, these are among the loveliest and the most subtle things in all the world, natural or man-made. It was in Sung times, too, that the control of the ceramic process to produce just the right kind of accident began—crude, irregular pots with blemishes in the glaze—as though they had been made by some half-blind, stumbling old peasant in a bonfire on the windy fields of Heaven. Fortunately, Sung pottery has influenced all the world since and, although not everyone can own a great Sung painting, anyone can have a pot of Japanese or American stoneware that embodies much of the achievement of the Sung potters.

And last, as a token of farewell, I would like to conclude with a tiny jade pitcher-shaped vase in the British Museum. There is nothing to it, it is only three and a half inches high, with a ring handle and a little ornamental band. It looks rather as though it might have held a royal baby's milk. But it is infinitely subtle, so much so that if you look too long at it in its case in the British Museum, it will hypnotize you. Its color is even more subtle than its form, the mottled olive and khaki and gray of the plugs of jade placed in the ears and nostrils of the distinguished dead. This little vase looks as though it might have lain against the heart of the buried Kuan Yin at the end of one of her many incarnations.

The Students Take Over

When the newspapers have got nothing else to talk about, they cut loose on the young. The young are always news. If they are up to something, that's news. If they aren't, that's news too. Things we did as kids and thought nothing of, the standard capers of all young animals, now make headlines, shake up police departments and rend the frail hearts of social workers. Partly this is due to the mythologies of modern civilization. Chesterton once pointed out that baby worship is to be expected of a society where the only immortality anybody really believes in is childhood. Partly it is due to the personal reactions of reporters, a class of men by and large prevented, occupationally, from ever growing up. Partly it is hope: "We have failed, they may do better." Partly it is guilt: "We have failed them. Are they planning vengeance?"

In talking about the Revolt of Youth we should never forget that we are dealing with a new concept. For thousands of years nobody cared what youth were doing. They weren't news. They were minding.

They aren't minding now. That isn't news. They haven't been minding since the days of John Held, Jr., *College Humor* and F. Scott Fitzgerald. In those days they were cutting loose. In the Thirties they were joining up, giving one last try to the noble prescriptions of their elders. During the McCarthy Epoch and the Korean War they were turning their backs and walking away. Today they are striking back. That is news. Nobody else is striking back. Hardly a person over thirty in our mass societies believes it is possible to strike back, or would know how to go about it if he did.

First published in The Nation, *July 2, 1960. Collected in Assays, 1961.*

During the past couple of years, without caring about the consequences, making up their techniques as they went along, organizing spontaneously in the midst of action, young people all over the world have intervened in history.

As the University of California student said at the recent Un-American Activities Committee riot in San Francisco, "Chessman was the last straw. I'm fed up." It's about time somebody got fed up, because, to mix the metaphor, all the chickens are coming home to roost. It has become only too apparent that we can no longer afford the old catch-as-catch-can morality with which civilization has muddled through to 1960. Sloth, rascality, predatory dishonesty, evasion, bluster, no longer work. The machinery has become too delicate, too complicated, too world-encompassing. Maybe it was once true, a hundred and fifty years ago, that the sum total of the immoral actions of selfish men produced a social good. It is no longer true. Maybe once, societally speaking, if wolf ate wolf long enough and hard enough, you produced a race of intelligent dogs. Not now. Pretty soon we are just going to have a world populated by dead wolves.

Toward the end of his life H. G. Wells remarked that "something very queer was creeping over human affairs." He saw a kind of foolish dishonesty, a perverse lust for physical and moral violence, and a total lack of respect for the integrity of the personality invading every walk of life, all the relationships of men, individual and global. He seemed to be not only troubled, but puzzled. In his own *In the Days of the Comet* the earth passes through the tail of a comet and a beneficent gas fills the atmosphere and makes all men good overnight. You feel that he suspected something very similar might have come upon us unawares out of outer space, but that in actuality the gas had turned out to be subtly and pervasively malignant. It is easy to see what he was getting at. Nobody sees it better today than the young student, his head filled with "the heritage of the ages," taught in school all the noblest aspirations of mankind, and brought face to face with the chaos of the world beyond the college gates. He's got to enter it, college will be over in a few months or years. He is entering it already fed up.

Think of the great disasters of our time. They have all been the result of a steadily growing immoralism. You could start indefinitely back—with Bismarck's telegram or the Opium War—but think of what those men alive have experienced: the First World War itself, a vast "counterrevolutionary" offensive; the Versailles Treaty; Fascism and Nazism with their institutionalization of every shoddy and crooked paranoia; the Moscow Trials; the betrayal of Spain; Munich; the Second World War with its noble utterances and its crooked deals; the horrible tale of fifteen years of peace and cold war; the Rosenbergs; the Hungarian Revolution; and, in the last few months, the rascality that has burst around our heads like exploding shrapnel—U-2, phony Summits, an orgy of irresponsibility and lies. This is the world outside the college gates. Millions of people are asked to enter it cheerfully each June, equipped with draft cards, social-security cards, ballots, job-application blanks countersigned by David Sarnoff, J. Edgar Hoover, Allen W. Dulles, the family physician and the pastor of the neighborhood church. Is it surprising that a lot of them should turn away at the door of this banquet hall, turn in their tickets and say, "Sorry, I'm already fed up"?

Marx believed that our civilization was born in the arms of its own executioner, twins who were enemies in the womb. Certainly ours is the only great culture which throughout its life has been accompanied by a creative minority which rejected all its values and claims. Almost all others have had a huge majority who shared in few, if any, of the benefits of civilization. Slaves and proletarians are nothing new, the words themselves are derived from another civilization. But a society which advances by means of an elite in permanent revolt and alienation is something new. In the last fifty years this elite itself has slowly gone under; it, too, has been overwhelmed by the society it both led and subverted. *L'Homme Révolté* has come to the end of his tether. One by one he has compromised and been compromised by all his thousand programs. Nobody believes him any more, so he has become a commercial stereotype, along with the cowboy and the Indian, the private detective, the war hero, and the bison and all other extinct animals. As the agent at MCA said to me three years back, "Revolt is the hottest commodity along The Street." The programs are used up and their promulgators are embarrassed. Youth is fed up with them too. And why not? Hitler fulfilled the entire emergency program of the Communist Manifesto, and in addition made May Day a legal holiday.

For the Bolsheviks, the good society would come automatically if the right power were applied to the right program. But power and program are not the question: what matters is the immediate realization of humane content, here, there, everywhere, in every fact and relationship of society. Today the brutal fact is that society cannot endure without this realization of humane content. The only way to realize it is directly, personally, in the immediate context. Anything else is not just too expensive; it is wrecking the machinery. Modern society is too complex and too delicate to afford social and political Darwinism any more. This means personal moral action. I suppose, if you wish to call it that, it means a spiritual revolution. Prophets and seers have been preaching the necessity for spiritual revolution for at least three thousand years and mankind has yet to come up with a bona fide one. But it is that kind of action and that kind of change that young people are demanding today.

Myself, past fifty, I cannot speak for the young. I am inclined to think they will fail. But that isn't the point. You might as well be a hero if society is going to destroy you anyway. There comes a time when courage and honesty become cheaper than anything else. And who knows, you might win. The nuclear explosion that you could not prevent doesn't care whether you were brave or not. Virtue, they say, in itself is intrinsically enjoyable. You can lose nothing, then, by striking back.

Furthermore, just because the machine is so vast, so complex, it is far more sensitive than ever before. Individual action does tell. Give a tiny poke at one of the insignificant gears down in its bowels and slowly it begins to shudder all over and suddenly belches out hot rivets. It is a question of qualitative change. Thousands of men built the pyramids. One punched card fed into a mechanical brain decides the gravest questions. A few punched cards operate whole factories. Modern society has passed the stage when it was a blind, mechanical monster. It is on the verge of becoming an infinitely responsive instrument.

So the first blows struck back were tiny, insignificant things. Not long after the last war Bayard Rustin got on a bus in Chicago and headed south. When they crossed the Mason-Dixon Line, he stayed where he was. The cops took him off. He "went limp." They beat him into unconsciousness. They took him to jail and finally to a hospital. When he got out, he got on another bus and continued south. So it went, for months—sometimes jail, sometimes the hospital, sometimes they just kicked him into the ditch. Eventually he got to New Orleans. Eventually Jim Crow was abolished on interstate carriers. Individual nonviolent direct action had invaded the South and won. The Southern Negro had been shown the only technique that had any possibility of winning.

Things simmered for a while and then, spontaneously, out of nowhere, the Montgomery bus boycott materialized. Every moment of the birth and growth of this historic action has been elaborately documented. Hour by hour we can study "the masses" acting by themselves. It is my modest, well-considered opinion that Martin Luther King, Jr., is the most remarkable man the South has produced since Thomas Jefferson—since, in other words, it became "the South." Now the most remarkable thing about Martin Luther King is that he is not remarkable at all. He is just an ordinary minister of a middle-class Negro church (or what Negroes call "middle class," which is pretty poor by white standards). There are thousands of men like him all over Negro America. When the voice called, he was ready. He was ready because he was himself part of that voice. Professional, white-baiting Negroes who thrill millionairesses in night clubs in the North would call him a square. He was a brave square. He is the best possible demonstration of the tremendous untapped potential of humanity that the white South has thrown away all these years. He helped to focus that potential and exert it. It won.

No outside organizers formed the Montgomery Improvement Association. They came around later, but they could never quite catch up with it. It is pretty hard to "catch up with," to institutionalize, a movement which is simply the form that a whole community has assumed in action. Although the force of such action is shaped by group loyalty, in the final analysis it must always be individual and direct. You can't delegate either boycott or nonviolence. A committee can't act for you, you have to act yourself.

The Montgomery bus boycott not only won where Negro Zealotism, as well as Uncle Tomism, had always failed, but it demonstrated something that had always sounded like sheer sentimentality. It is better, braver, far more effective and far more pleasurable to

act with love than with hate. When you have won, you have gained
an unimpeachable victory. The material ends pass or are passed
beyond. "Desegregated" buses seem natural in many Southern cities
today. The guiltless moral victory remains, always as powerful as the
day it was gained. Furthermore, each moral victory converts or
neutralizes another block of the opponents' forces.

Before the Montgomery episode was over, Bayard Rustin and
Martin Luther King had joined forces. Today they are world statesmen in a "shadow cabinet" that is slowly forming behind the
wielders of power, and the advisers and auxiliary leaders in the
councils of Negro Africa. At home in America the Montgomery
achievement has become the source from which has flowed the
moral awakening, first, of Negro, and following them, of white
youth.

Everything seemed to be going along nicely. According to the
papers and most of their professors, 99 and 44/100 per cent of the
nation's youth were cautiously preparing for the day when they
could offer their young split-level brains to GM, IBM, Oak Ridge or
the Voice of America. Madison Avenue had discovered its own pet
minority of revolt and tamed it into an obedient mascot. According
to *Time*, *Life*, MGM and the editors and publishers of a new,
pseudo avant-garde, all the dear little rebels wanted to do was grow
beards, dig jazz, take heroin and wreck other people's Cadillacs.
While the exurbanite children sat with the baby sitter and thrilled
to Wyatt Earp, their parents swooned in the aisles at *The Connection* or sat up past bedtime reading switch-blade novelists. The
psychological mechanisms were the same in both cases—sure-fire,
time-tested and shopworn.

But as a matter of fact, anyone with any sense traveling about the
country lecturing on college campuses during the past five years
could tell that something very, very different was cooking. Time and
again, hundreds of times, I have been asked, by some well-dressed,
unassuming, beardless student, "I agree with you completely, but
what shall we, my generation, *do*?" To this question I have been able
to give only one answer: "I am fifty. You are twenty. It is for you to
tell me what to do. The only thing I can say is, don't do the things
my generation did. They didn't work." A head of steam was building
up, the waters were rising behind the dam; the dam itself, the block

to action, was the patent exhaustion of the old forms. What was accumulating was not any kind of programmatic "radicalization," it was a moral demand.

Parenthetically, I might say that a legend of the Red Thirties was growing up too. Let me say (and I was there): as far as practically every campus except CCNY and NYU was concerned, the Red Thirties was pure myth. At the height of the great upsurge in California labor, led in its own imagination by the Communist Party, neither the Young Communist League nor the Young Peoples Socialist League was able to keep a functioning student cadre in continuous operation on the University of California campus. At least every four years they had to start over again. And the leadership, the real bosses, were middle-aged party functionaries sent in from "The Center." One of them, bellowing with early senility, was to show up at the recent Un-American Activities Committee riot in San Francisco and scandalize the students.

The plain fact is that today students are incomparably better educated and more concerned than their elders. As the young do, they still tend to believe things written on paper. For the past five years, bull sessions have been discussing Kropotkin, Daniel De Leon, Trotsky, Gandhi, St. Simon, Plato—an incongruous mixture of the world's cat bellers—looking for the answer. The gap between the generations has been closing up. Teaching them is a new group of young professors, too young to have been compromised by their actual role in the splendid Thirties, themselves realistic-minded products of the GI Bill; and neither ex-dupes nor ex-fellow travelers, but serious scholars of the radical past. It is only just recently that they have come up, only just recently that the creative minority of students has stopped assuming that just because a man stood at a podium he was *ipso facto* a fraud. So the head of steam built up, the waters mounted behind the dike.

And then one day four children walked into a dime store in a small Southern city and pulled out the plug. Four children picked up the massive chain of the Social Lie and snapped it at its weakest link. Everything broke loose.

Children had won at Little Rock, but they had not initiated the action, they had been caught in the middle in a conflict of equally dishonest political forces, and they had won only a token victory. All the world had marveled at those brave young faces, beautiful under the taunts and spittle. If they had not stood fast, the battle would have been lost; it was their bravery alone that won it. But it was a battle officered by their elders, and like all the quarrels among their elders nowadays, it ended in a morally meaningless compromise.

From the first sit-ins the young have kept the command in their own hands. No "regularly constituted outside authority" has been able to catch up with them. The sit-ins swept the South so rapidly that it was impossible to catch up with them physically, but it was even harder for routinized bureaucrats with vested interests in race relations and civil liberties to catch up with them ideologically. The whole spring went by before the professional leaders began to get even a glimmering of what was happening. In the meantime the old leadership was being pushed aside. Young ministers just out of the seminary, maverick young teachers in Jim Crow colleges, choir mistresses and schoolmarms and Sunday-school teachers in all the small cities of the South pitched in and helped—and let the students lead *them*, without bothering to "clear it with Roy." In a couple of months the NAACP found itself with a whole new cadre sprung up from the grass roots.

The only organization which understood what was going on was CORE, the Committee on Racial Equality, organized years ago in an evacuated Japanese flat, "Sakai House" in San Francisco, by Bayard Rustin, Caleb Foote and a few others, as a direct-action, race-relations offshoot of the Fellowship of Reconciliation (the FOR) and the Friends Service Committee. CORE was still a small group of intellectual enthusiasts and there simply weren't enough people to go around. To this day most Negroes know little more of CORE than its name, which they have seen in the Negro press, and the bare fact that its program is direct, nonviolent action. This didn't deter the high-school and college students in the Jim Crow high schools and colleges in Raleigh and Durham. They set up their own direct nonviolent-action organization and in imitation of CORE gave it a name whose initials spelled a word, COST. Soon there were COST "cells" in remote hill-country high schools, complete with codes, hand signals, couriers, all the apparatus of youthful enthusiasm. Needless to say, the very words frightened the older Negro leadership out of its wits.

The police hosed and clubbed the sit-inners, the Uncle Tom presidents of the captive Jim Crow colleges expelled them in droves, white students came South and insisted on being arrested along with the Negroes, sympathy picket lines were thrown in front of almost every chain variety store in almost every college town in the North. Even some stores with no branches in the South and no lunch counters anywhere found themselves picketed until they cleared themselves of any implication of Jim Crow.

The effect on the civilized white minority in the South was extraordinary. All but a few had gone on accepting the old stereotypes. There were good Negroes, to be sure, but they didn't want to mix. The majority were ignorant, violent, bitter, half-civilized, incapable of planned, organized action, happy in Jim Crow. "It would take another two hundred years." In a matter of weeks, in thousands of white brains, the old stereotypes exploded. Here were the Negro children of servants, sharecroppers and garbagemen—"their" servants and sharecroppers and garbagemen, who had always been content with their place—directly engaged in the greatest controlled moral action the South had ever seen. They were quiet, courteous, full of good will to those who abused them; and they sang, softly, all together, under the clubs and firehoses, "We will not be moved." Long protest walks of silent Negroes, two abreast, filed through the provincial capitals. A major historical moral issue looked into the eyes of thousands of white spectators in Southern towns which were so locked in "our way of life" that they were unaware they lived in a great world. The end of Jim Crow suddenly seemed both near and inevitable. It is a profoundly disturbing thing to find yourself suddenly thrust upon the stage of history.

I was at the first Louisiana sit-in with a girl from the local paper who had interviewed me that morning. She was typical, full of dying prejudices, misinformation and superstitious fears. But she knew it. She was trying to change. Well, the sit-in did a good job of changing her. It was terrific. A group of well-bred, sweet-faced kids from Southern University filed into the dime store, hand in hand, fellows and girls in couples, and sat down quietly. Their faces were transfused with quiet, innocent dedication. They looked like the choir coming into a fine Negro church. They weren't served. They sat quietly, talking together. Nobody, spectators or participants, raised his voice. In fact, most of the bystanders didn't even stare rudely. When the police came, the youngsters spoke softly and politely, and once again, fellows and girls hand in hand, they filed out, singing a hymn, and got in the paddy wagon.

The newspaper girl was shaken to her shoes. Possibly it was the first time in her life she had ever faced what it meant to be a human being. She came to the faculty party for me at Louisiana State that night. Her flesh was still shaking and she couldn't stop talking. She had come up against one of the big things of life and she was going to be always a little different afterward.

The response on the campuses of the white colleges of the South was immediate. There had always been interracial committees and clubs around, but they had been limited to a handful of eccentrics. These increased tremendously and involved large numbers of quite normal students. Manifestations of sympathy with the sit-ins and joint activities with nearby Negro schools even came to involve student-government and student-union bodies. Editorials in college papers, with almost no exceptions, gave enthusiastic support. Believe me, it is quite an experience to eat dinner with a fraternity at a fashionable Southern school and see a can to collect money for CORE at the end of the table.

More important than sympathy actions for and with the Negroes, the sit-ins stimulated a similar burst, a runaway brush fire, of activity for all sorts of other aims. They not only stimulated the activity, they provided the form and in a sense the ideology. Nonviolent direct action popped up everywhere—so fast that even the press wire services could no longer keep track of it, although they certainly played it up as the hottest domestic news of the day. The actions dealt with a few things: compulsory ROTC, peace, race relations, civil liberties, capital punishment—all, in the final analysis, moral issues. In no case were they concerned with politics in the ordinary sense of the word.

Here the ROTC marched out to troop the colors and found a line of students sitting down across the parade ground. In another school a protest march paraded around and through and between the ranks of the marching ROTC, apparently to everybody's amusement. In other schools the faculty and even the administration and, in one place, the governor joined in protest rallies against ROTC. There were so many peace and disarmament meetings and marches it is impossible to form a clear picture—they seem to have taken place everywhere and, for the first time, to have brought out large numbers. Off campus, as it were, the lonely pacifists who had been sitting out the civil-defense propaganda stunt in New York called their annual "sit out" and were dumbfounded at the turnout. For the first time, too, the courts and even the police weakened. Few were arrested, and fewer sentenced.

The Chessman execution provoked demonstrations, meetings, telegrams, on campuses all over the country. In Northern California the "mass base" of all forms of protest was among the students and the younger teachers. They provided the cadre, circulated petitions, sent wires, interviewed the governor, and kept up a continuous vigil at the gates of San Quentin. All this activity was unquestionably spontaneous. At no time did the American Civil Liberties Union or the regular anti-capital-punishment organizations initiate, or even take part in, any mass action, whatever else they may have done. Chessman, of course, had a tremendous appeal to youth; he was young, he was an intellectual, even an artist of sorts; before his arrest he had been the kind of person they could recognize, if not approve of, among themselves. He was not very different from the hero of *On the Road*, who happened to be locked up in San Quentin along with him. As his life drew to a close, he showed a beautiful magnanimity in all he did or said. On all the campuses of the country—of the world, for that matter—he seemed an almost typical example of the alienated and outraged youthful "delinquent" of the post-World War II era—the product of a delinquent society. To the young who refused to be demoralized by society, it appeared that that society was killing him only to sweep its own guilt under the rug. I think almost everyone (Chessman's supporters included) over thirty-five seriously underestimates the psychological effect of the Chessman case on the young.

At all points the brutal reactionary tendencies in American life were being challenged, not on a political basis, Left versus Right, but because of their patent dishonesty and moral violence. The most spectacular challenge was the riot at the hearing of the Un-American Activities Committee in San Francisco. There is no question but that this was a completely spontaneous demonstration. The idea that Communist agitators provoked it is ludicrous. True, all that were left of the local Bolsheviks turned out, some thirty of them—Stalinists and the two groups of Trotskyites. Even the "youth leader" who, twenty-eight years before, at the age of thirty, had been assigned to lead the YCL, showed up and roared and stomped incoherently, and provided comic relief. Certainly no one took him seriously. There was one aspect about the whole thing that was not spontaneous. That was the work of the committee. They planned it that way. Over the protests and warnings of the city administration they deliberately framed up a riot. When the riot came, it was the cops who lost their nerve and rioted, if rioting means uncontrolled mob violence. The kids sat on the floor with their hands in their pockets and sang, "We shall not be moved."

Spectacular as it was, there are actions more important than the San Francisco riot. Here and there about the country, lonely, single individuals have popped up out of nowhere and struck their blows. It is almost impossible to get information about draft resisters, nonregistrants, conscientious objectors, but here and there one pops up in the local press or, more likely, in the student press.

Even more important are the individual actions of high-school students whom only a hopeless paranoiac could believe anybody had organized. A sixteen-year-old boy in Queens, and then three in the Bronx, refused to sign loyalty oaths to get their diplomas. As kudos are distributed in a New York suburban high school, a boy gets up and rejects an award from the American Legion. Everybody is horrified at his bad manners. A couple of days later two of his prizes are offered to the two runners-up, who reject them in turn. This is spontaneous direct action if ever there was. And the important thing about it is that in all these cases, these high-school kids have made it clear that they do not object to either loyalty oaths or the American Legion because they are "reactionary," but because they are morally contemptible.

The Negro faculties and presidents of the Jim Crow colleges, who not only opposed the sit-ins but expelled dozens of the sit-inners, now found themselves faced with deserted campuses. They were overtaken by a tremendous groundswell of approval of their young-sters' actions from Negro parents, and were dumbfounded by the sympathy shown by a broad stratum of the white South. One by one they swung around, until Uncle Toms who had expelled students taking part in sit-ins during their Easter vacations in other states, went on public record as saying, "If your son or daughter telephones you and says he or she has been arrested in a sit-in, get down on your knees and thank God."

Not only did the New Revolt of Youth become the hottest domestic copy in years, but it reached the ears of all the retired and semiretired and comfortably fixed pie-card artists of every lost and every long-since-won cause of the labor and radical movements. Everybody shouted, "Myself when young!" and pitched in with application blanks. The AFL-CIO sent out a well-known leader of the Esperanto movement who reported that the kids were muddled and confused and little interested in the trade-union movement which they, mistakenly in his opinion, thought of as morally compromised. YPSL chapters of the Thomasite Socialists rose from the graves of twenty years. Youth experts with theories about what their grandchildren were talking about went on cross-country tours. *Dissent* had a subscription drive. The Trotskyites came up with programs. Everybody got in the act—except, curiously, the Communists. As a matter of fact, back in a dusty office in New York, they were grimly deadlocked in their last factional fight. Although the movement was a spontaneous outburst of direct nonviolent action, it didn't quite please the libertarians and pacifists. They went about straightening everybody out, and *Liberation* came out with an article defining the correct Line and pointing out the errors of the ideologically immature.

As the kids go back to school this fall, this is going to be the greatest danger they will face—all these eager helpers from the other side of the age barrier, all these cooks, each with a time-tested recipe for the broth. All over the world this kind of ferment is stewing on college campuses. In Korea and Japan and Turkey the students have marched and brought down governments, and they have humbled the President of the greatest power in history. So far the movement is still formless, a world-wide upheaval of disgust. Even in Japan the Zengakuren, which does have a sort of ideology—the Left communism against which Lenin wrote his famous pamphlet—has only been able to act as a cheerleader. It has failed to impose its leadership, its organization or its principles on the still chaotic upsurge. In France the official Neo-Gandhian Movement, in alliance with certain sections of the Catholic Left, does seem to have given some sort of shape and leaderhsip. I am inclined to think that this is due to the almost total ignorance of French youth of this generation—they had to go to the official sources for information and guidance, they just didn't have enough, themselves, to get started.

Is this in fact a "political" upsurge? It isn't now—it is a great moral rejection, a kind of mass vomit. Everybody in the world knows that we are on the verge of extinction and nobody does anything about it. The kids are fed up. The great problems of the world today are immediate worldwide peace, immediate race equality and immediate massive assistance to the former colonial peoples. All of them could be started toward solution by a few decisive acts of moral courage among the boys at the top of the heap. Instead, the leaders of the two ruling nations abuse each other like little boys caught out behind the barn. Their apologists stage elaborate military and ideological defenses of Marxian socialism and laissez-faire capitalism, neither of which has ever existed on the earth or ever will exist. While the Zengakuren howls in the streets, Khrushchev delivers a speech on the anniversary of Lenin's "Leftism, an Infantile Disorder" and uses it to attack—Mao! Meanwhile a boy gets up in a New York suburban school and contemptuously hands back his "patriotic" prize. He is fed up.

Turner and Whistler

In the little booklet *British Painting*, put out by the National Gallery of Art (Washington, D.C.), it says, "It seems curious, when looking at this vision of radiant light with its blues and golds, to realize that the painter was an uncouth boor, who lived under an assumed name in squalor with his common law wife." Well, well. I guess that's one way of looking at it. Considering its source, it is almost an official statement. Like most official statements it is not quite right factually, but it is an accurate reflection of a common emotional attitude.

Turner is vulgar. I think the man got it wrong way around. There was something rather aristocratic about his flaunting of polite society. Plenty of dukes have lived in squalor in big, dirty, rat-infested and leaking houses as Turner did. He didn't, most of the time, "live with" his mistress, he kept her in a cottage up the river, just like a duke. It is his paintings that are vulgar. Out of the painting of Venice in the National Gallery that prompted this remark came seventy years of chocolate boxes. Many of his romantic landscapes are even vulgarer. His water colors and graphic work are least so, but certainly their appeal is very obvious. Can good art be this common in its appeal?

Folk art is one thing—we accept its crudity as "natural" and value its simple, effective design. Naive artists are, when good, really eccentric rather than naive. Rousseau's slightly daffy vision of the world can be accepted as a different reality. As styles, however

---

Originally published in ARTnews November 1960, *under the title "Turner and Whistler: Aristocratic Vulgarian and Vice-Versa" (Copyright ARTnews Associates, 1960); used by permission. Collected in* Assays, 1961.

absurd, pass back in time, they cross a dividing line beyond which they become less and less offensive because they are no longer reacted against by our own taste. This isn't just up-to-dateness. Growth of the sensibility in society always rejects the immediate past and later reorganizes it in different terms, finds new values and meanings in the enduring work and forgets the rest. Styles blend together as they recede. Only trained observers can distinguish between the styles of Augustan and Hadrian Rome. Hadrian's artists considered themselves as revolutionary as the Fauves. "Messages" are first vital, then trivial, then acquire a nostalgic evocative power. Today nineteenth-century British anecdotal painting is popular again. One of my favorite paintings is Ford Madox Brown's *The Last of England.* Alma-Tadema, however, for me at least, has not been lent enchantment by time. A tear dims my eye whenever I regard Henry Farny's *Song of the Talking Wire,* but, closer to home, the funny-paper epics of Stanley Spencer and the WPA muralists leave me slightly nauseous.

Whistler is vulgar. He is vulgar in quite the opposite direction to Turner. He did not, to quote that catalogue, "turn his back on polite society." He was a social lion, a drawing-room pet, almost the first of his type in modern Society. Men like Reynolds or the modern clubman Academician are not pets of Society—they are themselves Society. Whistler was not Society, he was not even a gentleman. He was, in fact, close to being an intellectual gigolo.

An artist who is a gentleman has the dignity and craft secretiveness of a skilled mechanic or a good butler. He never lets on. He never peddles spurious initiations into the mysteries of his trade. He keeps his place and expects his customers to keep theirs. The old Scripps-Howard cartoonist Williams once drew a cartoon all voluble artists should take to heart. A battered old house painter in ragged overalls and walrus mustache is mixing paint. The Milquetoast-type client, interested in future do-it-yourself projects, asks, "What's that you're mixing with the paint?" Says the true craftsman, "Muriatic acid, it makes the paint stick better." Whistler taught idle women to chatter in a bad imitation of artists' shop talk. It is the heritage of Whistler's little ventures in high-toned Adult Education, far more than Karl Marx, which has led modern artists to refuse when asked out, and to bristle at the sight of a pulsating diamond choker.

At this date we come at both Turner and Whistler with a mass of prejudices and preformed judgments. Can we clear them away so that we can look at both without bias? Can good pictures be that pretty? Can a popinjay paint honest paintings? I think the answer to the first question is, "Yes." The answer to the second question is, "Yes." The third question, I am afraid, must be answered, "More or less." Turner, in the noblest sense of the words, knew his place, and kept his mouth shut. His paintings are redeemed by something greater than taste. Whistler, who inaugurated a worship of good taste, could never quite keep his ingrained charlatanism from peeping out of even his most devoted work. It is only one step from Whistler to Aubrey Beardsley, only another to Gustave Moreau, only a third to Dali. Whistler is a dangerous artist to like.

It is good to approach Turner through a large display of his water colors. In the first place, there is the purely mechanical fact that his colors have lasted better in that medium than in his oils. Many of his large oils, especially those in America, have faded terribly. The storm at sea in the Chicago Art Institute, for instance, is about as colorful as a steel engraving. Modern taste has to learn to adjust to his Romantic bravura. This is much easier to do in the more intimate, quiet art of water color. Sheer technical mastery in oil is a little beyond the layman (the world is full of people who still think Dali is a "great craftsman"). No one was ever a greater virtuoso of water color than Turner, and this virtuosity is sufficiently apparent to anyone who has never touched a brush, and is, as in the ink painters of the Far East, a delight in itself. Last, and most important, unless you moved an appreciable part of the Tate Gallery across the Atlantic, it would be quite impossible to organize an exhibition which would show Turner's steady development from picturesque landscape to what today we call abstract painting.

Arranged chronologically, water colors like the *Mer de Glace, Snowstorm on Mt. Cenis, St. Goar on the Rhine, Tell's Chapel, Lake Lucerne* show the steady growth of abstract considerations and the dwindling of picturesque detail. In each one it is necessary to mask a smaller and smaller area of representation and anecdote to obtain pure vortexes of light, cloud, wind and rock. Even in a painting like *Mt. Cenis*, the horses and wagons are there to give scale and set the drama. Eventually these effects are achieved by "painterly" means, and, in the last great water colors, even scale ceases to function. Like much recent painting, they depend on their own local space—the direct action of paint on paper.

It is doubtful if Turner knew much of anything about Far Eastern art. About all he could have seen was bric-a-brac and bijouterie. Yet, of all modern artists, he is closest to the great painters of China and Japan. Even the dim river scene *Mainz*, completely within the European tradition and painted rather early on, has the same feeling as the ink scrolls of the misty Yang-tse Kiang. Late paintings like *Tell's Chapel, Lake Lucerne* pass beyond even the ink-blot "discipline-of-occasion" tours de force of Sesshu and his disciples. This is organic painting of a new kind, dynamic, saturated space, all the forces of which are related like the strains and stresses, the vacuoles, vortices and pseudopods which make up the living processes of an amoeba.

In his life Turner was equally un-Western European. He was a totally devoted craftsman and a modest, unpretentious visionary. His mistresses were illiterate and housewifely. Their neighbors thought he was a retired sea captain. He and his father ran his career like a small but very successful business. He tried to hang on to all his best work, and when he died he left everything to his fellow countrymen. Remote heirs broke his will.

Whistler was not just immodest, he was shamelessly vain. His most conscientious portraits, of his mother and of Carlyle, are really Fantin-Latour, slightly flavored with Vermeer. He gave them ridiculously pretentious titles. They are not *Arrangements in Grey and Black* at all, they are just good, workmanlike portraits. *Arrangements of Rose and Silver* is no such thing, it is a studio portrait of a model in a kimono—a particularly exciting form of cheesecake in those days. Neither is it *La Princesse du Pays de la Porcelaine*. It is hard to understand how Whistler could look at so much Japanese art and talk so much about it and have such trouble seeing it. *Arrangement in Black* is simply a portrait of Sarasate with his fiddle, painted in a combination of the styles of Velásquez, van Dyck and Fantin-Latour. Re-do it in slashing brush work and you have Sargent. So it goes. There is nothing wrong with these paintings—except Whistler's lamentable inability to keep still.

Perhaps the best are the *Symphonies in White* and the other color-music jobs which are really exercises in a peculiar, weak, etiolated, precocious sexuality. They are very odd people, the Victorians. More went on than ever met the public eye. These weary children are not as rough as Lolita, but they are every bit as perverse. One step back, the sick nymphomaniacs of Rossetti and the mawkish boys of Burne-Jones, one step ahead, the silly brothel decorations of Aubrey Beardsley. Whistler's girls are far better, because they are convincing. Looking at them we not only know they once really existed, but we can extrapolate the whole world which produced them. This is no small virtue. But they are not *Symphonies*.

Face to face with the *Nocturnes* it is necessary to draw a deep breath. Whistler thought of them as transmitting the inspiration of Hiroshige and Hokusai. They do not. Those artists were gentlemen craftsmen, much like Turner. Both of them had an accurate and knowing eye and uncannily steady hands. Both were even more vulgar than Turner. Whistler's *Nocturnes* are all annoyingly imprecise. Where is the man standing on that barge? This is not calligraphy—it is just careless drawing. For once I think he was right in his choice of titles. These paintings have the same emotional vagueness, patchouli-scented sentiment and etiolated virtuosity as the less admirable piano works of that diseased and neurotic Pole. Once again, like the oddly sexy girls, these are fashionable paintings, embodiments of the most chic vapors of a bygone day.

Does this mean that Whistler is all bad? No. It just means that it requires a kind of censorship of the sensibility to appreciate him. Like highbrow movies, we have to be always on guard not to be taken in. And like highbrow movies, we have to be on guard in a special way—this is our kind of corn, designed specifically to take in just our caste. In Whistler, at least, it is sufficiently dated so that we can recognize it and perform the necessary surgery.

This leaves us with little more than an entertaining afternoon of sophisticated nostalgia, like three hours spent with *Traviata* or *The Merry Widow*. Some artists, of all periods, are inexhaustible in history. Whole art movements will be indebted to them for centuries to come. With Whistler we can only come away saying wryly, "Curious, life was like that once, at least for some people."

Gnosticism

There are two "culture clashes" (as anthropologists call them) of great importance in the history of religion. The first was the Persian conquest of Syria, Palestine and Egypt. The second was Alexander's conquest of Persia. They were not just sterile military conquests but wide and deep fusions of culture. Each was like the mixing of two chemical elements with the resulting effervescence, heat, and emergence of new chemical compounds. Out of the first came Judaism as we know it in the Scriptures. Out of the second came Christianity as we know it in the Christian Scriptures and in the writings of the early Fathers of the Church.

Tremendous energies are often released by the mingling of the right disparate elements—chemical explosions, nuclear fission—the strongest "radio star" in the sky is actually a pair of colliding nebulae. So, likewise, the spiritual and intellectual energies released by those ancient culture clashes are still affecting us today. Not only Judaism and Christianity, but Stoicism, Neo-Platonism, Mahayana Buddhism, the later mystery religions, Mithraism, the worship of Isis, Manicheism, all emerge from this cultural mixing. Even the old orthodox religions in Greece, Egypt, Syria, Persia and India were profoundly changed.

Religion was uprooted, quite literally. It was lifted from the soil of the strictly local rite and cult and was internationalized and generalized. Once you were born in a place and worshiped the god of the nearby hilltop and the goddess of the spring under it. They may

---

First published as "A Primer of Gnosticism," an Introduction to Fragments of a Faith Forgotten, *by G. R. S. Mead (New Hyde Park, New York: University Books, 1960). Collected in* Assays, *1961.*

have been called Zeus or Artemis, but as living deities they are bound to a place, their national character remained an unreal creation of the poets. Even in the Orient, the Great Gods—Amun or Marduk, Isis or Ishtar—owed their generalized worship to the fact that they were gods of the Palace Cult or the capital city. In daily life they were fragmented into hundreds of minor Amuns and Marduks and Ishtars and Isises, gods of the village or the field or the neighborhood. It was these local deities the people worshiped, except for the great national or royal ceremonies.

The uprooting of religion came when men were able to come and go freely through vast empires that stretched from one end of the ancient world to the other. Their deities acquired a theology, a gospel, a general myth and a theoretical justification. Such religions produced a propaganda and missionaries. Eventually there were shrines to Persian and Palestinian and Egyptian saviors on the borders of Scotland; religious sculptors and painters who had learned from Praxiteles and Apelles worked in the Gobi Desert and among the recently civilized Japanese.

Out of this immense seedbed or forcing-shed sprouted all the modern orthodoxies. Out of the same soil came heterodoxy. In fact, until this time the notion of heterodoxy could not exist. The famous Aten worship of Ikhnaten was not a heterodoxy—it was simply a different royal cult. The old folk religions had sanctified the seasons of the year and the rites of passage. The new world religions built on this foundation and gave the myths and practices of the cult an ethical content. At first they gave the individual only significance; later they came to offer him salvation; but this salvation was contingent on the co-operation of the worshiper's will and the assent of his faith. By the time of the first Greek nature philosophers, the world of science and the folk transcendental world had become incompatible. To Socrates, Anaxagoras was impious and crazy in trying to explain the mechanisms of the universe. Heterodoxy came into existence.

It is obvious, is it not, that the propaganda of a foreign or constructed religious cult must be that it will work where the old native faith does not. As against the ancestral faith which is taken on trust but which becomes insufficient to cope with the new facts, the proselytizers of the new religion must guarantee results. Also, the native religion is public by definition. Its rites and myths are an open expression of the entire society and any person who cares to learn the sacred scriptures can understand them. In contrast, the alien religion is occult. It is a secret doctrine because the very knowledge of the doctrine of itself insures salvation, and so it cannot be left accessible to the untested and uninitiated. The secret doctrine includes the actual scientific knowledge of the time, which is directly assimilated to the myth. Perhaps a better way of saying this is that the myth absorbs all the details of the knowledge of the world. So you have a religion which throughout approximates to magic. Its knowledge and its rites are coercive. The faithful can force the universe to the desired conclusion. Prayers are thought of as being as efficacious as chemical formulas. They are spells.

Of course, magical elements of this sort lie at the very sources of all the religions of the ancient world and reach their greatest development in Babylon and Egypt. Maturing civilization gives the magical formulas of the Book of the Dead a personal and ethical interpretation. But the individual crises of the soul which accompany the dislocations, deracinations, and insecurities of men living in world empires reinstate the securities of the primitive spell, the formula, the coercive rite, the knowledge of presumed absolute fact that insures salvation.

Our first record of a mystery religion of the later type is a fourth-century demotic papyrus, found in an ancient polyglot settlement in the Nile Delta, which must have been something like modern Alexandria. It is written in cursive Egyptian, but the language is Aramaic, the *lingua franca* of the Persian and Hellenistic Near East. It is a mystery play, a sacred marriage of the goddess Anat and Baal, after Anat has saved her consort from Mut, the god of death. There is also a trinity of couples and behind them all an overgod, Baal Shamain, the Lord of Heaven. These nine deities do not all come from one place, but from Canaan, Babylon, Assyria and the old Sumerian lands. They have been deliberately put together by some unknown "founder," a connoisseur of Near Eastern religion not unlike our twentieth-century religious window-shoppers. Furthermore, not only does the text handle the Egyptian characters in a most cavalier way, but *it is in code*. No Egyptian or Aramaic scribe could decipher it without the key. In addition, it is not in ordinary current Aramaic of its day, but in an artificial, pseudo-archaic language, like our bad classical translations in "Biblical prose." Before this, only the secrets of divination and astrology were written in cryptogram—because they were thought to have the efficacy of scientific procedures. Here we have a foreign cult in an alien land with a secret ritual, its myth is a recently constructed syncretistic fantasy, its rite is guaranteed to work, its deities parallel the scientific picture of the cosmos. We have, as I said, the first of the mystery religions of the later type known to us, and we have the first intimations of Gnosticism. In the next eight hundred years the pattern would change very little, it would only develop.

Gnosticism as such is only a few years older than Christianity but its origins, or at least the origins of its material, are lost in time. Some of this material it shares with Christianity, but Gnosticism is much more conservative, it uses far more of the past. Christianity takes from the past only a central religious drama, Gnosticism retains a whole cosmology and cosmogony.

Let us take one by one the cardinal points of the Gnostic creed and trace them back to their earliest appearance.

Emanationism is contemporary with the beginning of high civilization in Egypt. The "Memphite Theology" is a tractate from the Old Kingdom. In it, Ptah, the deity whom the Egyptians of Memphis considered the eldest of the gods, has emanate from him four couples of gods, male and female, in descending order of being. Ptah *thought, spoke,* and his word created them. Each god or goddess had no other being than the "heart and tongue of Ptah" and by them all things were made and without them was not anything made that was made. (Ptah himself, incidentally, is represented not with the ordinary body of a man, but as a swaddled mummy with a huge protruding phallus, the combination of life and death.) Earlier still than the Memphite Theology is the Ennead of Heliopolis, where the same four pairs are derived from the creator Atun. This, however, is an ordinary creation myth and does not share with the Memphis tract its remarkable philosophy. The unique idea of emanationism is that the Great God acts only through his emanations.

The war of Good and Evil and the debauching of creation are Babylonian and later Persian ideas. It never seems to have occurred to the Egyptians or the early Semites that there was anything seriously wrong with the world; but Mesopotamian and later Persian religions are haunted by the power of evil. This is an important distinction. The Egyptians were well aware of evil, but they granted it no metaphysical, let alone ontological importance. Isis and Osiris saved men from death. The saviors, the Saoshyanto, of Persian religion save from sin, against which, unaided, man, and all creation with him, could not prevail. We have an abundance of texts which indicate that the Egyptians, like the Quakers, found it relatively easy to be good. Farther east, the Babylonians, then the Persians, and after them the post-exilic Hebrews and then the majority of Christians, seem to have found it difficult indeed.

The Gnostics went still further. Although in Persian religion evil often functions as an autonomous principle, there is no suggestion that creation, matter, or man, is bad as such. This idea, of *the intrinsic evil of the world*, is the peculiar and distinguishing notion of most of the Gnostic cults.

From Persia comes the concept of the universe as a moral battleground, existence in itself as *the struggle of light against darkness*. We are familiar with this language in the New Testament and among the Jewish sectaries of the Dead Sea Scrolls. With it, into Gnosticism, came a whole physics and metaphysics of light which was to survive in various forms in Western thought for centuries.

Anyone who has ever seen a reproduction of one of the pictures from the Egyptian Book of the Dead is familiar with what is known as the Perils of the Soul, the belief that after death the soul passes before the inquisitors of the Underworld and to be saved must know the proper prayer or spell for each god as well as their secret names. By Persian times in Egypt the Ennead of Osiris had come to take the place of the original principal judges of the dead, although the unfortunate soul had to undergo a minor inquisition from dozens of petty deities or demons. Gnosticism equated these inquisitors of the soul with the cosmic powers, the rulers of the spheres of heaven. The Egyptian progress of the soul through the Underworld was changed to *the ascent of the soul, led by the descended and now ascending savior*, to the empyrean and the bliss of union with the unknown God from whom all creation and creators had emanated. But the magical process by which this ascent is achieved remains the same as in the Egyptian Underworld. The Gnostic soul is saved because it knows the secrets of the heavenly spheres and can give the correct answers.

The Enneads of Heliopolis or Memphis were not equated with the planets and the sun and moon until very late in Egypt. In Babylon, however, similar hierarchies were so identified at an early date. Once Babylonian astrology reached its full development, just before and during the Persian period, this (so to speak) *solar-system religion* spread over the whole Near East, eventually to influence not only the Greeks and Romans but also the Celts and Teutons.

The descent of the redeemer goddess, Ishtar or Anahit or Isis, long predates the organization of the pantheon into the solar system, but once the two notions are conjoined it is obvious that the cosmos becomes the theater of a tremendous drama. This cosmogony is not to be disdained. A millennium and a half later it was still meaningful to William Blake.

Other elements—serpent worship, erotic mysticism and ritual, the mystic marriage, the slain redeemer god—all these ideas, as it has so often been pointed out, are nearly universal and in most cases precede the coming of the historic populations into the Near East. They are Neolithic or even earlier. So, too, is *the strong matriarchal or at least antipatriarchal emphasis* of most Gnostic sects.

The gods of Homer and the Greek dramatists and, to a lesser degree, those of the Royal cults of Egypt or Babylon, go their way regardless of man. Gnosticism shares with Christianity, Judaism and Zoroastrianism the concept of creation and redemption as a great drama, focused on man, a drama in which the individual worshiper plays a primary role. Literal dramas of redemption, actual plays, are common throughout the ancient Near East. The Memphite Theology is in fact a play; so is the principle Ras Shamra codex, so is the Aramaic papyrus I mentioned before, so too is one form of the Gilgamesh Epic and of the Descent of Ishtar. Relics of this dramatic form survive in the Song of Songs, Job and Esther. These ancient dramatic performances conditioned the myths they portrayed, and conversely the new dramatic myths provided the framework for the myth as literature and eventually for the Passion of Christ as well as for the drama as a work of art. It is not for nothing that cranks have found in the tragedies of Shakespeare, but especially in *The Tempest,* the disguised rituals of an occult mystery religion. Dramatic episodes survive in the documents of Gnosticism, especially the famous dance and antiphonal chant in the Acts of John. The ancient ritual dramas before the great empires were social—they were concerned with objective reality, fruitfulness of the fields and the turning of the year. Acting in a great royal play in Memphis or Thebes, the Pharaoh is the god incarnate, but he functions only as the focus of Egyptian society, the nation ceremoniously embraces its bride, the land of Egypt. Gnosticism subjectivized the cosmic drama. Simon Magus is the god incarnate, going from place to place in the Levant like an ordinary man, and his bride, the mystic Helen, is literally a girl redeemed from a brothel. The Gnostic saviors are independent operators, come to save individual sinners without any of the sanctions of organized society.

I have dwelt at length on the origins of the mythological and ritual material of Gnosticism for the simple reason that Gnosticism is the main funnel through which these rites and doctrines reach modern times. The mysterious deity of the Templars or the erotic revels of the witches or the ceremonies of the Masons or Rosicrucians, all are aspects of a special heterodoxy that began with Gnosticism. For better or worse, the Gnostics were the founders of what we call occultism. Occultism is always a minority religion. Were it to become the religion of an empire, and for long enough, it would become folk, social, public, no longer occult.

Some critics have seen Gnosticism as a sort of international secret religion which was scattered all through the Near East in the years just before the Christian Era. They have stressed its Greek, Persian, Babylonian and Egyptian elements and its debt to vulgarized Neo-Platonism and Stoicism, and have tried to dissociate its formation from Judaism and Christianity. I think this is open to question. There is no doubt but that syncretistic cults of all kinds were flourishing in the Near East of those days, but actually we deduce this from Gnosticism, not the other way around. We have very little to substantiate it. There are a few documents, like the Aramaic papyrus from the Delta, but they are synthetic mystery religions, vulgarized Neo-Platonism, magic, Hermeticism, everything but Gnosticism. As a definite entity Gnosticism appears with Simon Magus, Menander and Saturninum, and it appears in an entirely

Jewish and Christian context. It is, in fact, generated by the action of Jewish heterodoxy upon the inchoate, formative years of Christianity. Gnosticism has transmitted many ancient ideas to later heretics and occultists, but it received them as transmuted and fused by Jewish eccentric speculation.

For instance, I myself have spoken of Kabbalism as Jewish Gnosticism. This is more or less true, but in the fantasies of the *Book of Baruch* (not the Book of Baruch of the Apocrypha) we have already a fully developed Jewish gnosis contemporary with the very beginnings of the Gnostic cults. The First Principle, the Ayn Soph of the Zohar, is, of all things, called Priapus in Baruch. He generates Elohim and his consort Eden, and they in turn generate twenty-four angelic forces, male and female couples, who together create the world and Adam and Eve. Elohim, believing himself the Lord, ascends to the summit of creation and is united with Priapus. Eden, left behind, becomes jealous and brings sin and death into the world. Then Elohim through his angel Baruch inspires Moses, Heracles and Jesus to lead men up to Priapus by the path Elohim has discovered; men go up not alone but in union with their spouses. The source of evil in the world is temporary, the result of Elohim's desertion of his bride and the resulting divorce and adultery. Heracles and Moses fail, but Jesus succeeds in teaching the gospel of redemption and himself ascending to God. Where are we? Is Gnosticism Christian Kabbalism? Except for the name of Jesus we are in a completely Jewish world. These are the mysteries of the Zohar and of the Hasidim. The sexual act is the foundation of all existence and its frustration or betrayal or misuse is the source of all evil. The relationship of two specific human individuals is not only reflected in the organization of the cosmos but each, macrocosm and microcosm, affects the other. This is Kabbalism, but is it Gnosticism? Certainly it lacks many of the distinguishing characteristics of Gnosticism: light metaphysics, the perils of the soul, an evil deity, the irredeemable nature of matter; most important, it does not presume to impart a mysterious, secret knowledge with which the member of the cult can coerce reality. Nevertheless, it is out of such a background of Jewish apocalyptic, eschatological and cosmological fantasy, out of the melting pot of religions that was Palestine at the beginning of the Christian era, that Gnosticism arose.

About Gnosticism as such, as it is revealed in the documents which survive to us, it is not necessary to correct George R. S. Mead. Since he gathered his anthology and commented upon it, sixty years of research and new discoveries have gone by, but his picture is still, in its essentials, correct. In recent years we have learned a great deal about one sect of heretical Judaism from the Dead Sea Scrolls, and in the Scrolls we can trace various germinal ideas that the Gnostics were to develop. It was not until 1955 that the *Berlin Papyrus*, Mead's *Akhmin Codex*, was published in its entirety in a critical edition, but Mead's summary of it is still sound. In 1945 a whole library of Gnostic books was discovered at Nag-Hammadi in Upper Egypt, thirteen volumes, forty-eight treatises, more than seven hundred pages. Unfortunately, economic and political vicissitudes have kept most of these from publication. So far only the Gnostic books which are contained also in the *Akhmin Codex* of Berlin, the *Gospel of Truth* and the *Gospel of Thomas*, have appeared. We know the others only through summaries by Jean Doresse. Our knowledge of Gnosticism has been deepened and enriched, but has not been changed in any fundamental way since Mead wrote. And nobody since has better understood what we know.

Fragments of a Faith Forgotten is a masterpiece of lucid, or as lucid as might be, exposition of an unbelievably complicated and difficult and ambiguous subject. Once in a while Mead's sympathies for the Gnostics make him a little sentimental, but he never permits his sympathies to destroy his objectivity. After sixty years he is still the most reliable guide to the corpus of Gnosticism that we have.

It might be desirable to add to what we learn from Mead a few words about the effects of Gnosticism on the evolution of orthodox Christianity. The Synoptic Gospels make of the Incarnation the climax of a *historical* drama. Paul, and to a lesser degree John, and the author of the Epistle to the Romans, constantly using Gnostic terms, reinterpreted in their own way, make of the Incarnation the climax of a *cosmic* drama. Gnostic angelology influenced Dionysius the Pseudo-Areopagite, and through him the whole Catholic and popular mythology of the organization of heaven. Traces of Gnostic cosmology are everywhere in Dante. The peculiar light physics and metaphysics which the Gnostics got from Persia influenced all Scholastic philosophy, and reached its culmination in St. Bonaventura. It reappears again in Jakob Boehme, along with a Gnostic theory of emanations (and who is to say that it does not survive, imperceptible to us, under the surface of the primary assumptions of modern physics?).

As Gnosticism died away in popularity its place was taken by Manicheism. Out of Manicheism came Paulicianism, Bogomilism, and out of them both a whole covey of Russian heresies and the famous Cathari of the Albigensian Crusade. In ways that are impossible to trace, much of the mythology of Gnosticism survived, underground, to emerge in the revival of occultism in the seventeenth century.

Finally, what did Gnosticism do for the practicing Gnostic of the first Christian centuries? As long as the Church was without power it was forced to suffer dissent. Some men seem to be naturally heterodox. It is a great psychological consolation to certain kinds of personalities to believe that the official Deity of the Old Testament and the Church is really the Devil. This is not as frivolous as it might sound; it is good for civilization to have Trotskyites around. We have found in our own day that an all-pervading orthodoxy dries up the sources of creativity. Since the official Church was patriarchal and authoritarian, Gnosticism gave expression to those matriarchal and libertarian tendencies which are there, suppressed or not, in all societies.

Furthermore, what the Gnostics projected onto the screen of their profound ignorance as a picture of the universe was in reality a picture of their own minds. Its mythology is a symbolic portrayal, almost a deliberate one, of the forces which operate in the structuring and evolution of the human personality. It is, more than almost any other religious system, because it is of all others, the most invented, the most "made up," an institutionalized panorama of what Jung has called the Collective Unconscious. The whole Gnostic heresy is a sort of socially therapeutic dream. (This notion, as Jung has pointed out, does not involve any mysterious undersoul shared by all men—it is a collective picture because all men respond to life in much the same way, because they all have the same physiological endowment.)

We can operate upon our minds by the manipulation of symbols if not on the cosmos; Gnosticism was fundamentally a magical theory of life, man, the universe, God, morality. The spirit-matter, good-evil, God-creature, omnipotence-freedom dilemmas posed by Christianity, Gnosticism attempted to solve with a magical doctrine of correspondences in which man and the cosmos reflected each other. As such, it was a step in the history of science as well as in the history of religion. It was a wrong step, but one which still influences thought, not just the Theosophists, but those who think that Heisenberg's Principle of Indeterminancy is an ontological discovery rather than a mathematical formula. Alchemy was Gnostic through and through, an attempt to achieve both wealth and salvation by parallel manipulation of the microcosm and the macrocosm. But the philosophy of Alfred North Whitehead is based on the same principle—an enormously sophisticated Smaragdine Tablet. We can learn nothing about the solar system from Gnosticism and little about good and evil in the world, but we can learn considerable about ourselves.

The Influence of
French Poetry on American

People, especially French and American people, tend to forget that the heart of the United States was once French. Not only was all of Canada and all of the Mississippi drainage from the Alleghenies to the Rockies under the French flag, as everybody knows, but French and French-Indian mountain men had penetrated to the West Coast before any of the officially recognized explorers and discoverers, for whom they were in fact often the guides. Deep in the Northern Rockies is the town of Coeur d'Alene, Idaho. In Nevada, Wyoming, Oregon, many of the leading merchants in the small towns are descended from the French, and they often still name their children Pierre, Jeanne and Yvonne—conspicuous among the recent rash of movie-star first names, dictated by the mysteries of Hollywood "numerology" which cause the Roman Catholic clergy such distress at baptism. Not only are towns all over the Middle West named such things as Prairie du Chien and Vincennes, not only are their leading families named Sublette and Le Sueur and Deslauriers, but—something very few people realize—French life survived intact in hundreds of small isolated communities until well into the twentieth century.

When I was a boy, during the First World War, I took a canoe trip down the Kankakee River from near Chicago to the Mississippi. We passed through many villages where hardly an inhabitant spoke a word of English and where the only communication was the

This essay was written in 1958 and published in Europe, *February 1959, in French, under the title "L'Influence de la poésie française sur la poésie américaine"—an introduction to an anthology of American poetry in translation. First collected in English in* Assays, *1961.*

wandering tree-lined river and a single muddy, rutted road out to the highway. There is a book about it, *Tales of a Vanishing River*, and there was a popular humorous dialect poet, Drummond, who used to recite his poems in high-school assemblies and on the Chautauqua Circuit (a kind of pious variety tent show for farmers, now vanished) back in those days. "I am zee capitan of zee *Marguerite* vat zail zee Kankakee." This was not off in the wilds somewhere—it was a long day's walk from the neighborhood of Studs Lonigan.

Midwestern Naturalism of the first quarter of the century was essentially a French-inspired movement. Its sources were in Zola and Turgenev, and in a lesser, but then more popular writer, Maupassant. In Theodore Dreiser, Zona Gale, Willa Cather, Hamlin Garland, down to Vardis Fisher and H. L. Davis in our own day, the very conception of the "family epic" is Balzacian, modified by Zola, and the locale is in each case—even Idaho and Eastern Oregon—a land first trod by French moccasins. Zola and Balzac taught the novelists of the early twentieth century method, Flaubert and the Goncourts taught them style. Not only is *Main Street* a flimsy and unironic imitation of *Madame Bovary*, but Sinclair Lewis never realized how very like Carol Kennicott's Gopher Prairie were the small French towns which broke the hearts of thousands of self-dramatizing Duses of the Second Empire.

I myself was born in South Bend, Indiana, on the site of an old portage of the *voyageurs*, and in sight of a monument to the Chevalier de La Salle, whose flowing locks in pigeon-limed bronze were my first intimation that people had not always looked like twentieth-century Americans.

Henry James, of course, owed everything to Flaubert—the conception of the novel as an extraordinarily complex organization of what a later generation was to call "abstract art." This is a false conception—there is nothing "abstract" about a novel—and the French influence in Henry James and his like is literary and artificial. Actually, he writes like an etherealized Trollope or Jane Austen. Nothing in criticism, unless it is some of the dreadful blunders of Sainte-Beuve, or the silly enthusiasms of Poe, is quite so comic as Henry James' book on French novelists, with its utter inability to understand what those novels were about. They might as well have been in Swahili or Etruscan for all Henry James understood them, for the simple reason that his life and background were totally different. The Midwest Naturalists responded to French nineteenth-century literature because it was about a life they could recognize as very much like their own, and its values and aims were theirs.

Baudelaire to Rimbaud, Balzac to Ibsen, there is one factor operating in Western European literature too seldom recognized, and for the suffering authors it was sometimes the most important. This is de-provincialization—the struggle for metropolitan community with the new, emancipated and uniform standards of a new level of capitalist culture. It is seriously open to question if the system of values represented by the lycanthrope Borel is superior to that of Charles Bovary. It is just more citified. By the end of the First World War, Ben Hecht in Chicago, who had just gone through the Munich Commune, thought of himself as completely a member of the same City State as Ernst Toller, Louis Aragon, Blaise Cendrars or George Grosz. In 1923 Sam Putnam, Lawrence Lipton and myself, led a Dadaist movement in Chicago known as "The Escalator" which was quite as lunatic as anything ever managed by Max Ernst or Francis Picabia or Tristan Tzara. Notice the names— German, Catalonian, Rumanian—the Western European City State community has not only arrived, it has grown sick of itself.

Where did Norah go when she escaped from the Doll's House? She went to town and got a job. Henry James' characters go to art galleries to resolve their mysterious tragedies. His women are already completely emancipated—as emancipated as the authoress or the heroine of the *Princesse de Clèves*. But this is artificial; like Malraux's art, it is writing which has fed on writing. In the long run archaism in the arts is of interest only to the very refined—it is a brave and very precious sort of soul that finds Abadie and Violet le Duc more exciting than Phidias, and Sacré Coeur more fun than Amiens. When the chi-chi has died away, cannibalism is an uncommon curiosity, in art as in anthropology.

It should be made clear, in a sort of parenthesis, that the New England tradition so ably reinstated by Van Wyck Brooks is neither characteristic of the rest of America nor really essentially British in inspiration. It is a reflection of the dominance of the German universities in the first half of the nineteenth century. Emerson, Longfellow and their friends were typically Teutonic in so many ways, and even Thoreau is not Rousseau in the woods near Boston but Rousseau as filtered through the German Romantic notion of natural self-sufficiency—a very different idea from Rousseau's essentially communal concept. As a matter of fact, the only Englishman all the New Englanders liked, and who liked all of them, was that most Teutonic Scot, Carlyle.

This brings us to Whitman. It is true that Whitman filled his poems with pidgin French. It is also true that his poem on the defeat of the Commune is the best poem, in any language, that still unhealed schism in the French soul inspired. It is true that he looked to what he thought of as the French spirit as the leader in a revolution of morals—especially sexual morals. But I am afraid he thought of France entirely in terms of Fourier, Proudhon, St. Simon, Blanqui—the mother of free communes and free love. America in those days was dotted with Fourierist Phalanxes, Etienne Cabot's *Icaries*, and similar French communalist experiments. The American Warren ran a Time Store in Cincinnati which not only anticipated Proudhon by several years, but which actually made "mutualism" work.

France, of course, in Whitman's day was not the France he imagined. That France existed largely in books read by cranks. It was in America that it came to life in Group Marriage, Comradely Love, Vegetarianism and Funny Money. Whitman, I am afraid, for all the doctors of comparative literature try to do with him, is an autochthone, a real original, and if his roots are anywhere except in the pre-Civil War North with its swarming cranks, reformers and humanists, they are in Isaiah.

Which brings us back to poetry and the twentieth century. How many Americans would be prepared to admit that the greatest American poet of the turn of the century did not write in English at all, but in French? How many have ever heard of him? Hardly any. I am referring of course to Stuart Merrill. Yet who is there to compete with him? Trumbull Stickney? George Santayana? I do not care for Edwin Robinson or Robert Frost myself, so I would say that Stuart Merrill remained the best American poet until the end of the First

World War, with the sole exception of Carl Sandburg. Of course, if you prefer, you can have Vielé-Griffin.

One of the most hilarious examples of intercultural error known to me is G. E. Clarcier's statement: "Merrill . . . fondant aux Etats-Unis le mouvement socialiste." The American Socialist movement is at least as old as Babeuf—and the Social Democracy of his day never heard of Merrill. Alas, he was what the Bolsheviks call "a petty bourgeois dilettante," although a very admirable one, but he loved to entertain French admirers around café tables with fairy tales of his career as a revolutionist in the States.

Before we go on, two minor points should be cleared up. Frost and Robinson are presented in the contemporary academy in America as intensely American writers. They are nothing of the sort. Robinson is a rather vulgar imitator of the early nineteenth-century British narrative poet Crabbe and, when he does not imitate those incredibly soft and sentimental productions, of the narrative poems of Tennyson. Robert Frost discovered himself as a British Georgian poet. In his young days he lived near and was greatly influenced by the man who has slowly emerged as the best of the Georgian poets—Edward Thomas—and he belongs squarely in that tradition.

Now we come full circle. Who was the idol of the Georgian poets? Francis Jammes. Now that the dust of the explosions of the epoch from Apollinaire to Georges Schéhadé is dying away, it does not sound so incredible to recall that the great international influences in poetry in the early years of this century were Jammes and Verhaeren. They wrote about different things in different ways, but they were two faces of the same coin, two poles of the same literary universe—the world of H. G. Wells and Theodore Dreiser, of Gerhart Hauptmann and Romain Rolland, the world which was given international viability in the criticism of Georg Brandes, and which found poetic expression in the English language in figures again as diverse as John Masefield in Britain and Carl Sandburg in America. The Marxists are perfectly right, incidentally, in pointing out that this literature, realistic if not naturalistic, and always with at least an undercurrent of social criticism, is the last artistic expression of capitalist culture to believe in its own health. All artistic expression after these times starts by *calling itself* decadent. Recently, when the Nobel Prize went to modern Russia for the first time it went to a poet who, whatever his varying favor with the Bolsheviks might be, was for one thing the leading living disciple of Francis Jammes.

Literary epochs play leapfrog with one another. French poetry after Apollinaire ignored the recent past and went back to Rimbaud and Mallarmé—finding in them of course not Symbolism, but a revolutionary syntax of the mind. The most powerful current immediately before the First World War was programmatically anti-Symbolist. If this was true in France it was even more true in the English-speaking world where Rimbaud, Verlaine and Mallarmé meant the sentimentalities of Oscar Wilde and Ernest Dowson, and the pallid *Art Nouveau* descendants of the Symbolists, the disciples of Maeterlinck, seeking the blue flowers of their souls under purple and green lights on a stage masked in heavy scrim, like pea soup.

Derème, Toulet, Carco and the poets of *Le Divan* could be thought to have had a considerable influence in America. There certainly existed a large number of poets, more or less their contemporaries, who wrote much like them. The average literate poet of the early years of this century owned and read the *Mercure* anthology. But I doubt if this was a real influence. Rather it was what biologists call "convergence." Modern taste has never revived these writers, and today the average young American poet has never heard of them. There is nothing to compare to the revival of Toulet and Carco in France—let alone to the remarkable contemporary reputation of O. V. Lubicz-Milosz. Arthur Davison Ficke, even the still living and quite good Witter Bynner, are largely forgotten, and only Edna St. Vincent Millay survives, read by passionate high-school girls.

Did Edna Millay read Renée Vivien or Lucie Delarue-Mardrus? Although she was married to a French intellectual, I would be willing to wager a considerable sum that she never heard of them. Instead, she attempted what is probably the worst translation of Baudelaire—a personality utterly beyond her—in any language. Again, as part of the revolt against provincialism and for a world-wide liberated urban culture, I imagine she thought of herself as standing for French values against New England Puritanism. But, alas, even worse than Whitman, I fear she thought of French culture pretty much the same way as a G.I. out for the night in Gay Paree. It is very simple—Tristan Derème is read today in France and Arthur

Davison Ficke is not read in America for the reason that Derème is an incomparably better writer.

The best poet of the *Divan* style in America is the critic Edmund Wilson, who has a genius for conveying the very taste and smell of old, unhappy, far-off seductions—a regular heterosexual Cavafis. His rigorously unsentimental contemporaries refuse to take him seriously as a poet.

Similarly, a large body of bad Parnassian or Verlainean verse might be extracted from bygone American magazines, but like minor and provincial French verse of the same kind it is better left forgotten. On the other hand, there is in America, as in France, a vast amount of good, but forgotten, provincial verse. For two generations the American hinterland has produced innumerable poets of the kind and quality of Pomairols.

While discussing this period it occurs to me to ask: Where was the Prince of Poetry in those days? The God of the Closerie des Lilas, did he have no influence in America? I think Paul Fort is too intensely French to travel. In certain formal and syntactical ways, yes, but in any real sense, no. Amy Lowell wrote a book titled *Six French Poets* (Regnier, Samain, Spire, Fort, Jammes and Verhaeren). In it she pays tribute to Fort. She borrowed several devices from him, notably what she called "polyphonic prose." Unfortunately, although she was an extremely powerful personality—a little like Gertrude Stein—she was not one of America's best writers and her influence never extended much further than the reach of her personality. "Polyphonic prose" was never taken up by anyone else.

Amy Lowell does, however, bring us to the first major climacteric in twentieth-century American poetry, the Imagist movement. This was a bona fide movement of the Parisian type, with members, leaders, its own tradition, its own magazine and annual. For this reason any number of doctoral theses have been written demonstrating its connection with French poetry. I think this is so much waste paper. The connection is almost nonexistent.

Did Imagist theories of free verse owe anything to the tireless propaganda of Vielé-Griffin? I think not. There is a simple, obvious reason why not. *Vers libre* is *"libre"* of the French alexandrine and the syllabic structure of French poetry. American free verse is free of the accentual pentameter and the quatrain. In fact, as free verse in

America became more sophisticated, it often adopted syllabic structures, as in Marianne Moore, whose verse is not free at all, but counted. Of course, poetry in the English language has always been free in Vielé-Griffin's sense. The rules of classical French poetry have no counterpart in even the strictest English prosody.

Imagism is part of the world-wide movement of the time—anti-Symbolism. If we had nothing but the Imagist Manifestoes to go by, we might think it was very like the poetry of Reverdy—that it was "literary Cubism." It was not. It was much more conventional syntactically and it was actually, however anti-Symbolist its program, influenced at second and third hand by certain Symbolists, notably Gourmont and Laforgue, who were favorites of two of the leaders, Richard Aldington and Ezra Pound. The notion of any intelligent influence can be dissipated instantly by a perusal of Ezra Pound's essay on leading French poets of those days, in which he names as the great hope of French poetry—Max Elskamp! This at the height of the careers of Apollinaire and his colleagues! Pound himself was a sort of late-born Symbolist, actually an *Art Nouveau* poet—the last of the Pre-Raphaelites. A bitter struggle broke out between Pound and Amy Lowell for leadership of the Imagists, and partly it revolved around who knew best what was the latest thing from Paris, France. Amy Lowell was a little out of date—Spire and Fort were getting *usé* in 1920—but at least she knew French poetry. But Pound was on the scene, he drank with Georges Fourrest and flirted with models who had slept with Willy, and he seized the loudspeaker of authority and clung to it. And today many an American Ph.D. thinks Pound is the "founder of Imagism and the first American to introduce modern French poetry to the United States." Georges Fourrest and Max Elskamp!

One American Imagist who was thoroughly conversant with the French poetry of his time was John Gould Fletcher. In fact his major work, a series of reveries called *Blue Symphony, Red Symphony, Green Symphony*, etc., can best be characterized as a deliberate attempt to turn Imagism into a kind of Neo-Symbolism. It is not easy to pinpoint any one French poet as the inspiration for these poems. None of the later Symbolists fit exactly. There are ideas derived from Merrill, Vielé-Griffin, St-Pol Roux, as well as the early work of Salmon and Apollinaire. But basically the resemblance is closest to the Belgians, and it is my opinion that the school of Maeterlinck is not Symbolist at all, but a literary parallel to *Art Nouveau* in the plastic arts. The theories behind John Gould Fletcher's practice, however, came straight from Remy de Gourmont . . . as might be guessed from the very idea of symphonies in color. The *Blue Symphony* in particular was very influential in its day and prepared the way for the long philosophical reveries which are so characteristic of modern American poetry—Eliot's *Waste Land*, Pound's *Cantos*, Williams' *Paterson*, Zukofsky's "A," Lowenfels' *Some Deaths*, Tyler's *Granite Butterfly* and much of the work of Conrad Aiken. Five long poems of my own are all deeply indebted to John Gould Fletcher. Had he written in French, Fletcher would have been a recognized landmark in literary history. As it was, he went out of fashion in his middle age, was little read, changed his style, much for the worse, and finally, as have thirty other important American poets in the twentieth century—committed suicide.

The British Imagist F. S. Flint, who later gave up writing altogether, did know contemporary French verse very well indeed. His translations of Cendrars, Aragon, Eluard, Soupault, Jacob and the rest, from their classical period, remain the best translations of modern French verse in English, and they were done over thirty-five years ago. They seemed to have no influence on the Imagists, however. They encouraged them in their practice of free verse, but the problems of French poetry in the early Twenties were either over the heads or outside the interests of English and American writers.

The leading Imagist, and the only one still read today, was H. D. (Hilda Doolittle, then the wife of Richard Aldington). She was more influenced by Meleager and the Choruses of Euripides than all of French literature rolled together. Her personality greatly resembles Renée Vivien; some of her poetry has the same scene and subject as *Les Chansons de Bilitis*. But there the resemblance ends. She is a far harder, brighter, cleaner poet than Louys or Vivien—a much better one, if you will.

Imagism was a revolt against rhetoric and symbolism in poetry, a return to direct statement, simple clear images, unpretentious themes, fidelity to objectively verifiable experience, strict avoidance of sentimentality. I suppose this is the actual *programme* of all good poetry anywhere. The Enemy of the Imagists was Tennyson and Victorianism generally. I doubt if anybody writing in France in 1912-25 was consciously engaged in a struggle against Lamartine or Hugo.

There was an important but usually ignored influence. All the Imagists were familiar with Judith Gautier's *Livre du Jade*—that precious minor classic of French letters. From it they got their first intimation of Chinese poetry—a poetry which fulfilled and surpassed the Imagist Manifesto beyond the abilities or dreams of even the best of the Imagists. Amy Lowell's (with Florence Ayscough) *Fir Flower Tablets*, Witter Bynner's *The Jade Mountain* (The 300 Poems of T'ang), Ezra Pound's *Cathay* are translations from the Chinese, and are in each case incomparably their respective author's best work. Judith Gautier not only was almost certainly the first inspiration for this interest, but she provided the Americans with her special interpretations of Chinese poetry—a mood of exquisitely refined weariness and excruciating sensibility which is not, as a matter of fact, characteristic of Chinese poetry until the eighteenth century. None of these authors, including Judith Gautier, read Chinese—yet they made the best translations in any language.

Even those Imagists who could not read *Le Livre du Jade* in French read beautifully translated selections in Stuart Merrill's *Pastels in Prose*. This was a translation of French prose poems from a wide variety of writers, mostly Symbolist, and was an attempt to acclimate the prose poem in America. It is the only work by which Merrill is known to most Americans. It failed in its purpose. Not only have few prose poems of any importance ever been written in English, but from Baudelaire to Léon Paul Fargue there are no good translations from the French. It seems to be a medium singularly unfitted to the spirit of American poetry. In fact, the only important prose poems in America are to be found in William Carlos Williams' *Kora in Hell*, a sort of prose *Vita Nuova* which shows a familiarity with Max Jacob and Fargue.

There is one other curious influence, one of those vagaries of history due to the "personal element" that eludes the strict mechanists. Pound knew Georges Fourrest and tried vainly to write witty epigrams like his—"Here lies George Fourrest under the sod./ He never feared the cops, syphilis or God." Pound never managed anything as good as that. But F. S. Flint knew a considerable poet then teaching in London—Jean de Bosschère. He introduced him to the other Imagists and their own concepts of free verse probably had some influence on Bosschère rather than the other way around. He certainly had a definite influence on Flint himself, to a lesser degree on Aldington, and probably on Pound's "Villanelle of the Psychological Hour"—the only poem Pound ever wrote in anything like the idiom of modern French verse. Then Bosschère published in London and Chicago in a *face en face* edition, French and English, his *Closed Door*. This contained the famous "Ulysses Builds His Bed," the first competent example of dissociation and recombination of elements in the "cubist" manner that most poets who read no French had ever encountered. Its effect was tremendous. Out of it came the germinal idea for Joyce's great epic. Out of it came the technique of *The Waste Land*. Anthropologists are familiar with phenomena like this in what they call "acculturation" or in "diffusion" of culture elements. Something not of primary importance in one culture will be transmitted to another almost by chance, and find a niche unoccupied in the other culture pattern and proliferate all over the place. It is like the spread of the English sparrow and the starling all over America, or rabbits in Australia. Pascal Covici, then a Chicago book dealer and later one of America's largest publishers, was especially fond of Bosschère and published practically everything he wrote, while Cendrars is, to the best of my knowledge, except for his *Anthologie Negre*, represented only by a poor translation of *L'Or*, made long ago. Such are the exigencies of the diffusion of culture and of comparative literature.

Meantime, literary cubism was coming into existence in English. Gertrude Stein's *Tender Buttons* and the abstract dissociative poems of Walter Conrad Arensberg antedate the fully developed style of Reverdy by ten years or more. Both were wealthy Americans who had lived for long periods in France and who were very much alive to what was going on in the most advanced circles. Arensberg gave up writing, became the leading exponent of the Baconian heresy— the idea that Bacon wrote Shakespeare—to prove which he spent thousands. He was a close friend of Marcel Duchamp, and, aided by

Duchamp, he built one of the two or three largest collections of modern painting in the world—now in the Philadelphia Museum. (It contains almost the entire *oeuvre* of Duchamp himself.)

Until just before the Second World War, when she became a great world celebrity like the Aga Khan or Brigitte Bardot or Princess Margaret, Gertrude Stein published her books at her own expense and was read only by a tiny coterie, mostly of Americans living abroad. She is one of the most intensely American writers that ever lived. Her words, her ideas, her materials, all are the purest Americanese, and even her extraordinary syntax is simply a development of tendencies latent in typically American speech. Yet she is also an American writer whose work stands fully in the mainstream of French poetry from Apollinaire to Surrealism.

Arensberg and Stein both lived abroad, they both wrote for small coteries of sophisticates, they both contributed to the magazine *Others* edited by Alfred Kreymborg, and it is with this magazine and the group that grew up around it that modernism in American poetry really begins. William Carlos Williams, Wallace Stevens, Marianne Moore, Mina Loy, T. S. Eliot, Conrad Aiken, Marsden Hartley, Wallace Gould, Alfred Kreymborg himself, Maxwell Bodenheim, and the socialist poets Lola Ridge and James Oppenheim, the anarchist Arturo Giovannitti, dozens of others—Kreymborg produced them all suddenly on the literary stage in America, like a conjurer pulling rabbits from a hat. The effect on the press and the conventional poetry circles was terrific. It surpassed by far the noise made by the Beat Generation or the alcoholics of the Hemingway-Fitzgerald Lost Generation. American literature was never the same again, and of course today many of these names are modern classics, poets loaded with honors and taught in the grammar schools and endlessly and exhaustively explicated in hundreds upon hundreds of Ph.D. theses. Their influences are, without exception, largely French.

French they may have been. Up to date, except with a few exceptions, they were not. It takes as long almost for new poetic idioms to cross a language barrier as it does for the use of the blowpipe to travel from one tribe to another in the Amazon. The time lag was considerable. Pound had just discovered Laforgue and was translating his prose extravaganzas and singing his praises to all comers. Laforgue is the principal influence on most of these people. All the early work of T. S. Eliot is extremely Laforguean. He now attributes that special spleen and irony to Corbière, but it is extremely doubtful if he had ever heard of Corbière prior to 1920. The real leader of the group to which Eliot and Pound belonged in London was the novelist, polemicist, and very great painter, Wyndham Lewis, and Lewis's narrative style is Laforgue reduced to a formula: "Describe human beings as though they were machines, landscapes as though they were chemical formulas, inanimate objects as though they were alive." This is pretty much the formula of the Laforguean poetry of the English poetess Edith Sitwell too, and she had a considerable influence on American poets. Marianne Moore is a poet very like Edith Sitwell, but without her depth. She not only took over the Laforguean aesthetic, but she wrote in syllabic verse which structurally often resembles specific poems of Laforgue's. Aiken's poetry was much like Laforgue's in its choice of inadequate, spleen-ridden and troubled narrators—the first person of the poem almost always sounds like Eliot's *Prufrock* or a slightly healthier Laforgue himself. But Aiken's long, mellifluous, easy line with its obvious sonorities and sentimental rhythms sounds much more like Valéry Larbaud. Dozens of Aiken's poems are pure Barnabooth.

It is very important to understand that modernist American poetry—and English, as well—of the generation just before and after the First World War, the generation of Supervielle and Cendrars, of Reverdy and Breton—was hopelessly stuck on Laforgue. This peculiar blockage is extremely difficult to understand and merits a long essay—or an American Ph.D. thesis—in itself. Puzzling about this, I comfort myself with the memory that shortly after the Second World War, Roger Caillois informed me that the best American novelist was Horace McCoy.

Actually the Socialist-Populist writers were more aware of contemporary French literature. They read the French socialist and anarchist press and wrote in a sort of international Whitmanesque revolutionary idiom like many of their now forgotten compeers in the French journals of the "movement." I suppose their favorite foreign poets were Verhaeren and the German, Richard Dehmel. But they were aware of what was going on, as the aesthetes of this period were not. They had a living contact with intellectuals in Paris, Amsterdam, Berlin, Munich, Geneva. The Laforgueans had derived their knowledge of the latest thing from courses in French literature at Harvard and I doubt if either Pound or Eliot has ever heard of Herman Gorter to this day. When Gorter and his friends seized power in postwar Rotterdam, weeping men and women recited hastily made translations of his poems from soapboxes to ragged crowds in the slums of New York and Chicago. Mayakovsky's poems were translated into American before they were into French. Sandburg wrote one of the first poems to Brancusi in any language, and it is still one of the best.

The large Yiddish-language press, then by far the most civilized journals in America, published translations of poetry from all over the world, and the American Yiddish poet Yehoash was translating Japanese *haiku* and introducing ideas derived from Apollinaire into Yiddish verse before anybody ever dreamed of doing such things in English. A section of New York, utterly unknown to the "real Americans," was an international capital with an international language into which literature from all over Europe was translated, dozens of magazines and newspapers of higher quality than anything in English, and the best theater in the Western hemisphere. It must not be forgotten that almost all Jewish poets of those days still read Yiddish, although they wrote in English, and were thus exposed to international influences unknown to their Gentile colleagues. "Cosmopolitanism" somebody in Russia called it a few years back.

If the proletariat had an international culture, so did the rich. Walter Conrad Arensberg moved from specific imitations of Mallarmé, *"Reflets dans l'Eau"*: "The swan existing/ Is like a song/ With an accompaniment/ imaginary . . ." through imitations of Toulet: "Sleepy head/ Lay aside your sandals/ That have fled/ Down a night of candles/ By the bed . . ." to the pure cubism of "A drink into home use indicates early Italian, otherwise the elements of how keep outside. Use what listens on Sundays and catchy elms will oxidize pillows. Blunders are belted in cousins . . ." to "abstract" poems with titles like "Axiom" and "Ohm," which can be compared only with Picabia, but which, quite unlike Picabia or Tzara, were written in dead earnest.

Mina Loy somewhat resembled the early Soupault, although when she wrote her best verse it is unlikely that she had ever heard of him. Later she married the boxer Arthur Craven, a famous figure of the great days of Dada. Gertrude Stein, of course, was plugging away, writing poetry and prose which might well have puzzled Barzun (the father, not the son), but she did not contribute much to literary magazines until ten years later.

Marsden Hartley was one of America's greatest painters. Working in Germany and Paris before the First World War, he was one of the first abstract expressionists and in those days he wrote some rather odd poetry, obviously French in inspiration. When he returned to the States he abandoned all this and painted for the rest of his life in a powerful, rocky, Fauve-like style the landscapes and seascapes and people of his native Maine. His poetry underwent a similar change. It is simple, direct, painfully honest, unabashedly personal. Little appreciated in the long period of academic English-inspired metaphysical verse of the self-styled Reactionary Generation, he is coming back into favor, at least among young poets.

Now we come to the last two poets of this group, whom I have held back because they are by far the best. (A comparative study like this must pass by, at least to an extent, questions of value and concentrate on historical connections. Arensberg, Oppenheim, Bodenheim, several others, are not very good writers. I forgot poor old Bodenheim, by the way. He was a sort of hobo Laforgue, a poor and rather absurd poet who spent his life cadging drinks in the Bohemian quarters of New York and Chicago and living off the fringes of "the movement"—first the anarcho-syndicalist IWW, later the Communists. Like all such pathetic people, he had a rather frightening dissolute integrity of his own. He was, I suppose, the most Laforguean of all, but Laforgue came to him through the worst of all channels, the English Decadents, Wilde, Dowson, Symons—and Ben Hecht!)

To resume the thread—Wallace Stevens and William Carlos Williams are poets of world importance, completely devoid of the provincial, derivative character that marks most of these people. They have, *vis à vis* French poetry, none of that flavor of the backwoodsman seeing Paris for the first time that we associate with even such important figures as Rubén Darío.

Wallace Stevens might be said to have fulfilled and completed Laforgue, more than anyone in French poetry, or any other language for that matter. (Rimbaud does not fulfill Laforgue—no two life attitudes could be less alike.) Stevens shares Laforgue's irony and his sensual wisdom, but he has something Laforgue lacks as a poet and lacked as a man—a very simple thing: good health. The bitterness of Laforgue's irony becomes a tonic rather than a corrosive bitterness in Stevens and produces a skepticism and animal faith, a completely *laique* affirmation beyond the capacity of a dying and unhappily exiled man. The pure Voltairean malice in the Laforgue tradition is revealed in all its innocence and grandeur.

Today it is William Carlos Williams who emerges as the greatest of this group—the classic American modernists—and as America's greatest living poet. He was partly educated in France. He has lived there for extended periods. He knows personally most of the heroic generation of post-World War I poets and has translated a novel of Soupault's. He was a friend of Valéry Larbaud and the American editor of *Commerce*. Intensely personal, local, antiliterary, absolutely devoted to the achievement of a truly American vision, he is none the less the one American poet who ranks with the best of his French contemporaries, who speaks to them as an equal in a language they can understand. I would say too that the ordinary French reader today could get more out of him than from any other American poet except Whitman. It is the true autochthones who circulate most freely in all lands. Williams could be said to belong in the Cubist tradition—Imagism, Objectivism, the dissociation and rearrangement of the elements of concrete reality, rather than rhetoric or free association. But where Reverdy, Apollinaire, Salmon, Cendrars, Cocteau and Jacob are all urban, even megalopolitan, poets of that Paris which is the international market of objects of *vertu*, vice, and art, Williams has confined himself in single strictness to the life before his eyes—the life of a physician in a small town twenty miles from New York. In so doing, his localism has become international and timeless. His long quest for a completely defenseless simplicity of personal speech produces an idiom identical with that which is the end product of centuries of polish, refinement, tradition and revolution.

The next generation, the young men and women who began to write during and just after the First World War, had more connections with France and were more alive to what was actually going on there. The reason was obvious—they were there. Many of them went abroad as soldiers and stayed on, traveling about Europe and living as cheaply as possible off the inflated currencies with their hard dollars. This is the famous Lost Generation. They weren't very lost. They had a ball in Europe. They all started publishing their books and selling their paintings in their early twenties. Most of them came back to the States to enormously successful careers or very highly paid jobs. Ernest Hemingway, on safari hunting rhinoceros, has never looked very "lost" to me.

Although the First World War broke the isolation of America and pulled it into the general orbit of Western civilization, the experiences of Europe in the war actually had little meaning for these young Americans. Malcolm Cowley, one of their leaders, and a poet who became a successful editor and publisher, wrote a book about those years, *Exile's Return*. It is a good book, and a fine study of the mind of his generation of Americans abroad, but it shows less than no understanding of what had happened to the European spirit. A good deal of it is taken up with the high days of Dada. To Cowley, and to most of his well-off friends, Dada was just a continuation of the American-college-boy pranks they had known at Princeton and Harvard. They might be able to write about it, but they could never understand in their hearts that the war and the counterrevolutions that followed it had destroyed the foundations of the Humanist tradition, that the very word *civilization* had come to stink of blood. Perhaps it was a Nazi who first said, "When I hear the word *culture,* I reach for my revolver." But it was Max Ernst who exhibited a billet of wood with an ax chained to it and the card, "If you don't like this piece of sculpture, you dirty bourgeois, make one for yourself." And who was it who wanted to show, in the same Rhineland Dada exhibition, a loaded pistol mounted in a frame and pointed at the spectator, with a little string on the trigger and the caption: *Please pull.* The state of mind behind this state of affairs was totally incomprehensible to the average American poet drinking Pernods which cost him two and a half cents American money on the *terrasse* of the Dome and congratulating himself on what a rebel he was—against American Prohibition. No happy man has so much *einfühlung* that he can truly comprehend a broken heart.

Still—they did their best. They bought drinks for the leading personages of the period if they could persuade them to visit their tables. They financed literary reviews. They helped stage demonstrations and plays in which people continuously shot off pistols and cranked klaxons. (Ah, the klaxons! The true Mona Lisas of the Twenties! Where would we have been without them?) The exiles were always good for a loan which seemed very sizable on the receiving end, translated into francs, but which was cheap at half the price. They bought a taste of the disorderly old age of a culture. In other words, they were like schoolboys who discovered they could make love to a decrepit and dissolute but unbelievably depraved duchess for less than the price of ten minutes in a short-order whorehouse back home.

Duchesses in dissolution, alas, are over the heads of schoolboys, and so, like Malcolm Cowley, the exiles returned—to good jobs. What had they accomplished, the young men of the Twenties, the expatriates? A good deal, some of it unwittingly. They broke for a moment the continuity of American culture. They introduced to America the alienated and outraged European avant-garde, and although few of them understood what they were doing, there were others, in America and expatriated, who did. They started a tradition of publishing the most vital American writing, as well as a lot of translation from modern French writing, in Paris—a tradition which persists, more or less on dying momentum, to this day. They ran a number of reviews, expensively gotten up by European standards, which may have had little public support but which were studied avidly by every alert writer and painter back home. Similar magazines, necessarily cheaper and less worldly, proliferated all over America.

The Little Review, edited by Margaret Anderson and Jane Heap, started in Chicago and moved to Paris, where it finally died in Gurdjieff's dude ranch in Fontainebleau. *Broom* was founded and edited by Alfred Kreymborg and Harold Loeb in Rome, Paris and Berlin, and eventually was taken over by Malcolm Cowley and Matthew Josephson and moved to America—where it promptly died. *Contact* was edited by William Carlos Williams and Robert MacAlmon and included a book-publishing venture. The *Transatlantic Review* was edited by the dynamic and endlessly fertile British novelist Ford Madox Ford, but published mostly American and French writers. There were many others. At the end there were still plenty, and they and their editors were more closely integrated with European life and more comprehending. Eugène Jolas' *transition* and Sam Putnam's *New Review* were even read by Frenchmen!

Most of these magazines also published good reproductions, and so laid the foundations, not only of modern American abstract art— but of the fabulously successful American art market. Institutions like the Museum of Modern Art, the Arensberg Collection, and the Barnes Collection in Philadelphia, the beautifully organized collection of modern French painting in the Chicago Art Institute, as well as the millionaire art dealers of New York—this would all have been a much poorer thing had it not been for these apostles of acculturation who often had to hide from their printers till money showed up at American Express from Grandma in Sheboygan, Wisconsin.

Then came the Stavisky riots, the manifesto for the United Front (signed by dozens of American writers and artists in France), the Spanish War, Munich—the thunderous footsteps of the Golem marching toward the door—and everybody left for America . . . except Henry Miller, who didn't have the fare and didn't believe in politics anyway.

Let us give what the American *commerçants* call a brief rundown on the leading poets of that period.

Malcolm Cowley started out as a populist poet, but from Harvard, not the Middle West. For five years in Europe his work was full of echoes of Apollinaire, Rimbaud, Cendrars, Soupault—(Soupault and Duchamp seem to have been very congenial minds to the Americans)—even Tristan Tzara and Roger Vitrac. Then he went back to the States, wrote the best poem on the death of Sacco and Vanzetti, gave up poetry and became an editor of a political weekly, *The New Republic.*

Hart Crane worshiped Rimbaud, or at least the Rimbaudian legend. He never learned to speak more than a few words of French, but his "Voyages" are the best recreation of Rimbaud that exist in English and his whole life was a sort of acting out of *Bateau Ivre.*

Formally, however, as a prosodist, he was quite conventional and influenced mostly by early Elizabethan blank verse—probably because he also thought of himself as an avatar of Marlowe. He spent quite a bit of time in France in the last years of his life, but he had more trouble with the police than he did contact with his French colleagues.

Harry Crosby and his wife Caresse ran a very ambitious publishing house, the Black Sun Press. They wrote together a book of beautiful erotic poems, *Sleeping Together,* which bears comparison with the Golls' *Dix Milles Aubes.* Then they returned to America and Crosby shot himself at a drunken party. His work somewhat resembled Artaud's, if Artaud had been mad for the sun instead of the way he was.

Archibald MacLeish lived in Paris in those days and his best poem is "Portrait of a Man," in memoriam to Harry Crosby. It is a very deliberate imitation of Apollinaire's *Zone.* Larbaud, St.-John Perse, Apollinaire, Cendrars—especially their use of tourism as a symbolic system—MacLeish was deeply influenced by them and he echoed and imitated them quite consciously. In his young days he was almost a new Stuart Merrill, whom he greatly resembled in personality.

Matthew Josephson wrote a sort of Dadaist poetry, went back to America, became first a successful advertising man and then an even more successful biographer and forgot about poetry, Dadaist or otherwise.

Jolas spent several years trying to shift the basis of Surrealism from Freud and Marx to Jung and St. John of the Cross, publishing in *transition* Joyce's *Finnegans Wake* and imitating it in polylingual poems full of neologisms which nobody read. He and his friends launched "The Revolution of the Word," complete with manifesto (which he persuaded all sorts of French personages to sign), but nothing came of it and he went back to America. As an apologist for his own brand of Surrealism, he was, if anything, a more cogent and learned polemicist than Breton himself, and to his door can be laid the beginning of the present popularity of Jungianism, with its chaos of undigested symbology and its antinomian mysticism. Out of him come the pseudo mahatmas of *On the Road*—but, alas, all devoid of his curious and amusing learning.

Yvor Winters suffered from tuberculosis and was forced to go from Chicago, not to Paris with all his colleagues, but to the New Mexican mining town of Raton, high in the desert mountains. He actually knew more about French literature than any other practicing American poet of his generation and in his early work did a better job of intelligent assimilation of the whole tradition from Baudelaire to Aragon and Breton than anybody else. He cannot be said to have shown specific French influence. Like William Carlos Williams, his work was his own completely but it was part of the world of modern European literature. Only he of all poet-critics of the time in America had any comprehension of the profound spiritual crisis which this evolution embodied. Suddenly he identified himself with the antimodernism of Valéry or Maritain and became the strictest of contemporary Parnassians. This is a phenomenon typically French again, so much so in fact that his poetic style and critical opinions are still very little understood in America. He once wrote a long attack on H. D. which was at the same time his own farewell to Imagism—hers and his own dissociative, Reverdy-like brand of it. Now this essay has an odd note about it of never quite comprehending H. D. and of somehow missing the whole point of her work. The reason is simple. In its original form it was not about H. D. It is very close to being a paraphrase of Charles Maurras' famous attack on Renée Vivien, *"Le Romantisme Féminin: Allégorie du Sentiment Désordonné."*

In the meantime, there was growing up in Vanderbilt University, one of the few institutions of learning in the American South, a little coterie of political reactionaries, under the leadership of their English professor, John Crowe Ransom. Their roots were in Europe, too, though not in the antimodernism of Maritain and Valéry, but in the antimodernism of Léon Daudet, Maurras, and in the theories of Pareto, Houston Stewart Chamberlain and Major Douglas—the "social credit," "classless syndicalism" and "new agrarianism" which came to so disastrous an end in a gas station in Milan and a fiery hole in Berlin. Their idol was T. S. Eliot, "Classicist, Anglo-catholic, Royalist." They tolerated Fernandez, but thought he was too broad in his tastes. They approved of Ezra Pound but wished he paid more attention to the rules of verse. They believed Nigras should be kept in their place. Their real mentor, who imported these ideas for them—they lacked the languages—was a political professor named Donald Davidson, whose writings somewhat resemble those of a literate Senator Eastland and who is one of the leading think tanks of the modern South.

They numbered one genuine poet in their ranks, a then young girl named Laura Riding. The association was fortuitous. She did not share their ideology. Like Williams, Stein, Winters, she was a genuinely autochthonous American modernist. Her poetry bore a slight resemblance to Reverdy's but I am sure this resemblance too was accidental—convergence again. She left the Ransom group (who called themselves "The Fugitives"—fugitives from modernism, liberalism, humanitarianism, socialism, interracialism, and all the other cusswords of the reactionaries), migrated first to London, where she was one of the early muses of W. H. Auden, and then to Paris and Majorca, where she ran a press and a magazine for several years with Robert Graves. She is without doubt America's most unappreciated good poet. Unfortunately her best poetry is small in bulk and came early. Later she broke down into a dull wordy chaos and then stopped writing altogether. She is one of the many casualties of the permanent crisis of the modern mind, like René Crevel, Rigaut, Artaud, Mayakovsky, Hart Crane, Harry Crosby, Dylan Thomas, and the rest—but for a while she was one of the very finest poets of her day in any language.

Walter Lowenfels lived in Paris for many years and was one of the better American contributors to *transition*. He published a series of books—printed by Darantière, who printed so many of these people—called "Some Deaths," the deaths being those of D. H. Lawrence, Apollinaire, Hart Crane, Rimbaud and a couple of others whom I have forgotten. Structurally they bear considerable resemblance to Apollinaire. Lowenfels, a fairly wealthy man, returned to America after the Stavisky riots (he was one of the first signers of the famous manifesto), gave up poetry and became a correspondent for *The Daily Worker* and editor of its Pennsylvania edition. Only in recent years, arrested under the Smith Act outlawing the Communist Party, was he moved to return to poetry. In his young days he was certainly one of America's best poets, and one of those most in the current of contemporary French life. He is, incidentally, the hero of the very amusing episode "Jabberwhorl

Cronstadt," in Henry Miller's *Black Spring*—which shows how much comprehension Henry has of the refinements of modernist verse. Miller, of course, is another writer so American he is completely assimilable to French culture and stands at ease in the small company of Restif, Céline, and Sar Péladan.

e. e. cummings lived in France after the First World War, but for him Paris seems to have been a place of beautiful streetwalkers and abundant liquor. He is a conventional and sentimental poet whose typographical and syntactic oddities are the pranks of an incurable Harvard Boy. They certainly have nothing to do with the sickness of the European heart which began in 1848 and became fatal in Père Lachaise in 1871. Everybody pretends not to notice that among his comical cut-ups are some of the most scurrilous bits of anti-Semitic doggerel in any language, including German. Anti-Semitism is unknown in America except among lunatics. So in the sense that he is a sane and educated man and an antidreyfusard, he may be said to show French influence. It is a little ominous that he is just beginning to be appreciated in France.

John Brooks Wheelwright was a different kind of Bostonian, a perfect descendant of the revolutionary humanists and eccentrics of the 1840's. Descended on both sides from ancient Mayflower families, and moderately wealthy, he lived for a while abroad and read a great deal of modern French poetry. But he had his own ideas about what kind of modernism he wanted, and he again was a true *indigène*, and so, a good European. Too hot for the orthodox, he became an impassioned Trotskyite, Anglocatholic and several other kinds of violent and peculiar exceptionalist. Walking home one night, he was killed by a drunken driver near the bridge across the Charles River in Boston which his father had built. Dead in his prime like so many American poets, he was not, like most of them, already burnt out. No one has ever taken the place of this dynamic, inexhaustible and lovable mind and completely original talent. Had he written in French, he would have died loaded with honors. As it is, few people have ever heard of him.

Already revolutionary politics has begun to intrude into this narrative. With the onset of the permanent world economic crisis, the rise of fascism and the development of war economies, the Americans went home from Paris, and other international movements than those founded by Picasso and Apollinaire captured the allegiance of American poets. Aragon's *Front Rouge* was recited to jazz trumpets and drums in John Reed clubs (the American Union of Revolutionary Writers) in San Francisco and Chicago—the "trip to Kharkov" caused all sorts of convulsions in advanced literary circles. Mimeographed magazines of Proletcult poetry flourished in provincial towns. The theses of Leopold Auerbach were passionately debated in unheated furnished rooms and rattling boxcars. This movement produced some excellent prose—the early work of Mike Gold, Dos Passos (Dos Passos was strongly influenced by the program, but not the practice, of Jules Romains' "*Unanisme.*" In fact, "*Unanisme,*" which had produced a poetry either monstrous or dull, or both, found in Dos Passos' *USA* its major realization), Farrell, Richard Wright and others, even Steinbeck in a sense—but the bitter fact is that it produced almost no poetry of any consequence whatsoever. The American Roman Catholic Church is the most ultramontane in the world. Similarly the American Communist Party has always been more Russian than the Russians, more Stalinist than Stalin. The witch-hunting—or "petty-bourgeois hunting"—of the bureaucracy, the tedious "let's play we all work at the Pulitov Iron Works" pseudo proletarianism of the Bohemians of Greenwich Village drove most bona fide writers away or out of proletarian literature and into actual trade-union work, and robbed those who stayed of the self-respect essential to poetry. With the exception of Mike Gold, who has not done any important writing in twenty-five years, all the novelists and short-story writers ended up bitter enemies of Bolshevism in all forms . . . many of them professional antibolsheviks, a very lucrative occupation in the States.

There was a moment when French influence was very important in American writing. From Kharkov to *Les Cloches de Basle,* all eyes were on Aragon. Would he be the leader of an assertion of the valid rights of literature against the anti-intellectualism of the bureaucracy? Nothing happened, and one by one the writers dropped away. The leading literary quarterly in America, bitterly reactionary, paranoid in its antibolshevism, was once an organ of the International Union of Revolutionary Writers and carried, along with myself, Louis Aragon on its masthead. No one of my generation is ever likely to forget Aragon's speech attacking Léger and praising as the pure representative of the working class—Gromaire!

When the split came, Breton did not carry any of the older American modernists with him. A whole new crop of American poets sprang up—specifically disciples of Breton's brand of Surrealism. The most important of these poets are Charles Henri Ford, Parker Tyler and Philip Lamantia, all still writing today. Together they edited one of the most dynamic magazines of *"Surréalisme Outremer"*—called *View*—which was livelier if less learned than *transition*. All three are certainly among the finest non-French Surrealists. Parker Tyler's *Granite Butterfly* is an excellent philosophic revery of the type written by Lowenfels, Zukofsky, myself, and others—a form which begins in France with *Un Coup de dés*. This poem of Mallarmé's—along with *Zone, Le Cimitière marin*, and even Carco's *L'Ombre*—has been of immense influence on American poets of my generation.

In the meantime, as a sort of effort to stave off disorganization, the poet Louis Zukofsky organized a "movement"—with manifesto—called Objectivism. It owed a good deal to Apollinaire and the Cubists and to the principles, but not the practice of the German *Neue Sachlichkeit*. Just at this moment people in France—notably Léger—were talking about "the return to the object." Zukofsky himself was deeply read in French poetry and had translated André Salmon, in fact, all of *Prikaz*. His own poetry somewhat resembled the Salmon of the days of *Prikaz* but owed even more to William Carlos Williams and Ezra Pound's *Cantos*. He has a peculiarly knotty, Kabbalistic sort of mind and his long philosophical-personal "epics," actually reveries, resemble nothing so much as the permanent crisis of the modern heart filtered through the baffling convolutions of the Zohar. Incidentally, he was a friend and translator of the great Yiddish modernist, Yehoash. Zukofsky included me, along with Williams, Pound, Horace Gregory, Lowenfels, Wheelwright, in fact, anybody who would say yes and didn't write sonnets, in his Objectivists—but after putting out a very stimulating anthology (printed by Darantière) the movement died for lack of interest on the part of its members. Zukofsky did discover the one American poet who is, without ever having heard of him, an almost exact replica of Reverdy—Carl Rakosi.

Rakosi was published by James Laughlin at New Directions. For over twenty years Laughlin alone imported French writers into America by the bucketful. He took up where Jolas stopped and has lasted four times as long. He has published everybody from Julien Gracq to Eluard, from Queneau back to Louise Labé. At one time he was very awake to what was going on in France. People were just beginning to talk about Michaux in St. Germain when Laughlin appeared with a bilingual *Selected Works of Michaux*. In 1940 the baby Surrealists in the American cornbelt cut their eye teeth on the *New Directions Annual* Surrealist number. In recent years he has been more interested in publishing the work of Asian writers in English and has turned away from the French writers of post-World War II. He is himself an excellent poet, a kind of *intimiste*, who owes much to the example of French poets as diverse as Toulet, Eluard, and Queneau.

The Second World War produced nothing in American poetry. Like most everybody else in the world, Americans seemed to be ashamed of themselves—fighting a war in the middle of the twentieth century; but unlike the more seasoned British, they were unable to write out this attitude in a mature way. Of course, there was nothing in America like the French press of the Resistance, which was by definition stimulating. However, anything that crossed the ocean by chance from North Africa was eagerly read and by the end of the war American poets who read French were well aware of the wartime work of poets like Char and Frénaud. *Les Editions de Minuit* and *Poésie* were easier to buy in America than in Paris.

Has the French poetry that has come after the Second World War had much influence? I think not. Modern American poetry now has a long tradition behind it and it is deeply involved in developments of its own. Poets like Allen Ginsberg, Robert Creeley, Denise Levertov, Lawrence Ferlinghetti, all of whom have lived for long periods in France, owe much to the classic period of French modernism, but they are now following roads which diverge widely from the poets represented in anthologies like Rousselot's and Bealu's. Ferlinghetti has translated Prévert and fancies that he himself writes like Prévert. Actually, if he resembles anybody, it is much more Queneau.

Kenneth Patchen is one of the Old Masters of the universe of discourse which is that of American poetry after the Second World War. Once again—see how often we come to these American writers, truly indigenous, who are so easily comprehensible to the French! The simplest definition of Patchen's style is that he writes as Aragon might have written if Lunacharski had been chairman of the Kharkov Conference. Aragon at the great turn said, "We do not need to concoct synthetic nightmares, the nightmares of the daily press can always surpass us in horror." Well, Patchen really captures that horror, in the way no social-realist ever could. He writes of a world in which every man has become Antonin Artaud, where René Crevel and Mayakovsky shoot each other at every street corner, and where every body of water six feet deep contains its own corpse of Hart Crane and every barroom floor a bloated Dylan Thomas lost in a coma from which there can be no return.

Ever since the wave of world-wide reaction which is a reflection of the by now admittedly incurable economic crisis and the economy of permanent war, American poetry has been in the hands of a coalition of the pillowcase-headdress school which originated at Vanderbilt so long ago, and the ex-Stalinist paranoiacs of a small circle of cocktail drinkers in New York. These people control the scholarships and fellowships that bring American intellectuals to Europe and French intellectuals to teach in Iowa State University's School of Creative Writing. They also publish lavish quarterlies subsidized by American millionaires. They also control that milk-soaked biscuit *Encounter*, which is not really what it seems—edited by John Foster Dulles—but is a publication of the international *beni oui-oui*. So they have given the impression abroad that this is what American poetry is today, a sort of hayseed imitation of Valéry at his most pompous, a bumpkin version of Patrice de la Tour du Pin at his most vapid. The truth is that, like the Proletcult Boys before them (many of them were Proletcult Boys!), they are not poets at all, but politicians, professors and manipulators of prizes, fellowships and scholarships. They are the present American Academy, even more ridiculous than the one which the Bull on the Roof recently entered as the last Dadaist joke of his extreme old age. No one of importance in American poetry takes them seriously, except their poor students, to whom, if they show any originality, they can always give a failing grade in "Creative Poetry 2679132 A."

The great trouble with transatlantic communication is that it is like short-wave radio—it gets distorted by the overpowering signals of the official stations. French people seldom really realize, having never seen the country, that America is a commercial civilization with a mass culture and an official literature which in no way reflects the actual life of the country. But its noncommercial culture is by no means underground; it is just not exported by the American State Department or Hollywood or the big slick magazines and the academic quarterlies. Except by accident, important American intellectuals never show up in Europe on Fulbright Fellowships. The entire official and academic, but not the privately sponsored, fellowship system is a kind of U.S. State Department Gold Curtain, through which only mice can pass.

Finally, although some of the people in the collection presented by *Europe* are important poets and good friends of mine, they show no perceptible French influence. Muriel Rukeyser, Langston Hughes, John Ciardi, Richard Eberhart, all speak French, are well-read in the language and have lived in France; perhaps for this very reason they have been little touched by French poetry. I myself have translated a great deal of French poetry and probably read more of it than I do American poetry, but since my early twenties I do not think I have been much influenced by it. French poetry influenced American in the days when it was changing rapidly, and when it, more than the poetry of any other language, was the first to catch the funeral music of the end of our civilization. Its influence was so powerful because it was so different from American.

Today America has not just been dragged into the orbit of Western Civilization. It, more than any other country except Japan, reflects the inner moral collapse of that civilization. Between Cartier and Champlain thousands of Indians in Northwestern Canada died from the diseases imported by a handful of men in a couple of small boats. The gulf that opened before Pascal, the black bile of Baudelaire, the *sacrificium intellectis* of Rimbaud, the cacodaemon in the bowels of Artaud, these are commonplaces in America today, as common as measles among the Iroquois. And just as common on both sides of the Atlantic are those highly exportable commodities, the castrated pimps of circumstance in the night of man. The world ill has long since smitten Bolivia and Afghanistan. French poetry and American poetry in the age of Strontium 90 are much alike.

The Poet As Translator

When discussing the poet as translator, from time immemorial it has been the custom to start out by quoting Dryden. I shan't, but I will try to illustrate Dryden's main thesis—that the translation of poetry into poetry is an act of sympathy—the identification of another person with oneself, the transference of his utterance to one's own utterance. The ideal translator, as we all know well, is not engaged in matching the words of a text with the words of his own language. He is hardly even a proxy, but rather an all-out advocate. His job is one of the most extreme examples of special pleading. So the prime criterion of successful poetic translation is assimilability. Does it get across to the jury?

If we approach the great historic translations this way it is easy to understand why they are great. It is obvious on the most general survey of English literature that the classic translations of the classics accompany the classics of English, occur in the periods of highest productivity and greatest social—what shall we say? cohesion? euphoria? Tudor, Jacobean, Caroline, Augustan or Victorian, many of the translations are themselves among the major English works of their time. Malory's *Morte d'Arthur*, North's Plutarch, Pope's Homer—and, of course, the King James Bible. All the great translations survive into our time because they were so completely of their own time. This means simply that the translator's act of identification was so complete that he spoke with the veridical force of his own utterance, conscious of communicating directly to his own audience.

Presented as a lecture at the University of Texas, and published in The Craft and Context of Translation, *edited by William Arrowsmith and Roger Shattuck (Austin: University of Texas, 1961). Collected in* Assays, *1961.*

Of course, many such translations are ethnocentric to a degree—
sometimes to the degree that they have turned the original into
something totally different. This is not true of many of the greatest
translations but it is true of some. Is Fitzgerald a translation of
Omar? Here the two cultures are so radically different, all that can
be said is that Fitzgerald was probably all of medieval Persia that
Victorian England was prepared to assimilate. The only real problem is Urquhart. It is hard to imagine anything less like the benign
humanism of Rabelais than this crabbed and cracked provincial
euphuism. The point of Rabelais is that he was the opposite of
eccentric—he was profoundly, utterly normal. Urquhart produced a
Scottish classic, and so for Englishmen Rabelais will always be an
oddity. This is unfortunate, but then, is Rabelais' normality normal
in the British Isles? I think not. Perhaps his Gallic magnanimity
could only cross the Channel tricked out in tartan stripes for a
harlequinade.

It is the custom to deride Pope's Homer. Nothing could be less
like Homer. But the eighteenth century certainly didn't think so—
on either side of the Channel. This was the Homer they were
prepared to accept. Of course, Pope was a neurasthenic, a dandy in
Baudelaire's sense, or Wallace Stevens's, a thoroughly urbanized
exquisite who had professionalized his nervous system. Whatever
his formal commitments (Pope was a Roman Catholic) his real
system of values was only a specialized hierarchy of nervous response. Certainly, nothing less like Homer could be imagined. But
each age demands its own image. The other eighteenth-century
Homers are not Homer either; they are just mediocre or bad. Is
Butler Homer? I suppose he is for those of us who are rationalist,
utilitarian, humanitarian. He is a fine Reform Club Homer. I still
prefer Butler to Butcher and Lang or William Morris, let alone
T. E. Lawrence. However, it is simply not true that the Butcher and
Lang version is any more false to the text than Butler. Butcher and
Lang is Homer for the readers of *The Idylls of the King.*

I am not proposing to dissolve all questions of authenticity in
some sort of vulgar pragmatism. The text is always there as a
control. The recent hair-raising performance of Robert Graves, for
instance, both violates the text and fails to transmit anything resembling Homer. This is not Homer for the readers of *Punch*; it is the

invasion of the text of Homer by the text of *Punch*. Here we have passed the limits of eccentricity. Pope's whole age was eccentric, as was Urquhart's. But theirs was a viable eccentricity; Graves's is not. It is an unpleasant eccentric eccentricity.

The first question must be: is this as much of Homer, or whomever, as can be conveyed on these terms to this audience? Second, of course: is it good in itself? Lord Derby or T. E. Lawrence are simply not good enough English. Graves is simply in bad taste, and the Heroic Age, by definition, was before bad taste was invented. It is possible, of course, that a given audience cannot assimilate enough of the original to justify the effort to achieve a significant resemblance. How much of *Les Liaisons Dangereuses* could be translated into the world of William Law? How much does Proust mean to a Chinese collective farmer and vice versa? Imagine Dante translated by Dorothy Parker or Shakespeare by Tristan Tzara. You don't have to imagine. Dante has recently been translated by someone not too unlike Dorothy Parker. Read it.

As time goes on all translations become dated. Before the language changes the society changes. The Butcher and Lang Homer is repugnant to us because society has changed, but has not changed so much that it has become strange to us. Pope, on the other hand, speaks a language that, considered purely linguistically, seems closer to our own, but his world has receded so far that we read him for his special and extraordinary insights and distortions. At length language changes so much that it becomes liturgical. This is a natural thing and can never be imitated. The nineteenth century made the mistake of thinking it could. Nothing sounds less like liturgical English than William Morris trying to imitate it. This led to terrible waste—I doubt if Morris's wonderful Saga Library was ever readable by anybody, and there the great sagas are, locked up in that ridiculous language. On the other hand, we never think of the Prophets as speaking like a committee of Jacobean Bishops; we think of the Jacobean Bishops as speaking like the Prophets. At last the language becomes really foreign. Chaucer's wonderful rendering of the *Consolation* of Boethius sounds splendid to us, and certainly seems by far the best ever made in any language. It didn't sound that way to generations closer to Chaucer, not even as far away as Dryden and Pope. They read Chaucer as still in their own language. We do not, but in another that we have no difficulty translating as we go along. Of course, there is here the special factor: Chaucer was an incomparably finer poet than his original.

What I have been trying to convey indirectly is what the poet does in the living relationship of translation, the actual act. Or at least what I think he does and what I presume I do myself. Although it is not itself a translation, consider such a poem as H. D.'s "Heliodora." It may seem dated to those who are not old enough to have mellowed to H. D.'s enthusiasms, to those who are not young enough to have never heard of her. Its language is very much the argot of Bloomsbury aestheticism with a strong lacing of the Chautauqua Circuit. Still, I think it does convey, all allowances being made, the excitement of translation of great poetry. It certainly does recall very vividly to me my own experience—my first translation from the Greek, a whole evening till after midnight spent in the continuously exalted discussion of one small Sapphic fragment with a friend who was then an undergraduate student of Paul Shorey's.

Here is the H. D.:

Heliodora*

He and I sought together,
over the spattered table,
rhymes and flowers,
gifts for a name.

He said, among others,
"I will bring"
(and the phrase was just and good,
but not as good as mine,)
"the narcissus that loves the rain."

We strove for a name,
while the light of the lamps burnt thin
and the outer dawn came in,
a ghost, the last at the feast
or the first,

---

*From H.D.'s *Collected Poems 1912–1944* (Copyright 1925 by Hilda Doolittle); used by permission of New Directions Publishing Corp.

to sit within
with the two that remained
to quibble in flowers and verse
over a girl's name.

He said, "the rain, loving,"
I said, "the narcissus, drunk,
drunk with the rain."

Yet I had lost
for he said,
"the rose, the lover's gift,
is loved of love,"
he said it,
"loved of love,"
I waited, even as he spoke,
to see the room filled with a light,
as when in winter
the embers catch in a wind
when a room is dank;
so it would be filled, I thought,
our room with a light
when he said,
(and he said it first,)
"the rose, the lover's delight,
is loved of love,"
but the light was the same.

Then he caught,
seeing the fire in my eyes,
my fire, my fever, perhaps,
for he leaned
with the purple wine
stained on his sleeve,
and said this:
"did you ever think
a girl's mouth
caught in a kiss,
is a lily that laughs?"

I had not.
I saw it now
as men must see it forever afterwards;

no poet could write again,
"the red-lily,
a girl's laugh caught in a kiss";
it was his to pour in the vat
from which all poets dip and quaff,
for poets are brothers in this.

So I saw the fire in his eyes,
it was almost my fire,
(he was younger,)
I saw the face so white,
my heart beat,
it was almost my phrase;
I said, "surprise the muses,
take them by surprise;
it is late,
rather it is dawn-rise,
those ladies sleep, the nine,
our own king's mistresses."

A name to rhyme,
flowers to bring to a name,
what was one girl faint and shy,
with eyes like the myrtle,
(I said: "her underlids
are rather like myrtle,")
to vie with the nine?

Let him take the name,
he had the rhymes,
"the rose, loved of love,
the lily, a mouth that laughs,"
he had the gift,
"the scented crocus,
the purple hyacinth,"
what was one girl to the nine?

He said:
"I will make her a wreath;"
he said:
"I will write it thus:

I will bring you the lily that laughs,
I will twine
with soft narcissus, the myrtle,
sweet crocus, white violet,
the purple hyacinth, and last,
the rose, loved-of-love,
that these may drip on your hair
the less soft flowers,
may mingle sweet with the sweet
of Heliodora's locks,
myrrh-curled."

(He wrote "myrrh-curled,"
I think, the first.)

I said:
"they sleep, the nine,"
when he shouted swift and passionate;
"that for the nine!
above the hills,
the sun is about to wake,
and to-day white violets
shine beside white lilies
adrift on the mountain side;
to-day the narcissus opens
that loves the rain."

I watched him to the door,
catching his robe
as the wine-bowl crashed to the floor,
spilling a few wet lees,
(ah, his purple hyacinth!)
I saw him out of the door,
I thought:
there will never be a poet
in all the centuries after this,
who will dare write,
after my friend's verse,
"a girl's mouth
is a lily kissed."

What H. D. was doing in this rather precious and somewhat dated little drama was objectifying the story of her own possession by the ghost of Meleager while translating his *stephanos,* his proem to his anthology. Whatever else she has done, she has conveyed the poignancy of that feeling of possession and the glamour of the beautiful Greek words as they come alive in one's very own English. Most of the epithets can be found in the lovely 147th Epigram of the 5th Book, and who will ever forget the first time he ever saw them, bright with their old Greek life on the page? That 147th Epigram has been translated by most of those who have taken the Anthology to English, but only H. D. brings over the glamour and excitement of the language.

Now let us look at a selection from the great number of translations of Sappho's "Apple Orchard," the poem I translated so long ago under identical emotional circumstances, and finally my own.

> . . . And by the cool waterside the breeze rustles amid
> the apple-branches, and the quivering leaves shed lethargy;
> > *J. M. Edmonds*

> And round about the cool water gurgles through apple-boughs,
> and slumber streams from quivering leaves.
> > *Henry Thornton Wharton*

> And by the cool stream the breeze murmurs through apple
> branches and slumber pours down from quivering leaves.
> > *Edwin M. Cox*

> Cool waters tumble, singing as they go
> Through appled boughs. Softly the leaves are dancing.
> Down streams a slumber on the drowsy flow,
> > My soul entrancing.
> > > *T. F. Higham*

> Through orchard-plots with fragrance crowned
> The clear cold fountain murmuring flows;
> And forest leaves with rustling sound
> Invite to soft repose.
> > *John H. Merivale*

> All around through branches of apple-orchards
> Cool streams call, while down from the leaves a-tremble
> > Slumber distilleth.
> > > *J. Addington Symonds*

By the cool water the breeze murmurs, rustling
Through apple branches, while from quivering leaves
    Streams down deep slumber.

Edwin M. Cox

   . . . about the cool water
   the wind sounds through sprays
   of apple, and from the quivering leaves
   slumber pours down. . . .

K. Rexroth

I hold no brief for my own translation, but at the time I did it, it was an entirely original experience with me, or rather, I should say, with us, for, as was the case with H. D.'s poem, there were two of us working on it together—and neither of us was familiar with any other English version. That evening was one of the memorable experiences of my life, just because of the completeness of projection into the experience of that great dead Greek woman. On inspection of these various versions it is obvious that what matters most is sympathy—the ability to project into Sappho's experience and then to transmit it back into one's own idiom with maximum viability.

There is a special factor here, something that comes up in almost all translations of Sappho from Catullus to our own day. There is a special, vertiginous exaltation in Sappho's language, not only in the phrases of a poem like the one to Anactoria, which is about such a state, but even in the very few words surviving in some of the fragments. Both H. D. and those two very exalted ladies who called themselves Michael Field not only felt this but they all wrote poems which are expansions of tiny fragments of Sappho, and which in each case attribute to the inspiring fragment precisely this supernatural luster. Is there any basis for this in fact? It is easy to see what an Englishwoman of Sappho's temperament could do with Fragment 27, *optais amme*, "you burn me . . ." but is there anything actually inflammatory about Fragment 106: *Met' emoi meli mete melissais*, "Neither honey nor bees for me." Does it bear H. D.'s almost hysterical expansion? I think not. Actually it means, "If I can't have roses without thorns I won't have them at all," and is a proverb quoted by Sappho. Here is a poem by Michael Field which is an expansion of Fragments 109 and 110: *Kotharos gar o chrysos io*

and *Dios gar pais est' o chrysos/ kenon ou sees oude kis/ dardaptois.
o de damnatai/ kai phrenon brotean kratiston.* *

> Yea, gold is son of Zeus; no rust
> Its timeless light can stain.
> The worm that brings men's flesh to dust
> Assaults its strength in vain.
> More gold than gold the love I sing,
> A hard, inviolable thing.

> Men say the passions should grow old
> With waning years; my heart
> Is incorruptible as gold,
> 'Tis my immortal part.
> Nor is there any god can lay
> On love the finger of decay.

This is a rather lovely little poem, perhaps the best in the Michael
Field volume of reconstructions of Sappho, *Long Ago*. But it is not
Sappho—it is very specifically the *fin de sièle* Lesbian sensibility
that flourished alongside the poetry of Wilde and his friends. It is
part of the same myth as *Les Chansons de Bilitis* and the poems of
Renée Vivien. The amusing thing about it is that the Greek "originals" are not originals at all, but paraphrases in Sappho's metre
from indirect references in Pausanias and a scholiast on Pindar. The
Sapphic legend was so powerful that anything was enough to set off
her late-born sisters. Here sympathy achieves a kind of translation
when the source does not even exist. In a few of the translations of
the "Apple Orchard" lack of sympathy leads to ludicrous effects—to
words (for instance, "gurgles") that would never have occurred to
anyone who bothered to project himself imaginatively into Sappho's experience.

Still there is the question of the awesome luster of Sappho's
simplest words. Is it there or do we read it into her fragments? Partly
it is a function of attention. If you isolate two sentences of a skillful
description of passion or of Nature and say, "Pay attention, these are
by the greatest lyric poet who ever lived," the mind will find values
in them which may have been there, but which would normally

---

*Transcription from the Greek texts in The Loeb Library *Lyra Graeca* volume,
edited by J. M. Edmonds. The Scholiast on Hesiod ascribes 110 to Pindar.

have been passed over. Prisoners with nothing else to do, their eyes focused on the stained ceilings of their cells for hours, can find more there to look at than they might in the Sistine Chapel. True, Sappho's apple orchard or her waning moon have all the intensity of Japanese *haiku*, but so do Frances Densmore's schematic translations of Chippewa and Teton Sioux poetry—and, we should never forget, so do hundreds of mediocre English translations of Japanese *haiku* themselves, which transmit none of the special virtues of the originals. I am afraid that I must admit that the supernatural gleam that seems to emanate from the *oio polu leukoteron* of Fragment 62, "far whiter than an egg," is a delusion, on a par with the mystical vision which comes with staring too long at an unshaded electric bulb or from taking one of Aldous Huxley's pharmaceutical nirvana-producers. But, still, in Sappho as in Homer, the simplest sentences do have a wonder, never equalled again in the West and never translated to any other language.

I am going to give you a little anthology of translations, all of them I think successful. They are not all successful for all the same reasons, and one of them is definitely eccentric, but I think they all exemplify a very high degree of imaginative identification with their originals:

The River-Merchant's Wife: A Letter*

While my hair was still cut straight across my forehead
I played about the front gate, pulling flowers.
You came by on bamboo stilts, playing horse,
You walked about my seat, playing with blue plums.
And we went on living in the village of Chōkan:
Two small people, without dislike or suspicion.

At fourteen I married My Lord you.
I never laughed, being bashful.
Lowering my head, I looked at the wall.
Called to, a thousand times, I never looked back.

At fifteen I stopped scowling,
I desired my dust to be mingled with yours

*From Ezra Pound's *Personae* (Copyright 1926 by Ezra Pound); used by permission of New Directions Publishing Corp.

Forever and forever and forever.
Why should I climb the look out?

At sixteen you departed,
You went into far Ku-tō-yen, but the river of swirling eddies,
And you have been gone five months.
The monkeys make sorrowful noise overhead.

You dragged your feet when you went out.
By the gate now, the moss is grown, the different mosses,
Too deep to clear them away!
The leaves fall early this autumn, in wind.
The paired butterflies are already yellow with August
Over the grass in the West garden;
They hurt me. I grow older.
If you are coming down through the narrows of the river Kiang,
Please let me know beforehand,
And I will come out to meet you
As far as Chō-fū-Sa.

Rihaku (Li Po)
Ezra Pound

The Shadow of the Orange-Leaves

The young girl who works
all day in her solitary chamber
is moved to tenderness if she
hears of a sudden the sound of
a jade flute.

And she imagines that she
hears the voice of a young boy.

Through the paper of the
windows the shadow of the
orange-leaves enters and sits
on her knees;

And she imagines that somebody has torn her silken dress.

"Tin-Tung-Ling"
Stuart Merrill's English of
Judith Gautier's French

Lugete, O Veneres Cupidinesque

Weep, weep, ye Loves and Cupids all
And ilka Man o' decent feelin':
My lassie's lost her wee, wee bird,
An that's a loss ye'll ken, past healin'.

The lassie lo'ed him like her een:
The darling wee thin lo'ed the ither,
And knew and nestled to her breast,
As ony bairnie to her mither.

Her bosom was his dear, dear haunt—
So dear, he cared no long to leave it;
He'd nae but gang his ain sma' jaunt,
And flutter piping back bereavit.

The wee thing's gane the shadowy road
That's never travelled back by ony:
Out on ye, Shades! ye're greedy aye
To grab at ought that's brave and bonny.

Puir, foolish, fondling, bonnie bird,
Ye little ken what wark ye're leavin':
Ye've gar'd my lassie's een grow red,
Those bonnie een grow red wi' grievin'.

Catullus
G. S. Davies

Me Nive Candenti Petit Modo Julia

White as her hand fair Julia threw
A ball of silver snow;
The frozen globe fired as it flew,
My bosom felt it glow.

Strange power of love! whose great command
Can thus a snow-ball arm;
When sent, fair Julia, from thine hand
Ev'n ice itself can warm.

How should we then secure our hearts?
Love's power we all must feel,
Who thus can by strange magic arts
In ice his flames conceal.

'Tis thou alone, fair Julia, know,
Canst quench my fierce desire;
But not with water, ice or snow,
But with an equal fire.

From the Petroniana
Soame Jenyns

Chorus of Troizenian Women

At high-tide,
the sea—they say—
left a deep pool
below the rock-shelf:
in that clear place
where the women dip
their water-jars,
my friend steeped her veils
and spread the scarlet stuff
across the hot ridge
of sun-baked rocks:
she first brought word
of my mistress:
"She lies sick,
faint on her couch
within the palace;
her thin veils
cast a shadow
across her bright locks.
I count three days
since her beautiful lips
touched the fine wheat—
her frail body
disdains nourishment:
she suffers—
some secret hurt
hastens her death."

Surely, O young queen,
you are possessed
by Pan, by Hecate,
by some spirit
of the Corybantic rites,

or by Cybele
from the hill-rocks!
or have you sinned,
that you suffer thus,
against Artemis?
Have you offered
no sacrificial cakes
to the huntress?
For she walks above earth,
along the sea-coast,
and across the salt trail
of the sea-drift.

Or is it that your lord,
born of Erechtheus,
the king most noble in descent,
neglects you in the palace
and your bride-couch
for another in secret?
Or has some sea-man,
landing at our port,
friendly to ships,
brought sad news from Crete?
or some great hurt
binds you to your couch,
broken in spirit.

Euripides
H. D.

An Elegy

I

O youngest, best-loved daughter of Hsieh,
Who unluckily married this penniless scholar,
You patched my clothes from your own wicker basket,
And I coaxed off your hair pins of gold, to buy wine with;
For dinner we had to pick wild herbs—
And to use dry locust-leaves for our kindling.
. . . Today they are paying me a hundred thousand—
And all that I can bring to you is a temple sacrifice.

II

We joked, long ago, about one of us dying,
But suddenly, before my eyes, you are gone.
Almost all your clothes have been given away;
Your needlework is sealed, I dare not look at it. . . .
I continue your bounty to our men and our maids—
Sometimes, in a dream, I bring you gifts.
. . . This is a sorrow that all mankind must know—
But not as those know it who have been poor together.

III

I sit here alone, mourning for us both.
How many years do I lack now of my threescore and ten?
There have been better men than I to whom heaven denied a son,
There was a poet better than I whose dead wife could not hear him.
What have I to hope for in the darkness of our tomb?
You and I had little faith in a meeting after death—
Yet my open eyes can see all night
That lifelong trouble of your brow.

Yüan Chên
Witter Bynner

Davies' Catullus has been put down, by a Sasenach, as a charming trick. Perhaps it is, but it is a moving poem in its own right and makes a comparison made many times before—the Celtic Catullus and the curiously Roman Burns. Also, Englishmen never really believe that Scots speak their own language. I prefer to think that Davies was so deeply moved and identified himself so closely with Catullus that he naturally turned to his most natural idiom—the Doric.

Soame Jenyns, not the curator of the British Museum, but the eighteenth-century churchman, seems to me to have achieved something very rare—a perfect translation of the most untranslatable type of Latin verse—those light lyrics and erotic elegies and little satires which are grouped in the *Petroniana* and which have otherwise only been captured by Ben Jonson and Herrick, and in their cases have been actually paraphrases. Not only is the English as close as possible to the metric of "Petronius," but the Latin and the English can both be sung to the same melody, "Phillis why shoulde we delaie?" by Waller with music by Henry Lawes. This can be found in Potter's *Reliquary of English Song,* and you can try it yourself if you like. Jenyns catches not only the tone of the original, but he handles language in exactly the same way. The only thing that is missing is the deep hidden undercurrent of ironic disillusion and memory of blood that haunts all these little poems and that led to their being attributed to Petronius in the first place.

Euripides was certainly a neurasthenic, always in quest of a new shudder of hyperaesthesia, and H. D. of all translators is closest to him in this. It is significant that she was herself so hung up on precisely this entranced intensity of response that she was unable to manage the whole plays—*Iphigenia* and *Hippolytus*—that she attempted, but translated only the high spots. They remain, nonetheless, the most Euripidean Euripides in English.

The greatest translators of Chinese—Judith Gautier, Klabund, Pound—knew less than nothing of Chinese when they did their best translations. In fact, Judith Gautier's lover and informant was a Thai, and himself had only the foggiest notions of the meanings of the Chinese text. Stuart Merrill was America's greatest poet between the New Englanders and the post-World War I moderns. He is practically unknown in this country because he lived and wrote almost exclusively in French. His English is definitely Edwardian or McKinleyan, and suffers from all the vices of *The Yellow Book.* Yet who could quarrel with this "translation"? It is a perfect transmission of one of the dominant themes of Chinese poetry and conveys exactly the neurotic lassitude and weakness of the sex-starved girls and deserted concubines who fill Chinese literature.

Pound worked from the notebooks of Fenollosa, who was himself badly informed by a Japanese whose knowledge of Chinese was already out of date, hopelessly Japonified for even the Japan of their day. Nevertheless this is one of the dozen or so major poems to be written by an American in the twentieth century, and still the best single translation from the Chinese.

I have included Witter Bynner's translation of Yüan Chên's elegy for his dead wife because I think it is, again, one of the best American poems of this country, incomparably Bynner's best poem, and, of all these poems, it conveys an overwhelming sense of identification with the situation of the original author. Mistakes, or at least dubious interpretations of a few words have been pointed out since it was made, and Bynner has discarded all the obliquity and literary reference of the original. Still, I think that from every point of view it is the second-ranking single translation from the Chinese out of all we have so far done.

Not only have the best "translators" not known Chinese, there is only one great translator who has, and only one in the second class—Arthur Waley, of course, and Bernhard Karlgren. Waley is a special case. He is a fine poet who has deliberately limited himself, as a kind of rigorous aesthetic discipline—a little like the self-imposed rigors of Paul Valéry—to translation from the Chinese and Japanese. Karlgren must be a special case, too, because he is the only Sinologist in any language who is any good at all as a translator. Possibly this is because he translates not into his own Swedish but into another foreign language—English.

I think this is due to the primitive state of Sinology. Most Sinologists are philologists. They are all too close to the language as such and too fascinated by its special very unEnglish and yet curiously very English-like problems ever to see the texts as literature. The grammarian takes over in the decadence of the study of a language; but he also takes over—in fact he is essential—in its infancy. Karlgren does as a matter of fact seem to sit very easy to Chinese; you can hear him ordering a meal in Cantonese or bawling out a bureaucrat in the National Language.

A bit of the GI approach to language—*Ou est, les cigarettes, les girls, le restaurant, le W.C.?*—would be a great help to contemporary Sinology and would go a long way to overcome the philologists' barbarism. After all, you can do nothing whatever with poetry until you comprehend that it too is about "the necessities of life."

One of the most engaging Hellenists of our time, Robert Byron, believed that all ancient Greek should be given the modern pronunciation. There is something to be said for this. Homer certainly did not sound like the waiter in the corner beanery, but it is possible that he sounded even less like the German and American professors, and it is certainly great fun to sit and eat pie à la mode after midnight and swap quotations with a lonely counterman. Somehow Pericles seems more available. This again is the virtue of the Italian and Roman Catholic pronunciation of Latin. The *Tantum Ergo* of Aquinas, known to children in the slums of Youngstown or Belfast, shades imperceptibly into the chirr of Horace's bracelets and back to the old Saturnian stomp. Communion is as important to the poet-translator as communication. I was taught the correct pronunciation of Latin, but I have never been able to take it seriously. On the other hand, who has ever forgotten the first time, on the streets of modern Rome, that he looked down at his feet and saw SPQR on a manhole cover?

Sympathy can carry you very far if you have talent to go with it. Hart Crane never learned to speak French and at the time he wrote his triptych poem "Voyages" he could not read it at all. His only informant was Allen Tate, a doubtful guide at best in this field, and his image of Rimbaud was an absurd inflation of the absurd Rimbaud myth. Yet "Voyages" is by far the best transmission of Rimbaud into English that exists—the purest distillation of the boyish hallucinations of the *"Bateau Ivre."*

Sympathy, or at least projection, can carry you too far. All sensible men to whom English is native are distressed at the French enthusiasm for M. Poë, the author of *"Jamais Plus."* Nobody in France seems to be able to learn ever, that Poe's verse is dreadful doggerel and his ratiocinative fiction absurd and his aesthetics the standard lucubrations that go over in Young Ladies' Study Circles and on the Chautauqua Circuit. The reason is, of course, that the French translate their whole culture into Poe before they even start to read him. They think his formalism is their formalism and his scientific speculation the speculation of d'Alembert. They think the giddy early nineteenth-century misses in Baltimore who swooned over the architectonics of *Eureka* are the same overcivilized courtesans who once bestowed their favors on the brocaded inventors of ingenious mathematical machines and, for that, on homespun Le Bon Franklin. In this they are exactly like the brave French Jesuits whose adroit questions taught the Iroquois to expatiate on the mysteries of the Great Spirit, a deity who had migrated unnoticed through the empyrean across the Atlantic from the court of Louis XV.

Finally, what does all this mean to the poet himself? What has it all meant to me? As Eliot, paraphrasing Dryden, has said, inspiration isn't always at its peak. Today we demand practically unrelieved intensity in poetry. The versified agricultural handbooks of the past are not for us—not even the verse novels of the Victorians. No poet ever could meet such a demand every day in the week. Translation, however, can provide us with poetic exercise on the highest level. It is the best way to keep your tools sharp until the great job, the great moment, comes along. More important, it is an exercise of sympathy on the highest level. The writer who can project himself into the exultation of another learns more than the craft of words. He learns the stuff of poetry. It is not just his prosody he keeps alert, it is his heart. The imagination must evoke, not just a vanished detail of experience, but the fullness of another human being.

Last and not least, translation saves you from your contemporaries. You can never really model yourself on Tu Fu or Leopardi or Paulus the Silentiary, but if you try you can learn a great deal about yourself. It is all too easy to model yourself on T. S. Eliot or William Carlos Williams or W. H. Auden or Allen Ginsberg—fatally easy— thousands do it every day. But you will never learn anything about yourself. Translation is flattering, too. I don't at all like feeling like T. S. Eliot or Allen Ginsberg. All through the world's literature there are people I enjoy knowing intimately, whether Abelard or Rafael Alberti, Pierre Reverdy or Tu Fu, Petronius or Aesculapius. You meet such a nice class of people.

What's Wrong with the Clubs

This is a very presumptuous piece; I don't really know enough about the subject to write about it. You'll probably be better off reading Nat Hentoff's book *The Jazz Life*, because he does know what he is talking about. Anyway, I'd like to explore what trade unions call "working conditions" and, in my opinion dependent on working conditions—and race—the living conditions under which many jazz men have to operate.

Music is an art, and its expression should be a joy, but the brutal fact is that the average jazz musician works far too hard, too long hours, under absurdly bad conditions, for too little pay. All musicians of course know this, but the lay public, including the jazz audience, does not. In San Francisco, where I live, a checker in a supermarket or chain grocery makes over four hundred dollars a month for a five-day week, eight-hour day, with fairly liberal time breaks. He, or she (women get the same wage as men), gets overtime, vacations, depending on the company, and often a considerable number of side benefits. The work is certainly nerve-racking, but the hours are normal, and the customers are ordinarily decent human beings.

Compare this with the lot of the average jazz musician. How many make four hundred dollars a month, every month in the year? How many have any prospects of steady employment at all? How many work in clean surroundings? Granted "meeting the public," even banging a cash register in a grocery, is no fun at best, how do the relations between a grocery clerk and the passing stream of

---

Published first in Metronome, *May 1961. Collected in* Assays *later the same year.*

housewives compare with the audience relationship enjoyed by a jazz musician in the average night club? What kind of people by and large go to night clubs? Swindlers, rascals and tyrants may, here and there, run grocery stores. How do the worst of them compare with the average night-club owner? How long would the average night-club owner stay in business if he were selling cornflakes to women with children? And how many grocery clerks have to kick back part of their salary to the owner?

You get the point. The final question of course is, why on earth does anybody go on playing jazz for a living? A lot of people don't. Like nursing, where the girls drop out early, most of them, and get married, jazz is pretty much an occupation of the young. The world is full of house painters, psychiatrists, bell captains, ship captains, who tell you, "I used to play trombone when I was in my twenties." As long as you are young and foolish enough to look on the working conditions of the jazz musician as romantic and glamorous, you may have fun. Come thirty, you've got to be pretty good and pretty devoted, or pretty dumb, to stick it out.

The working conditions of jazz have produced in much of the jazz audience, and in all too many musicians themselves, a kind of mystique—a glorying in the disabilities of jazz employment. Due to the fact that a majority of jazz musicians are Negroes, this has merged with a similar mystique—the glorification of the American Negro for the effects of his disabilities. I have always said of the leading Beat novelist that he has exactly the attitude toward the American Negro that any redneck gallus-snapping Southron chauvinist has. He is considerably less informed about the realities of Negro life than even Senator Eastland, who, I suppose, in his own evil way, does "know Nigras." The Beat novelist just likes them that way. Mailer was right when he said that the hipster was a white Negro—but he neglected to point out that the Negro model the hipster imitates is the product of white imaginations. One of the saddest things I ever saw in my life was a couple of Negro Beat bars out near Thirty-fifth Street in Chicago—misguided young Negroes industriously imitating silly white people imitating Negroes who don't exist. We are all familiar with this sort of thing in jazz. Long ago somebody called it "Crow-Jimism." You can find it on both sides of the color line—Negrophilism is not by any manner of means a purely white phenomenon. It used to be a mass sickness in France, and it's still pretty strong over there.

Did you ever hear Juliette Greco sing *"Dieu est Negre"*? It's about as corny a song as can be imagined—all about Tjeemmy, *le saxophone*, dying in the gutter in Place Pigalle, and saying, as he vomits blood, "God is a Negro." I have seen strong-minded French intellectuals weep in their Pernods as she sings it, totally unaware of its hidden chauvinism. Not only that—but Greco herself believes it so intensely that she carries a powerful conviction. She affects me, although I know that it is all tosh.

It is not easy to be a Negro in America. Discrimination has its effects and they are not all good by any manner of means. Anybody who considers the evil effects of discrimination as virtues is pretty silly, and he is unlikely to be a Negro—unless he has been corrupted, usually financially, by silly Negrophiles. True, there exists, to match Crow-Jimism, a kind of Tom Uncle-ism—Black Chauvinism as a commercial racket. Some people have found it very profitable. A few of them, unfortunately, have been jazz musicians.

Once again, this returns us to the question of the jazz audience relationship. It is because the audience is not a normal musical audience, sitting out there beyond the stand primarily to listen to music, that these stereotyped responses have grown up and been turned into rackets. It doesn't do any good to be "cool" and pretend there is nobody out there. They are out there all right, for better or worse. It doesn't do any good to get up with a horn and pretend that you are Elijah Muhammad and the Vassar girls at the front table are the Georgia mob that lynched your grandfather. You aren't and they aren't.

Jazz is music. Music is not black or white. Leonard Feather demonstrated that the musicians who said they could always recognize the race of anybody on a record not only couldn't tell Negro from white, but often couldn't even tell the race of men they had themselves played with for years. The important thing is to secure conditions where the jazz musician plays music for an audience which is there to listen to music.

Now, true, jazz is not chamber music. At least most jazz is not. Some of the best jazz still is dance music. Certainly most of it is social music—music for conviviality—music which needs a certain kind of audience participation to be most effective. There is nothing unusual about this. This is what all music was, everywhere, until the emergence of "serious" music in modern times and in Western European civilization.

How many clubs provide such a setting? The answer is: how many clubs are primarily in the business of selling music? How many club owners could distinguish between Miles Davis, a glockenspiel and a C clef? The fact is that the night club is a lineal descendant of the speakeasy, and is at least as much an underworld operation, in most cases, as ever was its parent. Jazz is permeated with the underworld. By this I do not mean that jazz musicians are underworld characters. Quite the opposite. The boy who works hard, studying piano or trumpet, gaining scholarships, living in a poor flat in a Negro ghetto, perhaps helped by a mother who works as a domestic, is about as far from the underworld, black or white, as could be. As a matter of fact, a large proportion of Negro musicians come from the middle class; two I know well are the sons of doctors who have always carried on an "integrated" practice. Certainly most musicians in their teens start out as what people call "church" rather than as hippies.

But the exploiters of the musicians are underworld characters, with only a few honorable exceptions. Managers, agents, cheap record companies, owners, bartenders, cocktail waitresses—they all bear a singular resemblance to the people who prey on boxers. Of course, pushing drinks with no chemically analyzable alcoholic content, and all the other little swindles of the trade, produce a grifters' mentality in even the best. An appreciable number of night clubs all across the country are run by the Mafia. Now, spreading out of Vegas, has come a new invasion of the entertainment business by a new kind of crook—naive, cheap, brassy and rich. Behind them, I suppose, lies the sophistication of the Mafia Old Guard, now the business executives of a major American enterprise. They themselves are straight out of Damon Runyon. I grew up on Chicago's South Side and was taught by my gangster friends that life's greatest motto was, "Keep your nose clean and don't volunteer." These boys are like the comic relief in an old George Raft picture.

What the hell kind of environment is this for the practice of an art? No wonder heroin is a problem among jazz musicians. Is it a problem among abstract painters? Members of the Symphony? Architects? Poets? Oh, I know, the Beat poets used to talk about heroin on TV, but the sight of a luer would make any of them faint, and besides, they couldn't afford it. They were just pretending to be like what they thought Negro jazz musicians were like, man. Dope is a problem in jazz because of the nature of the exploitation of the musician. If I had to work till 4 A.M., picking up casuals in gangster-run joints and living in Harlem or in a filthy pad in the New Village east of 2nd Avenue, I wouldn't take heroin, I'd take prussic acid.

Clellon Holmes's *The Horn* is as good a novel as has been written about jazz. Partly it's based on Lester Young's life—but it doesn't hold a candle to the facts. Cast as a novel, the true story of misery and exploitation would not have been believable. Lester Young was no more neurotic nor "insecure" than a good many painters and poets of his generation, Negro or white, but he is dead and they are still alive. What killed him was a working environment with which no artist but the most powerful could be expected to cope. I met Bird when he started out, and, as they say, a nicer young fellow you'd never want to meet.

What is the answer? I don't think the concert hall is the answer. Jazz is essentially, whatever the cool boys thought, an audience-participation art. The only place I have ever seen musical excitement so directly communicated as by Ornette Coleman in the crowded Five Spot was in a sand shuffle in a country dance in Little Egypt. Performing out here in California a few months later at the Monterey Jazz Festival, the whole group showed signs of acute unhappiness—the vital connection with the audience was gone. Some jazz survives the concert or the jazz festival. It seldom seems to matter to Count where the band is playing, the old gismo flows out regardless. But the concert hall could not have produced Count Basie. Moten, Basie, even Mary Lou came out of as close, as all-involving, an audience relationship—the intense and special dance halls and joints of the old Kansas City circuit—as ever was Congo Square.

Almost by definition the good clubs—the "jazz rooms"—in the States are those that book the Modern Jazz Quartet, Coleman, Coltrane, Mingus. This is not because these are modernist musicians, but because, by and large, a club that books them has an audience primarily interested in music. How many such clubs are there? Damn few, and even some of them are not all that good. Some of them are just night clubs that graduated into jazz rooms without the owners ever realizing it.

I would like to see the revival of the old-time cabaret of the 1900's. Plenty of room between the tables. Good food—not just packets of stale sandwiches to get by the law, but real high cuisine. Really fine wines and imported beers and a de-emphasis on hard liquor—or better, "limited license." No bar whatsoever. Waiters, or at least fully clothed, well mannered waitresses . . . that you have to call to get served. In other words—no pushing at all. Put the nut on the door. Floor show, if necessary, to match the quality of the jazz. There's plenty of this stuff now—Dick Gregory, Moms Mably, Les Frères Jacques, Greco, Montero, Severin Dardan and that group that played the Second City recently—imagine a prestidigitator who took rabbits out of people's ears babbling along like Mort Sahl. . . . Imagine a Negro girl singing songs like those of Apollinaire, Queneau, Prévert, MacOrlan, Carco—the stuff that made Greco famous. Why don't American poets write songs like that? Of course blues singers, too. But a bill that automatically reduces the audience to the kind of people the best jazz is for anyway. John Coltrane is not for drunks.

Of course, there already are a few clubs like that—most of them, significantly, not in New York—The Crystal Palace in St. Louis, the *hungry i* in San Francisco (there are several more in San Francisco), the Second City in Chicago. They are fairly expensive, and they don't feature jazz, but they could, or new places like them could. One of the most important things to my mind is to get the take off the drinks and put it on the door. Another, perhaps more important, is some sort of physical arrangement worked out with the authorities that control the sale of liquor so that older teenagers can have a section where they can drink pop or coffee, eat, and listen. The Blackhawk had a good setup here in San Francisco, but one day, without warning, they got knocked over by the town clowns.

The cops were unjust to the Blackhawk, but you can't expect a copper to know any better. They are right in thinking the average night club is no place for a teenager. It's no place for me either. And it is no place for a musician who considers himself a creative artist.

The Institutionalization of Revolt, The Domestication of Dissent

About six or seven years ago I was sitting in a bosky cocktail lounge off Mad Alley with an account executive or whatever they call them from MCA, who was trying to sign me up with the firm as a package—entertainer, lecturer, writer, TV personality, maybe actor. I was being kindly but positively negativistic. He said, "Rexroth, you don't know what you've got. You're riding the crest of the wave. Do you realize that within a year dissent is going to be the hottest commodity along The Street?"

I realized it. But as time passed and it realized itself, I realized I hadn't really realized it at all. I doubt if anybody was prepared for what happened. No one was expecting a new kind of meretriciousness, the kitsch of pseudo-alienation, to become the popular mass culture of the next decade. I thought I was. I gave talks and wrote articles mentioning such a possibility. But I always spoke in terms of precedents—comic tricksters like Dali, nihilists of the good thing like Hemingway, country house weekend revolutionaries and later disillusioned revolutionaries like Auden and Spender, Kierkegaard at PR-Time cocktail parties, all the factitiousness of the compromised.

There is a difference. Hemingway was certainly a thoroughly conventional personality—anyone who could sit for five minutes in Harry's Bar or spend a weekend in that hotel on Torcello is indisputably a square. His tough guy code was bluster and bullying, he was the model and idol of a generation of junior executives, especially the type Yale Man or *Time* editor, but he had talent and a

Published in Arts in Society, *Spring 1963, not previously collected.*

certain tragic feeling. Dali, of course, was master of the false technical polish of the old-fashioned commercial artist and a master
clown. Most of the other professional révoltées who became part of
the Establishment in the interbellum period were not nihilists at all
but disappointed socialists. Furthermore, they were most apparently
members of the clerkly caste—gentlemen of a sort, with well-bred
education, well-bred nerves, and a gentleman's modicum of taste.

In fact, the whole course of alienation, up through the Second
War, was a secession of the clerks from the middle class. One note
that runs through all the literature of revolt, from Baudelaire to
W. H. Auden is de-provincialization. In Emma Bovary and the
Ibsen girls it is obvious. When Sinclair Lewis came to set Emma or
Norah in a Minnesota village, as far as he could see that is all his
models were about.

Whenever the great rich gave the artist his head, accepted his
values, he was perfectly content. The Countesses de Naoilles, the
Princesse de Polignac, Peggy Guggenheim, the Crosbys, Lady Cunard and her odd daughter—the list, as they say, could be extended
indefinitely. These were not only the great patronesses of the period
between two wars; they were themselves very much a part of High
Bohemia. This was by no manner of means the old aristocrat-
courtly clerk relationship. Although some of these ladies had titles
they were all simply Grandes Bourgeoises, most of them of American birth.

As Wyndham Lewis pointed out long ago, this was Erewhon,
Utopia, the Land of Cockaigne, where the Revolution was over and
it was from each according to his ability, and unto each according
to his needs. It had its nastinesses, but once he was accepted, the
artist ignored them. He had been inducted into the ranks of the
civilized. What spleen he had left could be vented on the vulgar—
those outside.

The Romantic Credo may have presented the artist, and especially the poet, as prophet, as the permanent, irreconcilable critic of
society. There is almost no evidence to support this claim. Prophets,
like madmen or albinos, arise in all walks of life. Actually a personality like Blake is much more likely to be found among self-
educated skilled mechanics than among intellectuals, and of course
this is what Blake really was, a professional engraver who lived by

the sweat of his brow, almost the only self-supporting artist or poet of the entire Romantic tradition.

The battle with the nineteenth-century middle class was a battle over questions of taste, technical questions. To an Eskimo, let alone a Martian, there is singularly little to choose between Bourguereau and Gauguin or Béranger and Rimbaud. This is really what Oscar Wilde was saying over and over to the ruling class: "I am one of you; my morals and life values differ in no wise from yours. If you will just accept the judgment of myself and my friends in your interior decoration we will be glad to stop annoying you." This, too, is exactly what the new generation is saying to Chairman Khrushchev. They will win, because despots need the arts, and need them kept up to date, and artists, as all history teaches us, flourish under despotisms.

It is curious that the artist seldom appears in the ranks of the civilized. Henry Adams as a personality was not unique but typical. There are thousands of families like the Adamses in America, but they do not produce writers very often. It was his articulation that was special in Adams' case. Articulation in America, but in England and France as well, appears at the hot spot of a pressure point. It appears in that area of intense conflict and constant tension set up around the lower middle class Protestant family.

I grew up in the Jazz Age. I went to the dances at Merry Gardens and played spin the bottle at children's parties. Coming home one night to my Near North Side studio, I met my first wife, a young anarchist abstract artist. What happened to all these people? They did not replenish themselves, not in the arts. Today, just as in my day or my parents', the artists and their parasites, the Bohemians, come from small Middle Western towns and were spanked if they spent their Sunday School nickels for ice cream. What ever happened to the children of the people who drank bathtub gin, danced the Charleston, read H. D. and slept around?

The answer is simple. They grew up and went off and lived. They didn't have to write or paint. It had already been done for them.

The point I am making is that the artist of the long Romantic Agony was not rejecting society by any manner of means. He was simply demanding that it let him in, demanding that caste privilege decide certain technical questions which had been his by immemorial tradition. Today, by and large, and for better or worse, he has that caste position, that right, that technical expertise and competence.

Nothing is sillier than the benighted amateur sociologists of the literary quarterlies who think this struggle is still going on. "Kitsch, Masscult, Midcult." What on earth is the man talking about? What decade is he living in? He is terribly upset that Virginia Woolf and E. M. Forster are not read in the station wagon and cooperative apartment set. Oh, but they are. Not much, but still, some. What upsets the *Partisan Review* people, really, is that their own middlebrow taste, still clung to in spite of Hell and hydrogen bombs, never made it from the days when they were young. There is nothing more out of date than an out-of-date middlebrow. I know, it's terribly sad that people don't feel about Rachmaninoff and Edith Wharton and Derain the way they did when Dwight MacDonald was young, but they don't.

On the other hand, I can remember when the only Bach you could get without ordering the records from His Master's Voice in Canada was the "Air for the G-String." Today there is more Buxtehude and Machaut and Gesualdo coming out every season than I can keep track of. I used to lug home from the library the immense volumes of Tudor Church Music and pore over the scores. Today I am up to my ears in polyphony. Hot sellers on *Marlboro's* mail order list are Klee and Mondrian. The day when the classics have the wide circulation in America that Ezra Pound longed for in his poems has long since come. True, although Homer is a best seller with every paperback publisher that prints him, people don't read Dwight MacDonald's friends like they'd ought to. I mean, like they dig Thelonius Monk—they got Saul Bellow in school.

American culture by now has become omnivorously eclectic and at the same time immensely creative. It is Kitsch, it is Mass, it is Mid, but a great deal of it, consumed by all economic levels, is quite High indeed. What is happening is that the population is sorting itself out, sensibility wise. There is something for everybody. You like sadistic movies with Eisenstein angles? You like baroque flute? You like proletarian novels? You like found sculpture? You like metaphysical verse? We got it. It isn't as meretricious as it is so easy to make it sound. In fact, it is not meretricious at all, but it is certainly part of an immense, inexhaustible market, the child of the New Leisure and the GI Bill. This illimitable market can absorb anything, and does. It took about one year to absorb its professed irreconcilable enemies.

It is true, of course, that the role of enemy of society is a difficult one to play. Society cannot be escaped all that easily. It is not just that St. Simon Stylites is fed by hysterical rich women—society produces the social critic as a regulatory mechanism. As it also in fact so produces the revolutionary and the militant trade unionist. I once at a literary luncheon upset Mr. Vance Packard by asking him if he ever thought of himself as a hygienic functionary of the market he criticizes. Partly, of course, people like Packard and Galbraith are just narrow-minded Puritans. It annoys them that in a Keynesian economy considerable sums should be frittered away on hula hoops. They are outraged that women spend more time and money painting their faces than they do educating their children. Alas, life since at least the Neolithic revolution was always thus.

So the socialist and trade union movements in the West have functioned in reality—not just as governors to insure that steam is let off when the pressure gets too high, not just as what are now called "fail safe" devices, though they certainly are that—but as essential parts of the motive organization of capitalism, more, in other words, like carburetors that insure there will be just the right mixture of fuel and air for each new demand on the engine.

Most of the literature of alienation and revolt, as well as obviously that of social criticism properly so called—for instance Sinclair's *The Jungle*—has served the same purposes all through the nineteenth and the first half of the twentieth century. We forget that Baudelaire or Rimbaud or Jarry not only wrote, they were read, and by large numbers. Who modeled themselves on the dandy and immoralist created by Baudelaire? The *jeunesse dorée* of the Second Empire. Who laughed uproariously at the antics of that petty bourgeois upstart Père Ubu? Other bourgeois who had learned to tell a Chateau Haut Brion from a Pommard, a Corot from a Poussin. Society can absorb almost anything that purports to attack it. Usually its organ of digestion is what is called "Society" in caps in the newspapers. Its masticatory apparatus is that caste Riesman has ironically called "engineers of taste." These people can chew up anything into a fashionable cud. The most fashionable vulgarizer of philosophy in contemporary France wrote a book of insufferable priggery about Baudelaire, not because he really objected morally to Baudelaire, but because Baudelaire was going out of date. In his place he put the world's dullest psychotic windbag, Sade. Sade was frightfully fashionable for a while and his works could be found in very bourgeois homes, unread like the family Bible. You object to the word *bourgeois*? What do you think the bourgeoisie are like? George Babbitt? Tommy Manville was certainly neither an aristocrat nor a proletarian, nor is Dave Rockefeller, nor, for that matter were the first Medicis.

It is this nihilistic total rejection of modern society which is relatively new—new at least in its intensity, pervasiveness and almost immediate acceptance as a fad by the very people against whom it was directed. Dope, Dadaism, and destruction are domesticated today and part of all well-appointed middle class decor, like the antimacassar, the platform rocker and the *Idylls of the King,* were among the same class a century ago.

Movements like Cubism and Post-Impressionism were special revaluations of the humanist tradition. Today we realize that they were only aspects of the long classical movement in Western art which reflects one pole of the personality of European man. The veriest school child today knows that Picasso's "Red Tablecloth" is solidly based on Poussin and Raphael. Does he indeed? Only if he minded his lessons. Actually the constant reorganization of historic values that has characterized the evolution of art since 1860 has been totally misinterpreted by most laymen, especially by lecture-trotting and gallery-haunting laywomen with their heads full of art dealers' nonsense and their purses full of money. To them it has all been like crazy, man, or isn't it simply adorable—an onslaught on all civilized values as such. Today these are the people who buy the pictures, subscribe to the art magazines, and appoint the directors of art museums and art schools. If you tell them that there is no important difference in purely painterly means and intent between Jackson Pollock and Tintoretto or Mondrian and Vermeer, they think you are being funny. They think they are like Charlie Parker and Duke Ellington. That, of course, is quite possible too, but first one must know what these two musicians are like.

After the First World War a tremendous revulsion swept over the world. In the arts as in politics, those who were felt to be morally or ideologically responsible for the catastrophe were turned on by the young with violence and loathing. The whole structure of liberal humanitarianism was not only called into question; organized groups and disorganized individuals everywhere attacked it with dynamite.

The average man in Russia, whether worker or peasant or intellectual, was convinced he had been betrayed and was sick with disgust. The Bolsheviks were able to organize this revulsion into an antiliberal, antihumane political regime, and it was precisely the rejection of the humanistic values of German Social Democracy that attracted the young to the nationalist and proto-Nazi movements.

In the arts, Dadaism was the popular and sensational expression of this rejection and alienation. The artist who exhibited a log of wood with an axe attached, and the legend, "If you don't like this piece of sculpture, you dirty bourgeois, make one of your own," or the other who wanted to mount a loaded pistol pointing out from a frame, with a card attached to the trigger, *"Tirez s'il vous plaît!"*—these people did not believe the academy was reactionary; they believed it was lethal, and organized society along with it. And it should be remembered that they included in the academy the "modernists" who were their slightly older contemporaries, although they were to convert some of them (for instance, Picabia) for a while and influence others permanently.

Years later, Allen Ginsberg was to write one of his funniest lines, "who threw potato salad at CCNY lecturers on Dadaism," with no foreknowledge that he would himself shortly be part of the pseudo-Dada academy. But that is what happened. The nihilism and disorder (the technical term is anti-nomianism) which arose from the broken heart of Europe in 1918 has become a gimmick, peddled in all the academies of the world, a do-it-yourself kit complete with instruction book in thirty languages and pictographs for the boys with rising expectations who haven't mastered any alphabet as yet.

In 1918 the price was a broken heart. Today it doesn't cost a thing; it is one of the perquisites—or is it prerequisites?—of the Welfare State. Drop a card to UNESCO.

A couple of years back, my friend Léon-Gabriel Gros, editor of *Cahiers du Sud* and feature writer for the Marseille daily, *Le Provençal*, came up to see me in Aix, all agog. He was going to what was still French Equatorial Africa, on a story. He'd never been that far south and was very excited about the new culture being created by the lads with rising expectations, due to be liberated in a month or so. "Look," he said, "here in the Conakry paper it says they are having an exhibition of the local art students. I wonder what it will be like? I'm curious to see how the new generation is transmuting their heritage from the great tradition of African sculpture."

"Un-hunh," I said, "Gaby, you're very naive. I bet you 2000 francs it will be indistinguishable from the Rue de Seine, 10th Street, or the California School of Fine Arts."

Two weeks later he showed up for lunch with a large portfolio. Out of it, he took with a grin, six watercolors, done by a boy at lycée in Conakry, a boy whose father had been sentenced for cannibalism. They were mules, an infertile cross between Deborah Remington and Sam Francis. "Spengler was right!" said he.

In America after the Second War, there was a period of unbridled nihilism in official life, symbolized by the late Senator McCarthy, and objectified in the dragging futility of the Korean War. Nihilism in the power structure is immediately reflected in nihilism in the intellectuals, as in nineteenth-century Russia. The mirror image of Senator McCarthy is Jack Kerouac. The significant thing about this phenomenon is precisely that it is not rejection, alienation; it is specifically reflection. The Beat evaluation of American life is exactly that of the most extreme reactionaries; it's just that the plus and minus signs have changed places.

Read the Beat novelists on most any subject: their opinions differ in no wise from those of the squares with whom they are engaged in a tug of war. The two parties are pulling on opposite ends of a rope which even the most moderately sophisticated are aware does not exist. This is especially clear in the immense Beat and Hipster literature of the Negro. This is, in every detail, the Negro as believed in by Senator Eastland; it's just that the hippies like them that way. There is a well-known novel laid in San Francisco, but which in fact took place in New York. It is about a Negro dancer and drug addict, a Bohemian avatar of an African cannibal priestess with a bone through her nose and a coiffure of blood, cow dung and clay, shaking her primary and secondary sexual characteristics to the savage and inchoate rhythms of jungle drums while the missionary soup comes to a boil. I happen to know this girl. She is a modest little social worker who met the novelist when he was in the last stages of alcoholic collapse and took pity on him for a few days. True, she takes dancing at the New School For Social Research, but so does every other social worker under sixty within commuting distance of New York City. The jungle drums were in fact Charles Mingus' band, a group of disciples of unboiled missionaries like Stravinsky, Schoenberg, Boulez and Bartok.

Jazz, Negroes—the same story is repeated in the hippy's craze for Zen Buddhism. This is the fatuous and flatulent Inscrutable Wisdom of the Ancient East which has been peddled for a century by what are known in show business as Ragheads, on what is known in *Variety* as the Menopause Circuit. This is simply the craze for dime store orientalism of the club women immortalized by the late Helen Hokinson mixed up with a little pornography. But, in fact, go to one of these swami-led gatherings advertised in the newspapers on Saturday, held in a deteriorated office building or a sample room in a third-rate hotel. Mix with the effeminate men and middle-aged women who make up the congregation. I guarantee you will get more, and more attractive, invitations to commit the sin of impurity for mystical reasons than you will in a Greenwich Village coffee bar, even in one on the East Side in the New Village.

Again, the same story: the immoralism of the new aliénées is the immoralism of any country club; it flourishes among the badminton courts, the swimming pools, and the ranch wagons. And there it is more fun; the women are washed, the liquor is better, and there is much, much, less guilt to spoil the pleasure. Note that the appurtenances are the same—leotards and tights, carefully bleached and torn blue jeans, olive drab sneakers with holes in just the right places, "flower arrangements," hi-fi as loud and expensive as can be managed, "found sculpture" in the tokonoma, or maybe a bit of spontaneous calligraphy painted by the hostess under the influence of peyote. The Beat pad reaches its total realization among the $75-an-hour Bohemians of the canyons back of Beverly Hills or in the apartments of the top personalities of Madison Avenue.

This is true even of dope. The leading magazine of the Beatniks is difficult to distinguish from a house organ for a pharmaceutical house, financed by Chicago money; it is hard to believe it isn't a giveaway put out by the Mafia. There is only one trouble with this: the dope fiends of Beat literature are a square's idea of dope fiends. There is, of course, no such thing as a dope fiend; drugs don't have that effect at all. The drug addict is in fact nothing like this at all. He isn't like anything in particular, and this is his distinguishing characteristic—that the nonuser cannot distinguish him. As an old friend of mine, one of the original bop musicians and one of the most creative, once said to me, apropos of this matter, "Back in the days when I was a dope fiend, we were under the impression the fewer people knew about it the better. Now these boys show up for their television dates equipped with hypodermic and opium pipes."

What has produced this ridiculous charade of revolt amongst the most compromised members of our society? The same thing that has produced similar phenomena on an international political scale—idleness and rising expectations. Society has always produced a lumpen-proletariat. Today the ill-housed, ill-fed, ill-clothed, and illiterate live in glass houses, take lysergic acid, wear leotards, and send their children to progressive schools that specialize in Free Love for infants. We now have a lumpen-intelligentsia and a new kind of lumpen-bourgeoisie.

We complain today about the quality of our higher education. The fact is that the colleges swarm with youngsters from homes in which there has never been a book. An appreciable number of them are educable, but a large number are not and would be happier by far if they had never been taught to read and write. In the vast conspiracy of organized mediocrity that has been called, mistakenly, the Power Elite, they can go far. They can gain money, leisure; they can even be taught to go through the motions of having taste, as apes can be taught to ride bicycles. They can assume unlimited authority as long as it does not entail responsibility. However awe inspiring their titles and office furniture, they are the technological and professional fellahin of an epoch of lazers and mazers and transistors. Often, when they are young and fresh they give a reasonable imitation of their betters, but as their tissues age and their neurons lose resilience, the patterns of their progenitors reassert themselves.

The critical situations that brought forth new responses pass and the past returns. Solomon Reinach once said that the style of barbaric Iron Age Europe lay just below the surface of all Western Art since the fall of Rome; anything that breaks the neoclassic veneer reveals La Tene and Hallstadt. Always there, ready to reproduce the familiar patterns, the Celt and Gaul wait on the Greco-Roman humanist. Pareto called it "the congelation of the aggregates," a conglomeration of polysyllables sufficiently barbarous in itself to reveal something about Pareto.

Marx long ago in controversy with Bakunin pointed out that the lumpen-proletariat—which Bakunin, with what again Marx called his furor aristocraticus—idealized, were just impotent and impoverished bourgeois. So it is only natural that when this class rises to affluence and finds itself with a leisure on its hands for which it has no preparation, it should immediately start to behave as its parents thought the leisure class behaved, out of sheer idleness. *Sex and the Single Girl* is a splendid example of what happens when a Mandarin ethic falls into the hands of a person who has no birthright in the caste of Mandarins. This is upper-class morality as seen through the eyes of the scandal sheets and the shop girls' magazines. It's just that the working girl wants some too, and now is in a position to get it. So we get revolutionaries carefully acting out the roles attributed to the revolutionaries by *Time* magazine or the Chicago *Tribune,* poets who behave the way chiropractors and Baptist preachers in small isolated Iowa villages believe poets behave. Sugar Hill and Greenwich Village Negroes who suddenly start acting just the way the White Citizens' League says Negroes act. Madison Avenue long since discovered that all you have to do is create an Image; somebody will show up immediately to exemplify it.

There is only one trouble with this: these people breed. They fill suburbs and exurbs and cooperative apartments; they fill colleges and schools and PTAs; they pay taxes and vote. This means that they have the power to force themselves into strategic positions and to exert mass pressures. So today a college professor brings out a cramming syllabus on the Beat Generation. "Compare Allen Ginsberg with Antonin Artaud. Compare Denise Levertov with Christina Rossetti. Gregory Corso is: (A) a street in Rome; (B) a Beat poet; (C) a part played by the late George Raft. Marijuana is: (A) poison;

(B) a fun thing; (C) a stimulus to creativity . . . and so on." All well-appointed art schools give courses in found sculpture with weekly visits to the City Dump. Ph.D.'s at Juilliard join the Black Muslims. Jazz singers with one-sixteenth Negro blood throw away their hair straightener and found Back to Africa movements and lecture before suburban white women's clubs. Perhaps worst of all is music. Here the omnipotence of stereotyped modernism from serialism to John Cage is so absolute that never a peep or a squeak, not even an electronic one, breaks the overpowering total roar of the dullest sounds ever emitted on the earth by man, beast, or machine. The academic sterility of a contemporary music contest must be experienced to be believed, as anyone who has ever judged such will tell you.

What can be done about it? Nothing. For a long period the Prince Consort and the Empress Eugenie were arbiters of Europe's most cultivated taste. As they used to say in Anglo-Saxon, "That passed away; this will too."

Why Is American Poetry
Culturally Deprived?

André Malraux is famous for the remark that American literature is
the only contemporary literature not written by intellectuals. He
points out that general ideas of any subtlety or profundity are
unknown to all major American novelists, poets, and dramatists.
Partly of course this judgment was motivated by Malraux's own
taste. The only writers acceptable to him are Faulkner, Hemingway,
Tennessee Williams, Raymond Chandler, Dashiell Hammett, the
militantly mindless. In fact, shortly after the war, both Malraux and
Roger Caillois happened to have said to me that they considered
somebody named "Orass Mikwa" America's most significant writer.
It was some time before I figured out that this was the semi-literate
pulp magazine writer of the blood-on-the-bikini school, Horace
McCoy.

Nevertheless, Malraux's judgment is substantially correct. I have
known the leading exponents of all the movements in American
poetry which presumed ideological motivation, that at least attempted to assume the language of those general ideas which were
part of the storm and stress of international thought. Without
exception, these ideas came to their poet exponents only through
the most superficial literary journalism, were never comprehended,
either the simple elements or their consequences, and were never in
fact acted upon. Let me detail this. Carl Sandburg could stand as an
example of the Social Democratic and Populist writers of 1910, a
colleague of Richard Dehmel and Émile Verhaeren and Romain

Published in Arts in Society, *1963,* Tri-Quarterly, *Winter, 1967, and collected in* The Alternative Society, *1970.*

Rolland. Sandburg is usually considered to have bankrupted himself as an artist by betraying these ideas when America entered the First War. The fact is he didn't have any ideas to betray. His attitude towards "the people" was a compound of Chicago police-court reporter sentimentality, Midwest smalltown Populist oratory, and Hull House maidenly magnanimity. The picture of the young Sandburg breathlessly following the debates in the international Socialist movement over Bernstein's Revisionism, the Millerand crisis, Luxemburg and Kautsky disputing the questions of imperialism and the falling rate of profit is so ridiculous it is not even laughable.

The Modernist movement in verse, from the Imagists to the old masters of modern verse, first extensively published in Alfred Kreymborg's *Others*, the period of *Broom* and *The Little Review*, was a movement of technical reform of syntax and a cleaning up of the vocabulary of poetry. It has often been compared to the Symbolist movement in France. None of these poets, with the exception of Amy Lowell, John Gould Fletcher, Walter Conrad Arensberg, Ezra Pound, Wallace Stevens, William Carlos Williams, and T. S. Eliot, read European poetry or knew anything about it. In their French classes in college the last poet in the course had been Jules Laforgue. Therefore, insofar as they paid attention to their lessons, he represented for them the last word in French modernism. He died in 1887. He still represents the last word in French modernism for American academic versifiers. The profound revolutions of the sensibility, the climactic changes in the soul of modern man, so-called, which began with Baudelaire, Kierkegaard, Newman, Dostoyevsky, and Nietzsche and which represent in fact a systematic destructive criticism of the foundations of humanism and humanitarianism, and which have thrown up in the course of their ever-accelerating liquidation all the anti-humane art movements and philosophies of our time, were, to judge from the evidence, totally incomprehensible to the American imitators of their stylistic innovations—even at the remove of fifty years. It should never be forgotten that H. D. was a contemporary of the Dadaists. French and German literature was falling to pieces with heartbreak. The veriest schoolboy in Europe, as Lord Macaulay used to say, knew that civilization had betrayed itself. H. D. was dedicating herself to cleaning and brightening the idiom of the Sapphic poets, Michael Field and Renée Vivien. Over against such much abused esthetes there was only Midwest Populism, whose intellectual foundations never rose higher than an editorial in a Des Moines newspaper. Out of the ranks of what were to become the Classic Modernists, two young men from the remote hinterland rose in revolt, T. S. Eliot and Ezra Pound. Pound most emphatically was not a member of the international community of letters, any more than any other emigré café sitter, then or now. Drinking Pernod on the sidewalk of the Dôme then, or the Flore now, never made Pound a cubist nor has it, if you will forgive the French word, made any "foundation bum" an *existentialiste*. Pound was under the impression that his café companions, Max Elskamp and Georges Fourrest, were the leaders of French poetry. This, at the height of the careers of Reverdy, Éluard, Aragon, with Apollinaire only dead a year. Eliot, on the other hand, did attach himself to an international community—the movement of virulent obscurantism and clerical fascism led by Henri Massis and Maurras and given voice in *L'Action française.* It should not be forgotten that the real reason for the international failure of this movement was that it was so reactionary that practical politicians like Hitler and Mussolini found it unusable. When *L'Action française* said, "We are not interested in the opinions of an obscure Jewish carpenter who met a disgraceful death two thousand years ago, but in restoring to France the order and glory [*gloire*—a bit of French slang recently restored to currency] of Richelieu and Mazarin," the Holy Office excommunicated them by telegram. This is not an idle, an unsubstantiated accusation against Mr. Eliot. He is not only on record as being an anti-Semite, but on record as being in favor of eliminating the Jews, and a surprising number of the French contributors to *The Criterion* ended up in the dock as war criminals.

Now, it so happens that if any international community recruited English and American poets in the interbellum period, it was fascism—Pound, Yeats, Eliot are on record. This is not because American poets are exceptionally vicious men, although some of them are and have been. It is simply because fascism is so much more easily assimilated by simple and emotionally unstable minds—you don't have to read so many books. As the economic

depression deepened and their betters began talking about economics, most of this generation of American poets became money
cranks, followers of the Social Credit theories of Major Douglas.
This is an ancient American foolishness. I don't doubt for a moment
but what as the fur market moved inexorably westward to Michilli-
makinac, the Grand Sachems of the Iroquois believed they could
call it back by fooling with the wampum. Funny-moneyism is
precisely a symptom of the incorrigible provinciality of small-town
debtors in the American Outback. When the actual levers of power
are so remote as to be unimaginable, their victims always resort to
sympathetic magic. Although Mr. Eliot is reputed to have worked
in a bank, it didn't help. No one used to handling general ideas, no
one familiar with elementary facts of, to use a sound but old-
fashioned term, political economy, as those facts and general ideas
work themselves out in the real affairs of men, would ever fall for
such flimsy nonsense as Major Douglas's Social Credit.

Like a faint chorus of young birds in the nest, echoes of Mr. Eliot's principled reaction suddenly were heard amongst the moon-
shine of the Southern Hills. Mr. Ransom, Mr. Tate, and their
friends at Vanderbilt, meeting in the parlor of a Greek letter fraternity, launched the frail vessel of American reaction. Alas, the cargo
was too slight for even so puny a ship. Mr. Eliot's *The Criterion*,
carried on its manifest bales of Massis, Maurras, and Maritain, as
reinterpreted by Fernandez, Saurez, and Bernard Fay, and Pareto
and Major Douglas reinterpreted by Ezra Pound and Wyndham
Lewis, and the Almighty as reinterpreted by the followers of Gurdjieff. Mr. Tate, and Mr. Ransom, could manage no more than the
ideological residues of *Red Rock* and *The Clansman*. True, there
was vague echo of the Physiocrats but an echo bounced off the
surface of the thinker of the Fugitives' new agrarian group, a professor who seems to have been a ghost writer for a number of leading
Southern personalities from Governor Long and Senator Bilbo to
Governor Wallace. This is as near as serious thought amongst
American poets ever came to the international discussions which
raged throughout the interbellum period about the role of the élite,
the threats of mass culture, the relations of town and country.

Many of these people were connected with the absurd Humanist
movement of the pre-crisis Twenties. Today it is obvious that this

was just a power drive on the part of a number of young academicians to recapture book-reviewing jobs from the Populist disciples of H. L. Mencken, who threatened to monopolize them. It was successful, but unimportant in the arena of world thought.

Throughout the period of proletarian literature, I never knew a Communist poet who was able to read through the first, much less the third volume of *Capital*. It was looked upon as a dry, dull, exclusively technical book. Of course, what's wrong with it is its highly emotional rhetoric and its elementary sleight-of-hand mathematics. God knows, it's absorbing enough reading, as absorbing as the Isaiah to which it has often been compared, but the Marxists of the Thirties judged Marx as the contributors to *Commentary* of the Fifties judged Isaiah—dry, dull, excessively technical. American poets just don't read non-fiction.

Since the Second War the literary quarterlies which started out under an alliance of Southern reactionaries and ex-Trotskyites have, it is true, tried to give their readers some inkling of some of the intellectual currents in the maëlstrom of post-war European thought. This has meant, pretty much, Existentialism, but with the exception of Lionel Abel, no poet has contributed to this discussion. What is more significant, not a single autochthonous idea has come up in the literary quarterlies of the post-war period. We live in a time of continuous revaluation. It is a time when it seems less and less possible to do anything overtly and therefore a time given over to relentless subjective subversion. There is no sign of this revaluation in America—our think pieces in our leading intellectual quarterlies never rise above the *ABC of Zen Buddhism, What Is Existentialism, How to Appreciate the Theatre of the Absurd in Easy Lessons for Small-Town Clergymen, Over-read Clubwomen, and Candidates for Ph.D.'s*. Modern thought is haunted by a sense of crisis. We live in an eschatological age. This sense of crisis is not new. It began in the 1840's. But for the past two generations there has solidified a tradition of crisis-thinking which is now almost universal, a true universe of discourse from which no one seems to be able to escape. Niccolo Hartmann, Scheler, Berdyaev, Buber, Tillich, Marcel, Mounier—these men are in fact anti-Existentialist, but even they are swept up in the general mass movement of anguish and anxiety, I have never met an American poet who was familiar with Jean-Paul Sartre's attempts at philosophy, much less with the gnarled discourse of Scheler or Heidegger.

This is not quite true. Lionel Abel is an exception. He even went to Paris and met Jean-Paul Sartre personally, and for a year could be seen on the Boulevard St. Germain eavesdropping on his conversations with Simone de Beauvoir and Jean Wahl. There's only one trouble. Although he is a pretty good playwright, Lionel Abel is not a major poet. The same is true of Paul Goodman, who not only is part of the discourse of modern international thought, but who has certainly tried hard all his life to be an honestly original thinker. Again, he's not one of our most important poets. Similarly, in the Marxist epoch, John Brooks Wheelwright not only knew more about Marx than Earl Browder, he knew very much more about St. Thomas Aquinas than T. S. Eliot and Mortimer Adler rolled together. All three of these people, Goodman, Abel, Wheelwright—and the forgotten poet disciple of Wittgenstein, Lou Grudin—would be immensely important figures if they had written in French or even German or Italian. For over a generation, they have been the think tanks from which the editors of *The Partisan Review* drew their sustenance. They are, or were (Wheelwright is long dead), very dear friends of mine, but I would never claim them as America's leading poets.

The immense popularity of the Beats in Europe on both sides of the Iron Curtain is due to the fact that, although they may not reflect the eschatological emphasis of modern philosophy, they do reflect an emotional consciousness of the fact of apocalypse. What is the reason for this state of affairs? The answer is self-evident. From the death of Longfellow to the day Allen Ginsberg took off his clothes, the American poet was not an important factor in American life. He was not a factor at all. For this reason, the kind of young man who wished to participate in the decisions of his community went into business, engineering, or the professions. The boy who knew he could not or was afraid to participate wrote verse.

A generation or so ago the poet considered himself an outcast because he partook only minimally of the life of his society. Today he is very much an incast. Society has overtaken and surpassed him. Everybody gets very little out of life nowadays. The engineer who once went off in kepi, breeches, and puttees to build roads through the haunts of the headhunters now lives in a garden suburb, finds his sexual outlet in Saturday night dirty-movies parties, and for maximized living reads *On the Road* and subscribes to *The Evergreen Review*. His indistinguishable neighbor teaches creative poetry at the local college and writes slide-rule poems more indistinguishable still. What is wrong with the vast bulk of American society is that it is smug. The neurosis of the affluent society is not anxiety but *taedium vitae—accidie*—moral boredom.

Over the years since the First War there have been a number of poets who have given expression to certain general ideas of more or less social importance for our time. A list of them makes curious reading—Vachel Lindsay put into one-time immensely popular doggerel the mystic Midwest Populism that had come down from the communitarian experiments of the 1840's—Robert Owen and so on, and which found final expression in the sentimental manifestoes of Louis Sullivan and Frank Lloyd Wright. Eliot's *The Waste Land* is the only major work of "anxiety" in American poetry. Conrad Aiken was one of the very few writers anywhere before the Surrealists to attempt to use psychoanalysis as a basic philosophy of life. The Surrealists themselves were passionate evangelists of a dogmatic world view, which presumed to use art, in the words of André Breton, "to revolutionize the human sensibility as such." Eugène Jolas, the editor of *transition*, was a more learned man and a more ambitious thinker than Breton himself. Unfortunately, the whole program was fundamentally misconceived and resulted in poetry which today seems trivial and dull. The best long Surrealist poem by an American was Parker Tyler's *Granite Butterfly*. Reading it over today, it simply does not seem effective enough. Hart Crane's *The Bridge* failed precisely because of its total lack of intellectual content. Hart Crane certainly led a textured enough life. But what tortured him was inability to hold a job, unhealthy relations with his parents, inability to accept his own homosexuality gracefully, and alcohol. He was not tortured by any failure of life to provide him with significance. On the contrary, he was a rather simple-minded man, gusty and lusty with a great appetite for crude experience. His most ambitious poem is an impressive attempt to write again the patriotic epic exhortations of Walt Whitman. Insofar as it fails, it does so for no profound reason, but simply because

Hart Crane was not able to control his appetites. His intoxication with his own rhetoric defeats his gospel, and his poem is devoid of general ideas entirely. Other writers of long ruminative reveries (we used to call them philosophical epics) like Walter Lowenfels' *Some Deaths* or Louis Zukofsky's *A* or Charles Olson's *Maximus Poems*— in spite of all the avant-garde rhetoric—manage to say only quite conventional things. Of no one is this more true than of Gertrude Stein. A whole generation thought she must be deep because no one believed that anybody could take so much trouble to say such fatuous things as she seemed on the face of it to be saying. Late in life she suddenly started to write conventional English and revealed herself as possessed of the most extraordinarily ordinary intellectual endowment. Properly understood, she bears a strong resemblance to her contemporary, Edgar Guest. Who reflects the "age of anxiety" which is so much the concern of French intellectuals, German theologians, and American psychiatrists? W. H. Auden wrote a book called that. But W. H. Auden is English; his state of anxiety has conspicuously died down in the last few years, and he's considered very out of date. Leonard Bernstein wrote a symphony called *The Age of Anxiety* but I don't think the things that make him anxious could be classed as ontological *Angst*. It's perfectly true that George Barker, Dylan Thomas, Auden, David Gascoyne do give utterance to the kind of metaphysical terror which afflicts many people who confront the ultimate implications of the contemporary human condition. They are all British. Thomas is dead; the rest are middle-aged and not read by young English poets. "The Movement," so-called, which dominates English verse is not a movement at all. It is simply a reflection of the fact that English poets in recent years have, like their American counterparts, become well-paid professors of creative writing. Anything more flaccid and less creative it would be difficult to imagine. There are certain American poets, like Robert Lowell or Robert Creeley, whose work is haunted by anxiety, but this is, in each case, an individual psychological problem and very far from a judgment as to the meaning of life. This is the trouble with the most alienated of the Beats. Their alienation is a luxury product of the affluent society. They can afford to live in what Lawrence Lipton calls voluntary poverty (viz. no fourth TV set in the bathroom). Villon, Baudelaire, Van Gogh could not afford it and that's all the difference.

Does this mean that I think American poetry in the twentieth century is worthless? Quite the contrary. It serves society as it always has, as a symbolic criticism of value, but the values it concerns itself with are not those of philosophy or a metaphysics of the conscience. The one specifically philosophic American poet of the twentieth century has been Wallace Stevens and his work has been a kind of versification of the philosophy of George Santayana, of what Santayana called skepticism and animal faith. But Stevens' poetry is not of the great artistic merit that it is because it versifies Santayana. If that's what we want, it's better to go the original in Santayana's own prose. What is valuable about the poetry of Wallace Stevens is that it really does reorganize the human sensibility afresh in each poem in terms of quite simple elements of experience. This experience is never more profound than that accessible to the kind of man Wallace Stevens in fact was—a wealthy cultivated executive of a big insurance company.

So with William Carlos Williams, who for contemporary taste is the best of the generation of Classic Modernists. As a handler of general ideas, Williams is pathetic. As either aesthetic or epistemology, his favorite phrase, "No ideas but in things," is infantile. He thought of his great poem *Paterson* as a philosophic epic preaching precisely that profound philosophy. What it is, of course, is a profound organization of the life experience of a small-town doctor with all of a small-town doctor's infinite roots into a community into which he was born, practiced medicine, and never left except for vacations. To products of environments as troubled as those which produced Rilke, Mayakovsky, Paul Éluard, or Dylan Thomas, even the most tormented American poet must seem singularly content, but so it is.

Community Planning

Every month enough human beings to make a city the size of
Detroit are added to the world's population. In a few years it will be
a city the size of Chicago—every single month. The annual growth
of India's population is equal to the total population of Australia.

We are all aware of the population explosion, although with our
present economy of abundance and our still uncrowded country, we
are, most of us, only intellectually aware of it. And very few of us are
aware of how rapidly its effects are being felt in many parts of the
world. It is a pity that we can't travel in time and space and visit
Madras and Canton and Java in 1850, in 1900, and today. Those of
us who are old enough can at least compare life in our own cities, in
Paris and London and New York, a generation ago and today.

Man creates his own environment—and at an accelerated pace.
Create is hardly the word, so far he has simply made it, in the sense
in which we say, "Well, you've made your bed, now you'll have to
lie in it." It is obvious that it is on the verge, even in the richest and
most highly developed countries, of getting beyond him.

Most speculation about the dangers of the population explosion
are concerned with economic factors—especially with the dwindling food supply and the exhaustion of natural resources. There is
another, graver danger, the aesthetic danger. This may sound frivolous to some, but indeed it is not. On the organic, physiological,
neurological, emotional response of man to his environment depends his health as a species.

*First published as "Community Planning," an Introduction to Sergius I.
Chermayeff and C. Alexander,* Community and Privacy *(Garden City, N.Y.:
Doubleday, 1963). Collected in* The Alternative Society, *1970.*

We make fun of the word "togetherness" but there is nothing funny about the increasing failure of our own togetherness with ourselves and the rest of life on this planet. Ecology is the science of the togetherness of living things and their environment. Man is so radically altering the ecological situation out of which he emerged as a species, and altering it in such an irrational manner that he is endangering his own future.

If in the next century the world grows to five billion people (and at present rates it will grow to far more than that), all living in a hundred thousand or more Calcuttas and Harlems, it may be possible to feed everybody on tanks of algae in the cities, the farming of the sea, the synthesization of foodstuffs from minerals, and the growing of vast mountains of living meat in reservoirs of culture media, but something will have happened to the human species. If it survives under such conditions it will certainly survive only by beginning to turn into another kind of animal, and, from our point of view at least, not a very nice kind. We talk of the waning of the humanist tradition. It is specific humanness itself which is threatened. Montaigne or Sophocles could not flourish in present-day Jakarta. What are the beings that will be the fittest to survive when such communities have spread over the surface of the earth?

The probabilities are that man will discover ways to limit population during the next generation. Or perhaps the too probable nuclear war will solve the problem out of hand and reduce the population to a few millions in the Tropics and the Southern Hemisphere. Meanwhile, the inchoate spread of inhumane communities goes on. Urban renewal, what the French call *urbanisme*, suburbia, exurbia—aseptic slums proliferate.

We all remember the aquarium in our high-school biology class, where the colony of volvox grew over in one corner, in the spot of optimum light and temperature. Man is altering, as it were, the temperature and light and salinity of his own aquarium, irrationally, and with no knowledge of the possible results. Nobody knows what may happen.

Nature makes man. Man makes culture. Culture makes man. Man destroys nature. Consider the ecologically stable environment out of which man as a species probably developed. It must have been something like the climax formation of the Eastern United

States, a vast deciduous forest broken by parklands—only probably somewhat warmer. Where is that forest now? Does the present man-made environment of the Eastern United States bear any resemblance to it? How much of this kind of change can we stand? It is already greater than the ecological changes that set in in the late Jurassic and doomed the giant reptiles.

Archeologists and cultural anthropologists, and of course economists, often talk of culture as though it was just a mass of pots and arrowheads, ruined buildings, kinships, initiation ceremonies, food crops, value, price and profit—things and their relationships, sweeping inexorably through time, with no self-conscious chunks of human vitality around at all. Are we just vehicles for the evolution of our artifacts—which will eventually overwhelm and exterminate us?

This is the role of the architect, the landscape architect, the community planner—the creative reconstruction of our ecology. Today we have the knowledge and the techniques. It is perfectly possible to rebuild deliberately the human environment, in such a way that the ultimate result will be the widening and deepening of the life of the species as such, the augmenting increase of lifescope, aesthetic enrichment in the most profound sense. This, I suppose, is the only kind of "creative evolution" of which we are capable. But it is possible that we are capable of that.

This is the purpose of a book such as Serge Chermayeff's *Community and Privacy: Toward a New Architecture of Humanism.* What he is talking about is much more than the efficient organization of the shelter of a community. At least his discussion is posited on an unusually profound sense of the meaning of the word "efficient." Le Corbusier was wrong, a house is *not* a machine for living in. The ideal community structure—the actual fabric of buildings and land—should be like a culture medium, like the optimum part of the tank where the volvox flourished, a culture medium that stimulated and enriched, like a circumambient food, the creative responses of the community to its most human life.

We have a long tradition of community planning of this sort. We have a great deal of rather general or philosophical discussion. Geddes and Mumford are names known to every educated layman. But I know of few works that approach the problem so directly in terms of the actual physical structuring. What do we need for a biological optimum? How do we define these needs in terms of cubic feet of filled and empty spaces?

It would be easy to call Chermayeff's book a sort of exercise in human bio-technical engineering. It certainly is that, and masterfully so. It seems to me it is more than that. It is an exercise in creative or constructive humanism, but in a special sense. The guide here is such a work as Werner Jaeger's *Paideia*. We are to think in terms of a kind of higher hygiene—the planned ambience of the most abundant life.

What good will it all do? Can we possibly stop the avalanche of our own insensate constructions? I don't know. There are so many negative factors operating against the survival, let alone the evolution of the species, that the outlook is gloomy indeed. However, such books as Chermayeff's are a powerful force in the other direction. Who knows what single flicker of cosmic radiation once altered a gene somewhere back in geologic time and made all the difference? Certainly one book is a small but potent dose of creative evolution. Enough like it and the vast tides of our own biological history may, just may, turn.

The Heat

Recently police activity began to impinge upon my own life. I live in a San Francisco Negro district and I could see about me a noticeable increase—prowl cars were more evident at all times. On weekend nights they seemed to be everywhere, stopping and questioning many more people than formerly.

An art gallery was raided and welded sculpture illustrating the *Kama Sutra* was confiscated by the police. This was entirely a police action without civilian complaint. The police lost the case. Student parties in San Francisco's Haight-Ashbury district were raided again and again and everybody hauled off to jail. Even where the police claim to have found marijuana butts on the floor, the cases were usually dismissed. In New York two parties of the Artists' and Writers' Committee Against Vietnam, a group with no political affiliations, were raided without a warrant or complaint and several arrests made.

Friends of mine married to members of another race began to complain that they were frequently stopped by prowl cars and questioned when walking along the street with their spouses in broad daylight. After the Ginzburg decision there was a noticeable increase throughout the country in police censorship; in San Francisco bookshops were visited by police officers who told the proprietors, "Clean this place up or we'll take you in," but vouchsafed no information as to what books were in fact objectionable.

First published with the title, "The Fuzz," in Playboy, *July 1967. Rexroth's note in* The Alternative Society, *1970, read: "When this article appeared in* Playboy *they say the Boss Heat in San Francisco got me fired from three jobs at once, one of which I had held for almost ten years. Can I prove it? No. My informants 'refuse to testify.'"*

Certain costumes seem to be an open invitation to police questioning—beards, dirty jeans, bare feet, especially on juveniles, but more commonly still the uniform of the homosexual prostitute, the studbuster—T-shirt, leather jacket, tight jeans, heavy belt, boots. I began to get all sorts of complaints: a well-known jazz musician taking a breather in front of a perfectly respectable jazz room between sets and talking to his white wife was arrested, taken to the local station, held for two hours, insulted, and then let go. Another driving with his wife was arrested for a minor traffic violation, failure to signal a right-hand turn, and taken to the station.

No policemen had molested me in over forty years. I drink only wine at dinner. Marijuana has no effect on me. I haven't smoked it since adolescence. I am a very safe driver. However subversive my opinions, I am an exemplary law-abiding citizen. However, one night I parked my car in front of my own home, took my two daughters to the door, left my secretary in the car. When I returned the police, who obviously thought they were dealing with a racially mixed couple, had been questioning my secretary and because they hadn't liked the tone of her voice were writing a traffic ticket.

In the next block the same patrol had threatened a neighbor with arrest in a similar situation. A few blocks away a Negro youth leader had an appointment for lunch with a police officer. On the way to the lunch he was rousted by that very officer. A Negro high-school boy acting in a school play with my daughter was stopped as he was walking home from rehearsal along a well-lighted business street, rousted, and eventually forced to lie down on the sidewalk, but finally let go.

All of this happened in my immediate neighborhood, to people known to me, in one month. Yet San Francisco's police force is unquestionably one of the most professional in the country, with the extremely active community-relations detail led by a dedicated officer, an enlightened chief, lectures and classes on civil liberties, race relations, youth problems, and like matters. Reports in the press and from friends in other cities of increasing petty police harassment were far more shocking. It was apparent that The Heat was on—nationally. Why?

What exactly is The Heat and what turns it on? And why should it suddenly go on all over the country? The documentation of police brutality and violation of civil liberties in various cities about the country is staggering. But this is not what I want to write about.

In recent months there have been a number of magazine articles and serial newspaper features on "What's Wrong With the Police," and these have been answered in most cases by literate spokesmen for the police, not PR men, but working officers themselves. There's very little dialogue. One side makes flat accusations, usually well-documented, of police brutality, illegal entry or search, harassment, prejudice against the poor, racism, political reaction, third-degree, and other violations of the rights of those arrested. The other side simply denies that most of these things exist, and counters with the statement, "Police work is a profession with very special problems which the layman cannot understand any more than he can understand the special problems of medicine or law."

Both sides isolate the problem and treat the police as though they were members of a self-contained society—separate from the rest of us, like monks, professional soldiers, or the inmates of prisons and state hospitals. The problem is the functioning of the police as part of society, not as apart from it. Essential to any understanding is the definition of the roles that the police perform in the society in fact and the different roles which they are supposed to perform in theory, their own theories and those of their critics.

The following article recently appeared in *The Berkeley Barb*:

POLICE RAID NUDE FEST . . . LIKE "GANGBUSTERS"

Berkeley police with flashbulbs blazing ran swiftly through a gathering of about 40 nude men and women last Saturday. They were "investigating" possible lawbreaking at an East Bay Sexual Freedom League party. "It was like 'Gangbusters,'" EBSFL President Richard Thorne told BARB. "They came in very quickly and told us to hold it, stay where we were, and flashed cameras." The police searched the house and checked the I.D. of each guest. They stayed for about an hour, around midnight. "After I got dressed, I went to the lieutenant in charge and inquired on what grounds the police were present," Thorne said. "The lieutenant said that someone had issued a complaint which led them to suspect that there was the possibility of contributing to the delinquency of minors. 'Of what sort?' I asked him. He said, 'Alcohol'." Thorne and several other witnesses described the police investigation. Desks, chairs, bureaus, and clothes in closets were searched. Ashtrays were examined. Medicines were confiscated. Brown filipino cigarettes were peeled open. Guests who objected to showing their I.D.'s were given the choice of cooperating or being identified "at the station." At BARB presstime, no arrests had resulted from the investigation. One guest, who met a flashbulb as he emerged from the bathroom, described his conversation with the plain-clothesman who apparently admitted the other police:

"I asked him what had happened to give them the right to enter and search without a warrant.

"He said, 'Are you a lawyer?'

"I said, 'No.'

"'In that case, it's none of your business,' he said." Witnesses described the police demeanor as initially "rude," "sarcastic," "snide," and "up tight." As the hour passed, they "settled down" and became "mannerly" and "courteous," guests said. About 20 partygoers remained after the police departed. "Clothes came off again at a rapid rate after they left," one participant told BARB. "It was as if they wouldn't let the police intimidate them, and they wanted to release a pent-up rage. It became quite a party. A very fine, successful party."

Following the publication of this article I took it upon myself to question one of the members of the Berkeley Police Force regarding the matter. Our conversation was friendly and was not confined to the police raid although it covered the pertinent aspects. Pertinent portions of the interview were in sum and substance to this effect:

INTERVIEWER: What happened at the nude party?
POLICE OFFICER: Oh, we alleged that there were people below the age of 18 there but there weren't.
I: Did you really believe that there was someone below the age of 18?
P: No, we just used that as an excuse.
I: Well, what happened?
P: We busted into the place and there were several couples actually fornicating. So, we took some pictures and left.
I: What did you do with the pictures?
P: Oh, they're fun to pass around for all the boys to look at down at the station.
I: Isn't that illegal?
P: Well, I suppose so but they were having a nude party.
I: Didn't the attorney general of the state of California specifically say that nude parties were legal?
P: Oh, we know that there isn't anything illegal going on, but we feel that if you let this kind of thing happen it's like opening Pandora's Box.
I: Is the police department supposed to prescribe morals?

P: Somebody's got to.

I: Doesn't the Constitution of the United States specifically allow the citizenry to determine its own morals?

P: Well, you know how these things are.

I: Would you want the police busting into your home under these circumstances?

P: Well, I wouldn't be doing anything illegal.

I: Neither were they.

This example, however comic, poses the dilemma: the contradiction between the police as officers of order and officers of law. In the early days of the development of modern police forces perhaps their primary function was the preservation of social order and the enforcement of public morality. They dealt mostly with the poor, who, however unruly, accepted the same values. In a heterogeneous society such as America was in the days of massive immigration, most of the work of a patrolman on the beat in Hell's Kitchen, the lower East Side, Five Points, Back of the Yards, was extra-legal. He was not a law officer but a peace officer and if he invoked the law to handle all violations of public order he would have found himself hopelessly overwhelmed. Until recent years the Paris police force still operated this way in almost all their day-to-day work. The vicious, disorderly, the conspicuous violaters of common morals, were simply taken up an alley and "coated" with a weighted cape or worked over with a truncheon and kicked out on the street with a warning that if they were caught doing it again they'd get worse in the station house.

Vice (prostitution, gambling, narcotics) as distinguished from crime was "policed." Streetwalkers were protected on their stations from invasion by other whores or pimps, and guarded against robbery or attack by their customers. This type of relationship—which was usually effective—was always advanced in private conversation by American policemen as an excuse for payoff: "If you clout them, you control them." It still prevails in the Tenderloin districts of many American cities.

America has changed. It is becoming a homogeneous society and the divisions that do exist are of a new kind. First, of course, is the conflict over homogeneity itself to which the Negroes demand they be admitted. The second most important division, from the police point of view, is a change of values, the democratization of what was once the privilege of an élite of radical intellectuals—an entirely new moral code. Emma Goldman, free-lover and anarchist, was quite a sufficient bother to the police of her day. Today there are millions of Emma Goldmans, members of a new kind of middle class. This public resents the police as guardians of public morals. Younger people who live by moral codes which bear little resemblance to the lower-middle-class Irish Catholic morality of most of the police force look upon the policeman as a dangerous and ignorant disrupter of their own peaceful lives.

The police on the other hand believe that they have the right to control the lives of others for their own benefit, that they know better what others should do than they do themselves. They adjust the behavior of those who live by a different moral code to the stereotypes which they have inherited from the past. In its most extreme form: "If you see a nigger and a white woman together, chances are it's a pimp and a whore." "All those beatniks," referring to a bearded student of nuclear physics, "take dope." "If you watch you can catch one of them making a pass and you're sure to find marijuana or pills."

Both press and police commonly refer to marijuana, an intoxicant far less harmful than alcohol, and to LSD and the various barbiturates, tranquilizers, and stimulants as "dope" and "narcotics," and attempt to deal with the problem exactly the same way that they dealt with the morphine traffic and addiction of fifty years ago. It is significant that the use of most of these drugs results in relaxation and non-invasive behavior while alcohol stimulates aggressions. The police as the Arm of the Squares represent an aggressive lower-middle-class morality in conflict with life patterns of non-aggression which they find incomprehensible and interpret in terms of crime and vice—aggression—which they *can* understand.

What is it the spokesmen for the police are talking about when they say the public doesn't understand the nature of police work? Why don't they explain? The reason is that the contradiction, the dilemma of police work, is something they do not wish publicized. They wish to present to a society concerned about civil liberties the policeman as a functionary of the legal process. They are not prepared to face the fact that he is involved in a symbiotic relationship within the illegal communities that function as subcultures in the society.

It is a common charge of those interested in a reform of the methods of handling the narcotic problem that the federal, state, and, to a lesser degree, city police have a "vested interest," along with the Mafia, in preserving the status quo. This is an oversimplification. What has actually developed is a great web of petty crime, addiction, peddling which the narcotics officer hopes he can control and which is sensitive to his manipulation.

For instance, to begin at the beginning of the process: A narcotics addict arrested on a petty larceny charge can cooperate with the police in several ways. He can help clear the record by admitting to a number of unsolved petty thefts and he can give information which will lead to the arrest of his retail dealer, and his anonymity will be protected by the police and the charges against him will be reduced to a minimum. In the somewhat bigger time a felony charge can be reduced if the prisoner is willing to cooperate in the arrest of a narcotics wholesaler.

At the bottom of the ladder a prostitute known to have associates who are either thieves or narcotics pushers or both can cooperate simply by giving general information, or in cases where the police know that the girl has information they want, she is often given the choice between cooperation, being admitted to bail, and receiving only a fine at her trial, or refusing to cooperate, being held without bail for a medical examination, and then given a jail sentence.

All this is done with a great deal of indirection and evasive language but since narcotics control is something which the police must originate themselves—it is one of several "crimes without plaintiff" which is another definition of "vice"—gambling, prostitution and narcotics—the police can function only if they can keep a complicated machinery of information and actual social contact operating. And the fuel which keeps this machine going is bargaining power: each side has a commodity to exchange of value to the other. Each party to the transaction must make a profit. In this sense the police have a vested interest in the subculture of the underworld.

The remarkable thing about this subculture is that, although it may use the term "square," both police and criminals share the same system of value. The narcotics peddler, the gambler, or the prostitute may point out that their activities are civil-service occupations in some countries and if the public didn't want what they had to offer, they would go out of business. To some extent most policemen share this point of view, but both sides in private conversation usually will be found to be convinced that vice is morally wrong.

The underworld subculture does not have the self-confidence attributed to it in fiction. Again, this lack is a powerful psychological tool in the hands of the police. A prostitute who is treated by the arresting officer as "just a hard-working girl," the victim of hypocritical bluenosed laws which it is the officer's job to enforce, will be far more cooperative than a girl who feels she is being treated with contempt, most especially so because she herself has that contempt. Organizations like Synanon have made a therapeutic method out of the self-hate of the narcotics addict, but a policeman who used the language of a Synanon session would find himself with a very hostile prisoner indeed on his hands.

What the policeman does as a custodial officer within the underworld subculture is keep it abated and he applies these methods to other problems of social order.

For instance, for several years I knew a handsome young Negro intellectual who was a professional blackmailer. He would spot a wealthy young married woman slumming in bohemia, strike up an acquaintance, carry on an intellectual conversation, arouse her sympathy. After reciting T. S. Eliot at length he would divulge the information that he cried himself to sleep night after night because his skin was black and his hair was crinkly. As they parted he would thank her profusely, say that he never hoped to see her again but could he write her sometimes when the pain was more than he could bear. The exchange of letters led to an exchange of pictures and possibly even to an affair, and then one day the socialite housewife would get a telephone call that he was in a terrible jam and needed a thousand dollars that he had been offered by a newspaperman for the letters and pictures. Needless to say, journalism is no longer conducted this way but the girls usually paid up and those who were sleeping with him usually went right on doing so.

One night I was in a club in San Francisco's North Beach and watched the regular cop on the beat question only the mixed couples in the place and concentrate his hostility on this man and his new girl. As he went out the door he said to me, "O.K., Rexroth, say I'm prejudiced but what do you want me to do with that motherfucker? Go up to him and say, 'You're under arrest for blackmail'?"

Eventually this harassment may have paid off because the fellow left town for good. This instance explains a good many things. The police still believe that there are enough relationships of this kind, or worse, amongst mixed couples to justify a policy of general interrogation and of making those people who do not respond as the police think they should as uncomfortable as possible. Harassment is a method of abatement and the police consider it one which may work when there is no plaintiff or no visible commission of crime.

Take the case of homosexuality. Homosexual acts between consenting adults are no longer policed as such. The laws which the police attempt to enforce are essentially the same as those applied to heterosexuals. The bushes in parks and public toilets are not chosen by heterosexuals for sexual intercourse, and although assignations are made between men and women in bars, this has become socially acceptable in most cities, and it is usually not so obvious as the activities in a gay bar.

With the growing tolerance of homosexuality and the enormous increase in gay bars and other open manifestations of homosexuality socially, there has not only been a great increase in homosexual prostitution, especially amongst floating adolescents, but a tremendous increase in robbery and murder. Not only have a number of well-known personalities in recent years been found robbed and beaten to death in cities with a large homosexual population, but studbusting has become one of the commonest forms of "unexplained" homicide. Middle-aged men, many of them married and with children, are pulled out of the bushes dead, with a frequency the police prefer to say nothing about.

Here is the police problem. No one is going to complain. The partners in a homosexual relationship participate voluntarily. If one is robbed, he will not risk disgrace by going to the police. If he's dead, he's dead, and the circumstances of his murder provide no clue. The act itself takes only a brief time and is almost impossible to catch. So the police harass and embarrass the gay bar or the respectable-looking homosexuals frequenting parks or cruising certain well-known streets looking for "trade." The "trade," the homosexual prostitute, they make as uncomfortable as possible.

At one time entrapment was a common form of arrest, but the prejudice of the court and the public is so great that it is being abandoned. A judge is very likely to say, "What were you doing when the defendant was fondling your penis?" Besides entrapment does not catch the principal offender, the studbuster, who if he is experienced can recognize a plainclothesman no matter how plausibly disguised.

This leaves the police with degrading methods, peepholes in public toilets and such like which most officers rebel against using. Of course, in all these cases some policemen simply love this kind of work. The favorite term of contempt amongst police as in the underworld is "copperhearted." Fairy-killers and whore-hunters are not liked by their colleagues on the force, and although police will give all their skill and devotion to cracking a big case of narcotics wholesaling, most men on the narcotics detail sicken of the work with the petty addict and the round of desperation, pilfering, prostitution, squalor, and the hopelessness of changing it.

There is one outstanding factor in common in almost all arrests for "vice." The cop must *judge* to arrest, and in court in a legal process based on contest he must stick to his guns and the *esprit de corps* of the force must back him up all the way up the chain of command. A general cannot deny his troops. This is the reason that the chain of command almost invariably seems to the public to do nothing but whitewash whenever there is a complaint no matter how grievous. It is this paramilitary ethic, not corruption, which accounts for the runaround. Except for a few cities in the East, corruption from outside is dying out. If it exists today it comes from within the force. Outside the cities that are still controlled by the Organization, policemen, let alone high-ranking officers, are no longer directly controlled by corrupt political machines or by the "Mafia."

Modern police corruption is a more subtle thing. Many police departments are controlled by intra-departmental political structures, power *apparats*. Others are the battleground of conflicting groups of this sort, but they are more likely to be generated within the department and concerned exclusively with police rank and privilege than to come from outside. In fact the tendency is to keep such things from the attention of the public, even of the apparatus of the political parties.

In the case of a liberal and enlightened police chief the increasing polarization of American society is certain to be reflected in an opposition, usually clandestine but often organized, which considers him a nigger-lover and a red and whose members do everything they can to sabotage his efforts and to back each other up all along the chain of command as high as they can go. It is this type of reactionary opposition that accounts for the apparently successful John Birch Society recruitment campaign in the police forces of America, and it is here that you can find charges of whitewash and runaround in cases of police brutality, and especially of racism.

Payoff is, as I said, part of a system for control for which many otherwise honest, old-fashioned policemen will present strong if not convincing arguments. Big-time payoff is another thing and occurs only sporadically in a few Eastern cities. Criminal corruption again arises within a police force prompted only by the generally criminal character of American society.

Rings of thieves like those uncovered a couple of years ago in two police forces usually grow out of the general "knock-down" philosophy of American enterprise, particularly in relation to insurance claims. To quote Chief Stanley R. Schrotel:

> Most policemen recognize no wrong in accepting free admissions to public entertainment, discounts on their purchases, special favors and considerations from persons of influence, or tips and gratuities for services performed in the line of their regular duty. They choose to look upon these incidents as being strictly personal matters between themselves and the donors and are unwilling to recognize that moral obligations are involved. . . . No matter how much effort is expended in minimizing the derogatory effect of the acceptance of gratuities and favors by law-enforcement officers, the practice has become so prevalent that the public generally concedes that policemen are the world's greatest "moochers." Aside from the question of the effect of the practice upon the officers' effectiveness in enforcing the law, it is a certainty that a reputation for "mooching" does not elevate the standards of the profession in the public's mind.

This picture has a certain old-time charm: the copper in pith helmet and blue Prince Albert copping an apple off the pushcart. To quote again Banton's *The Policeman in the Community*, paraphrasing Morton Stern's article, "What Makes a Policeman Go Wrong": "A former member of the Denver police department, in discussing what went wrong there, stressed that a new recruit was not accepted by his colleagues unless he conformed to their norms. When investigating a burglary in a store, police officers might put some additional articles into their pockets. Indeed, they were sometimes encouraged to do so by the owners who pointed out they would recover from the insurance company anyway." In the Cops-as-Robbers scandals of a few years back, investigation soon revealed the step-by-step process of corruption. The robbery victim, owner of a shop or warehouse, expected and encouraged the investigating officers to help themselves to a couple of mink coats or television sets to run up the insurance claim. From there it was a short step to collusion between police, burglary gang, and would-be "victim," and from there a still shorter step, the elimination of the middle-man, until the police planned and carried out the robberies themselves and moved on to plain, old-fashioned robbery, without the connivance of the robbed.

The corruption that stems from gambling is a special case, although its effects are probably the most far-reaching. Few police anywhere are directly part of the organized narcotics business, and their involvement in prostitution is really trivial, however common, and mostly part of what they consider the necessary web of information. Gambling is different. Today when churches and supermarkets are gambling institutions, it is hard for the average policeman, who is likely to be an Irish Catholic whose church stages weekly bingo games, to take gambling seriously.

Payoff may start as part of the system of control, but since gambling is the major business of organized crime in America, it soon penetrates to the vitals of the police system. Since gambling is also the major bridge between politics and organized crime, it carries with it not only the corruption of vice but the additional corruption of vice-controlled politics.

Collusion with bookmakers and the proprietors of gambling rooms is turned up fairly frequently on the West Coast. Massive infection of the police department and the penetration of high-level, outside, political corruption seems to be far more common east of the Rockies. There is a psychological factor here which must be taken into account. A corrupt police force is a guilt-ridden police force, because with few exceptions policemen do believe in the lower-middle-class values even when they flout them. A guilty police force is likely to be both belligerently puritanical in its attempts to control unconventional behavior, and hostile, quick to react aggressively to any fancied assault on its own authority. Obviously, this sets up a vicious circle which goes round and round in an ever-accelerating separation of the police from the general population.

At the very best, as any honest policeman will tell you, the police live in a ghetto of their own and a great deal of the effort of the human-relations bureaus and details of the better police departments is devoted simply to getting through to the public, to breaking down the ghetto wall. But even with the best public relations the police as a subculture of their own are a garrison society. Policemen associate mostly with one another and have few civilian friends. Policemen's balls and picnics are characterized by a noisy but impoverished conviviality.

In the case of Negroes, the young man who joins the force is likely to meet with a total cutoff in his community and at the best find himself uncomfortable in his new one, the police society. A neighbor who was a graduate in law in a Southern Jim Crow university joined the force and discovered that he had even lost the friendship of his minister. After a couple of years of isolation, he quit. As a custodial officer in a Negro ghetto the policeman confronts a population in revolt to whom he is a soldier of an occupying army, as both James Baldwin and Bayard Rustin have said.

I have neglected to mention the only way in which the average citizen comes in frequent contact with the police—traffic violation. This is, as we all know, an area of continual exasperation on both sides, and one of the best things a city can do is to create a department of traffic-control officers for all violations short of crime completely divorced from the police department.

To sum up, these are the basic factors in the problem. The police are a closed community, socially isolated from the general population with a high level of irritability along the edges of contact. Police methods have developed in the day-by-day work of control of an underworld of petty crime and vice, in a period when most police work was with the poor, or at least the dwellers in slums and Tenderloin. As a control or custodial officer the typical policeman, in the words of Jerome H. Skolnick, "is inherently a suspicious person, fond of order and predictability. He reacts to stereotyped symbols of potential trouble—even oddities of dress or speech, and proceeds on the presumption of guilt, often while winking at the legal niceties of restraint in searches and arrests. Intent upon 'controlling crime,' the officer keenly resents having his results upset on the appellate level."

Skolnick found that the police feel frustrated by the court's affirmation of principles of due process, and generally consider the appellate judiciary as "traitor" to its responsibility to keep the community free from criminality.

We hear a great deal about the professionalization of the policeman from theorists and lecturers in police academies but on the part of the older or more conventional of these people, professionalism really means the development of a high degree of craft skill in playing the role described by Skolnick, a social custodial officer, with maximum efficiency and minimum social friction. This body of social servants with its own ideology and ethic is set over against a society which bears little resemblance to the one which produced it in the first place. To quote Thomas F. Adams, "Field Interrogation," *Police*, March-April, 1963:

A. Be suspicious. This is a healthy police attitude, but it should be controlled and not too obvious.
B. Look for the unusual.
   1. Persons who do not "belong" where they are observed.
   2. Automobiles which do not "look right."
   3. Businesses opened at odd hours, or not according to routine or custom.
C. Subjects who should be subjected to field interrogations.
   1. Suspicious persons known to the officers from previous arrests, field interrogations, and observations.
   2. Emaciated-appearing alcoholics and narcotics users who invariably turn to crime to pay for cost of habit.
   3. Person who fits description of wanted suspect as described by radio, teletype, daily bulletins.

4. Any person observed in the immediate vicinity of a crime very recently committed or reported as "in progress."
5. Known trouble-makers near large gatherings.
6. Persons who attempt to avoid or evade the officer.
7. Exaggerated unconcern over contact with the officer.
8. Visibly "rattled" when near the policeman.
9. Unescorted women or young girls in public places, particularly at night in such places as cafés, bars, bus and train depots, or street corners.
10. "Lovers" in an industrial area (make good lookouts).
11. Persons who loiter about places where children play.
12. Solicitors or peddlers in residential neighborhood.
13. Loiterers around public rest rooms.
14. Lone male sitting in car adjacent to schoolground with newspaper or book in his lap.
15. Lone male sitting in car near shopping center who pays unusual amount of attention to women, sometimes continuously manipulating rearview mirror to avoid direct eye contact.
16. Hitchhikers.
17. Person wearing coat on hot days.
18. Car with mismatched hub caps, or dirty car with clean license plate (or vice versa).
19. Uniformed "deliverymen" with no merchandise or truck.
20. Many others. How about your own personal experiences?

And Colin McInnes, *Mr. Love and Justice*:

The true copper's dominant characteristic, if the truth be known, is neither those daring nor vicious qualities that are sometimes attributed to him by friend or enemy, but an ingrained conservatism, and almost desperate love of the conventional. It is untidiness, disorder, the unusual, that a copper disapproves of most of all: far more even than of crime which is merely a professional matter. Hence his profound dislike of people loitering in streets, dressing extravagantly, speaking with exotic accents, being strange, weak, eccentric, or simply any rare minority—of their doing, in fact, anything that cannot be safely predicted.

Then Peter J. Connell, "Handling of Complaints by Police":

The time spent cruising one's sector or walking one's beat is not wasted time, though it can become quite routine. During this time, the most important thing for the officer to do is notice the *normal*. He must come to know the people in his area, their habits, their automobiles, and their friends. He must learn what time the various shops close, how much money is kept on hand on different nights, what lights are usually left on, which houses are vacant . . . only then can he decide what persons or cars under what circumstances warrant the appellation 'suspicious.'

All this was all right in a different world. At least the society didn't fall apart. Today what was once a mob is now a civil-rights demonstration, oddly dressed people are musicians, students, professors, members of the new professions generally (half of Madison Avenue seems to take the subway home to Greenwich Village at 5:00 P.M., shed the gray flannel suits and basic blacks, and get into costumes which the police believe are worn only by "dope fiends").

Why is the heat on all over America? For exactly the same reason it has always gone on in an American city after an outbreak of social disorder, a shocking crime, or a sudden rise in the crime rate. The police feel that they are dealing with a situation that is slipping away from their control and they are using the methods, most of them extra-legal, by which they have traditionally regained control—"discourage them and they'll go away."

Where the police once confronted unassimilated groups of the illiterate poor, they now face an unassimilable subculture of the college educated, unassimilable certainly to their own standards. Homosexuality, once a profitable source of shakedown, and a chance to release a few sadistic repressions, is now open and in fact tolerated. There are articles in theological magazines about the church's responsibility to the homosexual and an interfaith organization to implement such responsibility—"homophile" organizations of both men and women stage national conventions addressed by notabilities in law, psychiatry, and sociology, and even by a few enlightened police officers. Such organizations recently sued the State of California to gain the right to operate a booth at the State Fair.

Racially mixed couples are common on the streets of every Northern city and are beginning to appear in the South, and they are far more likely today to be students or professional people than denizens of the underworld. Outlandish costume has become the uniform of youth all over the world who are in moral revolt against a predatory society.

Today, when extra-marital sex is a commonplace, from grammar school to the senior-citizens' clubs, we forget that only a generation ago people were still serving sentences in American prisons for fornication, adultery, and oral sex between men and women, but the police have not forgotten, most of them anyway. A weekly book-review section that once refused advertising of all books whatsoever by Kenneth Patchen or Henry Miller now runs a "cover story" on *The Story of O*, a detailed, graphic description of the most extreme sado-masochism, homosexuality, and "deviance" generally. There are regular underground movie houses which publicly show movies which would shock even a police smoker. Due to their seriousness of intent, they still horrify the police but in a new way.

Adolescent Negro prostitutes in San Francisco when arrested "go limp," and put up long, highly sophisticated arguments for legalized prostitution and do everything but sing "We Shall Overcome." I must say that the police with whom I have talked who have been involved in such situations have enough sense of humor to think it's all just hilarious.

At one time marijuana and the various pharmaceutical kicks were part of a hard-dope subculture and unquestionably led in some instances directly to heroin addiction—"Whatsa matter, you chicken? When are you going to graduate?" This is certainly no longer true. The squares and the oldies have no conception of how common the use of marijuana is amongst the young. Pick-up and put-down pills are used by everybody to sleep or wake up and we have just gone through a craze for hallucinogens that seems to be levelling off. It is my impression that this was accompanied by a proportionate decline in the use of heroin except possibly in certain sections of New York City. Although large numbers of informed people believe that marijuana is harmless and that even the worst of the other drugs cause neither delirium tremens, polyneuritis, exten-sive brain damage nor lung cancer, the police, egged on by some of the press, persist in treating all users of all drugs and intoxicants except alcohol and nicotine as narcotic addicts.

Everybody talks back to the cop today. This "disrespect for law" has two contradictory sources—the general criminality that seeps through all American business and politics, and the growth of a new culture of revolt against precisely this "business ethic." In a sense the police are caught in the middle of a class war, a war between antagonistic moral rather than economic classes.

Most policemen come from conservative levels of the society, lower-middle and working-class families that have preserved an authoritarian structure and fundamentalist religion and puritanical attitude towards sex and a fear and contempt for any nonconformist behavior. The great majority of patrolmen in America have no more than a high-school education and that in substandard schools.

An additional factor seldom taken account of is the class hostility of the people on this social level for the educated, sophisticated, and affluent generally and most especially for those to whom the proper definition of bohemianism specially applies, those who mimic the habits of the idle rich without possessing their money or their reserves of power and who forego the commonly accepted necessities of life to enjoy the luxuries. This type, this model personality, is specifically designed to outrage the type or model policeman who is likely to be suspicious of anybody who drinks brandy instead of bourbon or smokes Turkish cigarettes, much less someone who thinks Juan Marichal must be an obscure Spanish poet.

At one time the great web of police custodial care could isolate such types in Greenwich Village or the Near North Side or North Beach. Today they are everywhere and increasing geometrically. If all of their activities, from peddling poetry on the streets or marching in demonstrations to smoking marijuana and attending nude parties, were suddenly to become accepted, the police forces of the country would be threatened with mass nervous breakdown. This may be one of those processes of historical change where the resistance of the past is not altogether valueless. For instance, laws against the possession of marijuana have become practically unenforceable. If everyone who smoked grass were arrested, we'd have to build concentration camps all over the country. Yet even today it would be quite impossible to legalize marijuana by referendum. It is doubtful if 1 per cent of the state legislators of this country would have the guts to go on record as voting yes on a law like the British one abolishing the criminality of homosexual acts between consenting adults.

The most dangerous social tensions between police and people is certainly in race relations. The most enlightened police chief, with the aid of the most dedicated community-relations detail, cannot control the policeman on the beat, in his personal relations with ignorant, poor, and obstreperous members of a race which he does not understand. The only solution for this within the police force is education and the changing of group pressures. As one police officer said, "We all use the word 'nigger' in the squadroom. You'd be looked on as a kook if you didn't, but I won't let my kids use it at home."

Most chiefs of police rise directly from the ranks and are often less well educated than the new generation of rookies. Most city charters forbid the recruitment of executive officers from outside the force. What this means is that the precinct captains are men from a less enlightened age who have risen by seniority to that point and are not competent to go further. They are the real bottlenecks and they can defeat all the efforts of an enlightened chief and police commission in their own bailiwicks.

The paramilitary structure of the police force is such that it is exceedingly difficult to create a board of review, or an office of complaints or of human relations within the force which will not be dominated by police politics and civil-service inertia. This is the reason for the ever-growing demand for outside surveillance—civilian policing of the police.

Most cities now have boards of police commissioners of various sorts but these are made up of well-to-do businessmen and politicians and seldom meet more than a couple of hours once a week and have at the best only a small secretarial staff. Negro members are usually lawyers and politicians or pastors of respectable churches. It would be possible totally to reorganize such commissions, make them representative, give them power, and a large working staff.

Within the police force itself it is possible to set up an inspector general's office, outside the chain of command, which would process, investigate, and act on all citizen complaints. This is the common proposal of the more enlightened spokesmen from within the police system.

It would be possible to set up in each city an Ombudsman office with the job of clearing all manner of citizens' dissatisfactions with functioning of the city and its employees. This has worked in Scandinavia from which the word comes, but the vision of pandemonium which the prospect of such an American office conjures up is frightening. It is doubtful if it would be possible to get people to take the jobs and certainly not to stay on them.

A civilian review board, either elected or appointed by the mayor from completely outside all political apparatus, would be ideal but the very terms contain a contradiction. How is this going to come about? It is a popular proposal with the civil-rights organizations and the one most fervently resisted by the police. Although it is true, as Bayard Rustin says, that it would protect the unjustifiably accused officer, it would strip naked the paramilitary structure which the police consider essential, not just to their morale but to their actual function.

In some cities, Seattle and Los Angeles amongst others, the civil-rights organizations have set up civilian patrols who prowl the prowl cars. They follow the police and stand by during arrest, politely and usually silently. They must be made up of citizens of all races, of unimpeachable respectability who are willing to donate eight hours at least once a week to difficult and unpleasant work. Obviously they will obtain from the officers in the patrol cars the most elaborate compliance with all the amenities of the etiquette of arrest. How much effect this has in the long run is questionable and by its nature a civilian patrol program is not likely to endure beyond a few critical months. People are unlikely to engage in such activity night after night, year after year.

What is the best of these alternatives? Only experience can tell. If we were to set up in American cities a kind of neighborhood civil militia which checked on all police activity, we would soon find that we had created a police system like that of the Russians in which the law and the police and their party and neighborhood representatives function as agents of public order and education in social ethics. This may be an estimable theory of how to run a society but it is in total contradiction to every principle of British-American law and social organization. We do not want the police as custodians but as instruments of a law which regards all men as equal and at liberty to run their affairs to suit themselves as long as they do not inflict damage on others.

The police spokesmen are perfectly right in saying that what should be done is truly to professionalize police work. This means changing the class foundation of the police force itself. A professional is a man with a salary at least comparable to that of a small-town dentist, with at least one college degree, with an advanced technical and at the same time broadly humanistic education and whose work demands that he keep abreast of its latest developments. The thought of turning all the policemen in America into such persons staggers the imagination. However, the nursing profession, which by and large is recruited from exactly the same level of society as the police, has been professionalized in one generation in everything but salary. An executive nurse in a big-city health department may have more years of college than most of the doctors working with her. She is lucky indeed if she makes $800 a month.

What is the answer? I have no idea. This is one of those many regions of frustration which are spreading across all of modern life, blotches on the skin of a body which is sick within with a sickness of which all diagnoses differ. I suppose society will smell its way to some sort of solution, muddle through the muddle. This is not a very hopeful prognostication for what is, after all, one aspect of a grave crisis, but none of the other prognostications about any of the other aspects is hopeful either.

TOM SAWYER IN TROUBLE

A bearded Tom Sawyer, nattily clad in a policeman's tunic and blue jeans, had a run-in with authority here yesterday.

Unlike his Mark Twain namesake, San Francisco's Sawyer lost this round to a pair of policemen.

Officers Tony Delzompo and Jim Bailey, in fact, found the wearing of parts of police uniforms so unamusing they arrested Sawyer.

Sawyer, 23, of 1253 Willard Street in the Haight-Ashbury district, was booked on suspicion of possession of stolen property.

The officers admitted that there was no report of stolen police jackets on file, but said that Sawyer's uniform, nonetheless, might well be stolen.

Sawyer, questioned at 7 P.M. at Frederick and Stanyan streets by the officers, told them he got the jacket from a friend.

Perhaps an explanation for the officers' investigative zeal could be found in Sawyer's substitute for the police badge, a large lapel button pinned on the left side of the tunic. It read:

"Overthrow the Government."

—*San Francisco Chronicle*, August 22, 1966

The Spiritual Alchemy
of Thomas Vaughan

Alchemy is the one field of past human endeavor which it is almost impossible even to begin to understand. No two modern authors agree about it and no two alchemists agree with each other. Thomas Vaughan is supposed to be the leading "spiritual alchemist" of the entire literature, and yet the majority of modern writers on alchemy deny flatly that such a thing as spiritual alchemy ever existed.

Most of the books which do purport to explain the mysteries of spiritual alchemy are suspect. Their scholarship is shoddy or invented or non-existent, their logic is cracked if not paranoid. Most of them occupy the far outer reaches of occultism, along with theories that the works of Shakespeare were written by a committee of mahatmas on Atlantis, or that the equations which disprove Einstein are embodied in the dimensions of the Great Pyramid. Such books are amusing reading if not too barbarously written—Ignatius Donnelly, for instance, is one of America's most entertaining authors. But Thomas Vaughan is far from being light bedside reading and equally far from being a barbarous writer. He is certainly in deadly earnest about something, and he is almost as beautiful a writer as his brother Henry, one of the greatest poets of the language. Even to begin to comprehend what he is in earnest about requires an extraordinary effort of imaginative projection into a universe of discourse utterly unlike anything to be found, at least in respectable intellectual circles, today.

First published as an Introduction to The Spiritual Alchemy of Thomas Vaughan (*New Hyde Park, New York: University Books, 1967*). *Collected in* With Eye and Ear, *1970.*

As a guide, A. E. Waite is not much help. His *The Secret Tradition in Alchemy* is an exasperating, elusive book. It is nothing to put in the hands of a novice, for it itself requires an explanation which, like everything else connected with alchemy, it would seem, is intrinsically implausible.

Waite belonged to a number of "secret brotherhoods" and was the founder and leader of at least one such group. As an initiate into practically every organization of occultists of his day which was not patently lunatic, he was bound by all sorts of solemn vows and oaths of secrecy. His works and his autobiography make it sufficiently evident that he took these vows seriously indeed. He wrote a set of books, treating systematically and one by one the major cruxes or problems of what might be called the scholarship of the occult tradition—the Holy Grail legends, Freemasonry, Alchemy, Rosicrucianism, the Tarot cards, Ritual Magic, the Kabbalah; and a number of important personages in the history of the occult, Raymond Lull, St. Martin, Eliphas Levi.

With the sole exception of *The Holy Kabbalah* where for once Waite's language is very thinly veiled—perhaps for the reason that what he was talking about is sufficiently well known at least to Jewish scholarship—all these books purport to deny what Waite is in actual fact, not so much proving, as quietly exposing to those who have eyes to see. Until you catch on, this device can be, to put it mildly, misleading, and it never ceases to be exasperating. *The Secret Tradition in Alchemy* claims to deny and disprove the existence of a secret tradition. It does nothing of the sort. If that had been Waite's real end in view, he would never had written the book, it would have been, in his language, "work of supererogation." However, it is certainly misleading. It misled Carl Jung.

For years Jung, in all his voluminous writings about alchemy, ignored Waite. In volume XII of *The Collected Works*, published in the Bollingen Series, where all of Jung's writings on alchemy are gathered up, *The Works of Thomas Vaughan* is not mentioned, nor are the original editions under his own name or Eugenius Philalethes. *The Secret Tradition* appears at last, along with four other alchemical works by Waite, including the alchemical works of E. Kelley, and the original editions of Eirenaeus Philalethes—works important almost exclusively because of the connection with certain controversies around Thomas Vaughan. This in a bibliography of 540 books and 58 manuscripts. In the essay, "Religious Ideas in Alchemy," the only place Jung mentions Waite by name, he attacks him precisely at a point (the Lapis-Christus parallel) where Waite is covering his tracks.

Why no mention at all of Vaughan? In the whole history of alchemy, this is the one author who really, indisputably, gives away the show, divulges the secret. One would think that Vaughan would have been Jung's favorite author, outranking even Rider Haggard and the Kalevala. To believe that Jung's silence is deliberate and designed, in his turn, to cover *his* tracks, is to tempt oneself with the little paranoias of the crackpots who beset this subject enough as it is. Still, it is surely very mystifying.

Alchemy as a subject is not just mystifying, it is intrinsically improbable. It is as though a textbook of chemistry, another of mining engineering, another of gymnastics and breathing exercises, another of pharmacology, several sex manuals, and many treatises of transcendental mysticism had been torn to pieces and not just mixed up together, but fused into a totally new chemical compound of thought. In fact it is not just "as though," looked at from the viewpoint of twentieth-century scientific world-view, this is pretty much what alchemy is—the humorous description is close to exact.

There is no use trying to explain Thomas Vaughan in our terms; he is inexplicable, and can only be appreciated with the subconscious, like a dream or a Surrealist poem. He, and many other alchemists, were in fact favorite reading matter of the Surrealists, who appreciated them for their resonance rather than their significant meaning. There is a good deal more to Vaughan than that, and a good deal more than can be comprehended under the terms of Jungian integration of the personality. Carl Jung's extensive writings on alchemy are illuminating to anyone coming fresh to the subject, but they are inadequate. The flaw in Jung's exposition is his assumption that the alchemists are not talking about anything real. "Man projects himself into his ignorance." A pseudo-science that concerns itself entirely with matters and procedures that have no objective reality must of necessity be really concerned with the unconscious of its devotees. This interpretation differs little from that of André Breton or Eugène Jolas, and as a matter of fact the

Jungians and the surrealists greatly influenced each other's notions about alchemy.

However, as long as alchemy is considered only a symbolic dramatization of the unconscious, works like Thomas Vaughan's little tracts will have only a fortuitous, alogical coherence, the coherence of dream, and will have only evocative rather than communicative meanings to offer us. Not only does Vaughan mean something, but his works form a kind of spiritual autobiography which comes to its climax in one of the more pathetic tragedies of English literature. Waite knew this, though he made no comment, he printed those poignant fragments from the notebooks which tell the story for those who can understand.

Nor is there any point in trying to explain Vaughan in an exegetical way, such an exegesis would only sound crazy to the uninitiated. Since all other alchemical works in Europe are far more "in code" than Vaughan's—which, as I said, really give the show away—I think it is best to lay the whole problem aside and turn to a place where these matters are all made quite explicit. Theoretically this should be India. I think it highly likely that alchemy did arise in India sometime before the appearance of systematized Tantric Buddhism in which it plays an important role. Yogic practices which are assumed into alchemy go back to the beginning of civilized life in the sub-continent. The seal from Mohenjo-Daro of the man in the lotus position, rapt in trance, with an erect penis, might well come from Woodroffe's *Serpent Power* or serve as a woodcut illustration for Ko Hung, the greatest of the Chinese alchemists. However, the most extensive work on this subject is still P. C. Ray's *A History of Hindu Chemistry*, published in two volumes in 1904 and 1925. Not only is it out of date but it is curiously exasperating in its ethnocentric conceit—as well as being quite unreliable as to dates. My objection to Indian writing in this field is the same as that of the Chinese critics of the T'ang Dynasty who concerned themselves with it. It is all so vague, full of shifting amorphous symbols, and impossible to date. So it is to Chinese alchemy I will turn to try to convey to you what a seventeenth-century Welsh mystic and poet and alchemist is talking about. Here we will be dealing with clear statements and definite dates and in all the body of alchemical literature such conveniences exist nowhere else.

The earliest sure date in Western alchemy is the treatise of Bolos of Mendes, the pseudo-Democritus, who wrote in the second century B.C. This survives only in Syriac, one of the clearer statements being, "The pledge has been imposed on us to expose nothing clearly to anyone." Next comes the collection of magical papyri in Leyden, with which are associated a number of tracts of what might be called proto-alchemy. Then come the miscellaneous Greek chemical writings contained in a manuscript collection in the library of St. Mark's. With few exceptions all of these deal exclusively with the adulteration of metals and the fabrication of false jewelry. However, they are couched in a special language of mystification. Furthermore, they and later documents like them are associated physically with the various tractates of the Hermetic literature. No one has ever given a satisfactory explanation of why these recipe books in the art of fraud should have been grouped by Byzantine and late Egyptian librarians and copyists with that corpus of Gnostic, Neo-Pythagorean and Neo-Platonic mysticism.

Flinders Petrie, to the scandal of his scholarly colleagues, dated the formation of the Hermetic tradition to Persian Egypt. There is, in fact, much to be said for this unorthodox opinion, but the works of "Hermes Trismegistus" begin to appear in European speculation in the late Middle Ages, and the originals are assumed to date from the first three centuries of the Christian Era. It is remarkable that, although medieval alchemists constantly refer to "Hermes," they show no knowledge of the mystical and philosophical tractates. However, I do believe that Gnosticism, and even the specific notions of Jewish Kabbalism, arose first in Persian and Hellenistic Egypt, when that country was a melting pot of speculations, cults and mysteries from all over the civilized world—including, at second or third hand, India and China.

The earliest appearance of alchemical, or rather proto-alchemical ideas in China are considerably earlier. The *Shan Hai Ching*, the *Classic of Mountains and Rivers*, in a passage which may date from the fifth century B.C. mentions six *wu*, shamans, who carry the corpse of the man-eating dragon Cha-Yu and have in their hands the death-banishing drugs which drive him away. Si Huang Ti, the Ch'in emperor, sends an expedition out to sea to search for the mystical isles where beautiful *wu* girls guarded the medicines of immortality. The greatest of Chinese historians, Ssu-ma Ch'ien (B.C. 145–79), tells anecdotes of the quest of emperors for the elixir of life in the Ch'in Dynasty (B.C. 221–207), and a long story of the Han emperor, Wu Ti (B.C. 140–87) and his many dealings with alchemists. Prompted by his chief alchemist Lao Shao Chun, this emperor established a regular budget for alchemical researches.

Many Han, and reputedly earlier, works of alchemy survived into T'ang times—the eighth century A.D.—and were subject to extensive commentary. However, in the Sung Dynasty, the tenth to thirteenth centuries, all these which revealed any of the sexual techniques for attaining trance and longevity were purged from the canon of Taoist texts and survived from then on only clandestinely and in Japan.

T'ang intercourse with Persia and Inner Asia led to a proliferation of popular alchemy. Ch'ang An, the capital, swarmed with alchemists and magicians, along with Nestorian monks and shamans from Siberia. Li Mi-li, a Persian alchemist, after a period at the T'ang court, crossed over to Japan and was a factor in the civilizing activities of the court at Nara. It is in Japan that the largest collection of early texts of explicitly sexual yogic-alchemical practices survives today, although there are certainly plenty of late and more popular treatises of this sort to be found now in China.

During the T'ang period Buddhist monks visiting India were on the lookout for alchemists, and the famous traveller Hsuan-ch'ao, under instructions of the Chinese court, sought out the leading Indian alchemist and persuaded him to visit China. I give all these facts simply to show that there was a great deal of alchemy coming and going, beginning sometime prior to the third century before Christ.

Chinese lists of metals and inorganic substances with typical alchemical parallels or synonyms and correlations with parts of the body and the constellations date back to at least the fifth century, possibly to Tso Yuan in the fourth century B.C., and include quite sophisticated substances—arsenic, sulfide, sulfur, arsenious acid, mercuric sulfide, mercury, sal ammoniac, alum, diamonds, lodestones and other metals and their compounds. Mineral acids are described by the earliest Chinese travellers to India. Paraphrases of no crucial importance of passages from the Indian alchemist and

Tantric philosopher Nagajuna (second century A.D.) occur in the writings of the founder of Neo-Taoist science and of fully developed spiritual alchemy, Ko Hung of the fourth century.

The illustrations of which Carl Jung makes so much in his *Secret of the Golden Flower* are in fact illustrations for Ko's *Pao P'u Tzu*. They were lifted from a nineteenth-century edition of his work and used by a syncretistic slum sect, of the type of our Holiness churches, Jehovah's Witnesses or the I Ams, without any understanding of their original significance. The most important illustration of all does not appear in Jung's book—it is a nude figure of a man in a position of meditation. In his body, corresponding in place to the major autonomic nervous system plexuses, are the various instruments of alchemy—retort, furnace and so on. This one illustration answers all the disputed questions, once and for all.

By the early Sung period Chinese alchemy was very highly developed on both fronts. Yogic practices, that is, autonomic nervous-system gymnastics, sexual techniques and methods of achieving several kinds of trance, were as advanced as any to be found in India. "Several kinds of trance" needs explanation. It is only in recent years when neurological research has turned its attention to yoga that we have come to realize that, although these practices include auto-hypnosis, they are primarily concerned with the production of states, which, although entranced, are psychologically and even neurologically speaking exactly the opposite of the hypnotic state. At the same time alchemy by the twelfth century was busy with chemical phenomena that European science would not begin to explore until the end of the eighteenth century. Not only had they developed a crude but comprehensive chemistry of the common acids, bases, metallic salts, sulfur, invented gunpowder and greek fire, burning glasses, artificial pearls, discovered the use of coal and petroleum (Peking man used coal), but they had occupied themselves quite intelligently with various mysteries and intriguing phenomena, luminescence, magnetism, production of a vacuum and so on. Exactly as in Europe most of this literature is at least quasi-Hermetic with mysterious and misleading terms for sulfur, magnitite, mercury and the rest.

As Neo-Taoism matured it produced hundreds of alchemical tracts and dozens of major expositions, an output which was to come to an end only in recent times. Even the great Sung Dynasty Neo-Confucian philosopher Chu Hsi wrote a short treatise on, and more or less against alchemy. After the eighth century Tantric Buddhism became common in China, and brought with it from India essentially the same esoteric practices divorced however from any connection with transmutation of metals and given a Buddhist philosophical basis. The frontispiece to Woodroffe's *Serpent Power* represents, in Tantric terms, the same method of yogic trance as do the illustrations to the *Pao P'u Tzu*.

Not only were the sexual techniques of alchemy assumed to develop internal processes which paralleled operations leading to the production of gold, the philosopher's stone, or the growth of precious metals, cinnabar, and sulfur in the wombs of the uprising mountains. This idea can be found in Proclus in the West and continues to dominate medieval ideas until the translation of Avicenna's *Treatise Against Alchemy*. The hierogamos literally fecundates the earth. At the same time it achieves salvation for the soul.

Meditation; mental exercise which reduces the mind to a single point of awareness; breathing gymnastics which are a form of sustained hyperventilation; concentration of the mind on the major autonomic plexuses of the body, beginning with the lumbar or pubic plexus and rising to the head; orgasm without ejaculation—which by pressure of the heel on the perineal region is diverted into the bladder—all this by oneself or with a woman in the sexual act: is the entire literature of alchemy just a code communicating the secrets of this method of achieving trance and illumination?

No. Mary Anne Atwood, whose *A Suggestive Inquiry into the Hermetic Mystery* introduced alchemy into modern occultism in 1850, apparently thought this was the essence of the matter—but there is more to it than that. It is inconceivable that so immense a body of literature in so many languages over so long a period should be no more than an infinitely complicated rebus or cryptogram for a relatively simple discipline of the nervous system which can be revealed in a sentence and explained in a few pages.

Thomas Vaughan and his wife, his *soror mystica*, wrapped in entranced embrace at the Pinner of Wakefield, were, it is true, blundering into a region of revelation which they little understood and which, it would seem, eventually destroyed both of them. They were doing what Chinese adepts had done at least four hundred years before Christ and what others may have done in the Indus Valley three thousand years before. But they were also, and concomitantly, performing a chemical experiment, and they believed that neither could be successful without the other.

The doctrine of the interaction, and in most cases of the transcendental identity, of the macrocosm and the microcosm is as old as alchemy. It is alchemy. By manipulating oneself one achieves illumination. By simultaneous and parallel manipulation of physical reality, one achieves the philosopher's stone, or potable gold, or whatever may be the chemical end in view. (The final achievement of the Great Work is always thought of as the term of an enormously long and difficult process—both chemically and, to coin a word, yogically.) But both processes are thought of as equally real. It is curious that the "objective" chemical operation has been proven to be illusory, while the psychological, or neurological one is as operable today as ever.

It may be objected that I have not explained in literal detail exactly what Thomas Vaughan and his wife were up to. The reason should be obvious. It killed them. Tantric and yogic works are full of warnings of the dangers of unguided autonomic nervous-system experiments. The neophyte is told again and again that he can learn only by submitting himself to the personal guidance of a teacher—guru. If not, he is warned that he will certainly come to a bad end. Furthermore, all texts all over the world of this type of mysticism point out that the pre-condition and essential foundation for all such practices is right living, the fulfillment of the commonplace injunctions of Buddhist, Christian or Chinese morality. Without this foundation the would-be adept is, as the experience of millenniums has shown, inevitably doomed.

I am well aware that following hard on the heels of Carl Jung have come a horde of apostles of irresponsible do-it-yourself ecstasy. Alchemy, Gnosticism, Tantrism are today part of a world characterized also by hallucinogenic drugs, folk songs, peace marches and black stockings. The great trouble with these people is that they confuse transcendence with sensationalism. Thomas Vaughan was a wise, disciplined and careful man, yet vision was too much for him. His work may be an inspiration but it is certainly also a warning.

The Cubist Poetry of Pierre Reverdy

The poets associated with Cubism are Guillaume Apollinaire, Blaise Cendrars, Jean Cocteau, Max Jacob, André Salmon and Pierre Reverdy. As the years have passed and *cette belle époque* recedes into perspective, for us today, Pierre Reverdy stands out from his fellows as the most profound and most controlled artist. This is part of a general revaluation which has taken place as the latter half of the century has come to judge the first half. So Robert Desnos has risen above his Surrealist colleagues and competitors. So independents like Supervielle, Milosz and Léon-Paul Fargue are more appreciated today than they were in their lifetimes. Just as Francis Jammes has almost overwhelmed the poetic reputations of the beginning of the century and the once world-famous Verhaeren is hardly read at all, so from the Fantaisistes, the poets of *Le Divan*, Toulet and Francis Carco almost alone survive. Although time has seldom worked so quickly, I am more or less confident that those revaluations will stand. Certainly Pierre Reverdy's present position should be secure. International literary taste has learned the idiom, the syntax that was so new and strange in 1912. Fortuitous novelty has fallen away and this has enabled comprehension and judgment. Neither Reverdy nor Tristan Tzara can shock anybody any more. And so those values once masked by shock enter into the judgment of a later generation.

Juan Gris was Pierre Reverdy's favorite illustrator, as he in turn was the painter's favorite poet. No one today would deny that they share the distinction of being the most Cubist of the Cubists. This is

Published as the Introduction to Rexroth's translation of Selected Poems, *by Pierre Reverdy (New York: New Directions, 1969).*

apparent to all in Juan Gris. But what is Cubism in poetry? It is the conscious, deliberate dissociation and recombination of elements into a new artistic entity made self-sufficient by its rigorous architecture. This is quite different from the free association of the Surrealists and the combination of unconscious utterance and political nihilism of Dada.

When I was a young lad I thought that literary Cubism was the future of American poetry. Only Walter Conrad Arensberg in his last poems, Gertrude Stein in *Tender Buttons* and a very few other pieces, much of the work of the young Yvor Winters and others of his generation of Chicago Modernists, Laura Riding's best work and my own poems later collected in *The Art of Worldly Wisdom* could be said to show the deliberate practice of the principles of creative construction which guided Juan Gris or Pierre Reverdy. It is necessary to make a sharp distinction between this kind of verse and the Apollinairian technique of *The Waste Land, The Cantos, Paterson,* Zukofsky's A, J. G. MacLeod's *Ecliptic,* Lowenfels' *Some Deaths,* the youthful work of Sam Beckett and Nancy Cunard and, the last of all, David Jones's *Anathemata.*

In poems such as these, as in Apollinaire's "Zone," the elements, the primary data of the poetic construction, are narrative or at least informative wholes. In verse such as Reverdy's, they are simple, sensory, emotional or primary informative objects capable of little or no further reduction. Eliot works in *The Waste Land* with fragmented and recombined arguments; Pierre Reverdy with dismembered propositions from which subject, operator and object have been wrenched free and restructured into an invisible or subliminal discourse which owes its cogency to its own strict, complex and secret logic.

Poetry such as this attempts not just a new syntax of the word. Its revolution is aimed at the syntax of the mind itself. Its restructuring of experience is purposive, not dreamlike, and hence it possesses an uncanniness fundamentally different in kind from the most haunted utterances of the Surrealist or Symbolist unconscious. Contrary to what we are taught, it appears first in the ultimate expressions of Neo-Symbolism in Mallarmé, in his curious still lifes like "*Autre Éventail,*" in occult dramatic molecules like "*Petit Air,*" and, of course, above all in his hieratic metaphysical ritual, *Un Coup de dés.* It is in this tremendously ambitious poem in fact that all the virtues and the faults of the style, whether practiced by Reverdy, Laura Riding or myself, can be found.

These faults, as well as those virtues which he decided were in fact faults, led Yvor Winters to condemn all verse of this kind as the deliberate courting of madness. What he objected to in essence was the seeking of glamour, that effulgence which St. Thomas called the stigmata of a true work of art, as an end in itself. What James Joyce translates "wholeness, harmony and radiance" are qualities not only of all works of art but they are often sought deliberately. Paul Valéry's objectives are the same as Reverdy's but he presents them in a syntactical context that can be negotiated throughout general experience.

When the ordinary materials of poetry are broken up, recombined in structures radically different from those we assume to be the result of causal, or of what we have come to accept as logical sequence, and then an abnormally focused attention is invited to their apprehension, they are given an intense significance, closed within the structure of the work of art, and are not negotiable in ordinary contexts of occasion. So isolated and illuminated, they seem to assume an unanalyzable transcendental claim. Accompanying, as it were garbing, this insistent transcendence are sometimes certain projected physical responses induced or transmitted in the person undergoing the poetic experience, whether poet or reader. Vertigo, rapture, transport, crystalline and plangent sounds, shattered and refracted light, indefinite depths, weightlessness, piercing odors and tastes, and synthesizing these sensations and affects, an all-consuming clarity. These are the phenomena that often attend what theologians call natural mysticism. They can be found especially in the poetry of St. Mechtild of Magdeburg and St. Hildegarde of Bingen, great favorites of the psychologists who have written on this subject, but they are equally prominent in the poetry of Sappho or Henry Vaughan or the prose of Jakob Boehme, as well as in many modern poets. They have often been equated with the idioretinal and vasomotor disturbances caused by drugs, migraine, or other dissociations of personality, or *petit-mal* epilepsy. At the present moment the quest of such experiences by way of hallucinogenic drugs is immensely fashionable.

I think what Winters meant was that intense hyperesthesia of this type, when it occurs in modern poetry without the motivation of religious belief, is pathological in its most advanced forms and sentimental in its less extreme ones. It is true of course that any work of art that coerces the reader or spectator into intense emotional response for which there is no adequate warrant or motive is by definition sentimental, but I do not think that this is exactly what happens in poetry like that of Reverdy, Mallarmé or Valéry. The putative justifications given by Valéry for the extremities to which he pushes his quest for effulgence are really sops to the reader. His seemingly ordinary informative syntax masks only slightly the same unanalyzable transcendental claim.

We still know almost nothing about how the mind works in states of rapture nor why the disjunction, the ecstasis, of self and experience should produce a whole range of peculiar nervous responses, sometimes quite conscious as in St. Hildegarde, sometimes almost certainly subliminal as in Reverdy or the early poems of Yvor Winters. I am inclined to believe that the persistence of this vocabulary among visionary poets is not a defect but a novitiate. Until rapture becomes an accepted habit, a trained method of apprehending reality, an accustomed instrument, the epiphenomena that accompany its onset will seem unduly important. Since only the intimations of rapture are all that most people are ever aware of, Henry Vaughan's ring of endless light will always serve as an adequate symbol of eternity. Kerkele saw the same idioretinal vision as a very finite ring of carbohydrates.

We are dealing with a self-induced, or naturally and mysteriously come-by, creative state from which two of the most fundamental human activities diverge, the aesthetic and the mystic act. The creative matrix is the same in both, and it is that state of being that is most peculiarly and characteristically human, as the resulting aesthetic or mystic experience is the purest form of human act. There is a great deal of overlapping, today especially, when art is all the religion most people have and when they demand of it experiences that few people of the past demanded even of religion. But a painting by Juan Gris or a poem by Pierre Reverdy is self-evidently not a moment of illumination in the life of St. Teresa of Avila nor even her description of it. It is the difference between centripetal and centrifugal. A visionary poem is not a vision. The religious experience is necessitated and ultimate. The poet may have had such an experience in writing the poem, although probably only to a limited degree, or he would not have had the need to write the poem. But there is nothing necessitated about the poem. We can take it or leave it alone, and any ultimates we find in it we must first bring to it ourselves.

History accustoms the public for poetry, as experience accustoms the poet, to this idiom of radiance. Returned to today, *Un Coup de dés*, or the poems of Reverdy or Laura Riding seem negotiable enough and the similar poems of Yvor Winters seem only passionate love poems or rather simple philosophic apothemes. Reverdy, in fact, in most of his poems is hardly a mystic poet. He simply uses a method which he has learned from his more ambitious poems. It is ambitious enough. He seeks, as all the Cubists did, to present the spectator with a little organism that will take up all experience brought to it, digest it, reorganize it and return it as the aesthetic experience unadulterated. All works of art do this. Artists like Reverdy or Juan Gris sought to do it with a minimum of interference. When they were successful their artifacts were peculiarly indestructible. Today, like the paintings of 1910, Reverdy's poems have become precious objects indeed. They have a special appeal now because, although rigorously classical—(I suppose my description of their method could be called a definition of an hypertrophied classicism, which in a sense was precisely what Cubism was)—they are not in the least depersonalized. Quite the contrary—they are rather shameless. So many of the poems are simple gestures laying bare the heart. For this reason Reverdy has influenced personalist poets like Robert Creeley and Gary Snyder and through them whole schools of younger people.

Reverdy was aware of the final deductions to be made from his poetry as a whole and from his poetic experience when in his most illuminated poems he pushed it to its limits. It is not necessary that the poet have any special religious belief, or any at all, but if poetic vision is refined until it is sufficiently piercing and sufficiently tensile, it cuts through the reality it has reorganized to an existential transcendence. In Reverdy's case the consequences were more specific. In 1930 he retired to the Benedictine Abbey of Solesmes and lived there as a lay associate until his death in 1960 with only rare visits to Paris on business trips or to see old friends.

The revolution of the sensibility that began with Baudelaire became in the latter work of Mallarmé a thoroughgoing syntactical revolution in the language because it was realized that the logical structure of the Indo-European languages was an inadequate vehicle for so profound a change in the sensibility. In actual fact, although Apollinaire is usually considered the watershed of modern poetry, no single poem of his represents as thoroughgoing a change in method as Mallarmé's.

The only attack on the language that was as drastic was the Simultaneism of Henri Barzun, the father of the American critic. Unfortunately the quality of Barzun's work leaves much to be desired and his impact was slight. Gertrude Stein and Walter Conrad Arensberg both went further than anyone writing in French, both in their attempts to provide a new syntax of the sensibility and more simply in applying the methods of Analytical Cubism to poetry. Pierre Reverdy is the first important French poet after *Un Coup de dés* to develop the methods of communication explored by Mallarmé.

The syntactical problems and possibilities of a language are peculiar to that language so the poetry of Reverdy makes unusual demands upon the translator. Certain of his devices would be irrelevant if transmitted directly into English. I have tended to avoid his purposive confusions of tense and mood and used mostly the present or the simple past or future. The subjunctive of course is no longer part of American speech and its use would have destroyed the wry colloquialism so characteristic of Reverdy. Similarly I have used the simple English meanings where Reverdy uses slang of some special métier—for instance, show business. We simply do not have such terms for spotlights and one-wheeled bicycles. Again, "one" is not American speech, and sometimes it has been necessary to use more than one pronoun to translate the French "*on*" when Reverdy is talking about "you," "they" and "I" in the same poem. Otherwise I have tried to keep the translation reasonably literal although there is probably a tendency to assimilate Reverdy's language to that of my own Cubist poetry, Gertrude Stein's *Tender Buttons* or Walter Conrad Arensberg's "For Shady Hill."

Of all modern poets in Western European languages Reverdy has certainly been the leading influence on my own work—incomparably more than anyone in English or American—and I have known and loved his work since I first read *Les Épaves du ciel* as a young boy.

Who Is Alienated From What?

For years alienation has been the favorite catch word of the American literary establishment, as triangulated by the *Partisan Review*, *Commentary*, and the *New York Review of Books*. What they mean is that since these establishment members lost their jobs in Army Intelligence after the war, the ruling circles of American society have forgotten they exist and no longer ask them out.

On the other hand, there has been growing up in Europe what amounts to a systematic philosophy or sociology of alienation. Several intellectual currents have converged to form what is today a stream of thought that is practically unchallenged. Since the publication of the philosophical notebooks of the young Marx just before the war, people who broke with the Communist Party but remained Marxists have come to emphasize the problem of alienation as fundamental.

From Kierkegaard to Sartre and Merleau-Ponty alienation has been a central concept of the Existentialists. In the tremendous intellectual upsurge in the Catholic Church that has followed Pope John's *aggiornamento*, modern Catholics have pointed out what has been obvious to everyone else for a long time, that anyone who tries to model his life on Christ and his apostles is by definition alienated from a predatory society.

Today the dialogue between these groups has begun to be overheard even within the ranks of the European Communist parties, most especially the Italian and Polish. The unorthodox Yugoslavs have been leaders in the movement for a long time. This discussion is where intellectual life is today in Europe, but it has had little

---

Written in 1967 and collected in The Alternative Society, *1970.*

259

influence in America. Even theoretical socialist magazines like *Dissent* or libertarian ones like *Liberation* devote little or no space to the discussion of alienation, and the middlebrow magazines are aggressively unaware of its existence.

Partly this is due to the American theory that general ideas are the exclusive province of college professors, hired to teach them for grades or theses. Partly it is the American, and particularly the American labor movement's lack of interest in anything but bread-and-butter issues, and partly it is due to the fact that in America today even an unfavorable serious discussion of ideas that have any connection with the name of Marx is immediately labelled Communist, and anyone who embarks upon such a discussion is in danger of investigation.

David Herreshoff in *American Disciples of Marx* comments on Earl Browder's farewell to Marxism, "Through Browder's *Marx and America* runs an implicit identification of the level of wages and the level of well-being of the workers. The Marxist concept of alienation is not once alluded to in this work purportedly concerned with the relevance of Marx to American experience." Browder's book is primarily an attack on the theory of progressive impoverishment. It never occurs to him that Marx gave a symbolic "material" existence to a moral critique of his society and that today his categories are deserting their materialist vestures and returning to their old etherealization.

Alas, the same is substantially true of Herreshoff's book itself, although Daniel De Leon, to whom Herreshoff gives most space, was acutely aware that human self-alienation was the very reason for being of the revolt against industrial civilization. Behind his unfortunate addiction to mixed metaphors in the William Jennings Bryan fashion, which apparently the age demanded, De Leon shows a better understanding of the fundamental problems raised by Marxism than Lenin, Kautsky, or Plekhanov. After the Third Congress of the Comintern, Left Communism's very memory has been effectually obliterated.

The present efforts of the American Left to reorganize itself are little influenced by the tremendous Marxist *aggiornamento* which has been sweeping the Iron Curtain countries, the French and Italian Left, and is even beginning to penetrate the sealed minds of the Workers' Fatherland itself. I used the word *"aggiornamento"* advisedly, because there has been a most remarkable convergence with the development of a new philosophy of man in the Roman Catholic Church. These two movements in fact are the most significant and exciting in contemporary Europe. In America there is a considerable number of Catholic thinkers who have launched a dialogue with the Marxist *aggiornamento.* As far as any answers have appeared they have come from across the Atlantic or from Japan. Certainly there has been little response from anybody identified with any Marxist party in America. This is curious indeed, because the entire movement of what has been called the "psychoanalytic Left" is American-based and is quoted constantly by Marxist writers trying to develop a contemporary philosophy of man in Yugoslavia, Poland, Japan, or Italy.

There are several reasons for this. American Marxism has been dominated for over a generation by a mindless, vulgar bureaucracy principally distinguished by a militantly execrable taste in all aspects of life and a scorn for thought of any sort. There is no essential difference in values and manners, between the bureaucrats of American Marxism, the House of Representatives, and any Board of Aldermen. They all represent the American Political Way of Life. It is the system of values known by this name which of course is what makes the alienated alienated.

An American theory of alienation significantly has come from practical clinicians, confronted every day in their practices with patients made profoundly sick by a scale of values which has for its summit the reduction of all things and all men to commodities. It is the treatment of the mentally ill with manifest moral lesions which has shifted the bases of psychoanalysis in America from the Sixth to the Tenth Commandment. The besetting sin of modern society is certainly not adultery—it is covetousness. In modern America it is so besetting that the average educated person encountering the word in the Bible believes it is some ritual violation peculiar to the ancient Hebrews, like eating crayfish.

The runaway pornography of the American entertainment business—including pseudo-highbrow publishers who concentrate on dope and homosexual prostitution—is not motivated by sex, but by the reduction of sex to a commodity whose advertising lures must be continuously escalated and which can never be satisfied. This is a commonplace. Since all critics of our society say this, it is strange that America has not developed what might be called a systematic philosophy of its own morbidity. Working psychiatrists, even of the psychoanalytic Left, still function in an atmosphere of pandemic pressure, like traumatic surgeons in an air raid. It's the laity who read the theoreticians—whether Erich Fromm, Leslie Farber, or Abraham Maslow.

An important factor in the failure of American socialism to produce any kind of philosophical Marxism is the profoundly uncongenial temper of Hegelianism to the dominant pragmatism and pluralism of American philosophy. There has not been a socially significant Hegelian thinker in America since Josiah Royce. It is interesting that behind his soft and well-bred prose lurk some extraordinarily revolutionary ideas, precisely those so influential in Europe today: his notion of the Absolute as the Beloved Community, and, of course, the doctrine of reification, the idea that the turning of men into things was the essence of alienation or original sin.

These ideas are central to the leaders of political *aggiornamento* in Yugoslavia or Italy, but in America any mass movement of head-on attack on alienation as such is largely confined to the most intelligent members of the notorious Revolt of Youth. The only trouble with the Revolt of Youth or the New Left is that it has been defenseless against its main enemy. It took only a year for that caricature of Big Business and the Big Business ethic—Organized Vice—to take over the Hippies; and the movement itself, by the pressure of idle youngsters of the upper middle class, was turned into a craze for the conspicuous expenditure of senseless commodities—beads, couch cover serapes, and worn-out squirrel skin chubbies. This is also the general tendency of American literature and art. Where Poland produces Gombrowicz staged by Growtowski, and France and Ireland cooperate in producing Beckett, we come up with Andy Warhol, just a messier variety of chic.

Who is alienated from what? The writings of the young Marx which discuss the subject and which have become so influential today are actually ambiguous and contradictory. At times Marx speaks as Hegel; alienation is the very principle of creativity, the

Absolute self alienates itself in creation. Sometimes he speaks of all work as alienating. Again he speaks of man engaged in what later he would call the commodity production of capitalism as being alienated from his product, from his fellows in work, and from the work itself. What he never mentions, but himself perfectly exemplifies, is the alienation of the intellectual, clerkly caste from the new ruling class. In this he was only the latest of a long line of *aliénés* who began to appear contemporaneously with the rise of that class itself. This is an historically unparalleled phenomenon, characteristic only of Western European civilization since the rise of the middle class.

All important works of art, from the middle of the eighteenth century on, have rejected all the distinguishing values of the civilization which produced them. Rousseau, Blake, de Sade, Hölderlin, Baudelaire, Byron, Stendhal, these are only the most conspicuous and extreme *révoltés*. Not even the apostles of the middle class's own revolution—Marat, Robespierre, Saint-Just—thought they were waging that revolution for the values of that class. If we project this situation back on the Rome of Virgil, the Greece of Sophocles, or the China of Tu Fu, its historical peculiarity is of course apparent. Catullus may be angry and neurotic but he is anything but alienated.

The clerkly caste had been as important in the Middle Ages as ever they had been in Egypt or Babylon. In a commercial, industrial civilization they became "minions," skilled servants deprived of self-determination, even more of a personal, determinative role in society. It is this sudden loss of power, and of personal autonomy, that has fed the wider concepts of alienation.

It is from literature and art that the alienated personality has spread, first to the technical and professional intelligentsia, the very pets of the society, and from them to an ever deepening stratum of the working class. The shocking exploitation—worse than chattel slavery—characteristic of British business enterprise in its primitive days, which was so well described by Engels and others—did not produce "alienation" in the intellectual sense of the word. The naked child dragging a coal cart in a narrow tunnel did not become alienated; he became dead. The young Marx—and seventy-five years after him, Trotsky, in *Literature and World Revolution*—often speak like William Morris. Creative intellectuals themselves, they imagined that if the work of the industrial worker could be made creative, like that of the artist, he would cease to be alienated.

As a matter of fact, my experience with industrial workers has led me to suspect that most of them do not resent the low level of personal participation in the production process. Charlie Chaplin may have considered a job on the assembly line destructive of the personality. This was not an opinion widely shared in the United Auto Workers Union, and now the assembly-line worker himself is disappearing. In a completely automated and computerized system of production, most of the small number of workers required would in fact be able to participate creatively. In the heaviest, and once most onerous, extractive industries this is already becoming true. But in the automated Western world, and equally in the socialized East, personal alienation increases, even amongst the most favored beneficiaries of the new society. Account executives and commissars mimic Baudelaire. As slavery was a substitute for machinery, Bolshevik "socialism" is a substitute for automation.

On the other hand, immense numbers of people are becoming physically alienated from productive society altogether. The word here should not be alienated, but redundant. As labor power steadily loses its role as the primary source of economic value, whole races and nations become redundant. Except for the Talented Tenth, the American Negro today is born alienated. His black skin has led him to being sifted down to the bottom of the economic pile where he has nothing to sell but his labor power, and that labor power, which once built railroads and picked cotton, finds no buyers. Africa and the rest of the former colonial world has been liberated because the metropoles, the former imperialist nations, have discovered that imperialism is unprofitable.

Where once the current of rejection of the dominant society flowed from the intellectuals down and out into the common people, today the current is reversed. Dick Gregory, James Baldwin, LeRoi Jones, Frantz Fanon, Charles Mingus, Miles Davis, the most militant artist spokesman for the alienated black common people, have themselves enjoyed specially favored upbringing and a plethora of endowments from the "power structure." They participate in modern society far more than most white intellectuals—with a vengeance. At least their vengeance strives to be creative. They are eminently successful and doing creative work. Society has discriminated in their favor. They are black. As black men the current of society's rejection and reciprocal rejection of society flows up from the unwanted black common people. The child coal picker in 1840 England may have died of overwork, but her work was needed. Nobody needs the thousands and thousands of unskilled workers who are now entering a third generation on welfare, housed, or rather economically embalmed and stowed out of sight, in housing projects and other slums. This is an entirely different kind of alienation from the one Marx diagnosed in the labor process. The conviction that "nobody wants me, nobody needs me, nobody knows I exist" may be the birthright of the ghetto, but it is coming to pervade all levels of modern society, even the most productive and favored.

At the top of the social heap the children of the upper middle class turn on, tune in, and drop out in herds and droves. This is true of the children of factory managers in East Berlin just as much as it is true of the girls from Sweetbriar wrapped in bedspreads and running barefoot in the Haight-Ashbury.

The most fashionable artists strive desperately to invent some new nihilism and sell it to idle rich women. Andy Warhol and Kenneth Anger are far more fashionable with far richer people than ever was John Singer Sargent. The assumption is that when a rich woman spends $12,000 for a three-foot square of masonite painted an even coat of solid blue, or on a rusted, pressed automobile body, or on an exact ceramic reproduction of human feces, and puts the thing in her penthouse, it will destroy her. Unfortunately for the neo-Dadaist revolutionaries, she spends $12,000 or more a year on a psychoanalyst to keep that from happening, and never misses the money for either Dadaist or doctor.

Meanwhile, throughout the society, millions of mute inglorious people, surfeited with commodities and commodity relationships, become ever more divorced from their work, their fellows, their spouses and children, their lives and themselves.

"Why did you set all those fires?" "Why did you shoot thirty people on the university campus?" "Why did you kill those seven nurses?"

"I didn't know who I was." "I wanted to do something so that I could prove to myself I was really existing."

This goes all the way to the top. "Why are you dropping napalm on children?" "Why are you tempting a mighty nation to drop its hydrogen bombs on you?" Almost certainly the answer is, "I have the titles of power but I can't tell who I am."

The Influence of Classical Japanese Poetry on Modern American Poetry

There is a perceptive book on this subject, *The Japanese Tradition in British and American Literature,* by Earl Miner. It is close to definitive but it culminates with the work of Ezra Pound and William Butler Yeats and has little to say about developments since. In the last twenty-five years the influence of Japanese poetry has become far more pervasive than it has ever been. The postwar development has been quite different, a difference of distance. Japan was once for the West a far away world of lotus dreams, a paradise of decadent sensualists. Whatever it is now, it is certainly that no longer.

The first influence of Japan on Western culture came through the reports of the Jesuit mission in the sixteenth century, with their similar but more extensive reports and translations from China. For the *philosophes* of the eighteenth century, Far Eastern civilization was a model of rational order. As is well-known, specifically Japanese influence began with the wood block prints discovered used as packing and wrapping paper for Dutch imports of porcelain, tea, silk, and other commodities, and the influence of their asymmetric, dynamic balance on the then modern painters was revolutionary.

At the turn of the century art nouveau, directly imitative of Japanese art, coincided with a fad for things Japanese, from cheap porcelain in the ten cent stores to sword furniture and *netsuke* lovingly displayed in the homes of the rich. Then, too, the first great collections of important Japanese paintings were formed in the

---

Speech delivered at a P.E.N. conference in November 1972. Collected in The Elastic Retort, *1973.*

West, and the first imitations and translations of Japanese poetry were published.

It is amusing to think that in America the founder of the "discipline" with which we are concerned here was Sadakichi Hartmann, a bohemian of bohemians if ever there was one. In many ways Hartmann was a wise and witty man. As a poet he was dreadful, and he began a long tradition of vulgarization and sentimentalization of Japanese classical poetry in translation. The translations and imitations of Yone Noguchi and Lafcadio Hearn, and of E. Powys Mathers, from the French, were considerably better, yet no better than the best sentimental verse of the first years of the twentieth century. They established Japan in the literary imagination as a reverse image of America, a society whose system of values had been moved through the fourth dimension so that left was right and up was down. Japan became a dream world in the metaphorical sense—a world of exquisite sensibility, elaborate courtesy, self-sacrificing love, and utterly anti-materialist religion, but a dream world in the literal sense, too, a nightside life where the inadequacies and frustrations of the American way of life were overcome, the repressions were liberated and the distortions were healed. This isn't Japan any more than materialist, money-crazy America is America, but like all stereotypes some of the truth can be fitted into it. There are forms and expressions of the Japanese sensibility purified beyond anything in the West, where something quite unlike the spirit of Western civilization is to be found—for instance, Ashikaga ink paintings, the Nō drama and a great deal of the best classical Japanese poetry.

Modern Western civilization produces in most of its more sensitive spokesmen a profound alienation. Classical Japanese culture provides for some Americans one satisfying answer to that alienation. In Modern Japan the classic past can never become such a compensatory dream world for any but a few romantic, archaizing intellectuals any more than stories of George Washington, Thomas Jefferson and Abraham Lincoln can satisfy alienated American intellectuals. After all it's one's own world one is alienated from. Unless this is understood it is impossible to understand the peculiarly selective nature of the influence of Japanese poetry on American. "The Japanese do everything just the opposite to how we do," said the GI's of the Occupation. That is the point. Classic Japanese culture provided those nutriments for which the West was starved, or at least Western intellectuals persuaded themselves it did. A hundred Americans have read Arthur Waley's translation of *The Tale of Genji* for one who has read Kawabata Yasunari's novels. A very few poets may have read translations of Yosano Akiko, but after her, contemporary Japanese poetry is almost totally unknown. Translations exist, but their sales have been infinitesimal.

The Nō drama had a revolutionizing influence on both Ezra Pound and William Butler Yeats. There is a fairly large literature of Western plays more or less in the form of Nō. Kabuki has influenced contemporary playwrights, sometimes via Bertolt Brecht, but I seem to be one of the few Westerners who ever goes to the Shimpa theater. The excellent modern Japanese theater is unknown in the West with almost the sole exception of a dramatic adaptation of Kobayashi Takiji's *Cannery Boat* in the early thirties.

The myth of Japan provides a dream world in which the suppressed half of Western civilization can find imaginary fulfillment, but also, by a remarkable example of historical cultural convergence, the forms of Japanese poetry, of the Nō drama, and even of the Japanese language itself happen to parallel the development of poetry in the West from Baudelaire to Rimbaud, to Mallarmé, to Apollinaire, to the Surrealists. Ezra Pound was very aware of this, and beginning with his first little imagist epigram:

In a Station of the Metro

The apparition of these faces in the crowd;
Petals on a wet, black bough.

he called it "superposition." This example does resemble the structure of many classic *waka*, but is nothing strange to Western literature. It is scarcely a metaphor, rather a simile with the connective "like" suppressed. As Pound developed, the language of poetry became for him a vast field of metaphors in which relations could be established at the option of the poet to produce genuinely novel meanings, so that superposition becomes originative of new meanings as in the famous poems of Hitamaro's, *Ashibiki no*:

> The pheasant of the mountain,
> Tiring to the feet,
> Spreads his tail feathers.
> Through the long, long night
> I sleep alone.

whose complex of meanings so many translators have dismissed as purely formal and irrational. (Assuming of course that that is the meaning of the poem, which, as is well known, is disputable.) Before Pound little poems of Mallarmé like *"Petit air"* had already reached the same point—radical dissociation and recombination as in a Cubist painting. As Pound moved on into his long, final work, *The Cantos*, this method which he was to call "ideographic" became his almost exclusive style.

In spite of inaccuracies, Pound's translations of three of the greatest Nō plays have never been equalled either as poetry or as conveying the dramatic essence of Nō. As he, and following him, William Butler Yeats realized, the Nō drama does not move through a deductive logical process to climax and resolution following the recipes of Aristotle's *Poetics*. The Surrealist leader André Breton once pointed out that the development of modern poetry in the West could be interpreted as a revolt against Aristotelian logic and Greek grammar.

Nō drama creates an atmosphere, but one defined in sharp, definite, imagistic terms, an atmosphere of unresolved tensions or longings or irresolutions, and this dramatic situation is resolved by an aesthetic realization which evolves from the dramatic situation as its own archetype. The dance and the songs accompanying the dance have been compared to a crystal of sugar dropping into a supersaturated solution—the dissolved sugar crystallizes around the introduced crystal until the solution is no longer saturated. What eventuates is not resolved climax but realized significance. Yeats's *Plays for Dancers* do accomplish in their own terms the objectives of the Nō drama with, by and large, its methods. There are long tracts of Ezra Pound's *Cantos* that are not successful, but the great passages owe their success to the same method, the aesthetic of Nō and the technique of radical superposition derived from Chinese and Japanese poetry.

Critics with some knowledge of the Chinese written language have made fun of Pound's essay on the Chinese written character and of his advocacy of the ideographic method as a new syntax of the sensibility for Western poetry. He got his ideas of course from the Japanese informants of Ernest Fenollosa and although now the dissecting or parsing of Chinese characters has gone out of fashion, it was once an intellectual indoor sport amongst the more cultivated literati of the Far East.

If Japanese, or for that matter, Chinese poetry is translated into Western syntax and all the spark gaps of meaning are filled up, what results is a series of logically expressed epigrams, usually sentimental, with a vulgar little moral interpretation attached, or at the best a metaphorical epigram of a moment of sensibility like Pound's "Metro," which most resembles, not classical Japanese tanka or even the best haiku, but the more sentimental work of the late Yeddo period. It is this compulsion to fill up the gaps and interpret the poem for Western readers which vitiates the work of so many translators, both Western and Japanese. They too often believe that Westerners could not possibly understand a Japanese poem in all its simplicity. Bashō's "Frog" is self-evident in any language, and yet hundreds of words have been wasted extending and explicating it. As Western logical processes became popular with Japanese translators, and of course with Japanese poets writing in the modern style, Western poets were moving in the opposite direction.

Frances Densmore, one of the first American ethnomusicologists, published many volumes of Indian song—music, text and translation. The songs of some tribes consist of a large number of "abstract" vocables and a few meaningful syllables. In her translations Miss Densmore discarded all but the "real words" and so produced little poems which bear a remarkable resemblance to Japanese poetry:

> As my eyes
> Search the prairie,
> I see the summer in the spring.

> In the heavens
> A noise,
> Like the rustling of the trees.

• • •

The bush
Is sitting
Under a tree
And singing.

The deer
Looks at a flower.

It is quite possible that Miss Densmore modelled these translations on Japanese haiku. They had a profound influence on the American poet Yvor Winters (and, by the way, on myself) who produced about 1924 a book of one line poems similar to haiku.

Hunter

Run in the magpie's shadow

Sleep

O living pine, be still.

In the thirties and forties American poetry in the international modern idiom lived on more or less underground. Imitation of English poetry of the Baroque era was the reigning fashion. The influence of Japanese poetry is apparent in those young poets like Louis Zukofsky, George Oppen and Carl Rakosi who were followers of Pound and of William Carlos Williams, who was a master of the epigram of the sensibility, of poems which resemble the late post-classical haiku and *senryū*.

The first really satisfactory translations from the Japanese appeared in Arthur Waley's *Japanese Poetry, The Uta*, a book which unfortunately was never very easy to obtain, which had an excellent introduction, an elementary grammar and vocabulary and the Japanese text *en face*.

During the Occupation, as has happened so often in history, captivity took captivity captive. Thousands of young Americans learned a little Japanese and came to appreciate the virtues of the Japanese way of life. A smaller number gained an adequate knowledge of the language, and a still smaller number, but still a large one, was converted, not to contemporary Japanese life and thought, but to the traditional religion and culture. For over a generation the work of D. T. Suzuki had been slowly making its way amongst Westerners interested in Buddhism. It is true that Zen as interpreted by Suzuki is a special religion and philosophy which differs in some ways from any common form of the religion in Japan. It has been called "Zen for Westerners." Perhaps so. Certainly it was eminently successful and became the popular American form of Existentialism, much more influential than the work of Jean-Paul Sartre or Karl Jaspers, possibly because it was more meaningful and gave more profound answers. As a new generation matured after the war, Pound and Williams became old masters of the new American poets and their poetic practice and aesthetics along with those of French poets like Mallarmé, Apollinaire and Reverdy and the classical Japanese and Chinese as expounded by Suzuki all converged to produce poets like Robert Creeley, whose best short poems are like those of Japanese poets who have wedded a thoroughly modern sensibility to the classical forms. The last twenty years have seen a growing flood of such poetry.

There is too much of it to discuss in detail. Western civilization is experiencing that secession of the elites and schism in the soul described by Arnold Toynbee. The poetic expression of the counter-culture, which has turned away from the values of the dominant society, has sought and perhaps found new life meanings in the Far East. What was once a social phenomenon confined to a small number of highly sophisticated intellectuals is now a mass movement.

Outstanding among the leaders of this movement are a number of poets who have lived for extended periods in Japan, who speak Japanese, are well read in classic Japanese and Chinese literature, who are usually Buddhists, either Zen or Shingon, and who have meditated long on the words of the Avatamsaka and Lankavatara Sutras. Gary Snyder, Philip Whalen and Cid Corman are outstanding. In the Far East such ideas are usually connected with reactionary politics, but these Western writers are about as radical politically as they could well be, and their criticisms of their own society are fundamental. Long before ecology became a world-wide fad, Snyder and Whalen, still in college, were talking about an ecological aesthetic, a blending of American Indian and Far Eastern philosophies of cooperation with, rather than conquest of, nature. The

Tao Te Ching, the writings of the Zen masters, the meditations of American Indian medicine men, provided them with the foundations for a life philosophy at avowed cross purposes with that of the dominant society. If the counterculture has an ideologist, it is Gary Snyder. In the last fifteen years this life philosophy has proliferated into all levels of American society accompanied with a poetry indebted to classic Japanese examples—from collections of *haiku*, both translated and American, for young children learning to read, to little poems scattered here and there through the works of most younger poets—small crystals of meditation, of the poignancy of nature, or of wit, to *haiku* contests sponsored by small-town women's clubs. American *haiku* and *tanka* show every variety of knowledge or ignorance of their Japanese exemplars or the classic Japanese sensibility, from true, original zen koans or profoundly Buddhist poems comparable to Lady Izumi's, to embarrassingly sentimental nonsense.

Of the more significant young poets who have come up since 1955, a climacteric year in American poetry, at least twenty-five have written several, sometimes many, poems in Japanese style, and in longer poems the influence is more subtly pervasive. It can be safely said that classic Japanese and Chinese poetry are today as influential on American poetry as English or French of any period, and close to determinative for those born since 1940. I have tried to explain why this is so. Classic Far Eastern poetry speaks for all those elements of a complete culture, or factors of the human mind, of man at his most fulfilled, which are suppressed or distorted by Western civilization. This projection of a hunger in the West explains the weak interest in contemporary Japanese poetry, itself the expression, locally modified, of what, for better or worse, has become a world civilization. The contemporary Japanese poets best known in the West are Kitasono Katue, a translator and once somewhat of a follower of Ezra Pound, now one of the very finest concrete poets in the world, and the small group of friends of Gary Snyder who call themselves *harijans*, and who for a while lived in a commune on a remote volcanic island in the Ryukyus.

The Art of Literature

Definitions of the word literature tend to be circular. *The Concise Oxford Dictionary* says it is "writings whose value lies in the beauty of form or emotional effect." The nineteenth-century critic Walter Pater referred to "the matter of imaginative or artistic literature" as a "transcript, not of mere fact, but of fact in its infinitely varied forms." But such definitions really assume that the reader already knows what literature is. And indeed its central meaning, at least, is clear enough. Deriving from the Latin *littera*, "a letter of the alphabet," literature is first and foremost mankind's entire body of writing; after that it is the body of writing belonging to a given language or people; then it is individual pieces of writing.

But already it is necessary to qualify these statements. To use the word writing when describing literature is itself misleading, for one may rightly speak of "oral literature" or "the literature of preliterate peoples." The art of literature is not reducible to the words on the page; they are there because of the craft of writing. As an art, literature is the organization of words to give pleasure; through them it elevates and transforms experience; through them it functions in society as a continuing symbolic criticism of values.

Literature is a form of human expression. But not everything expressed in words—even when organized and written down—is counted as literature. Those writings that are primarily informative—technical, scholarly, journalistic—would be excluded from the rank of literature by most, though not all, critics. Certain forms

Published in The Encyclopædia Britannica, *15th edition, 1974. Copyright* © *1974 by Encyclopædia Britannica, Inc.; reprinted by permission.*

of writing, however, are universally regarded as belonging to literature as an art. Individual attempts within these forms are said to
succeed if they possess something called artistic merit and to fail if
they do not. The nature of artistic merit is less easy to define than to
recognize. The writer need not even pursue it to attain it. On the
contrary, a scientific exposition might be of great literary value and
a pedestrian poem of none at all.

The purest (or, at least, the most intense) literary form is the lyric
poem, and after it comes elegiac, epic, dramatic, narrative, and
expository verse. Most theories of literary criticism base themselves
on an analysis of poetry, because the aesthetic problems of literature
are there presented in their simplest and purest form. Poetry that
fails as literature is not called poetry at all but verse. Many novels—
certainly all the world's great novels—are literature, but there are
thousands that are not so considered. Most great dramas are considered literature (although the Chinese, possessors of one of the
world's greatest dramatic traditions, consider their plays, with few
exceptions, to possess no literary merit whatsoever).

The Greeks thought of history as one of the seven arts, inspired by
a goddess, the muse Clio. All of the world's classic surveys of history
can stand as noble examples of the art of literature, but most
historical works and studies today are not written primarily with
literary excellence in mind, though they may possess it, as it were, by
accident.

The essay was once written deliberately as a piece of literature; its
subject matter was of comparatively minor importance. Today most
essays are written as expository, informative journalism, although
there are still essayists in the great tradition who think of themselves
as artists. Now, as in the past, some of the greatest essayists are critics
of literature, drama, and the arts.

Some personal documents (autobiographies, diaries, memoirs,
and letters) rank among the world's greatest literature. Some examples of this biographical literature were written with posterity in
mind, others with no thought of their being read by anyone but the
writer. Some are in a highly polished literary style; others, couched
in a privately evolved language, win their standing as literature
because of their cogency, insight, depth, and scope.

Many works of philosophy are classed as literature. The *Dialogues* of Plato are written with great narrative skill and in the finest prose; the *Meditations* of the second-century Roman emperor Marcus Aurelius are a collection of apparently random thoughts, and the Greek in which they are written is eccentric. Yet both are classed as literature, while the speculations of other philosophers, ancient and modern, are not. Certain scientific works endure as literature long after their scientific content has become outdated. This is particularly true of books of natural history, where the element of personal observation is of special importance. An excellent example is Gilbert White's *Natural History and Antiquities of Selbourne.*

Oratory, the art of persuasion, was long considered a great literary art. The oratory of the American Indian, for instance, is famous, while in classical Greece, Polymnia was the muse sacred to poetry and oratory. Rome's great orator Cicero was to have a decisive influence on the development of English prose style. Abraham Lincoln's Gettysburg Address is known to every American schoolchild. Today, however, oratory is more usually thought of as a craft than as an art. Most critics would not admit advertising copywriting, purely commercial fiction, or cinema and television scripts as accepted forms of literary expression, although others would hotly dispute their exclusion. The test in individual cases would seem to be one of enduring satisfaction and, of course, truth. Indeed, it becomes more and more difficult to categorize literature, for in modern civilization words are everywhere. Man is subject to a continuous flood of communication. Most of it is fugitive, but here and there—in high-level journalism, in television, in the cinema, in commercial fiction, in westerns and detective stories, and in plain, expository prose—some writing, almost by accident, achieves an aesthetic satisfaction, a depth and relevance that entitle it to stand with other examples of the art of literature.

If the early Egyptians or Sumerians had critical theories about the writing of literature, these have not survived. From the time of classical Greece until the present day, however, Western criticism has been dominated by two opposing theories of the literary art, which might conveniently be called the expressive and constructive theories of composition.

The Greek philosopher and scholar Aristotle is the first great representative of the constructive school of thought. His *Poetics* (the surviving fragment of which is limited to an analysis of tragedy and epic poetry) has sometimes been dismissed as a recipe book for the writing of potboilers. Certainly, Aristotle is primarily interested in the theoretical construction of tragedy, much as an architect might analyze the construction of a temple, but he is not exclusively objective and matter of fact. He does, however, regard the expressive elements in literature as of secondary importance, and the terms he uses to describe them have been open to interpretation and a matter of controversy ever since.

The first-century Greek treatise *On the Sublime* (conventionally attributed to the third-century Longinus) deals with the question left unanswered by Aristotle—what makes great literature "great"? Its standards are almost entirely expressive. Where Aristotle is analytical and states general principles, the pseudo-Longinus is more specific and gives many quotations; even so, his critical theories are confined largely to impressionistic generalities.

Thus, at the beginning of Western literary criticism, the controversy already exists. Is the artist or writer a technician, like a cook or an engineer, who designs and constructs a sort of machine that will elicit an aesthetic response from his audience? Or is he a virtuoso who above all else expresses himself and, because he gives voice to the deepest realities of his own personality, generates a response from his readers because they admit some profound identification with him? This antithesis endures throughout Western European history—Scholasticism versus Humanism, Classicism versus Romanticism, Cubism versus Expressionism—and survives to this day in the common judgment of our contemporary artists and writers. It is surprising how few critics have declared that the antithesis is unreal, that a work of literary or plastic art is at once constructive and expressive, and that it must in fact be both.

Critical theories of literature in the Orient, however, have been more varied. There is an immense amount of highly technical, critical literature in India. Some works are recipe books, vast collections of tropes and stylistic devices; others are philosophical and general. In the best period of Indian literature, the cultural climax of Sanskrit (*c.* 320–490), it is assumed by writers that expressive and constructive factors are twin aspects of one reality. The same could be said of the Chinese, whose literary manuals and books on prosody and rhetoric are, as with the West, relegated to the class of technical handbooks, while their literary criticism is concerned rather with subjective, expressive factors—and so aligns itself with the pseudo-Longinus' "sublime." In Japan, technical, stylistic elements are certainly important (Japanese discrimination in these matters is perhaps the most refined in the world), but both writer and reader above all seek qualities of subtlety and poignancy and look for intimations of profundity often so evanescent as to escape entirely the uninitiated reader.

Far Eastern literary tradition has raised the question of the broad and narrow definitions of poetry (a question familiar in the West from Edgar Allan Poe's advocacy of the short poem in his "Poetic Principle"). There are no long epic poems in Chinese, no verse novels of the sort written in England by Robert Browning or Alfred Lord Tennyson in the nineteenth century. In Chinese drama, apart from a very few of the songs, the verse as such is considered doggerel. The versified treatises on astronomy, agriculture, or fishing, of the sort written in Greek and Roman times and during the eighteenth century in the West, are almost unknown in the Far East. Chinese poetry is almost exclusively lyric, meditative, and elegiac, and rarely does any poem exceed 100 lines—most are little longer than Western sonnets; many are only quatrains. In Japan this tendency to limit length was carried even further. The ballad survives in folk poetry, as it did in China, but the "long poem" of very moderate length disappeared early from literature. For the Japanese, the tanka is a "long poem"; in its common form it has 31 syllables; the *sedō-ka* has 38; the *dodoitsu*, imitating folk song, has 26. From the seventeenth century and onward, the most popular poetic form was the haiku, which has only 17 syllables.

This development is relevant to the West because it spotlights the ever-increasing emphasis which has been laid on intensity of communication, a characteristic of Western poetry (and of literature generally) as it has evolved since the late nineteenth century. In the Far East all cultivated people were supposed to be able to write suitable occasional poetry, and so those qualities that distinguished a poem from the mass consequently came to be valued above all others. Similarly, as modern readers in the West struggle with a "communication avalanche" of words, they seek in literature those forms, ideas, values, vicarious experiences, and styles that transcend the verbiage to be had on every hand.

In some literatures (notably classical Chinese, Old Norse, Old Irish), the language employed is quite different from that spoken or used in ordinary writing. This marks off the reading of literature as a special experience. In the Western tradition, it is only in comparatively modern times that literature has been written in the common speech of cultivated men. The Elizabethans did not talk like Shakespeare nor eighteenth-century people in the stately prose of Samuel Johnson or Edward Gibbon (the so-called Augustan plain style in literature became popular in the late seventeenth century and flourished throughout the eighteenth, but it was really a special form of rhetoric with antecedent models in Greek and Latin). The first person to write major works of literature in the ordinary English language of the educated man was Daniel Defoe, and it is remarkable how little the language has changed since. *Robinson Crusoe* is much more contemporary in tone than the elaborate prose of nineteenth-century writers like Thomas De Quincey or Walter Pater. (Defoe's language is not, in fact, so very simple; simplicity is itself one form of artifice.)

Other writers have sought to use language for its most subtle and complex effects and have deliberately cultivated the ambiguity inherent in the multiple or shaded meanings of words. Between the two world wars, "ambiguity" became very fashionable in English and American poetry and the ferreting out of ambiguities—from even the simplest poem—was a favorite critical sport. T. S. Eliot in his literary essays is usually considered the founder of this movement. Actually, the platform of his critical attitudes is largely moral, but his two disciples, I. A. Richards in *Principles of Literary Criticism* and William Empson in *Seven Types of Ambiguity,* carried his method to extreme lengths. The basic document of the movement is Charles Kay Ogden and I. A. Richards' *The Meaning of Meaning,* a work of enormous importance in its time. Only a generation later, however, their ideas were somewhat at a discount.

Certainly, William Blake or Thomas Campion, when they were writing their simple lyrics, were unaware of the ambiguities and multiple meanings that future critics would find in them. Nevertheless, language is complex. Words do have overtones; they do stir up complicated reverberations in the mind that are ignored in their dictionary definitions. Great stylists, and most especially great poets, work with at least a half-conscious, or subliminal, awareness of the infinite potentialities of language. This is one reason why the essence of most poetry and great prose is so resistant to translation (quite apart from the radically different sound patterns that are created in other-language versions). The translator must project himself into the mind of the original author; he must transport himself into an entirely different world of relationships between sounds and meanings, and at the same time he must establish an equivalence between one infinitely complex system and another. Since no two languages are truly equivalent in anything except the simplest terms, this is a most difficult accomplishment. Certain writers are exceptionally difficult to translate. There are no satisfactory English versions, for example, of the Latin of Catullus, the French of Baudelaire, the Russian of Pushkin, or of the majority of Persian and Arabic poetry. The splendour of Sophocles' Greek, of Plato at his best, is barely suggested even in the finest English versions. On the other hand, the Germans insist that Shakespeare is better in German than he is in English, a humorous exaggeration perhaps. But again, Shakespeare is resistant to translation into French. His English seems to lack equivalents in that language.

The very greatest translations may become classics in their own right, of enduring literary excellence (the King James Version of the Bible, appearing in 1611, is the outstanding example), but on the whole the approximate equivalent of most translations to their originals seems to have a very short life. The original work remains the same, of lasting value to its own people, but the translation becomes out of date with each succeeding generation as the language and criteria of literary taste change. Nothing demonstrates the complexity of literary language more vividly. An analogous process takes place when a reader experiences a literary work in his own language; each generation gets a "new version" from its own classics.

Yet the values of great literature are more fundamental than complexity and subtleties of meaning arising from language alone. Works far removed from contemporary man in time and in cultural background, composed in a variety of languages utterly different from one another in structure, have nevertheless been translated successfully enough to be deeply moving. The twentieth century has seen an immense mass of the oral literature of preliterate peoples and of the writings of all the great civilizations translated into modern languages. Understanding the growth of literature and its forms in other civilizations has greatly enriched the understanding of our own.

Literature, like music, is an art of time, or "tempo": it takes time to read or listen to, and it usually presents events or the development of ideas or the succession of images or all these together in time. The craft of literature, indeed, can be said to be in part the manipulation of a structure in time, and so the simplest element of marking time, rhythm, is therefore of basic importance in both poetry and prose. Prosody, which is the science of versification, has for its subject the materials of poetry and is concerned almost entirely with the laws of metre, or rhythm in the narrowest sense. It deals with the patterning of sound in time; the number, length, accent, and pitch of syllables; and the modifications of rhythm by vowels and consonants. In most poetry, certain basic rhythms are repeated with modifications (that is to say, the poem rhymes or scans or both) but not in all. It most obviously does neither in the case of the "free forms" of modern poetry; but neither does it in the entire poetry of whole cultures. Since lyric poetry is either the actual text of song or else is immediately derived from song, it is regular in structure nearly everywhere in the world, although the elements of patterning that go into producing its rhythm may vary. The most important of these elements in English poetry, for example, have been accent, grouping of syllables (called feet), number of syllables in the line, and rhyme at the end of a line (and sometimes within it). Other elements such as pitch, resonance, repetition of vowels (assonance), repetition of consonants (alliteration), and breath pauses (cadence) have also been of great importance in distinguishing successful poetry from doggerel verse, but on the whole they are not as important as the former, and poets have not always been fully conscious of their use of them. Greek and Latin poetry was consciously patterned on the length of syllables (long or short) rather than on their accent; but all the considerations of "sound" (such as assonance and alliteration) entered into the aesthetically satisfactory structure of a poem. Similarly, both the French and Japanese were content simply to count the syllables in a line—but again, they also looked to all the "sound" elements.

The rhythms of prose are more complicated, though not necessarily more complex, than those of poetry. The rules of prose patterning are less fixed; patterns evolve and shift indefinitely and are seldom repeated except for special emphasis. So the analysis of prose rhythm is more difficult to make than, at least, the superficial analysis of poetry.

The craft of writing involves more than mere rules of prosody. The work's structure must be manipulated to attract the reader. First, the literary situation has to be established. The reader must be directly related to the work, placed in it—given enough information on who, what, when, or why—so that his attention is caught and held (or, on the other hand, he must be deliberately mystified, to the same end).

Aristotle gave a formula for dramatic structure that can be generalized to apply to most literature: presentation, development, complication, crisis, and resolution. Even lyric poems can possess plot in this sense, but by no means are all literary works so structured, nor does such structure ensure their merit—it can be safely said that westerns, detective stories, and cheap melodramas are more likely to follow strictly the rules of Aristotle's *Poetics* than are great novels. Nevertheless, the scheme does provide a norm from which there is infinite variation. Neoclassical dramatists and critics, especially in seventeenth-century France, derived from Aristotle what they called the unities of time, action, and place. This meant that the action of a play should not spread beyond the events of one day and, best of all, should be confined within the actual time of performance. Nor should the action move about too much from place to place—best only to go from indoors to outdoors and back. There should be only one plot line, which might be relieved by a subplot, usually comic. These three unities—of time, place, and action—do not occur in Aristotle and are certainly not observed in Classical Greek tragedy. They are an invention of Renaissance critics, some of whom went even further, insisting also on what might be called a unity of mood. To this day there are those who, working on this principle, object to

Shakespeare's use of comic relief within the tragic action of his plays—to the porter in *Macbeth,* for instance, or the gravediggers in *Hamlet.*

Assiduous critics have found elaborate architectural structures in quite diffuse works—including Miguel de Cervantes' *Don Quixote,* Sterne's *Tristram Shandy,* Casanova's *Icosameron.* But their "discoveries" are too often put there after the event. Great early novels such as the Chinese *Dream of the Red Chamber* and the Japanese *Tale of Genji* usually develop organically rather than according to geometrical formulas, one incident or image spinning off another. Probably the most tightly structured work, in the Neoclassicists' sense, is the Icelandic *Njál's saga.*

The nineteenth century was the golden age of the novel, and most of the more famous examples of the form were systematically plotted, even where the plot structure simply traced the growth in personality of an individual hero or heroine. This kind of novel, of which in their very diverse ways Stendhal's *The Red and the Black* and Dickens' *David Copperfield* are great examples, is known as *Bildungsroman.* Gustave Flaubert's *Madame Bovary* is as rigorously classicist in form as the seventeenth-century plays of Racine and Corneille, which were the high point of the French classical theatre, although Flaubert obeys laws more complex than those of the Aristotelians. Novels such as Tolstoy's *War and Peace,* Dostoyevsky's *Brothers Karamazov,* and the works of Balzac owe much of their power to their ability to overwhelm the reader with a massive sense of reality. The latter nineteenth and early twentieth centuries witnessed an attack on old forms, but what the new writers evolved was simply a new architecture. A novel like James Joyce's *Ulysses,* which takes place in a day and an evening, is one of the most highly structured ever written. Novelists such as Joseph Conrad, Ford Madox Ford, Virginia Woolf, and, to a lesser extent, Henry James developed a multiple-aspect narrative, sometimes by using time shifts and flashbacks and by writing from different points of view, sometimes by using the device (dating back to Classical Greek romances) of having one or more narrators as characters within the story. (This technique, which was first perfected in the verse novels of Robert Browning, in fact reached its most extreme development in the English language in poetry: in Ezra Pound's *Cantos,* T. S.

Eliot's *The Waste Land,* William Carlos Williams' *Paterson,* and the many long poems influenced by them.)

The content of literature is as limitless as the desire of human beings to communicate with one another. The thousands of years, perhaps hundreds of thousands, since the human species first developed speech have seen built up the almost infinite systems of relationships called languages. A language is not just a collection of words in an unabridged dictionary but the individual and social possession of living men, an inexhaustible system of equivalents, of sounds to objects and to one another. Its most primitive elements are those words that express direct experiences of objective reality, and its most sophisticated are concepts on a high level of abstraction. Words are not only equivalent to things, they have varying degrees of equivalence to one another. A symbol, says the dictionary, is something that stands for something else or a sign used to represent something, "as the lion is the symbol of courage, the cross the symbol of Christianity." In this sense all words can be called symbols, but the examples given—the lion and the cross—are really metaphors: that is, symbols that represent a complex of other symbols, and which are generally negotiable in a given society (just as money is a symbol for goods or labor). Eventually a language comes to be, among other things, a huge sea of implicit metaphors, an endless web of interrelated symbols. As literature, especially poetry, grows more and more sophisticated, it begins to manipulate this field of suspended metaphors as a material in itself, often as an end in itself. Thus, there emerge forms of poetry (and prose, too) with endless ramifications of reference, as in Japanese *waka* and *haiku,* some ancient Irish and Norse verse, and much of the poetry written in western Europe since the time of Baudelaire that is called modernist. It might be supposed that, at its most extreme, this development would be objective, constructive—aligning it with the critical theories stemming from Aristotle's *Poetics.* On the contrary, it is romantic, subjective art, primarily because the writer handles such material instinctively and subjectively, approaches it as the "collective unconscious," to use the term of the psychologist Carl Jung, rather than with deliberate rationality.

By the time literature appears in the development of a culture, the society has already come to share a whole system of stereotypes and archetypes: major symbols standing for the fundamental realities of the human condition, including the kind of symbolic realities that are enshrined in religion and myth. Literature may use such symbols directly, but all great works of literary art are, as it were, original and unique myths. The world's great classics evoke and organize the archetypes of universal human experience. This does not mean, however, that all literature is an endless repetition of a few myths and motives, endlessly retelling the first stories of civilized man, repeating the Sumerian *Epic of Gilgamesh* or Sophocles' *Oedipus the King*. The subject matter of literature is as wide as human experience itself. Myths, legends, and folktales lie at the beginning of literature, and their plots, situations, and allegorical (metaphorical narrative) judgments of life represent a constant source of literary inspiration that never fails. This is so because mankind is constant—men share a common physiology. Even social structures, after the development of cities, remain much alike. Whole civilizations have a life pattern that repeats itself through history. Jung's term "collective unconscious" really means that mankind is one species, with a common fund of general experience. Egyptian scribes, Soviet bureaucrats, and junior executives in New York City live and respond to life in the same ways; the lives of farmers or miners or hunters vary only within narrow limits. Love is love and death is death, for a South African Bushman and a French Surrealist alike. So the themes of literature have at once an infinite variety and an abiding constancy. They can be taken from myth, from history, or from contemporary occurrence, or they can be pure invention (but even if they are invented, they are nonetheless constructed from the constant materials of real experience, no matter how fantastic the invention).

As time goes on, literature tends to concern itself more and more with the interior meanings of its narrative, with problems of human personality and human relationships. Many novels are fictional, psychological biographies which tell of the slowly achieved integration of the hero's personality or of his disintegration, of the conflict between self-realization and the flow of events and the demands of other people. This can be presented explicitly, where the characters talk about what is going on in their heads; either ambiguously and with reserve, as in the novels of Henry James, or overtly, as in those of Dostoyevsky. Alternatively, it can be presented by a careful arrangement of objective facts, where psychological development is described purely in terms of behavior, and where the reader's subjective response is elicited by the minute descriptions of physical reality, as in the novels of Stendhal and the greatest Chinese novels like the *Dream of the Red Chamber*, which convince the reader that through the novel he is seeing reality itself, rather than an artfully contrived semblance of reality.

Literature, however, is not solely concerned with the concrete, with objective reality, with individual psychology, or with subjective emotion. Some deal with abstract ideas or philosophical conceptions. Much purely abstract writing is considered literature only in the widest sense of the term, and the philosophical works that are ranked as great literature are usually presented with more or less of a sensuous garment. Thus, Plato's *Dialogues* rank as great literature because the philosophical material is presented in dramatic form, as the dialectical outcome of the interchange of ideas between clearly drawn, vital personalities, and because the descriptive passages are of great lyric beauty. Karl Marx's *Das Kapital* approaches great literature in certain passages in which he expresses the social passion he shares with the Hebrew prophets of the Old Testament. Euclid's *Elements* and St. Thomas Aquinas' *Summa theologica* give literary, aesthetic satisfaction to some people because of their purity of style and beauty of architectonic construction. In short, most philosophical works that rank as great literature do so because they are intensely human. The reader responds to Pascal's *Pensées*, to Montaigne's *Essays*, and to Marcus Aurelius' *Meditations* as he would to living men. Sometimes the pretense of purely abstract intellectual rigor is in fact a literary device. The writings of the twentieth-century philosopher Ludwig Wittgenstein, for example, owed much of their impact to this approach, while the poetry of Paul Valéry borrows the language of philosophy and science for its rhetorical and evocative power.

Throughout literary history, many great critics have pointed out that it is artificial to make a distinction between form and content, except for purposes of analytical discussion. Form determines content. Content determines form. The issue is, indeed, usually only raised at all by those critics who are more interested in politics, religion, or ideology than in literature; thus, they object to writers who they feel sacrifice ideological orthodoxy for formal perfection, message for style.

But style cannot really be said to exist on paper at all; it is the way the mind of the author expresses itself in words. Since words represent ideas, there cannot be abstract literature unless a collection of nonsense syllables can be admitted as literature. Even the most avant-garde writers associated with the Cubist or Non-Objective painters used language, and language is meaning, though the meaning may be incomprehensible. Oscar Wilde and Walter Pater, the great nineteenth-century exponents of "art for art's sake," were in fact tireless propagandists for their views, which dominate their most flowery prose. It is true that great style depends on the perfect matching of content and form, so that the literary expression perfectly reflects the writer's intention; "poor style" reveals the inability of a writer to match the two—in other words, reveals his inability to express himself. This is why we say that "style expresses the man." The veiled style of Henry James, with its subtleties, equivocations, and qualifications, perfectly reflects his complicated and subtle mind and his abiding awareness of ambiguity in human motives. At the other extreme, the style of Theodore Dreiser—bumbling, clumsy, dogged, troubled—perfectly embodies his own attitudes toward life and is, in fact, his constant judgment of his subject matter. Sometimes an author, under the impression that he is simply polishing his style, may completely alter his content. As Flaubert worked over the drafts of *Madame Bovary*, seeking always the apposite word that would precisely convey his meaning, he lifted his novel from a level of sentimental romance to make it one of the great ironic tragedies of literature. Yet, to judge from his correspondence, he seems never to have been completely aware of what he had done, of the severity of his own irony.

Literature may be an art, but writing is a craft, and a craft must be learned. Talent, special ability in the arts, may appear at an early age; the special personality called genius may indeed be born, not made. But skill in matching intention and expression comes with practice. Naive writers, "naturals" like Samuel Pepys, Restif de la Bretonne, Henry Miller, are all deservedly called stylists, although their styles are far removed from the deliberate, painstaking practice of a Flaubert or a Turgenev. They wrote spontaneously whatever came into their heads; but they wrote constantly, voluminously, and were, by their own standards, skilled practitioners.

There are certain forms of literature that do not permit such highly personal behavior—for instance, formal lyric poetry and classic drama. In these cases the word "form" is used to mean a predetermined structure within whose mold the content must be fitted. These structures are, however, quite simple and so cannot be said to determine the content. Racine and Corneille were contemporaries; both were Neoclassic French dramatists; both abided by all the artificial rules—usually observing the "unities" and following the same strict rules of prosody. Yet their plays, and the poetry in which they are written, differ completely. Corneille is intellectually and emotionally a Neoclassicist—clear and hard, a true objectivist, sure of both his verse and the motivations of his characters. Racine was a great romantic long before the age of Romanticism. His characters are confused and tortured; his verse throbs like the heartbeats of his desperate heroines. He is a great sentimentalist in the best and deepest meaning of that word. His later influence on poets like Baudelaire and Paul Valéry is due to his mastery of sentimental expression, not, as they supposed, to his mastery of Neoclassic form.

Verse on any subject matter can of course be written purely according to formula. The eighteenth century in England saw all sorts of prose treatises cast in rhyme and metre, but this was simply applied patterning. (Works such as *The Botanic Garden* by Erasmus Darwin should be sharply distinguished from James Thomson's *The Seasons*, which is true poetry, not versified natural history—just as Virgil's *Georgics* is not an agricultural handbook.) Neoclassicism, especially in its eighteenth-century developments, confused—for ordinary minds, at any rate—formula with form and so led to the revolt called Romanticism. The leading theorists of that revolt, William Wordsworth and Samuel Taylor Coleridge, in the "Preface" to *Lyrical Ballads* urged the observance of a few simple rules basic to all great poetry and demanded a return to the integrity of expressive form. A similar revolution in taste was taking place all over Europe and also in China (where the narrow pursuit of formula had almost destroyed poetry). The Romantic taste could enjoy the "formlessness" of William Blake's prophetic books, or Walt Whitman's *Leaves of Grass*, or the loose imagination of Shelley—but careful study reveals that these writers were not formless at all. Each had his own personal form.

Time passes and the pendulum of taste swings. In the mid-twentieth century, Paul Valéry, T. S. Eliot, and Yvor Winters would attack what the latter called "the fallacy of expressive form," but this is itself a fallacy. All form in literature is expressive. All expression has its own form, even when the form is a deliberate quest of formlessness. (The automatic writing cultivated by the Surrealists, for instance, suffers from the excessive formalism of the unconscious mind and is far more stereotyped than the poetry of the Neoclassicist Alexander Pope.) Form simply refers to organization, and critics who attack form do not seem always to remember that a writer organizes more than words. He organizes experience. Thus, his organization stretches far back in his mental process. Form is the other face of content, the outward, visible sign of inner spiritual reality.

In preliterate societies oral literature was widely shared; it saturated the society and was as much a part of living as food, clothing, shelter, or religion. In barbaric societies, the minstrel might be a courtier of the king or chieftain, and the poet who composed liturgies might be a priest. But the oral performance itself was accessible to the whole community. As society evolved its various social layers, or classes, an "elite" literature began to be distinguishable from the "folk" literature of the people. With the invention of writing this separation was accelerated until finally literature was being experienced individually by the elite (reading a book), while folklore and folk song were experienced orally and more or less collectively by the illiterate common people.

Elite literature continuously refreshes itself with materials drawn from the popular. Almost all poetic revivals, for instance, include in their programs a new appreciation of folk song, together with a demand for greater objectivity. On the other hand folk literature borrows themes and, very rarely, patterns from elite literature. Many of the English and Scottish ballads that date from the end of the Middle Ages and have been preserved by oral tradition share plots and even turns of phrase with written literature. A very large percentage of these ballads contain elements that are common to folk ballads from all over western Europe; central themes of folklore, indeed, are found all over the world. Whether these common elements are the result of diffusion is a matter for dispute. They do, however, represent great psychological constants, archetypes of experience common to the human species, and so these constants are used again and again by elite literature as it discovers them in folklore.

There is a marked difference between true popular literature, that of folklore and folk song, and the popular literature of modern times. Popular literature today is produced either to be read by a literate audience or to be enacted on television or in the cinema; it is produced by writers who are members, however lowly, of an elite corps of professional literates. Thus, popular literature no longer springs from the people; it is handed to them. Their role is passive. At the best they are permitted a limited selectivity as consumers.

Certain theorists once believed that folk songs and even long, narrative ballads were produced collectively, as has been said in mockery "by the tribe sitting around the fire and grunting in unison." This idea is very much out of date. Folk songs and folk tales began somewhere in one human mind. They were developed and shaped into the forms in which they are now found by hundreds of other minds as they were passed down through the centuries. Only in this sense were they "collectively" produced. During the twentieth century, folklore and folk speech have had a great influence on elite literature—on writers as different as Franz Kafka and Carl Sandburg, Selma Lagerlöf and Kawabata Yasunari, Martin Buber and Isaac Bashevis Singer. Folk song has always been popular with bohemian intellectuals, especially political radicals (who certainly are an elite). Since World War II the influence of folk song upon popular song has not just been great; it has been determinative. Almost all "hit" songs since the mid-century have been imitation folk songs; and some authentic folk singers attract immense audiences.

Popular fiction and drama, westerns and detective stories, films and television serials, all deal with the same great archetypal themes as folktales and ballads, though this is seldom due to direct influence; these are simply the limits within which the human mind works. The number of people who have elevated the formulas of popular fiction to a higher literary level is surprisingly small. Examples are H. G. Wells's early science fiction, the western stories of Gordon Young and Ernest Haycox, the detective stories of Sir Arthur Conan Doyle, Georges Simenon, and Raymond Chandler.

The latter half of the twentieth century has seen an even greater change in popular literature. Writing is a static medium: that is to say, a book is read by one person at a time; it permits recollection and anticipation; the reader can go back to check a point or move ahead to find out how the story ends. In radio, television, and the cinema the medium is fluent; the audience is a collectivity and is at the mercy of time. It cannot pause to reflect or to understand more fully without missing another part of the action, nor can it go back or forward. Marshall McLuhan in his book *Understanding Media* became famous for erecting a whole structure of aesthetic, sociological, and philosophical theory upon this fact. But it remains to be seen whether the new, fluent materials of communication are going to make so very many changes in civilization, let alone in the human mind—mankind has, after all, been influenced for thousands of years by the popular, fluent arts of music and drama. Even the most transitory television serial was written down before it was performed, and the script can be consulted in the files. Before the invention of writing, all literature was fluent because it was contained in people's memory. In a sense it was more fluent than music, because it was harder to remember. Man in mass society becomes increasingly a creature of the moment, but the reasons for this are undoubtedly more fundamental than his forms of entertainment.

Literature, like all other human activities, necessarily reflects current social and economic conditions. Class stratification was reflected in literature as soon as it had appeared in life. Among the American Indians, for instance, the chants of the shaman, or medicine man, differ from the secret, personal songs of the individual, and these likewise differ from the group songs of ritual or entertainment sung in community. In the Heroic Age, the epic tales of kings and chiefs that were sung or told in their barbaric courts differed from the folktales that were told in peasant cottages.

The more cohesive a society, the more the elements—and even attitudes—evolved in the different class strata are interchangeable at all levels. In the tight clan organization that existed in late medieval times at the Scottish border, for example, heroic ballads telling of the deeds of lords and ladies were preserved in the songs of the common people. But where class divisions are unbridgeable, elite literature is liable to be totally separated from popular culture. An extreme example is the classic literature of the Roman Empire. Its forms and its sources were largely Greek—it even adopted its laws of verse patterning from Greek models, even though these were antagonistic to the natural patterns of the Latin language—and most of the sophisticated works of the major Latin authors were completely closed to the overwhelming majority of people of the Roman Empire.

Printing has made all the difference in the negotiability of ideas. The writings of the eighteenth-century French writers Voltaire, Rousseau, and Diderot were produced from and for almost as narrow a caste as the Roman elite, but they were printed. Within a generation they had penetrated the entire society and were of vital importance in revolutionizing it.

Class distinctions in the literature of modern times exist more in the works themselves than in their audience. Although Henry James wrote about the upper classes and Émile Zola about workingmen, both were, in fact, members of an elite and were read by members of an elite—moreover, in their day, those who read Zola certainly considered themselves more of an elite than did the readers of Henry James. The ordinary people, if they read at all, preferred sentimental romances and "penny dreadfuls." Popular literature had already become commercially produced entertainment literature, a type which today is also provided by television scripts.

The elite who read serious literature are not necessarily members of a social or economic upper class. It has been said of the most ethereal French poet, Stéphane Mallarmé, that in every French small town there was a youth who carried his poems in his heart. These poems are perhaps the most "elite" product of western European civilization, but the "youths" referred to were hardly the sons of dukes or millionaires. (It is a curious phenomenon that, since the middle of the eighteenth century in Europe and in the United

States, the majority of readers of serious literature—as well as of entertainment literature—have been women. The extent of the influence that this audience has exerted on literature itself must be immense.)

Hippolyte Taine, the nineteenth-century French critic, evolved an ecological theory of literature. He looked first and foremost to the national characteristics of western European literatures, and he found the source of these characteristics in the climate and soil of each respective nation. His *History of English Literature* is an extensive elaboration of these ideas. It is doubtful that anyone today would agree with the simplistic terms in which Taine states his thesis. It is obvious that Russian literature differs from English or French from German. English books are written by Englishmen, their scenes are commonly laid in England, they are usually about Englishmen and they are designed to be read by Englishmen—at least in the first instance. But modern civilization becomes more and more a world civilization, wherein works of all peoples flow into a general fund of literature. It is not unusual to read a novel by a Japanese author one week and one by a black writer from West Africa the next. Writers are themselves affected by this cross-fertilization. Certainly, the work of the great nineteenth-century Russian novelists has had more influence on twentieth-century American writers than has the work of their own literary ancestors. Poetry does not circulate so readily, because catching its true significance in translation is so very difficult to accomplish. Nevertheless, for the past 100 years or so, the influence of French poetry upon all the literatures of the civilized world has not just been important, it has been pre-eminent. The tendentious elements of literature—propaganda for race, nation, or religion—have been more and more eroded in this process of wholesale cultural exchange.

Popular literature on the other hand is habitually tendentious both deliberately and unconsciously. It reflects and stimulates the prejudices and parochialism of its audience. Most of the literary conflicts that have seized the totalitarian countries during the twentieth century stem directly from relentless efforts by the state to reduce elite literature to the level of the popular. The great proletarian novels of our time have been produced, not by Russians, but by American Negroes, Japanese, Germans, and—most proletarian of all—a German-American living in Mexico, B. Traven. Government control and censorship can inhibit literary development, perhaps deform it a little, and can destroy authors outright; but, whether in the France of Louis XIV or in the Soviet Union of the twentieth century, it cannot be said to have a fundamental effect upon the course of literature.

A distinguishing characteristic of modern literature is the peculiar elite which it has itself evolved. In earlier cultures the artist, though he may have been neurotic at times, thought of himself as part of his society and shared its values and attitudes. Usually the clerkly caste played a personal, important role in society. In the modern industrial civilization, however, "scribes" became simply a category of skilled hired hands. The writer shared few of the values of the merchant or the entrepreneur or manager. And so the literary and artistic world came to have a subculture of its own. The antagonism between the two resultant sets of values is the source of what we call alienation—among the intellectuals at least (the alienation of the common man in urban, industrial civilization from his work, from himself, and from his fellows is another matter, although its results are reflected and intensified in the alienation of the elite). For about 200 years now, the artistic environment of the writer has not usually been shared with the general populace. The subculture known as bohemia and the literary and artistic movements generated in its little special society have often been more important—at least in the minds of many writers—than the historical, social, and economic movements of the culture as a whole. Even massive historical change is translated into these terms—the Russian Revolution, for instance, into Communist-Futurism, Constructivism, Socialist Realism, Western European literature could be viewed as a parade of movements—Romanticism, Realism, Naturalism, Futurism, Structuralism, and so on indefinitely. Some of the more journalistic critics, indeed, have delighted to regard it in such a way. But after the manifestos have been swept away, the meetings adjourned, the literary cafés of the moment lost their popularity, the turmoil is seen not to have made so very much difference. The Romantic Théophile Gautier and the Naturalist Émile Zola have more in common than they have differences, and their differences are rather because of changes in society as a whole than because of conflicting literary principles.

At first, changes in literary values are appreciated only at the upper levels of the literary elite itself, but often, within a generation, works once thought esoteric are being taught as part of a school syllabus. Most cultivated people once thought James Joyce's *Ulysses* incomprehensible or, where it was not, obscene. Today his methods and subject matter are commonplace in the commercial fiction of the mass culture. A few writers remain confined to the elite. Mallarmé is a good example—but he would have been just as ethereal had he written in the simplest French of direct communication. His subtleties are ultimately grounded in his personality.

Literature has an obvious kinship with the other arts. Presented, a play is drama; read, a play is literature. Most important films have been based upon written literature, usually novels, although all the great epics and most of the great plays have been filmed at some time and thus have stimulated the younger medium's growth. Conversely, the techniques required in writing for film have influenced many writers in structuring their novels and have affected their style. Most popular fiction is written with "movie rights" in mind, and these are certainly a consideration with most modern publishers. Literature provides the libretto for operas, the theme for tone poems—even so anomalous a form as Nietzsche's *Thus Spake Zarathustra* was interpreted in music by Richard Strauss—and of course it provides the lyrics of songs. Many ballets and modern dances are based on stories or poems. Sometimes, music and dance are accompanied by a text read by a speaker or chanted by a chorus. The mid-nineteenth century was the heyday of literary, historical, and anecdotal painting, though, aside from the Surrealists, this sort of thing died out in the twentieth century. Cross-fertilization of literature and the arts now takes place more subtly, mostly in the use of parallel techniques—the rational dissociation of the Cubists or the spontaneous action painting of the Abstract Expressionists, for example, which flourished at the same time as the free-flowing uncorrected narratives of some novelists in the 1950s and '60s.

Critics have invented a variety of systems for treating literature as a collection of genres. Often these genres are artificial, invented after the fact with the aim of making literature less sprawling, more tidy. Theories of literature must be based upon direct experience of the living texts and so be flexible enough to contain their individuality and variety. Perhaps the best approach is historical, or genetic.

What actually happened, and in what way did literature evolve up to the present day?

There is a surprising variety of oral literature among surviving preliterate peoples, and, as the written word emerges in history, the indications are that the important literary genres all existed at the beginning of civilized societies: heroic epic; songs in praise of priests and kings; stories of mystery and the supernatural; love lyrics; personal songs (the result of intense meditation); love stories; tales of adventure and heroism (of common peoples, as distinct from the heroic epics of the upper classes); satire (which was dreaded by barbaric chieftains); satirical combats (in which two poets or two personifications abused one another and praised themselves); ballads and folktales of tragedy and murder; folk stories, such as the tale of the clever boy who performs impossible tasks, outwits all his adversaries, and usually wins the hand of the king's daughter; animal fables like those attributed to Aesop (the special delight of Black Africa and Indian America); riddles, proverbs, and philosophical observations; hymns, incantations, and mysterious songs of priests; and finally actual mythology—stories of the origin of the world and the human race, of the great dead, and of the gods and demigods.

The true heroic epic never evolved far from its preliterate origins, and it arose only in the Heroic Age which preceded a settled civilization. The conditions reflected in, say, the *Iliad* and *Odyssey* are much the same as those of the Anglo-Saxon *Beowulf*, the German *Nibelungenlied*, or the Irish stories of Cúchulainn. The literary epic is another matter altogether. Virgil's *Aeneid*, for instance, or Milton's *Paradise Lost* are products of highly sophisticated literary cultures. Many long poems sometimes classified as epic literature are no such thing—Dante's *La divina Commedia*, for example, is a long theological, philosophical, political, moral, and mystical poem. Dante considered it to be a kind of drama which obeyed the rules of Aristotle's *Poetics*. Goethe's *Faust* is in dramatic form and is sometimes even staged—but it is really a philosophical poetic novel. Modern critics have described long poems such as T. S. Eliot's *Waste Land* and Ezra Pound's *Cantos* as "philosophical epics." There is nothing epic about them; they are reveries, more or less philosophical.

Lyric poetry never gets far from its origins, except that some of its finest examples—Medieval Latin, Provençal, Middle High German, Middle French, Renaissance—which today are only read, were actually written to be sung. In the twentieth century, however, popular songs of great literary merit have become increasingly common—for example, the songs of Bertolt Brecht and Kurt Weill in German, of Georges Brassens and Anne Sylvestre in French, and of Leonard Cohen, Bob Dylan, and Joni Mitchell. It is interesting to note that, in periods when the culture values artificiality, the lyric becomes stereotyped. Then, after a while, the poets revolt and, usually turning to folk origins, restore to lyric poetry at least the appearance of naturalness and spontaneity.

The forms of satire are as manifold as those of literature itself—from those of the mock epic to the biting epigram. A great many social and political novels of today would have been regarded as satire by the ancients. Many of the great works of all time are satires, but in each case they have risen far above their immediate satirical objectives. The sixteenth-century medieval satire on civilization, the *Gargantua and Pantagruel* of Rabelais, grew under the hand of its author into a great archetypal myth of the lust for life. Cervantes' *Don Quixote*, often called the greatest work of prose fiction in the West, is superficially a satire of the sentimental romance of knightly adventure. But, again, it is an archetypal myth, telling the adventures of the soul of man—of the individual—in the long struggle with what is called the human condition. *The Tale of Genji* by Murasaki Shikibu has sometimes been considered by obtuse critics as no more than a satire on the sexual promiscuity of the Heian court. In fact, it is a profoundly philosophical, religious, and mystical novel.

Extended prose fiction is the latest of the literary forms to develop. We have romances from classical Greek times that are as long as short novels; but they are really tales of adventure—vastly extended anecdotes. The first prose fiction of any psychological depth is the *Satyricon*, attributed to Petronius Arbiter. Though it survives only in fragments, supposedly one-eleventh of the whole, even these would indicate that it is one of the greatest picaresque novels, composed of loosely connected episodes of robust and often erotic adventure. The other great surviving fiction of classical times is the *Metamorphoses* (known as *The Golden Ass*) by Apuleius. In addition to being a picaresque adventure story, it is a criticism of Roman society, a celebration of the religion of Isis, and an allegory of the progress of the soul. It contains the justly celebrated story of Cupid and Psyche, a myth retold with psychological subtlety. Style has much to do with the value and hence the survival of these two works. They are written in prose of extraordinary beauty, although it is by no means of "classical" purity. The prose romances of the Middle Ages are closely related to earlier heroic literature. Some, like Sir Thomas Malory's *Le Morte d'Arthur*, are retellings of heroic legend in terms of the romantic chivalry of the early Renaissance, a combination of barbaric, medieval, and Renaissance sensibility which, in the tales of Tristram and Isolt and Lancelot and Guinevere, produced something not unlike modern novels of tragic love.

The Western novel is a product of modern civilization, although in the Far East novels began a separate development as early as the tenth century. Extended prose works of complex interpersonal relations and motivations begin in seventeenth-century France with *The Princess of Cleves* by Madame de Lafayette. Eighteenth-century France produced an immense number of novels dealing with love analysis but none to compare with Madame de Lafayette's until Pierre Choderlos de Laclos wrote *Les Liaisons dangereuses*. This was, in form, an exchange of letters between two corrupters of youth; but, in intent, it was a savage satire of the *ancient régime* and a heart-rending psychological study. The English novel of the eighteenth century was less subtle, more robust—vulgar in the best sense—and is exemplified by Henry Fielding's *Tom Jones* and Laurence Sterne's *Tristram Shandy*. The nineteenth century was the golden age of the novel. It became ever more profound, complex, and subtle (or, on the other hand, more popular, eventful, and sentimental). By the beginning of the twentieth century it had become the most common form of thoughtful reading matter and had replaced, for most educated people, religious, philosophical, and scientific works as a medium for the interpretation of life. By the late 1920s the novel had begun to show signs of decay as a form, and no works have since been produced to compare with the recent past. This may prove to be a temporarily barren period, or else the novel may be losing its energy as a narrative art form and in this sense giving way to the medium of film.

Like lyric poetry, drama has been an exceptionally stable literary form. Given a little leeway, most plays written by the beginning of the twentieth century could be adjusted to the rules of Aristotle's *Poetics*. Before World War I, however, all traditional art forms, led by painting, began to disintegrate, and new forms evolved to take their place. In drama the most radical innovator was August Strindberg, and from that day to this, drama (forced to compete with the cinema) has become ever more experimental, constantly striving for new methods, materials, and, especially, ways to establish a close relationship with the audience. All this activity has profoundly modified drama as literature.

In the twentieth century the methods of poetry have also changed drastically, although the "innovator" here might be said to have been Baudelaire. The disassociation and recombination of ideas of the Cubists, the free association of ideas of the Surrealists, dreams, trance states, the poetry of preliterate people—all have been absorbed into the practice of modern poetry. This proliferation of form is not likely to end. Effort that once was applied to perfecting a single pattern in a single form may in the future be more and more directed toward the elaboration of entirely new "multimedia" forms, employing the resources of all the established arts. At the same time, writers may prefer to simplify and polish the forms of the past with a rigorous, Neoclassicist discipline. In a worldwide urban civilization, which has taken to itself the styles and discoveries of all cultures past and present, the future of literature is quite impossible to determine.

Research by scholars into the literary past began almost as soon as literature itself—as soon as the documents accumulated—and for many centuries it represents almost all the scholarship that has survived. The most extensive text of the Sumerian *Epic of Gilgamesh*, the first of the world's great classics, is a late Assyrian synthesis that must have required an immense amount of research into clay tablets, written in several languages going back to the beginning of Mesopotamian civilization. Many Egyptian poems and the philosophic creation myth known as the "Memphite Theology" survive in very late texts that carefully reproduce the original language of the first dynasties. Once the function of the scribe was established as essential, he invented literary scholarship, both to secure his position and to occupy his leisure. The great epoch of literary scholarship in ancient times centered on the library (and university) of Alexandria from its foundation in 324 B.C. to its destruction by the Arabs in A.D. 640. Hellenistic Greek scholars there developed such an academic and pedantic approach to literary scholarship and scholarly literature that the term Alexandrine remains pejorative to this day. To them, however, is owed the survival of the texts of most of the Greek classics. Roman literary scholarship was rhetorical rather than analytic. With the coming of Islām, there was established across the whole warm temperate zone of the Old World a far-flung community of scholars who were at home in learned circles from India to Spain. Judaism, like Islām, was a religion of the book and of written tradition, so literary scholarship played a central role in each. The same is true of India, China, and later Japan; for sheer bulk, as well as for subtlety and insight, Oriental scholarship has never been surpassed. In a sense, the Renaissance in Europe was a cultural revolution led by literary scholars who discovered, revived, and made relevant again the literary heritage of Greece and Rome. In the nineteenth century, literary scholarship was dominated by the exhaustive, painstaking German academician, and that Germanic tradition passed to the universities of the United States. The demand that every teacher should write a master's thesis, a doctor's dissertation, and, for the rest of his career, publish with reasonable frequency learned articles and scholarly books, has led to a mass of scholarship of widely varying standards and value. Some is trivial and absurd, but the best has perfected the texts and thoroughly illuminated the significance of nearly all the world's great literature.

Literary criticism, as distinguished from scholarly research, is usually itself considered a form of literature. Some people find great critics as entertaining and stimulating as great poets, and theoretical treatises of literary aesthetics can be as exciting as novels. Aristotle, Longinus, and the Roman rhetorician and critic Quintilian are still read, although Renaissance critics like the once all-powerful Josephus Scaliger are forgotten by all but specialized scholars. Later critics, such as Poe, Sainte-Beuve, Taine, Vissarion Belinsky, Matthew Arnold, Walter Bagehot, Walter Pater, and George Saintsbury, are probably read more for themselves than for their literary judgments and for their general theorizing rather than for their applications (in the case of the first three, for instance, time has confounded almost all the evaluations they made of their contemporaries). The English critics have survived because they largely confined themselves to acknowledged masterpieces and general ideas. Perhaps literary criticism can really be read as a form of autobiography. Aestheticians of literature like I. A. Richards, Sir C. M. Bowra, Paul Valéry, Suzanne Langer, and Ernst Cassirer have had an influence beyond the narrow confines of literary scholarship and have played in our time something approaching the role of general philosophers. This has been true on the popular level as well. The Dane Georg Brandes, the Americans James Gibbons Huneker, H. L. Mencken, and Edmund Wilson—these men have been social forces in their day. Literary criticism can play its role in social change. In Japan, the overthrow of the shogunate, the restoration of the emperor, and the profound change in the Japanese social sensibility begins with the literary criticism of Moto-ori Norinaga. The nineteenth-century revolution in theology resulted from the convergence of Darwinian theories of evolution and the technical and historical criticism of the Bible that scholars had undertaken. For many modern intellectuals, the literary quarterlies and weeklies, with their tireless discussions of the spiritual significance and formal characteristics of everything from the greatest masterpiece to the most ephemeral current production, can be said to have filled the place of religion, both as rite and dogma.

Lafcadio Hearn and Buddhism

In attempting a book upon a country so well trodden as Japan, I could not hope—nor would I consider it prudent attempting—to discover totally new things, but only to consider things in a totally new way. . . . The studied aim would be to create, in the minds of the readers, a vivid impression of *living* in Japan—not simply as an observer but as one taking part in the daily existence of the common people, and *thinking with their thoughts*.

So Lafcadio Hearn wrote to *Harper's* magazine in 1889 just prior to leaving for Japan. He kept this promise so well that by his death in 1904 (as Koizumi Yakumo, a Japanese citizen) he was acclaimed as one of America's greatest prose stylists and the most influential authority of his generation on Japanese culture. That reputation has dimmed somewhat since then. Changing tastes in literary styles have made Hearn's work seem old-fashioned, and Japan's astonishing absorption of Western industrial methods and industrial values have made him for a time irrelevant.

Now interest in ancient Japanese culture and religion is again on the rise, and Hearn's work, devoted as it is to what he perceived as lasting and essential in Japanese life, is experiencing a revival. From his essays and stories emerges a sensitive and durable vision of how Buddhism was and still is lived in Japan—the ancient Buddhist traditions, rituals, myths, and stories that are still preserved, and their effects upon the beliefs and daily life of ordinary Japanese people.

Published as the Introduction to The Buddhist Writings of Lafcadio Hearn *(Santa Barbara: Ross-Erikson, 1977); not previously collected.*

Lafcadio Hearn was born on the Ionian island of Santa Maura in either June or August 1850 and died in Ōkubo, Japan in 1904. His father was an Irish surgeon major stationed in Greece and his mother a Greek woman, famous for her beauty. It was she who named him Lafcadio, after Leudakia, the ancient name of Santa Maura, one of the islands connected with the legend of Sappho. In a relatively short lifespan of fifty-four years he managed to live several different literary lives.

From Greece, at two years of age, he went to Ireland, where his father soon obtained a dissolution of marriage from his mother. She was sent back to Greece. His father quickly re-married and went off to India. That is the last Hearn saw of either of them.

His formal education consisted of one year at a Catholic school in France (he just missed Guy de Maupassant, who entered the school a year later and who later became one of his literary idols), and four years at St. Cuthbert's in England, where he lost one eye in a playing field accident. The disfigurement (the blinded eye was whitened, the good eye protruded from overuse) helped to make Hearn a painfully sensitive and shy person for the rest of his life. At seventeen, as a result of financial and personal misfortunes in the family, he was withdrawn from school. A year later, his uncle gave him passage money to America and advised him to look up a distant relative in Cincinnati. From then on Hearn had to make his own way in the world.

After a year of homelessness and near-starvation in Cincinnati, Hearn got a job as an editor for a trade journal and then as a reporter for the daily *Enquirer*. His assignment was the night watch, his specialty sensational crimes and gory murders. He had good contacts in the coroner's office, and his small, shy figure and one-eyed face did not arouse suspicion among the street people. His stories, with their ghastly descriptions, were frequent features that titillated the *Enquirer*'s readers. The editor reluctantly fired Hearn when rumors began to circulate that he was living with a mulatto woman whom he insisted he had married. (He had, but Ohio law refused to recognize mixed marriages.)

Another daily newspaper, the Cincinnati *Commercial*, hired him immediately. Here Hearn was allowed to contribute brief scholarly essays, local color stories, and prose poems, as well as the sensational stories that had got him his reputation. But he was restless with this kind of newspaper work, and sick of Cincinnati. In 1877 he quit the *Commercial* and left for New Orleans.

There he found work as a reporter for the struggling *Item*, though what he reported was anything he fancied, most often sketches of Creole and Cajun life. His *Item* essays were eccentric, flamboyant, and often self-indulgent, but they caught the eye of New Orleans' literary establishment. When the city's two largest newspapers merged to form the *Times-Democrat*, Hearn was invited to be its literary editor. He translated and adapted French stories (principally Gautier, Maupassant, Flaubert, and Loti—none of whom yet had a reputation in America); he wrote original stories in the lavish prose style he was perfecting at that time; and he collected local legends and factual narratives. His subjects ranged from Buddhism to Russian literature, from popularizations of science to European anti-Semitism. Altogether he offered the people of New Orleans such unpredictable and exotic fare that his reputation soon spread throughout the South. By this time he had become a disciple of his contemporary, Robert Louis Stevenson (or perhaps vice-versa: they developed similarly mellifluous prose styles and shared a fondness for fantastic and exotic subject matter). Hearn was enormously popular. From these years in New Orleans date *Stray Leaves From Strange Literatures*, 1884, *Some Chinese Ghosts*, 1887, and a novel, *Chita*, 1889.

In 1887 Hearn went to the West Indies for *Harper's Magazine* and produced *Two Years in the French West Indies*, 1890, and his last novel, *Youma*, 1890, an unprecedented story about a slave rebellion.

In 1890 he went to Japan for *Harper's* but soon became a school teacher in Izumo, in a northern region then little influenced by Westernization. There he married Koizume Setsuko, the daughter of a Samurai. In 1891 he moved to Kumamoto Government College.

Hearn was by now well known in America as an impressionistic prose painter of odd peoples and places. For this he was at first celebrated and later deprecated. Yet much of his Japanese work is of an entirely different quality and intention. He wrote to his friend Chamberlin in 1893, "After for years studying poetical prose, I am forced now to study simplicity. After attempting my utmost at ornamentation, I am converted by my own mistakes. The great point is to touch with simple words." *The Atlantic Monthly* printed his articles on Japan and syndicated them to a number of newspapers. They were enormously popular when they appeared and became even more so when they were published in two volumes as *Glimpses of Unfamiliar Japan*, 1894.

In 1895 Hearn became a Japanese citizen and took the name of Koizumi Yakumo. In 1896 he became professor of literature at Tokyo Imperial University, a most prestigious academic position in the most prestigious school in Japan. From then until his death he produced his finest books: *Exotics and Retrospectives*, 1898, *In Ghostly Japan*, 1899, *Shadowings*, 1900, *A Japanese Miscellany*, 1901, *Kwaidan*, 1904, *Japan, An Attempt at Interpretation*, 1904. These were translated into Japanese and became at least as popular in Japan as they did in America.

During the last two years of his life, failing health forced Hearn to give up his position at Tokyo Imperial University. On September 26, 1904, he died of heart failure. He had instructed his eldest son to put his ashes in an ordinary jar and to bury it on a forested hillside. Instead, he was given a Buddhist funeral with full ceremony, and his grave is to this day a place of pilgrimage perpetually decorated with flowers.

At the turn of the century, Hearn was considered one of the finest, if not the finest, of American prose stylists. He was certainly one of the masters of the Stevensonian style. As literary tastes changed, he was thought of more as a writer of pretty but dated essays about Japanese tame crickets and of sentimental ghost stories. After his death, his literary reputation was further damaged by the publication of several collections of his florid earlier work. His all-but-final reputation was as a lush, frothy stylist whose essays and stories were about as important as the pressed flowers likely to be found between their pages.

In fact, Hearn's Japanese writings demonstrate economy, concentration, and great control of language, with little stylistic exhibitionism. Their attitude of uncritical appreciation for the exotic and the mysterious is as unmistakably nineteenth century as the fine prose idiom with which it is consistent.

In spite of the incredible changes that have taken place in Japan since Hearn's death in 1904, as an informant of Japanese life, literature, and religion he is still amazingly reliable, because beneath the effects of industrialization, war, population explosion, and prosperity much of Japanese life remains unchanged. For Hearn the old Japan—the art, traditions, and myths that had persisted for centuries—was the only Japan worth paying attention to. Two world wars and Japan's astonishing emergence as a modern nation temporarily extinguished the credibility of Hearn's vision of traditional Japanese culture. But both in the West and in Japan interest in the old forms of Japanese culture is increasing. In Tokyo there are still thousands of people living the old life by the traditional values alongside the most extreme effects of Westernization. Pet crickets, for example, still command high prices, and more people apply their new prosperity to learning tea ceremony, calligraphy, flower arrangement and *sumi-e* painting than ever before. Ghost stories like those told by Hearn are popular on television; three of his own were recently combined to make a successful movie that preserves his title, *Kwaidan.*

One of the foreigners' (and Westernized, secularized Japanese intellectuals') myths of Japan is that the Japanese are a fundamentally secular, irreligious people. Nothing could be less true. The great temples swarm with pilgrims and are packed during their major festivals. Buddhism is more popular than ever. Shintō and Shingon and Tendai Buddhism perpetuate rites that began long before the dawn of Japanese history.

Although it is no longer true, if it ever was, that Japan is totally "Westernized," it is certainly the most Post-Modern of all the major nations today. With an economy which has ceased to be based on the mechanical, industrial methods of the nineteenth century (really because the old industrial capital structure was destroyed and everything dates from 1946), Japan has moved into the electronic age more completely than any other nation. Yet any Japanese who wishes can still make immediate contact with the Stone Age.

Hearn foresaw the industrialization of Japan and her development of imperialist ambitions. As much as possible he avoided the atmosphere of modernization, spending his summers away from Tokyo at Yaizu, a small fishing village where today there is a Hearn monument. His happiest period in Japan was the early years he spent as a country school teacher in Matsue on the southwest coast. His house and garden there are still preserved, and a Hearn museum is located next door. The essay "In a Japanese Garden" in his book *Glimpses of Unfamiliar Japan* describes his home and Matsue.

Beginning with Charles Eliot's *Japanese Buddhism,* there has grown up an immense bibliography of Buddhological works in Western languages. Since World War II, there is an ever greater store in the United States of books on Zen, which has become a popular form of Existentialism. There is no interpreter of Japanese Buddhism quite like Hearn, but he is not a Buddhologist. Far from it. Hearn was not a scholar, nor was he in the Western sense a religious believer. What distinguishes him is an emotional identification with the Buddhist way of life and with Buddhist cults. Hearn is as good as anyone at providing an elementary grounding in Buddhist doctrine. But what he does incomparably is to give his reader a feeling for how Buddhism is *lived* in Japan, its persistent influence upon folklore, burial customs, children's riddles, toys for sale in the marketplace, and even upon the farmer's ruminations in the field. For Hearn, Buddhism is a way of life, and he is interested in the effects of its doctrine upon the daily actions and common beliefs of ordinary people. Like the Japanese themselves, he thinks of religion as something one does, not merely as something one believes, unlike the orthodox Christian whose Athanasian Creed declares: "Whosoever would be saved, it is necessary before all things that he believe . . ."

One of the things Hearn admires about Buddhism is its adaptability to the spiritual and historic needs of a people. If they need a pantheon of gods, Buddhism makes room for them. If they need to fix upon a savior, Buddhism provides one. But the Buddhist elite, the more learned monks, never lose sight of the true doctrine. I will never forget a symposium in which I once took part along with a number of Buddhist clergy. A Westerner asked the leading Shinshu abbot, "Do you really believe in the existence of supernatural beings like Amida and Kannon, and in a life after death in the True Land Paradise of Amida?" The abbot answered very quietly, "These are conceptual entities." In fact the Diamond and Womb Mandalas with their hundreds of figures (sometimes represented by quasi-

Sanskrit letters) are tools for mediation. The monk moves from the guardian gods at the outer edge, in to the central Buddha—the Vairocana—and at last beyond him to the Adi Buddha—the Pure, unqualified Void.

Yet, popular rather than "higher" Buddhism is Hearn's main subject, and he always is careful to distinguish between the metaphysically complex Buddhism of the educated monks and the simpler, more colorful Buddhism of the ordinary people.

The only peculiarity in Hearn's Buddhism is his habit of equating it with the philosophy of Herbert Spencer, now so out of date. However, this presents few difficulties for the modern reader, as his Spencerianism can be said to resemble Buddhism more than his Buddhism resembles Herbert Spencer. Also, it is not Spencer's Darwinism, "red in tooth and claw," but Spencer's metaphysical and spiritual speculations that have influenced Hearn's interpretation of Buddhism. We must not forget that Teilhard de Chardin, who certainly is not out of date, is, in the philosophical sense, only Herbert Spencer sprinkled with holy water. Philosophies and theologies come and go, but the group experience of transcendence is embedded in human nature, and when it is abandoned, theology, philosophy, and eventually culture, perish.

It is difficult to think of a better guide to Japanese Buddhism for the completely uninformed than Hearn, though there are others who may be his equals. Certainly the popularizers of Zen are not. Zen, after all, is a very special sect, in many ways more Vedantist or Taoist than Buddhist. And of course as the religion of the Japanese officer caste and of the great rich it plays in Japan a decidedly reactionary role. Hearn's Buddhism is far less specialized than Zen. It is the Buddhism of the ordinary Japanese Buddhist of whatever sect.

The first distinction to be made in any consideration of Buddhism itself is that Christianity is the only major religion whose adherents live lives and hold beliefs diametrically opposed to those of its founder. Nothing could be less like the life of Jesus than that of the typical Christian, clerical or lay. Imagine thirteen men with long beards, matted hair, and probably lice, in ragged clothes and dusty bare feet, taking over the high altar at St. Peter's in Rome or the pulpit of a fashionable Fifth Avenue sanctuary. The Apostolic life survives in only odd branches of Christianity: the Hutterites, some Quakers, even Jehovah's Witnesses, but not, as everyone knows, in official and orthodox denominations. Catholicism carefully quarantines such people in monasteries and nunneries where a life patterned on that of the historic Jesus is not wholly impossible to achieve. The opposite is true of Buddhism. No matter how far the sect—Lamaism, Zen, or Shingon—may have moved from the Buddhologically postulated original Buddhist Order, all sects of Buddhism are pervaded by the personality of the historic Siddhartha Gautama.

The historicity of almost all the details of what are generally considered to be the earliest Buddhist documents is subject to dispute and in many instances is improbable. The earliest surviving Life of Buddha was written hundreds of years after his death. The prevailing form of Buddhism in Japan, Mahayana, seems to Westerners more like a group of competing, highly speculative philosophies than a religion. The complete collection of Hinanya, Mahayana and Tantric Buddhist texts makes up a very large library. In addition, there are many thousands of pages of noncanonical commentary and speculation. Yet out of it all emerges, with extraordinary clarity, a man, a personality, a way of life and a basic moral code.

Buddha was born in Kapilavastu, now Rummimdei, Nepal, sometime around 563 B.C. and died about 483 B.C. in Kusimara, now Kasia, India. His personal name was Siddhartha Gautama. Buddha, The Enlightened One, is a title, not a name, as is Sakumuni, the saint of the Saka clan. In Japan, the historic Buddha is commonly known as Shakya. He was a member of the Kshatriya warrior caste, the son of the ruler of a small principality.

For six years Buddha lived with five other ascetics in a grove at Uruvela practicing the most extreme forms of self-mortification and the most advanced techniques of Hatha Yoga, until he almost died of starvation. He gave up ascetic life, left his companions, and traveled on. At Bodh Gaya he seated himself under a Bo tree (*ficus religiosa*) and resolved not to get up until he had achieved true enlightenment. Maya, the personification of the world's illusion, with his daughters and all the attendant incarnate sins and illusions, attacked him without success. Gautama Siddhartha achieved final illumination, entered Nirvana and arose a Buddha: an Enlightened One. He returned to his five companions at Uruvela and preached to them the Middle Way between self-indulgence and extreme asceticism. They were shocked and repudiated him, but after he had preached to them the Noble Eight-Fold Way and the Four Truths, they became the first Buddhist monks.

The first Truth is the Truth of suffering: birth is pain, old age is pain, sickness is pain, death is pain, the endless round of rebirths is pain, the five aggregates of grasping are pain. The second Truth is the cause of pain: the craving that holds the human being to endless rebirth, the craving of the passions, the craving for continued existence, the craving for non-existence. The third Noble Truth is the ending of pain: the extirpation of craving. The fourth Noble Truth is the means of arriving at the cessation of pain: the Noble Eight-Fold Path, which is right views, right intentions, right speech, right action, right livelihood, right effort, right mindfulness, right concentration (or contemplation). This doctrine is the essence of Buddhism, common to all of its otherwise divergent sects. It is always there, underlying the most extreme forms of Tantrism or Amidism. It produces in the personality of the devout Buddhist what the Japanese would call the *iro*, the essential color of the Buddha-life.

As Hinduism was taking form in the Upanishads, it began to teach the doctrine of the identity of the individual self, the Atman, and of the universal self, Brahman as Atman. Buddha attacked the Atman doctrine head-on, denying the existence of the individual or absolute self. He taught that the self is simply a bundle of *skandas*, the five aggregates of grasping: body, feeling, perception, mental elements, and consciousness. The *skandas* that comprise the self are momentary and illusory in the flux of Being—but they do cause and accumulate *karma*, the moral residue of their acts in this life and in past lives. It is *karma* which holds the aggregates embedded in the bonds of craving and consequence until the *skandas* disintegrate in the face of Ultimate Enlightenment. In the most philosophical teaching of Buddhism, it is the *karma* and the *skandas* which reincarnate. The individual consciousness or soul, as we think of it, disappears. But the universal belief in the reincarnation of the individual person has always overridden this notion. The ordinary Buddhist in fact believes in the rebirth of the self, the *atman.*

It is these doctrines which distinguish Buddhism. Many ideas which we think of as especially Buddhist are actually shared by Hinduism, by Jainism, and in fact by many completely secular modern Indians—transmigration, Yogic practices (some modern Buddhologists have held that Buddhism is only a special form of Yoga, anticipating its final synthesis in the Yoga Sutras of Patanjali). Vedic gods appear at all the crucial moments in Buddha's life, from his conception to his entry into final Nivrana. Some time after its inception, Buddhism developed the practice of *bhakti*, personal devotion to a Savior, parallel to that of Hinduism. But always what distinguishes Buddhism is the Buddha Way, the Buddha-life, the all-pervasive personality of its founder, as the personality of Krishna in the *Bhagavad Gita* does not.

The fifty years after his illumination Buddha spent traveling and preaching, usually with a large entourage of monks. In his eightieth year he stopped at the home of Cunda the smith, where he and his followers were given a meal of something to do with pigs. The language is obscure—pork, pigs' food, or something that had been trampled by pigs. Buddha became ill and later stopped in the gardens of Ambhapala, where he announced to his monks that he was about to enter Paranirvana, the final bliss. He lay down under the flowering trees and died, mourned by all creation, monks, laymen, gods, and the lowest animals. His last words were, "The combinations of the world are unstable by nature. Monks, strive without ceasing."

This is the account preserved by the Pali texts, the sacred books of the Theravada Buddhists, of the religion of Ceylon, Burma, and the countries of the Indo-Chinese peninsula. Pali is a dialect of a small principality in Northern India, now forgotten in its homeland. The Pali texts are earlier than all but fragments of Buddhist Sanskrit documents, but this does not necessarily mean that the Hinayana ("The Lesser Vehicle") Buddhism which they embody is the most primitive form of the religion. Theirs is simply the religion of the Theravada, "The religion of the Elders," one of the early sects. However, up until the reign of Ashoka, the saintly Buddhist emperor who ruled more of the Indian sub-continent than anyone before him, Buddhism seems to have been a more or less unified religion resembling the later Hinayana. From the reign of Ashoka to the beginning of the Christian era two currents in Buddhism began to draw more and more apart until Mahayana, "The Greater Vehicle," became dominant in the North and in Java. All the forms of Japanese Buddhism with which Hearn came into contact are rooted in the Mahayana tradition.

The many Mahayana texts are differentiated from the postulated Buddha Word as it appears in Pali by several radically different, indeed contradictory, beliefs and practices. In Hinayana man achieves Nirvana, or advances towards it in a future life, solely by his own efforts to overcome the accumulated evil *karma* of thousands of incarnations. There is devotion to the Founder as the Leader of the Way, but no worship, because there is nothing to worship. The difference is the same as that which the Roman Catholic Church calls *dulia*, adoration of the saints, and *latria*, adoration of God. Mahayana introduced the idea of saviors, *Bodhisattvas*, who have achieved Buddhahood but who have taken a vow not to enter Nirvana until they can take all sentient creatures with them. As saviors they are worshipped with a kind of *hyper-dulia*, as is the Blessed Virgin in Roman Catholicism. Buddhism was influenced by the great wave of personal worship that swept through India, *bhakti*, the adoration of Krishna, the incarnation of Vishnu, or of Kali, the female embodiment of the power of Shiva. At least theoretically above the Bodhisattvas arose a pantheon of Buddhas of whom Vairocana was primary. Later, an Adi-Buddha was added above him. It is disputable if either properly can be called the Absolute. If there is any absolute in Buddhism, it is Nirvana, which in fact means the religious experience itself. From Vairocana emanate the four Dhyana Buddhas, the Buddhas of Contemplation, of whom Amida is the best known, and of whom the historic Shakyamuni is only one of four, although in his most transcendental form he can be equated with Vairocana or the Adi Buddha.

The story of the development of Mahayana as it spread from what is now Afghanistan and Russian Turkestan to Mongolia and Indonesia to Tibet, China and Japan, while it died out in India, would take many thousands of words to tell. There are traces of Buddhism in China two hundred years or more before the Christian era. Its official introduction is supposed to have occurred in the first century A.D. From then until the Muslim conquest of India, Chinese pilgrims visited India and brought back caravan loads of statuaries and *sutras* (sacred texts) which were translated into Chinese.

Indian missionaries emigrated to China and taught and translated. Buddhism was introduced into Korea in the fourth century and had thoroughly established itself in the three countries of the peninsula by the seventh. From there it passed to Japan in the sixth century.

The first missionaries converted the Soga Clan, which was then the power behind the Japanese throne. For the greater part of a century Buddhism was almost exclusively the religion of a faction of the nobility, and its fortune varied with the factional struggles of the court. In 593 A.D. Prince Shōtoku became the effective head of state. His knowledge of Buddhism and of the more profound meanings of Mahayana was extraordinary. He not only saved Buddhism from rapidly becoming a cult of magic and superstition, but like Ashoka in India before him, he went far to make it a religion of the people. He copied *sutras* in characters of gold on purple paper. He preached the doctrines of Mahayana to the common people as well as to the court. He established hundreds of monasteries, nunneries and temples. Not least, he promulgated a kind of charter which modern Japanese called The Seventeen Article Constitution, in which Buddhist ethics and, to a lesser degree, Confucianism were established as the moral foundations of Japan. To this day he is regarded by many as an avatar of Avalokitesvara, *Kuan Yin* in Chinese and *Kannon* or *Kwannon* in Japanese—the so-called Goddess of Mercy and the most popular of all Bodhisattvas.

By the eighth century Buddhism had become Japan's official state religion, a feat Hearn credits to Buddhism's absorption and expansion of the older Shintō worship of many gods, ghosts, and goblins (the gods, Buddhas or Bodhisattvas, the ghosts beings in transit from one incarnation to another, and the goblins, *gakis*, beings suffering in a lower state of existence). By the thirteenth century most of the major forms of Japanese Buddhism—a religion quite distinct from Buddhism elsewhere in the world—had been established, though minor sects continued to proliferate.

Ten large sects dominate Japanese Buddhism. The oldest of these are Tendai and Shingon. First was Tendai, established by the monk

Saichō in 804 on Mt. Hiei northeast of Kyoto (*Heian kyo*), facing
the most inauspicious direction. Not long afterwards the monk
Kukai returned from China and introduced Shingon, which became
the Japanese form of Tantric Buddhism. In China, Tendai attempted a synthesis of the various schools and cults in the great
complex of monasteries on Mt. T'ien Tai. The similar monastic
city on Mt. Hiei sheltered a wide variety of cults, doctrines, and
philosophies. Basically, however, Japanese Tendai modified what in
India was known as "right-handed" Tantrism, which we see today in
the Yellow Hat sect of Tibetan Lamaism in exile. All the great
Buddhist *sutras* were studied, the doctrine of the Void, the doctrine
of Mind Only, the vision of reality as the interpenetration of compound infinitives of Buddha natures of the Avatamsaka Sutra, and
the complex panpsychism of the Lankavatara Sutra. Most popular,
however, was the Lotus Sutra (*Hokkekyo* in Japanese), the Sad-
dharma Pundarika Sutra, the only major Buddhist document a
Japanese lay person is at all likely to have read. Tendai is a ceremonial religion, and only in recent years has it done much for the laity
except to permit them to participate in pilgrimages and to watch
public ceremonies.

Shingon is even more esoteric than Tendai and is in fact Japanese
Lamaism. Its doctrines are occult, its mysteries are not divulged to
the people, and many of its rites are kept secret. The worship of
Buddhas and Bodhisattvas as sexual dualities or as terrifying wrath-
ful figures is not as common in Japan as in Tibet, though in both
cultures the emphasis on magic formulas, gestures, spells and special methods of inducing trance remains essential. It is not known
how many Tantric *shastras* (scriptures secondary to *sutras*) survive
and are studied in Shingon monasteries, but recent discoveries and
paintings of this literature are read by the more learned Japanese
monks. "Lefthanded" Tantrism, with its cult of erotic mysticism,
survives underground in Tachigawa Shingon.

The worship of Amida which began in India around the advent
of the Christian era, almost certainly under the influence of Persian
religion, effected a complete revolution in Japanese Buddhism when
it was introduced in the ninth century. Originally sheltered within
the Tendai sect, Amidism grew to be the most popular form of

Buddhism in Japan—and the one with which Hearn was most familiar. Amida is the Buddha of Endless Light whose paradise, The Pure Land, is in the west. He has promised that any who believe in him and call on his name will be saved and at death will be reborn in his Pure Land. Buddha, of course, insisted that by oneself one is saved and thus achieves, not paradise, but Nirvana, which far transcends any imaginable paradise. Hearn, however, observed that few Japanese even knew of the concept of Nirvana. For them Amida's Pure Land was the highest heaven imaginable. Buddha also forbade worship of himself or others and considered the gods inferior to human beings because they could not escape the round of rebirths and enter Nirvana. Amidism, as a gesture to orthodoxy, teaches that the older Buddhism is too hard for this corrupt age and that the Pure Land, unlike other paradises, provides a direct stepping stone to Nirvana. As the Amidist sects developed in Japan, the doctrine of salvation by faith became more and more extreme. At first, it was necessary to invoke the name of Amida many times a day and especially with one's last words, but finally one had only to invoke it once in a lifetime. This was enough to erase the *karma*, the consequences, of a life of ignorance and sin.

The Japanese monk Nichiren, who played a role not unlike that of the Hebrew Prophets, taught that salvation could be won by reciting the words "*Namu Myōhōrengekyō*," "Hail to the Lotus Sutra!" The Lotus Sutra is a sort of compendium of Mahayana Buddhism, lavishly embroidered with miraculous visions, with thousands upon thousands of Buddhas, Bodhisattvas, gods, demigods and lesser supernatural beings. But its important chapter is the Kannon (*Avalokitshivara*), which raises the Bodhisattva to a position similar to that of Amida, The Savior of the World, "He Who Hears The World's Cry." The earliest Kannon statues and paintings seem to have reached Japan from the oasis cities of Central Asia. Their peculiar sexlessness led the Japanese, as it did the Chinese, to think of the Bodhisattva as a woman. Not just Westerners, but most Japanese, refer to him as the Goddess of Mercy, and cheap modern statues which depict him holding a baby bear a striking resemblance to popular representations of the Virgin Mary.

The secret of the tremendous success of Amidism and Nichiren-ism is that they are congregational religions. The largest of all Buddhist sects, the Amidist Jodo-Shinshu, is in this sense much like a modern Christian denomination. But, in other respects, and despite its tremendous pilgrimages, Buddhism seems inaccessible to the common Japanese. Very few people know anything about the profound and complex metaphysics of the Mahayana speculation. A surprising number do know the life of Buddha as it is told in Hinayana, which scarcely exists in Japan, and do try to model their lives on the Buddha-life—with remarkable success. But for most secular Japanese, a Buddhist monk is just a kind of undertaker, to be called upon only when somebody dies.

Zen Buddhism cultivated a special sensibility that many Japanese people think of as Japanese. The tea ceremony, *sumi-e* ink painting, the martial arts (archery, sword play, *jiu-jitsu judo, aikido,* wrestling), flower arrangement, pottery, and *haiku* survive as creative expressions of the Zen sensibility in pursuit of perfection. But this sensibility has weakened in most modern Japanese.

Zen is often translated as Enlightenment (*Ch'an* or Dhyana), but it means something like illumination, specifically illumination achieved by systematic religious meditation of the kind we identify as yoga. It is supposed to have been introduced to China by a missionary Indian monk, Bodhidharma, probably in the sixth century. It spread to Japan in the thirteenth as the long civil wars were beginning, became popular with the military castes and the great rich, and for a long time dominated the intellectual and artistic life of the country. Zen owed its powerful influence to the fact that it began as a revolt against the Buddhist cults of its time and reverted to what the nineteenth century was to call "Primitive" Buddhism. It rejected the salvation by faith and the devotional worship of Amidism, the cults of Kannon and the Lotus Sutra ("By yourself alone shall you be saved," says Gautama). It reinstated yogic meditation with a view to final enlightenment as the central and essential practice of the Buddhist religious life. Finally, it reinstated Shakyamuni himself, Shaka, as he is known in Japanese: its special interpretation of the Buddha-life is modeled on his.

Since World War II, Zen Buddhism has become enormously popular in the West, and largely in response to its reception here it has seen an intellectual revival in Japan. Although Hearn was familiar with Zen theories and practices, and had Zen Buddhist friends, he wrote little about the sect that was to become the most influential in the West. Neither Zen as a manifestation of aristocratic traditions nor Zen as a popular fad interested him. Instead, he kept his eye on what had persisted in Japanese Buddhism through the centuries among the farmers, fishermen, and other poor folk. Many of their beliefs inform their stories, and many of their customs in turn have stories behind them. It was the survival of Buddhism in such forms that above all else engaged Hearn.

Hearn's role in the spread of Buddhism to the West was a preparatory one. He was the first important American writer to live in Japan and to commit his imagination and considerable literary powers to what he found there. Like the "popular" expressions of Buddhist faith that were his favorite subject, Hearn popularized the Buddhist way of life for his Western readers. And he was widely read, both in his articles for *Harper's Magazine* and the *Atlantic Monthly*, and in his numerous books on Japan. Hearn's essays, with their rich descriptions and queer details, almost never generalizing but staying with a particular subject, always backed by the likeable and enthusiastic personality of Hearn himself, and always factually reliable, satisfied the vague and growing curiosity of his American readers about the mysterious East.

At St. Cuthbert's school, at age fifteen, Hearn had discovered that he was a pantheist. That is not unusual for a fifteen-year-old, and the fact that pantheism is unaccepted in Christian doctrine or in Western philosophical thought normally suffices to extinguish the common adolescent philosophy or to transmute it to something less vulnerable. But the idea stuck with Hearn, and when finally, at forty, he arrived in Japan, he was delighted to find that he could now exercise and explore his intuition of God-in-All. If Hearn entered Japanese culture and achieved understanding of Japanese Buddhist (and Shintō) thought with unprecedented rapidity for a Westerner, it is because his own spirit had always longed for an atmosphere in which his belief in the sentience and blessedness of all Nature could flourish.

Hearn never became a Buddhist, and he remained skeptical about certain of Buddhism's key doctrines—such as the relationship of *karma* and rebirth—but he passionately believed that Buddhism promoted a far better attitude toward daily life than did Christianity. It would be up to more scholarly and less imaginative writers to begin to translate and preach specific Buddhist doctrines, but Hearn has done much to translate the spirit of Japanese Buddhism and to prepare Western society for it.

Index

Abel, Lionel, 213, 214
Adams, Henry, 199
Adams, Thomas F., 235–236
Aiken, Conrad, 151, 154, 155, 215
Aldington, Richard, 19, 150, 151, 153
Algren, Nelson, 49, 50
Anderson, Margaret, 160
Apollinaire, Guillaume, 43, 45, 51, 147, 150, 156, 158, 161, 162, 164, 166, 167, 196, 211, 252, 253, 257, 269, 273
Apuleius, 298
Aquinas, St. Thomas, 4, 92, 188, 214, 254, 287
Aragon, Louis, 145, 151, 166, 169, 211
Arensberg, Walter Conrad, 153–154, 156, 157, 210, 253, 257
Aristotle, 270, 277–278, 283, 285, 297, 300, 301
Armstrong, Louis, 70
Arnold, Matthew, 9, 301
Arp, Hans, 32, 46, 109
Artaud, Antonin, 38, 53, 56, 75, 76, 162, 164, 170
Ashoka, Emperor, 312, 314
Atwood, Mary Anne, 250
Auden, W. H., 164, 190, 197, 198, 216
Auerbach, Leopold, 41, 166
Augustine, St., 11, 13, 81
Auric, Georges, 69
Avicenna, 250

Bakunin, Mikhail, 94, 207
Baldwin, James, 234, 264
Balzac, Honoré de, 144, 145, 284
Banton, Michael, 233
Barth, Karl, 38, 77, 81
Barzun, Henri, 257
Bashō, 271

Basie, Count, 195
Baudelaire, Charles, 2, 11, 20, 45, 51, 66, 105, 145, 148, 152, 170, 172, 198, 201, 202, 210, 217, 257, 263, 269, 281, 285, 289, 300
Beardsley, Aubrey, 29, 129, 131
Beat Generation, 204–206, 207–208, 214, 216
Beckett, Samuel, vii, 50, 53, 75, 76, 253, 262
Beowulf, 297
Bernstein, Leonard, 216
Black Mask, 48
Blake, William, 2, 10, 12, 26, 66, 137, 198, 263, 280, 290
Blavatsky, Mme. Helena, 82, 86
Bodenheim, Maxwell, 154, 157
Boehme, Jakob, 141, 254
Bolos of Mendes, 247
Bosschere, Jean de, 29, 153
Bowra, Sir C. M., 302
Brancusi, Constantin, 32, 109, 156
Brandes, Georg, 147, 302
Brassens, Georges, 298
Brecht, Bertolt, 269, 298
Breton, André, 46, 51, 155, 162, 167, 215, 245, 270
Bridges, Robert, 9
Briggs, Ernie, 47
Brooks, Van Wyck, 145
Broonzy, Big Bill, 68
Browder, Earl, 214, 260
Brown, Ford Madox, 128
Browning, Robert, 105, 279, 284
Buber, Martin, viii, 62, 77–78, 80–84, 89, 91–101, 213, 291
Buddhism, 58, 98, 104, 106–108, 110, 111, 205, 246, 250, 251, 273, 274, 303, 307, 308–319

Burrow, Trigant, 14, 100
Butcher, Samuel, 172, 173
Butler, Samuel, 172
Bynner, Witter, 148, 152, 185–186, 187–188
Byron, Robert, 188

Caillois, Roger, 155, 209
Callahan, Kenneth, 27, 47
Calvert, Edward, 26
Carco, Francis, 148, 167, 196, 252
Carlyle, Thomas, 130, 146
Cassirer, Ernst, 302
Cather, Willa, 144
Catullus, 11, 58, 179, 183, 186, 263, 281
Céline, Louis-Ferdinand, 50, 53, 56, 75, 76, 98, 165
Cendrars, Blaise, 145, 151, 153, 155, 158, 161, 162, 252
Cervantes, Miguel de, 284, 298
Chagall, Marc, 89
Chandler, Raymond, 48, 209, 292
Les Chansons de Bilitis, 151, 180
Char, René, 168
Chaucer, Geoffrey, 173–174
Chermayeff, Serge, 220–221
Chessman, Caryl, 114, 123
Chesterton, G. K., 38, 113
Chu Hsi, 107, 250
Chu Shu Chen, 111
Ciardi, John, 170
Classic of Mountains and Rivers (trans. of *Shan Hai Ching*), 247
Cocteau, Jean, 158, 252
Cohen, Leonard, 298
Coleman Ornette, 195
Coleridge, Samuel Taylor, 289
Coltrane, John, 195, 196
Confucianism, 98, 103, 104, 106–108, 109, 110, 111, 314
Connell, Peter J., 236–237
Conrad, Joseph, 284
Corbière, Tristan, 155
Corman, Cid, 53, 273
Corneille, Pierre, 284, 289
Covici, Pascal, 153
Cowley, Malcolm, 159, 160, 161
Crane, Hart, 45, 161–162, 164, 189, 215–216
Creeley, Robert, 53, 168, 216, 256, 273
The Criterion, 211, 212

Cros, Charles, 68
Crosby, Caresse & Harry, 162, 164, 198
Crotty, Ron, 68, 70
Cubism, 22, 33, 45, 153, 202, 252, 253, 256, 257, 270, 288, 296, 300
cummings, e.e., 64, 165
Cunard, Nancy, 198, 253

Dadaism, 202, 203, 210, 253
Dali, Salvador, 129, 197, 198
Danby, Francis, 26
Dante Alighieri, 4, 98, 141, 173, 297
Darwin, Erasmus, 289
Davidson, Donald, 164
Davies, G. S., 183, 186
Davis, H. L., 144
Davis, Miles, 44, 45, 194, 264
Defoe, Daniel, 280
Dehmel, Richard, 155, 209
de Kooning, Willem, 26, 46
De Leon, Daniel, 119, 260
Densmore, Frances, 181, 271–272
Derème, Tristan, 148, 149
Dickens, Charles, 284
"Dieu est Negre" (song), 193
Doolittle, Hilda (H. D.), 15, 19, 51, 151, 163, 174–178, 179, 184–185, 187, 210
Dos Passos, John, 166
Dostoyevsky, Fyodor, 210, 284, 287
Douglas, Major C. H., 163, 212
Dowson, Ernest, 4, 51, 148, 157
Dream of the Red Chamber, 284, 287
Dreiser, Theodore, 144, 147, 288
Dryden, John, ix, 2, 5, 171, 173, 189
Duchamp, Marcel, 153–154, 161
Duncan, Robert, 53, 54, 61–62, 64
Durrell, Lawrence, ix
Dylan, Bob, 298

Eberhart, Richard, 53, 170
Eliezer Baal-Shem, Rabbi Israel ben (Baal Shem Tov), 87, 91, 100
Eliot, Charles, 308
Eliot, T. S., ix, 4, 5, 6, 20, 22, 51, 52, 98, 151, [153], 154, 155, 156, 163, 189, 190, 210, 211, 212, 214, 215, 253, 280, 285, 290, 297
Ellington, Duke, 70, 202
Éluard, Paul, 45, 51, 54, 151, 168, 211, 217
Emerson, Ralph Waldo, 146

Emerson, Richard, 53
Emmanuel, Pierre, 61, 62
Empson, William, 280
Epic of Gilgamesh, 286, 300
Ernst, Max, 46, 145, 159
Esposito, Frank, 70
Euclid, 287
Euripides, 151, 184–185, 187
Everson, William, 54, 60–61, 64
Existentialism, 80–82, 83, 213, 259, 273, 308

Fa-ch'ang, 110
Fa-ch'ang (Mu Ch'i), 111
Fanon, Frantz, 264
Fargue, Léon Paul, 152, 252
Farny, Henry, 128
Farrell, James, 50, 166
Fearing, Kenneth, 50, 53
Fenollosa, Ernest, 187, 271
Ferguson, Allyn, 70, 71
Ferlinghetti, Lawrence, 54, 63–64, 168
Field, Michael, 179–180, 211
Fielding, Henry, 299
Fisher, Vardis, 144
Fitzgerald, Edward, 172
Flaubert, Gustave, 144, 284, 288, 289, 305
Fletcher, John Gould, 150–151, 210
Flint, F. S., 19, 151, 153
Foote, Caleb, 120
Ford, Charles Henri, 167
Ford, Ford Madox, 16, 17, 19, 52, 161, 284
Fort, Paul, 149, 150
Fourrest, Georges, 64, 150, 152–153, 211
Francesca, Piero della, 32
Freud, Sigmund, 11, 14, 97, 162
Frost, Robert, 146, 147

Galbraith, John Kenneth, 201
Gale, Zona, 144
Garland, Hamlin, 144
Gascoyne, David, 61, 62, 216
Gautama, Siddhartha (Buddha), 310–312, 316, 317
Gautier, Judith, 152, 182, 187
Genêt, Jean, 50, 53, 75, 76
Georgian Poetry, 1911–1912 (ed. Edward Marsh), 8

Ginsberg, Allen, 54, 55, 62–63, 64, 168, 190, 203, 214
Gnosticism, 24, 84, 85, 86, 87, 92, 96, 135–142, 247, 251
Goethe, Johann Wolfgang von, 100, 297
Gold, Mike, 166
Goodman, Paul, 214
Gorter, Herman, 94, 156
Gould, Wallace, 19, 154
Gourmont, Rémy de, 150, 151
Graham, W. S., 45
Graves, Morris, 26–34, 47, 48
Graves, Robert, 37, 164, 172–173
Greco, Juliette, 193, 196
Greene, Robert, 2
Gregory, Dick, 196, 264
Gris, Juan, 252, 253, 255, 256
Gros, Léon-Gabriel, 204
Gustafson, Gus, 70

Hammett, Dashiell, 48, 209
Hardin, Lil, 70
Hardy, Thomas, 9–10
Hartley, Marsden, 154, 157
Hartmann, Sadakichi, 268
Hasidism, 83–85, 87–93, 95, 96, 98, 100, 101, 139
Heap, Jane, 160
Hearn, Lafcadio, viii, 268, 303–309, 313, 314, 316, 318–319
Hecht, Ben, 145, 157
Hegel, Georg, 262
Hemingway, Ernest, 48, 159, 197, 209
Hentoff, Nat, 191
Herberg, Will, 80, 93
Herreshoff, David, 260
Hildegarde of Bingen, St., 254, 255
Hiroshige, 131
Hitamaro, 269–270
Hokusai, 131
Hölderlin, Friedrich, 66, 263
Holmes, Clellon, 195
Homer, [97], 171, 172–173, 181, 188, 200, [297]
Honneger, Arthur, 69
Hopkins, Gerard Manley, 9
Horace, 43
Hsia Kuei, 110
Hsu Tao-ning, 110
Hugel, Baron von, 66, 77, 78, 82, 92

Hughes, Langston, 68, 170
Huneker, James Gibbons, viii, 302

Imagism, 149–153, 210

Jacob, Max, 151, 152, 158, 252
Jaeger, Werner, 221
James, Henry, ix, 45, 48, 144–145, 284, 287, 288, 293
James, William, 78, 100
Jammes, Francis, 51, 147–148, 149, 252
Jeffers, Robinson, 60
Jenyns, Soame, 183–184, 186–187
Jolas, Eugène, 161, 162, 167, 215, 245
Jones, David, 253
Jones, LeRoi, 264
Jonson, Ben, 2, 5, 21, 186
Josephson, Matthew, 160, 162
Joyce, James, 3, 61, 153, 162, 254, 284, 296
Jung, Carl, 14, 24, 78, 82–83, 141, 162, 244–245, 249, 251, 285, 286

Kabbalism, 84–87, 90, 91, 96, 98, 101, 139, 247
Karlgren, Bernhard, 188
Katz, Fred, 69, 71
Kawabata Yasunari, 269, 291
Keats, John, 2, 4
Kelley, E., 244
Kerouac, Jack, 50, [123], [162], 204, [215]
Kierkegaard, Sören, 38, 81, 82, 197, 210, 259
King, Martin Luther, Jr., 117–118
Kipling, Rudyard, 80
Kitasono Katue, 274
Ko Hung, 246, 249, [250]
Kobayashi Takiji, 269
Koizume Setsuko, 305
Kreymborg, Alfred, 154, 160, 210

Laclos, Pierre Choderlos de, 299
Lafayette, Mme. de, [145], 299
Laforgue, Jules, 51, 52, 150, 154–155, 157, 158, 210
Lamantia, Philip, 53, 54, 61, 167
Landor, Walter Savage, 5
Lang, Andrew, 172, 173
Langer, Suzanne, 302
Lao Shao Chun, 248

Larbaud, Valéry, 155, 158, 162
Larsson, R. E. F., 52, 61
Laughlin, James, 64, 167–168
Lawrence, D. H., ix, 8–25, 164
Lawrence, Frieda, 10, 11, 15, 16, 17, 18
Leadbelly, 68
Le Corbusier, 220
Léger, Fernand, 166, 167
Levertoff, Paul, 86
Levertov, Denise, 53, 54, 168
Levi, Eliphas, 86, 244
Lewis, Sinclair, 144, 198
Lewis, Wyndham, 155, 198, 212
Li Ch'ing-chao, 111–112
Li Mi-li, 248
Lindsay, Vachel, 63, 215
Lipton, Lawrence, 42, 69, 71, 145, 216
Loeb, Harold, 160
Longfellow, Henry Wadsworth, 146, 214
Longinus, 278, 279, 301
Lowell, Amy, 51, 149, 150, 152, 210
Lowenfels, Walter, 151, 164, 167, 216, 253
Loy, Mina, ix, 52, 154, 157
Lu Hsiang-shan, 107
Lu Yu, 111
Lull, Raymond, 244
Luxemburg, Rosa, 38, 39

Ma Yüan, 110
MacAlmon, Robert, 161
McClure, Michael, 54
McCoy, Horace, 48, 155, 209
McInnes, Colin, 236
MacLeish, Archibald, 162
MacLeod, J. G., 253
McLuhan, Marshall, 292
McTaggart, J. M. E., 81, 94
Maeterlinck, Maurice, 148, 151
Mailer, Norman, 49, 192
Mallarmé, Stéphane, 54, 61, 148, 156, 167, 253, 255, [256], 257, 269, 270, 273, 293, 296
Malory, Sir Thomas, 171, 299
Malraux, André, 145, 209
Mann, Harold, 74
Marcus Aurelius, 277, 287
Maritain, Jacques, 33, 81, 212
Marlowe, Christopher, 2
Martin, St., 244

Martin, John, 26
Marx, Karl, 25, 75, 115, 162, 207, 213, 214, 259, 260, 262, 263, 265, 287
Masefield, John, 8, 15, 147
Massis, Henri, 211, 212
Mattick, Paul, 35
Maupassant, Guy de, 144, 304, 305
Maurras, Charles, 163, 211, 212
Mayakovsky, Vladimir, 156, 164, 217
Mead, George R. S., 140
Mechtild of Magdeburg, St., 254
Meleager, 15, 151, 178
Meltzer, David, 54
Mencken, H. L., viii, 213, 302
Merrill, Stuart, 146, 150, 152, 162, 182, 187
Meyer, Adolph, 100
Mi Fei, 110
Michaux, Henri, 168
Milhaud, Darius, 69
Mill, John Stuart, 6
Millay, Edna St. Vincent, 148
Miller, Henry, ix, 50, 54, 161, 164–165, 238, 288
Mills, Dick, 70, 71
Milton, John, 4, 297
Miner, Earl, 267
Mingus, Charles, 69, 195, 205, 264
Mitchell, Joni, 298
Mondrian, Piet, 19, 200, 202
Montaigne, Michel de, 287
Moore, Brew, 70
Moore, Marianne, 51, 150, 154, 155
Moreau, Gustave, 26, 48, 129
Morris, William, 54, 172, 173, 264
Motherwell, Robert, 26, 46
Moto-ori Norinaga, 302
Murasaki Shikibu, [269], [284], 298

Nagajuna, 249
Nashe, Thomas, 2
Newman, Cardinal John Henry, 78, 210
Nibelungenlied, 297
Nietzsche, Friedrich, 210, 296
Njál's saga, 284

Ogden, Charles Kay, 280
Old Testament, 76, 96–97, 98
Oliver, King, 70

Olson, Charles, 53, 216
Oppen, George, 272
Oppenheim, James, 19, 154, 157
Others, 154, 210
Otto, Rudolf, 77

Packard, Vance, 201
Paitch, Marty, 71
Palmer, Samuel, 26
Pareto, Vilfredo, 163, 207, 212
Parker, Charlie (Bird), 42, 43, 44, 45, 202
Pascal, Blaise, 11, 37, 170, 287
Patchen, Kenneth, 53, 68, 70, 71, 168–169, 238
Pater, Walter, 275, 280, 288, 301
Peele, George, 2
Pena, Ralph, 71
Perkoff, Stuart, 71
Perrin, Fr., 36, 39
Perse, St.-John, 162
Petrie, Flinders, 247
Petronius Arbiter, 183–184, 186–187, 190, 298
Philalethes, Eireneaus, 244
Picasso, Pablo, 24, 33, 166, 202
Plato, 3, 109, 119, 276–277, 281, 287
Poe, Edgar Allan, 189, 279, 301
Pollok, Jackson, 26, 44, 45, 46, 202
Pope, Alexander, 5, 171, 172, 173, 290
Potamkin, Harry Allen, 1, 2
Pound, Ezra, 4, 13, 19, 22, 51, 53, 98, 150, 151, 152–153, 154, 155, 156, 163, 167, 181–182, 187, 200, 210, 211, 212, 253, 267, 269, 270, 271, 272, 273, 274, 284, 297
Powers, James F., 49, 60
Prévert, Jacques, 63–64, 168, 196
Price, Clayton, 27, 47
Putnam, Samuel, 145, 161

Queneau, Raymond, 64, 168, 196

Rabelais, François, 172, 298
Racine, Jean, 284, 289
Rakosi, Carl, 167, 272
Ransom, John Crowe, 52, 55, 163–164, 212
Ray, P. C., 246
Redon, Odilon, 26, 48, 63

Reinach, Solomon, 207
Restif de la Bretonne, Nicolas-Edme, 165, 288
Reverdy, Pierre, 43, 51, 61, 150, 153, 155, 158, 167, 190, 211, 252–258, 273
Rexroth, Kenneth, vii–x, 50, 53, 54, 63, 68, 70, 71, 76, 111, 145, 151, 167, 170, 179, 197, 253, 254, 257, 258, 269, 272
Richards, Ivor, 12, 52, 54, 280, 302
Ridge, Lola, 19, 154
Riding, Laura, 164, 253, 254, 256
Rihaku (Li Po), 181–182
Rimbaud, Arthur, 1, 2, 4, 44, 51, 56, 65–67, 75, 76, 145, 148, 158, 161, 164, 170, 189, 201, 269
Robinson, Edwin, 146, 147
Rogers, Shorty, 70, 71
Romains, Jules, 166
Rothko, Mark, 26, 46
Rousseau, Jean Jacques, 146, 263, 293
Roux, St-Pol, 150
Royce, Josiah, 81, 262
Rukeyser, Muriel, 53, 170
Rustin, Bayard, 116–117, 118, 120, 234, 241
Ryder, Albert Pinkham, 26

Sade, Marquis de, 202, 263
Salmon, André, 51, 150, 158, 167, 252
San Francisco Renaissance, 54, 55, 57–64
Sandburg, Carl, 19, 51, 63, 147, 156, 209–210, 291
Santayana, George, 146, 217
Sappho, 178–181, 254, 304
Sartre, Jean-Paul, 82, 214, 259, 273
Schlesinger, Arthur, Jr., 74
Schrotel, Stanley R., 232
Schweitzer, Albert, 77
Sesshu, 28, 30, 31, 46, 110, 130
Shahn, Ben, 27
Shakespeare, 21, 137, 153, 243, 280, 281, 284
Shakyamuni, 313, 317
Shapiro, Karl, 54
Shelley, Percy Bysshe, 4, 290
Shōtoku, Prince, 314
Simenon, Georges, 49, 292
Sitwell, Edith, 44, 155

Skolnick, Jerome H., 235
Snyder, Gary, 54, 256, 273, 274
Soupault, Philippe, 151, 157, 158, 161
Spencer, Herbert, 309
Spicer, Jack, 68
Ssu-ma Ch'ien, 248
Stein, Gertrude, 3, 45, 54, 61, 153, 154, 157, 216, 253, 257
Steinbeck, John, 166
Stendhal, 263, 284, 287
Stern, Morton, 233
Sterne, Laurence, 284, 299
Stevens, Wallace, 51, 154, 157–158, 172, 210, 217
Stevenson, Robert Louis, 305, 306
Still, Clyfford, 26, 46
Stravinsky, Igor, 69
Strayhorn, Billy, 70
Strindberg, August, 300
Su Hsiao-hsiao, 105
Su Tung-p'o, 102, 105–106, 108, 109, 111
Sullivan, Harry Stack, 100
Sung culture, 27, 28, 30, 32, 102–112, 248, 249
Supervielle, Jules, 155, 252
Surrealism, 26, 45, 77, 80, 162, 167, 168, 215, 245, 253, 290, 296, 300
Suzuki, D. T., 92, 273
Sylvestre, Anne, 298
Symons, Arthur, 51, 157

Taine, Hippolyte, 294, 301
Taoism, 58, 98, 100, 104, 109, 110, 248, 249
Tate, Allen, 45, 52, 189, 212
Taylor, Jeremy, [24], 25
Teilhard de Chardin, Pierre, 309
Tennyson, Alfred, Lord, 147, 152, 279
Thibon, Gustave, 36, 39
Thomas, Dylan, 42, 43, 44, 45, 164, 216, 217
Thomas, Edward, 147
Thomson, James, 289
Thoreau, Henry David, 146
Tiepolo, Giovanni, 46, 47, 105
Tillich, Paul, 38, 77, 213
"Tin-Tung-Ling," 182
Tintoretto, Jacopo, 27, 30, 47, 202
Tobey, Mark, vii, 27, 28, 30, 47, 48

Tolstoy, Leo, 284
Toulet, J. P., 148, 156, 168, 252
transition, 161, 162, 164, 167, 215
Traven, B., 49, 294
Trotsky, Leon, 119, 263
Tung Yüan, 110
Turgenev, Ivan, 144, 289
Turner, Joseph M. W., 26, 127–131
Tyler, Parker, 52, 151, 167, 215
Tyrrell, George, 77, 78
Tzara, Tristan, 145, 156, 161, 252

Urquhart, Sir Thomas, 172, 173

Valéry, Paul, 20, 45, 52, 54, [167], 188, 254, 255, 287, 289, 290, 302
Vaughan, Henry, 243, 254, 255
Vaughan, Thomas, 243–246, 250–251
Verhaeren, Émile, 147, 149, 155, 209, 252
Vielé-Griffin, Francis, 147, 149–150
View, 167
Virgil, 263, 289, 297
Vivien, Renée, 148, 151, 163, 180, 211

Waite, A. E., 244–5, 246
Waley, Arthur, 188, 269, 272
Walton, William, 69
Wang An-shih, 102, 108
Weber, Max, 83, 94
Weil, Simone, 35–40, 82, 83
Weill, Kurt, 298
Wells, H. G., 50, 114, 147, 292
Whalen, Philip, 54, 273
Wheelwright, John Brooks, 52, 165, 167, 214
Whistler, James A. McNeill, 128–131

White, Gilbert, 277
White, William Alanson, 100
Whitman, Walt, 18, 19, 53, 146, 158, 215, 290
Wilde, Oscar, 148, 157, 180, 199, 288
Willey, Clair, 70
Williams, Jonathan, 53
Williams, William Carlos, 51, 53, 54, 63, 151, 152, 154, 157, 158, 161, 163, 167, 190, 210, 217, [253], 272, 273, 285
Wilson, Edmund, viii, 149, 302
Winters, Yvor, 52, 163, 253, 254, 255, 256, 272, 290
Wisdom, John, 81
Witt-Diamant, Ruth, 54
Wittgenstein, Ludwig, 214, 287
Woman in White (Sung painting), 111
Woodroffe, John, 246, 250
Woolf, Virginia, 200, 284
Wordsworth, William, 289
Wright, Richard, 166
Wu Ti, 248

Yeats, William Butler, 5, 6, 10, 16, 211, 267, 269, 270
Yehoash, 89, 156, 167
Ying Yu-chien, 110
Yosano Akiko, 269
Young, Lester, 44, 45, 46, 76, 195
Yüan Chên, 185–186, 187

Zen Buddhism, 205, 273, 274, 308, 309, 310, 317–318
Zevi, Sabatei, 84
Zola, Émile, 144, 293, 295
Zukofsky, Louis, vii, 52, 151, 167, 216, 253, 272